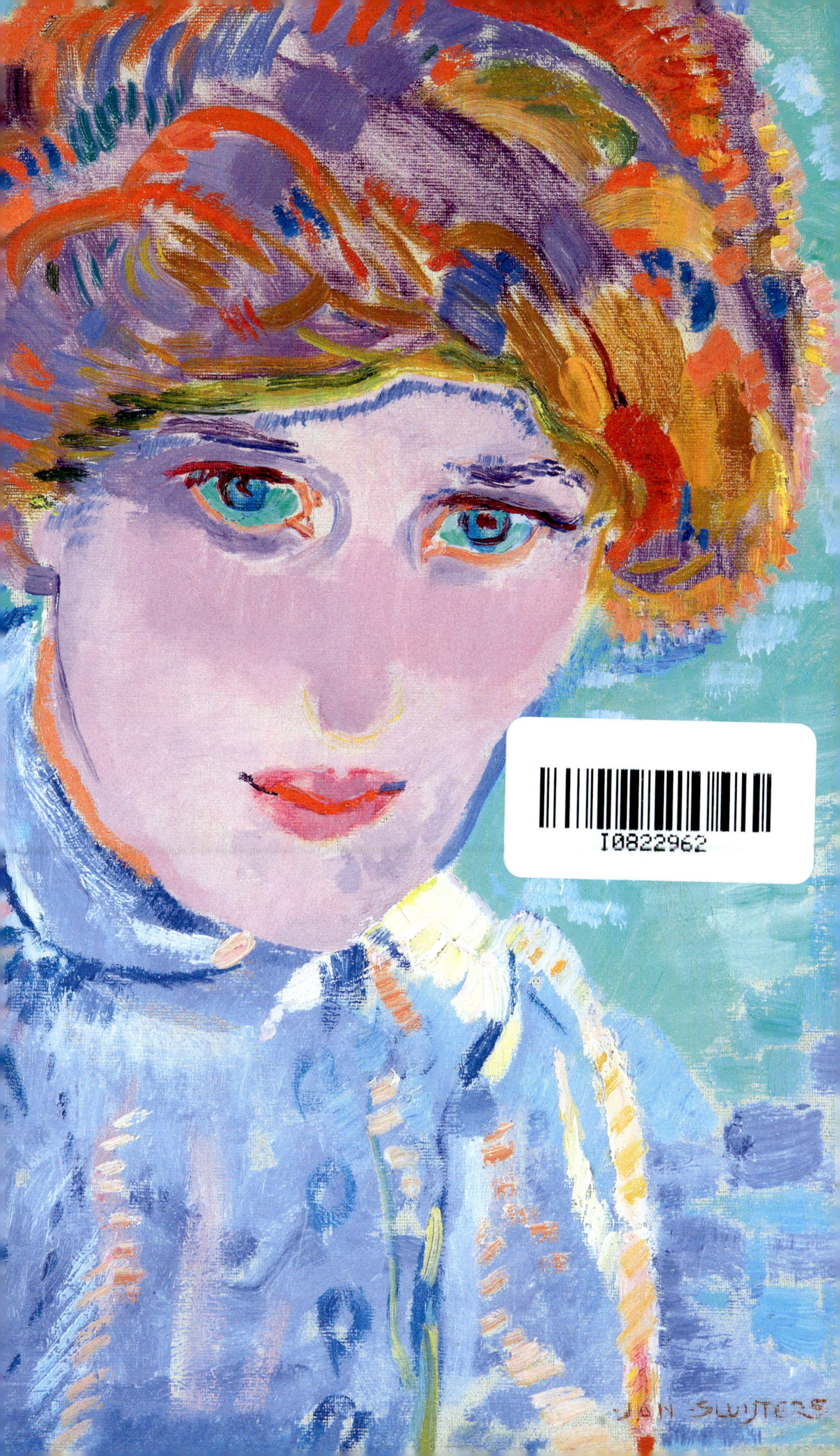
JAN SLUIJTERS

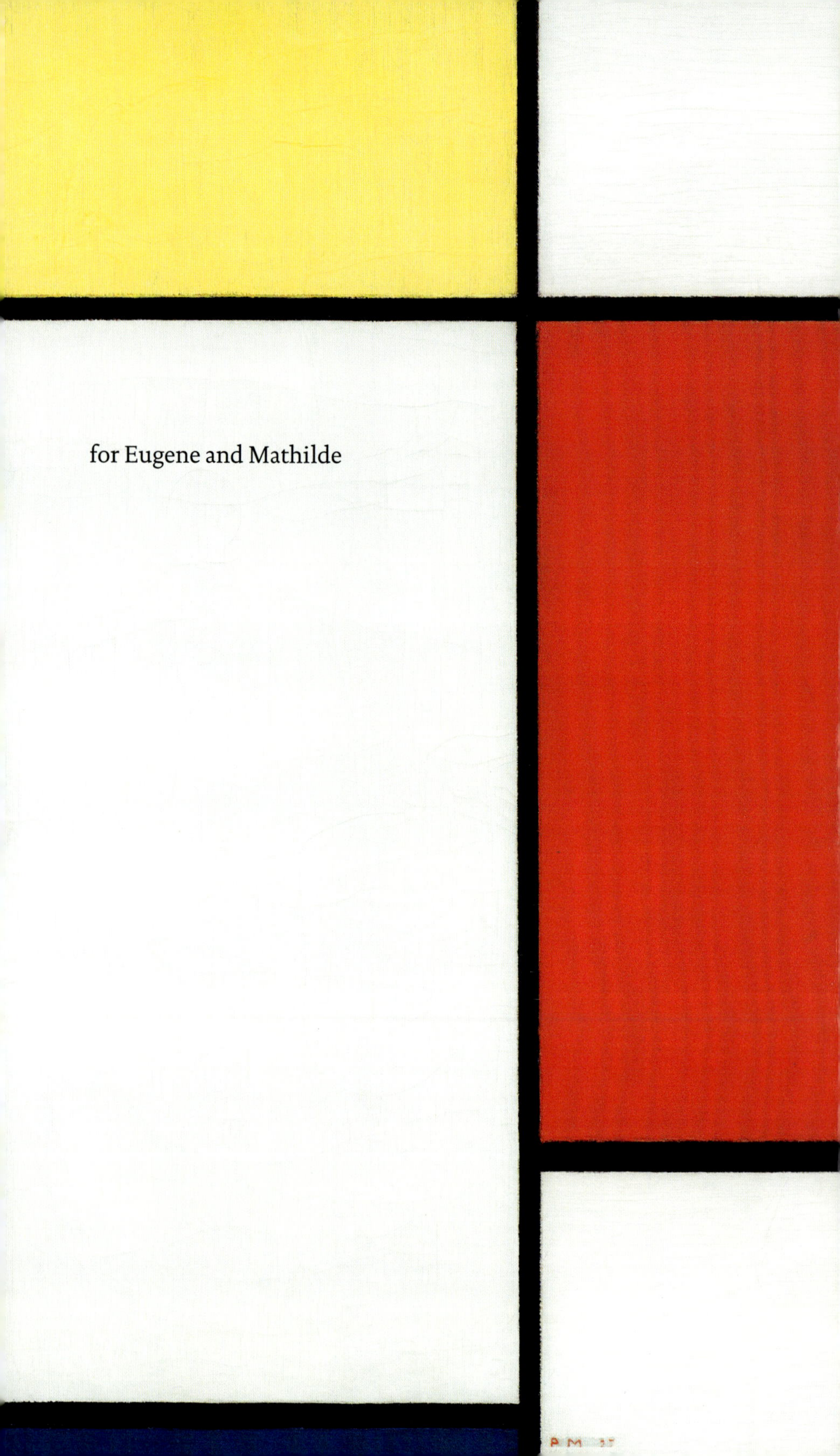

for Eugene and Mathilde

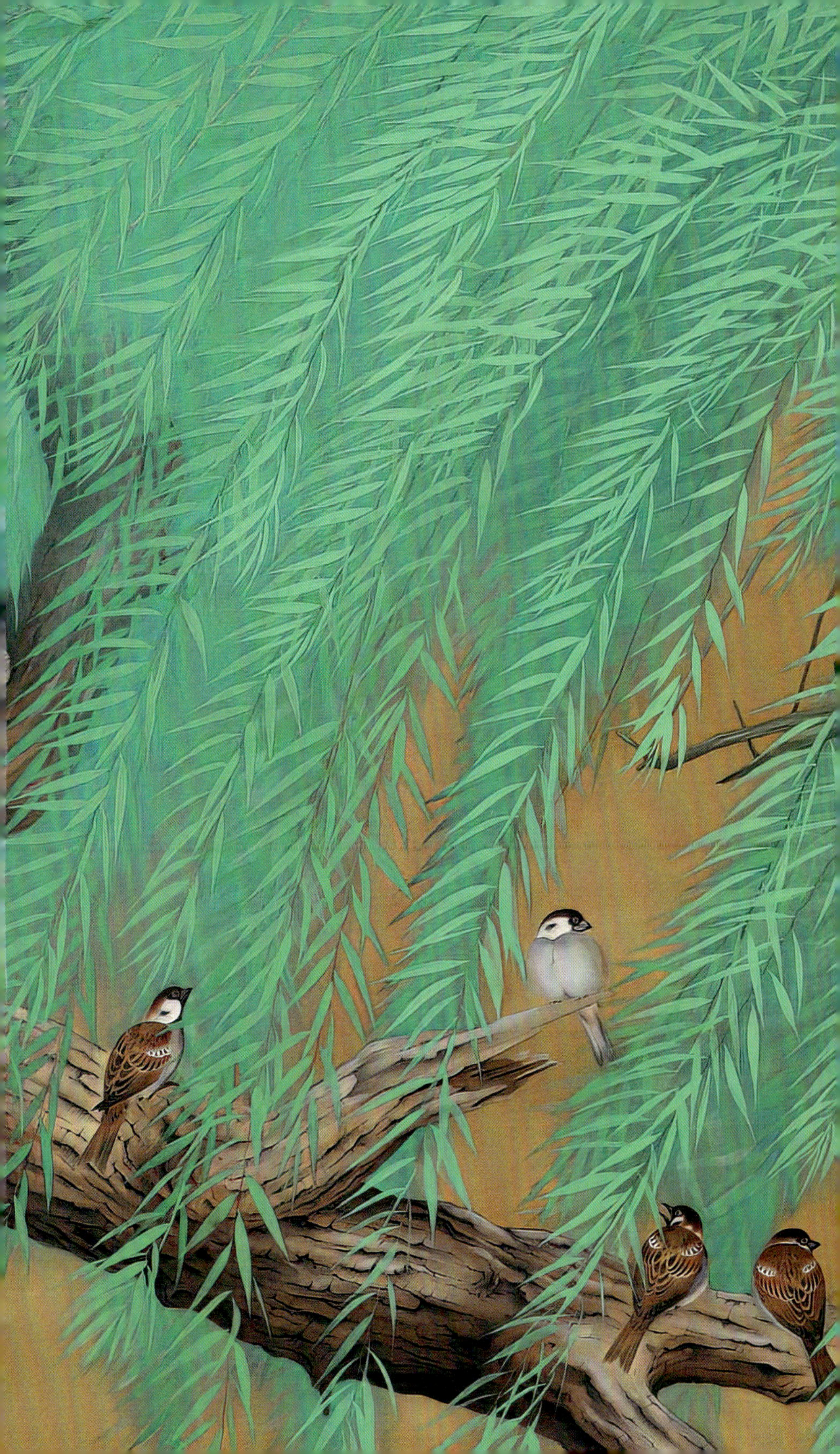

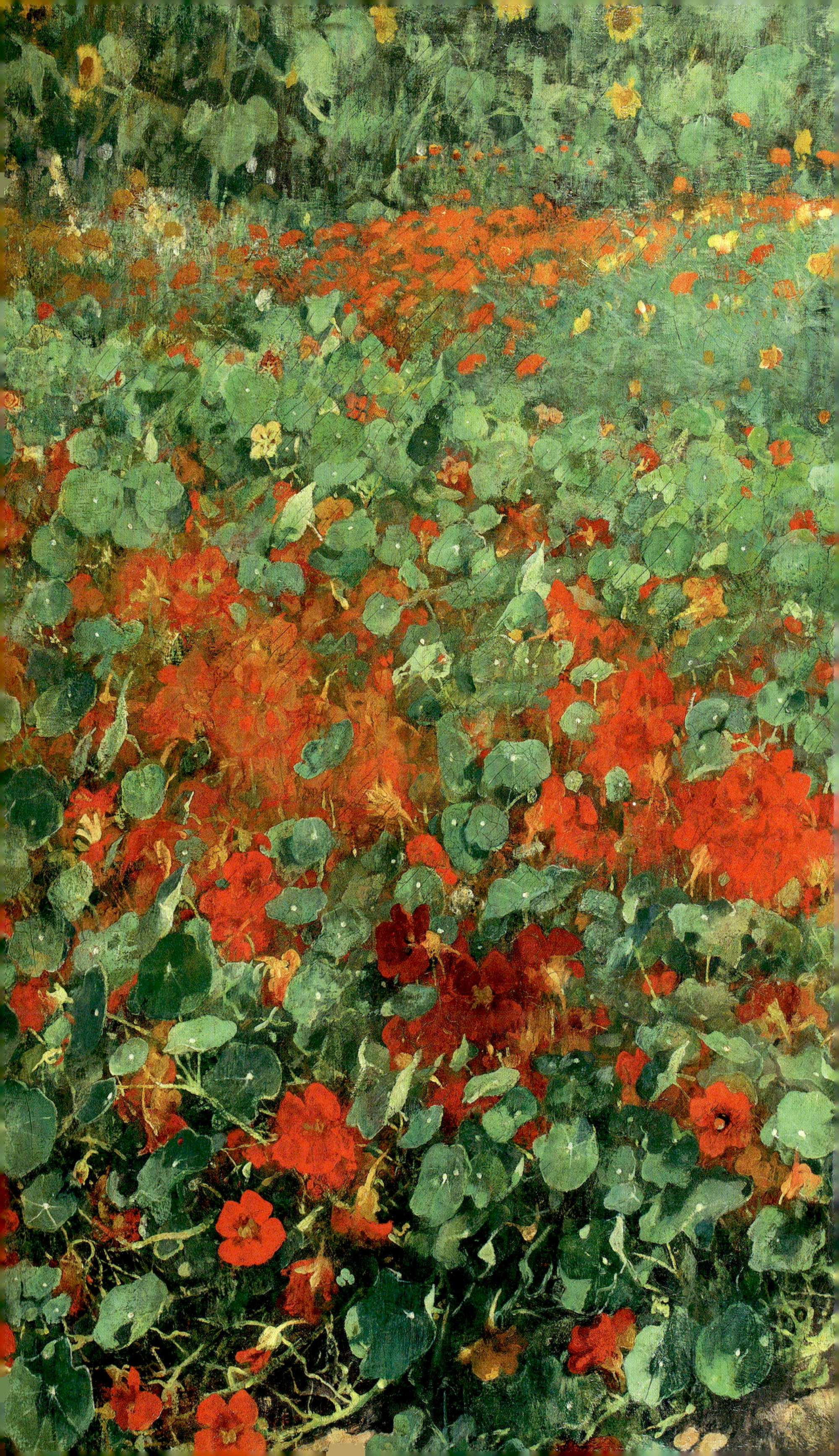

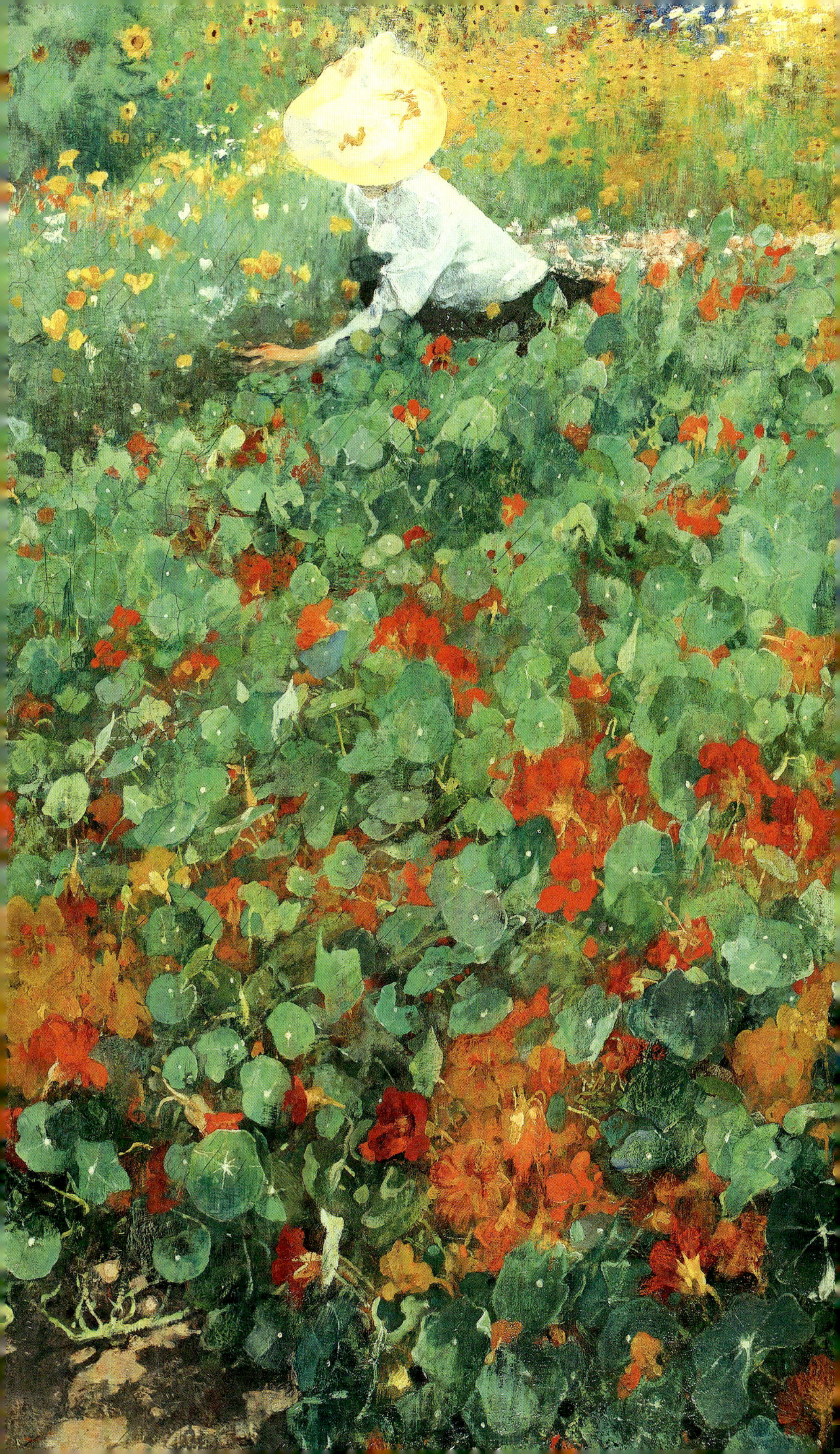

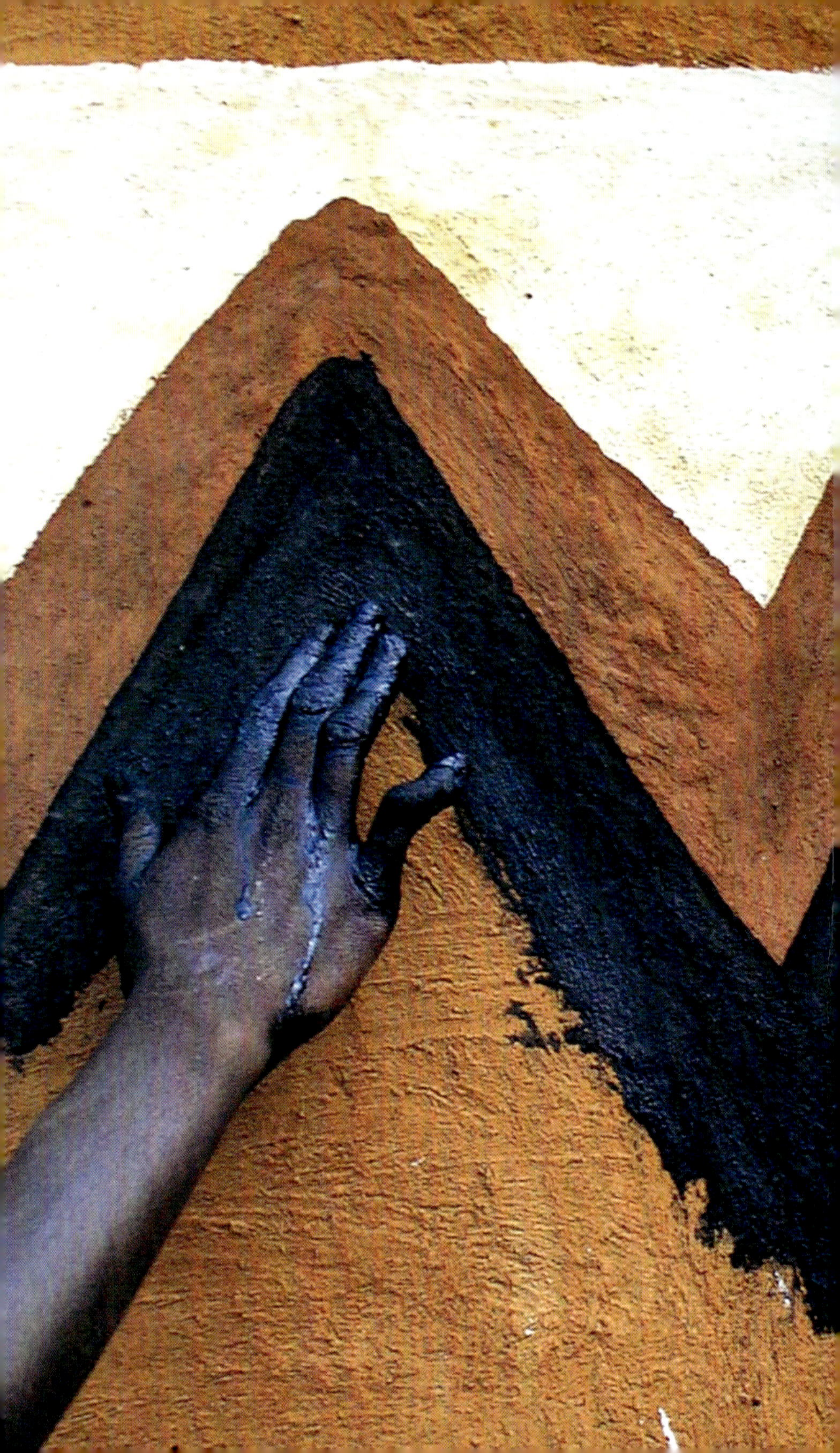

From Colour to Art

monica rotgans

Waanders Publishers, Zwolle

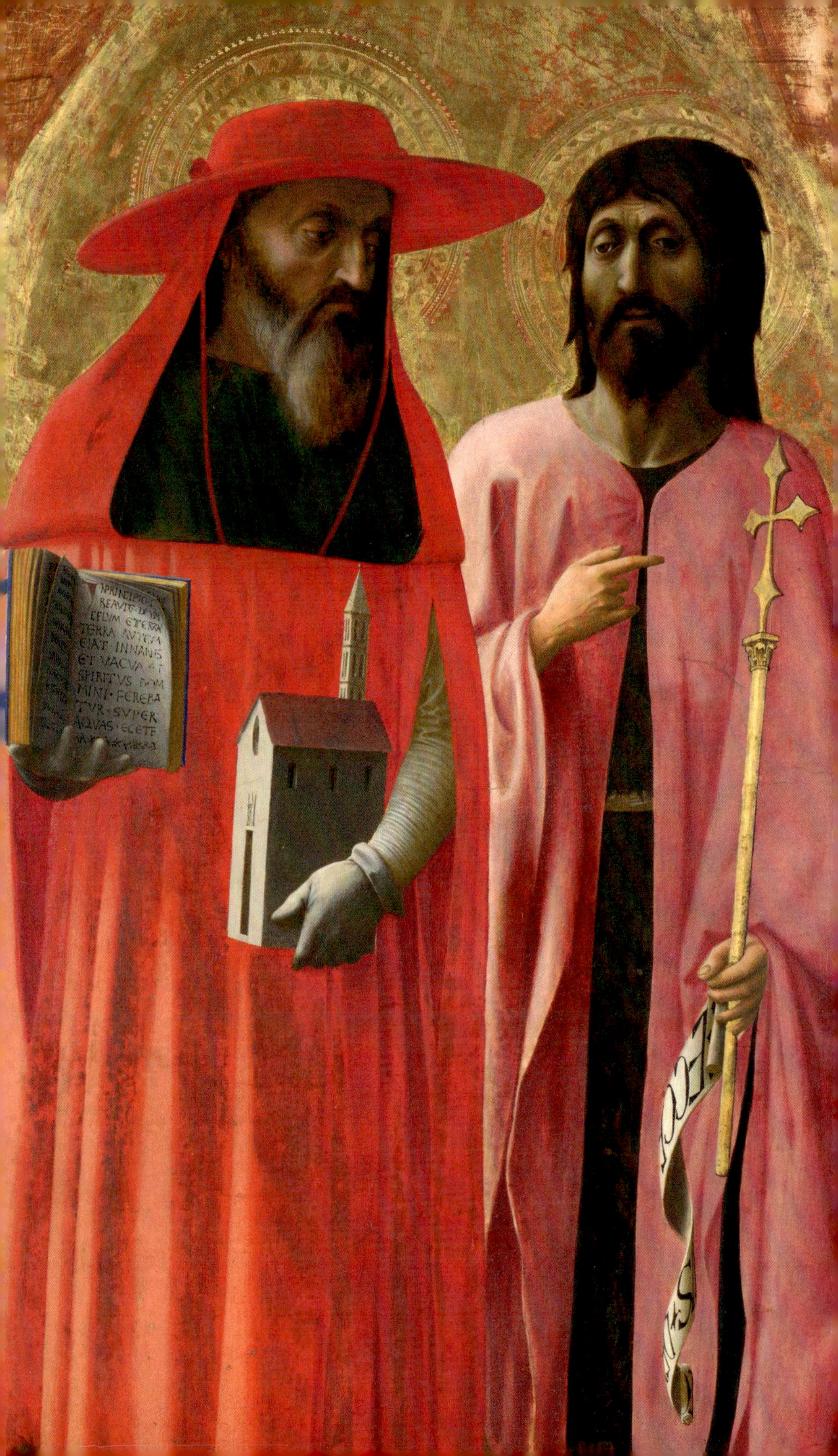
REAVIT
CELVM
TERRA
EIAT INNANIS
ET VACVA
SPIRITVS
MINI FEREBA
TVR SVPER
AQVAS

Contents

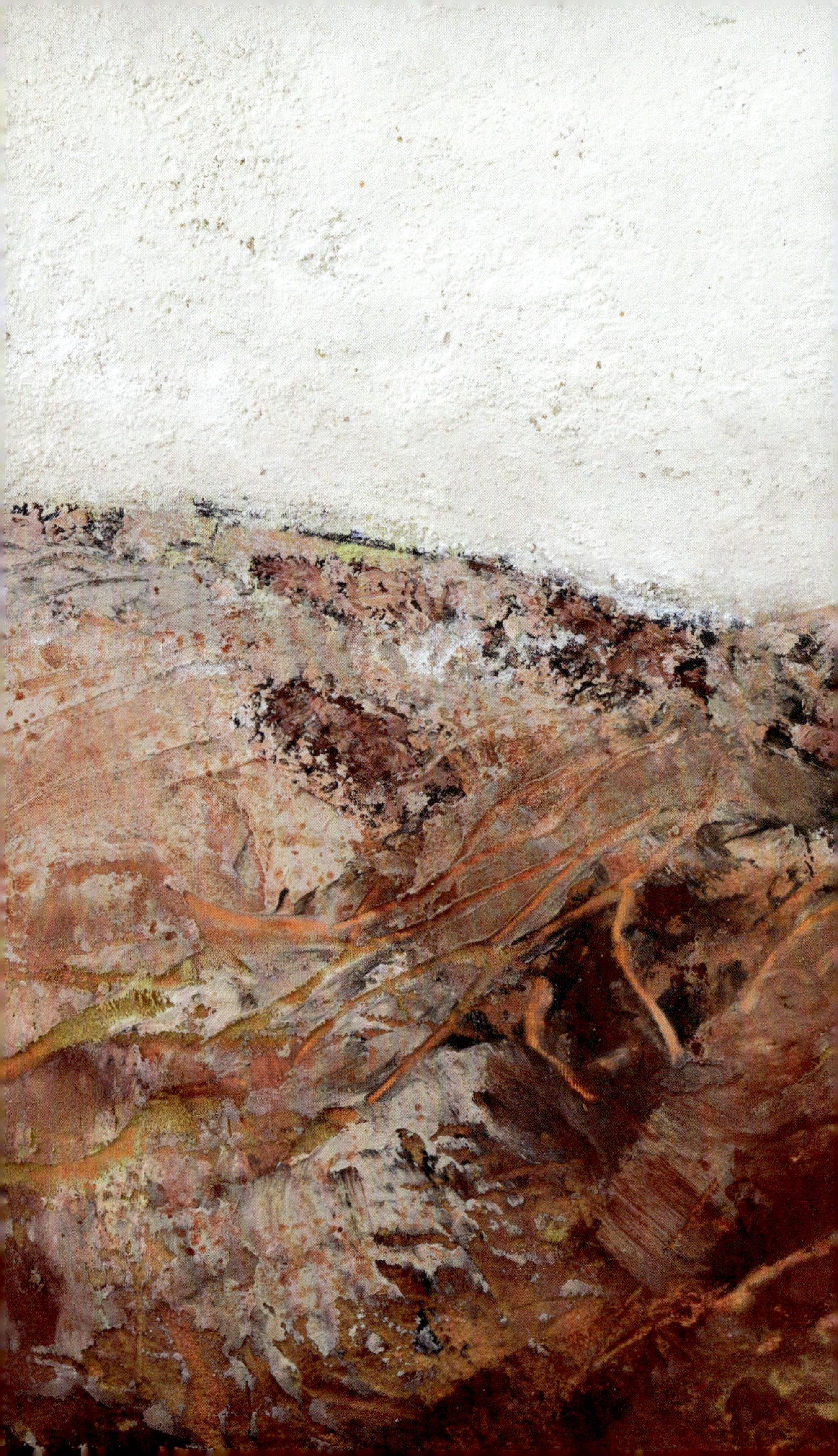

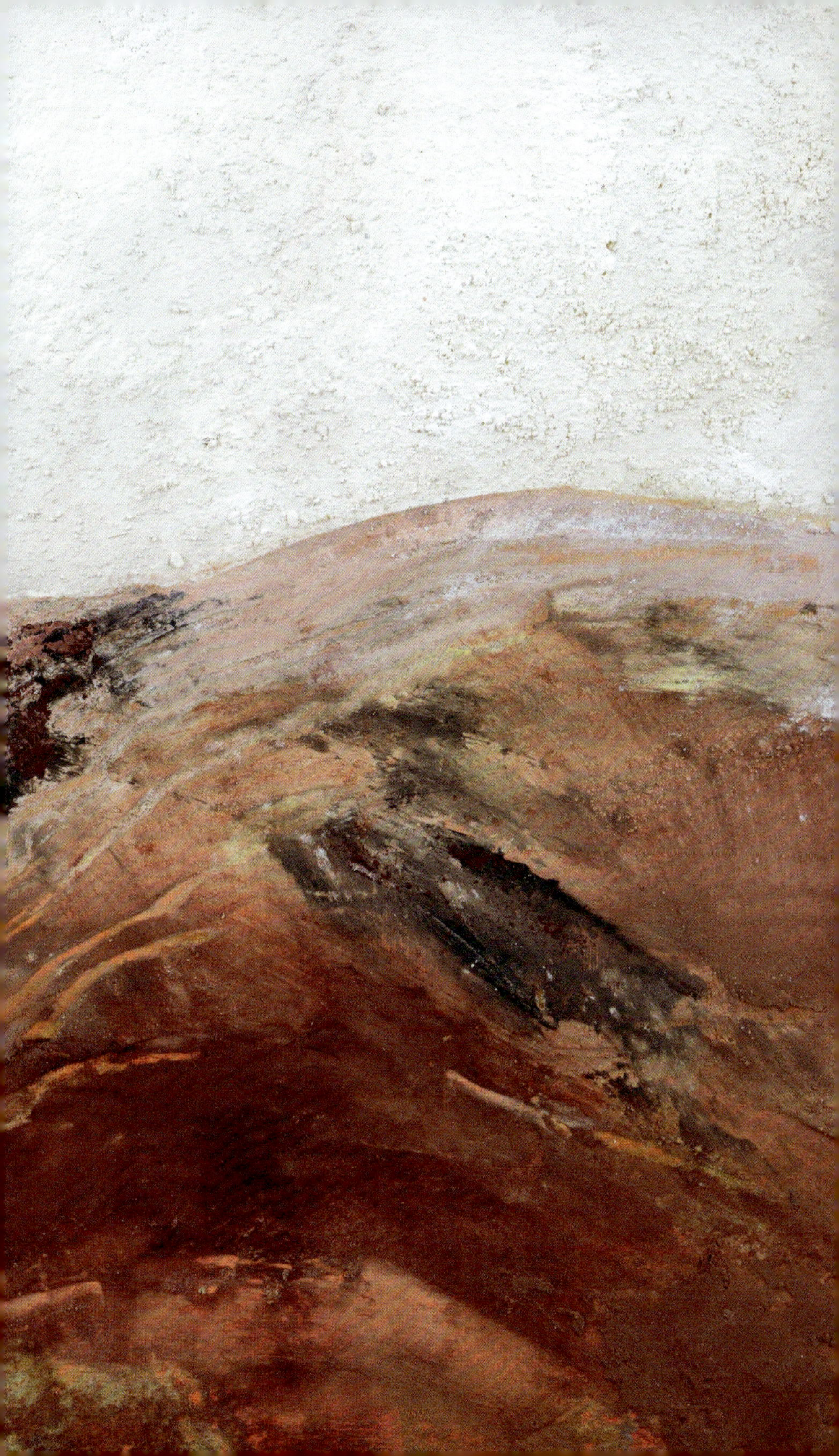

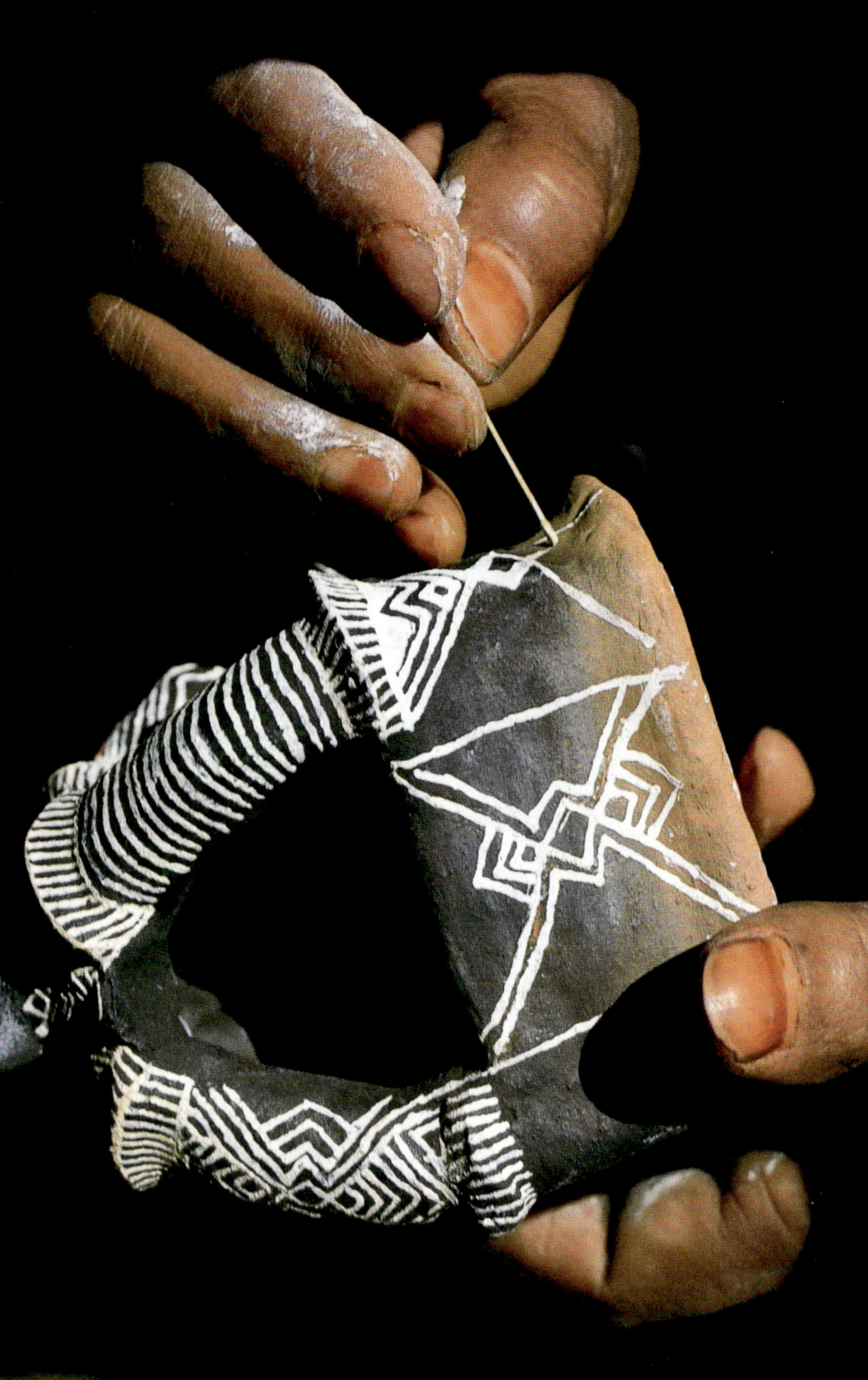

Introduction

'Colour never comes alone'

Antjie Krog – South African
poet and writer

It began with earth and charcoal. The first and actual primary colours: red, yellow, white and black coloured earth.
They can be found almost everywhere in the world, with an additional black provided by charred wood. This palette was later expanded with the colourful sap of plants, fruits, flowers, fungi, and animal fluids. Much later, probably around 7000 years ago, humans discovered the use of minerals for paint: the green and blue of copper ore, the bright red of vermillion (cinnabar), and a white, orange, and yellow from lead ore. The beginnings of our current abundance.

< Painting an incense burner, Oualata, Mauritania

Eucalyptus gum, Australia

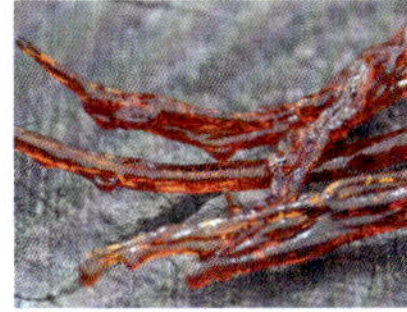

Since earliest prehistory, millions of hands have created paints. Paint to adorn the body, objects, and surroundings. Humans began to distinguish themselves from nature and others. Creating images allowed for the sharing of ideas, as demonstrated by preserved prehistoric cave drawings. Even after tens of thousands of years, these drawings have lost little of their original vitality. This is due to both the protection offered by the caves and to the stability of the earth colours with which they were made.

Ochre Point, South Australia

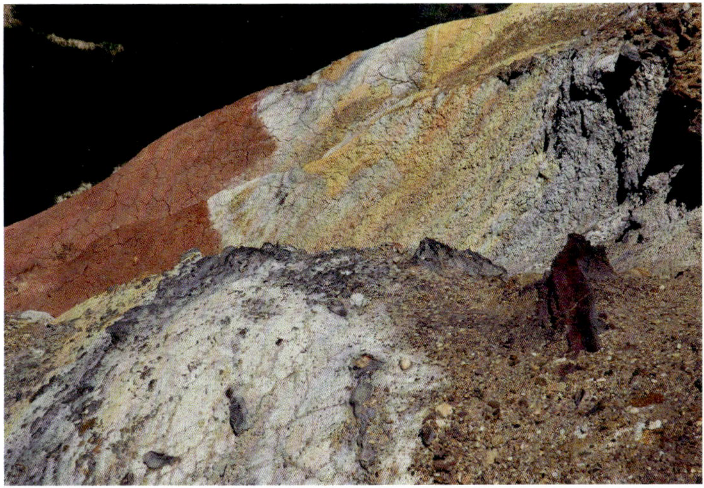

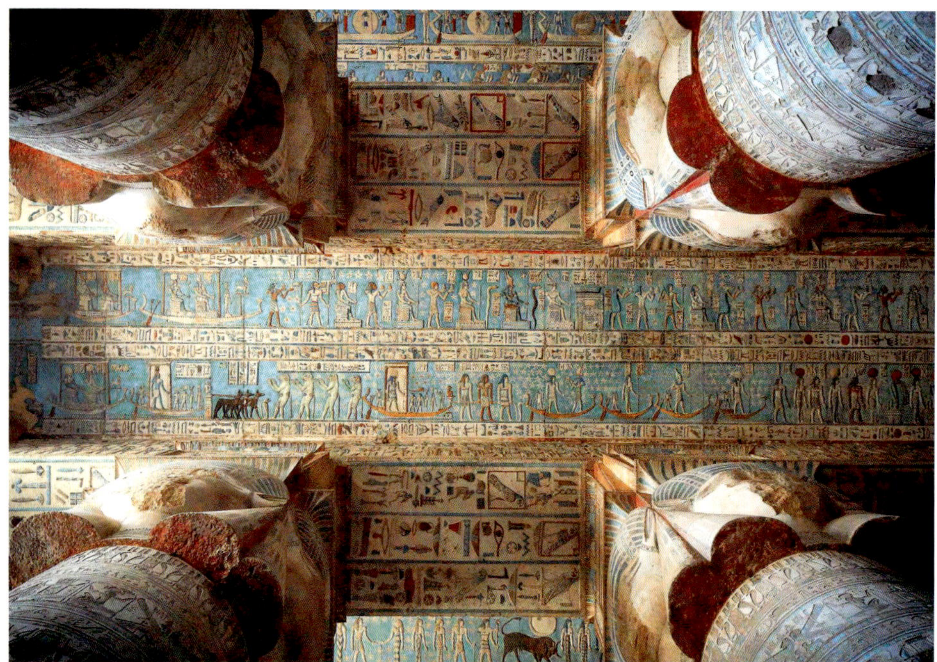

Painted ceiling of the Hall of Pillars at the Dendera Temple near Qena, Egypt

I knew very little of the preceding when I started my studies at the original, classical, Rijksakademie in Amsterdam.. Like most of us, I was familiar with the cave drawings of aurochs and horses from Altamira and Lascaux. That was the extent of my knowledge. Not much was yet known about how they were made and what materials were used. The same counted for the images of artworks shown to us during art history classes. I can vividly recall the numerous examples of temples and cathedrals, the paintings of well-known artists, the sculptures, the genres and movements, the shared influences. However, there was nothing about the colours. Nothing about pigments. In our first year of painting, the closest we came was when we were taught how to stretcha canvas, prepare painting grounds, and turn dry pigments into paint. But we painted with tube paint. The training aspect of our education was focused on developing skills, and a dexterity for form, as the basis for our individual style. All the while, as young artists, we each had our idols whom we wanted to emulate. Virtually all our idols were artists who had achieved their results precisely due to their craftsmanship and knowledge of pigments, materials, and colours. Studying the artworks of our idols came down to, basically, looking without actually understanding what we were seeing.

It wasn't until I began teaching that I realised what was missing: the knowledge of what colour and paint are and what they do. This is the rudimentary foundation for anyone who wants to work effectively with colour. At the time, in the early 1990s, professional literature concerning the subject was still scarce and not comprehensibly written. I decided to fill the gap myself by delving into the history of the painting palette and the history of pigments and colour. The more I discovered, the more I marvelled at the enormous variety of knowledge and available material. I was awed by the limitless connection of people and cultures using colour. My view on the profession drastically changed.

This book addresses the most essential pigments. It would be impossible to provide a complete overview of all pigments for the following reasons:

- many historical pigments are barely or no longer used
- specific and local pigments, the so-called everyday household pigments, are not (yet) known
- the enormous range of modern synthetic pigments
- the overabundance of mixtures

The last refers to a colour composed of several pigments. A large portion of the colours produced by paint manufacturers are mixed colours consisting of two or more pigments. This applies to the manufacturers of both general use paint and art paints. The first time I became aware of this was when a colour I often used was suddenly no longer available. Enquiries sent to the manufacturer informed me it was a mixture of two simple earth pigments, a red and a yellow, and easy to make. Something I hadn't realized.

The palette of Willem Roelofs Jr., one of the founders of Oudt Hollandse Olieverven Makerij; to the right Old Holland's current offer

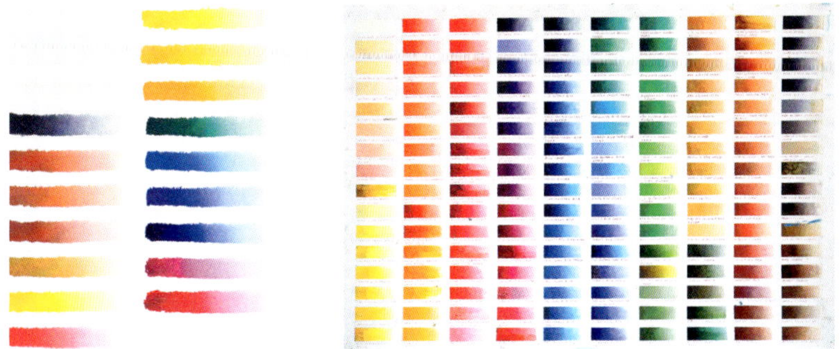

A good example of the difference between a manufacturer's supply and a classic basic palette is found in two colour charts from a long-standing producer of traditional artists paint in the Netherlands, the *Oudt Hollandse Olieverveven Makerij*, now Old Holland. Shown on the left colour chart is the palette used as a standard by one of its founders, the 19th-century painter Willem Roelofs Jr. Eighteen colours in total, including two different whites, enough to work with freely. On the right is the current chart overview of Old Holland with one hundred and sixty (!) colour variations. The enrichment lies mainly in the hues that are difficult, or cannot, be made with Roelofs' palette: violets, oranges, warm greens, and the so-called lake pigments, the transparent paints.

The deluge of colours to choose from today is almost incomprehensible. This superabundance we can mostly attribute to the Industrial Revolution of the 19th century. During the period when new pigments were created, and the industrial paint factories emerged, and the convenient paint tube was invented (around 1841). As a result, our direct contact with pigments, the process of making paint, has practically been lost from view and vanished from everyday life.

CRAFTMANSHIP

How *did* people make paint? Raw materials were (and still are) readily available. That is to say, every environment had a series of basic pigments to offer, the so-called common household colours. Plants, flowers, different types of soil, wood varieties, and minerals. These basics could be supplemented, as needed, with those available from merchants and pharmacies (Latin *apothe-ca*: 'storehouse'). We know pharmacies today as only dispensaries for medicine. Originally, various earths, herbs, minerals, tree products, dried fruits, insect specimens, oils, and spices passed over the counter. All served multiple purposes: as medicines, preservatives and cleaning agents, cosmetics, paints and dyes, or as flavouring. In this book you will frequently see examples of these combinations named.

The strict separation of disciplines, of craft and science, of 'labour' and 'domestic work', is a relatively modern phenomenon. It results from the growing urbanisation and industrialisation during the past three hundred years. Such a process happens gradually and occurs everywhere at a different rate. The raw materials in a painting studio or a dyer's workshop could be found at a physician's medical practice or in a private household. People were more or less self-reliant. Manuals for 'the young housewife' were still being published as late as the early 20th century. They featured formulas for making inks, varnishes, waxes, and basic dyes. Knowledge that is still readily available outside the urbanised world.

As with cooking, making paint is something you gradually master. Each pigment and each binder has specific properties. Through understanding, skill, and ability, these properties could be employed for the various techniques worked with by the artist. To the dry, raw materials were added glue, egg, or oil, to make paints in the studio or workshop. This was usually carried out by an assistant who, according to the master's requirement, prepared the needed colours and placed them on the palette or stored them in jars, or in pig's bladders. Before you continue reading, take a good look at the examples shown here from different times and cultures. The 15th-century woman paints with tempera, the 18th-century artist Horemans with oil, and the Tiébélé woman with a glue-based paint. The paints are made on location, and all the needed ingredients are visible. Their similarities are more relevant than their differences.

Horeman's painting provides a good idea of the ins and outs of an artist's studio, and how apprentices were trained, as was practised for hundreds, perhaps thousands, of years. The master himself is the focal point of the composition. He looks to the assistant, busily preparing paint. Perhaps they discuss the amount of oil, how fine the pigment should be ground, or how long before a colour is ready. The aroma of linseed oil seems tangible. Behind the painter, an apprentice with more experience uses a painting stick to add details to a work set up by his master. To the right of the easel stands a boy, with a sketch in his hands, apparently waiting for approval or instructions. His drawing board with a sheet of blue paper, to practice working with half-tones, his charcoal, chalk,

Jan Josef Horemans, *An Artist's Studio*, 1st half 18th cen., oil on canvas, 49 x 60 cm, Nationalmuseum, Stockholm

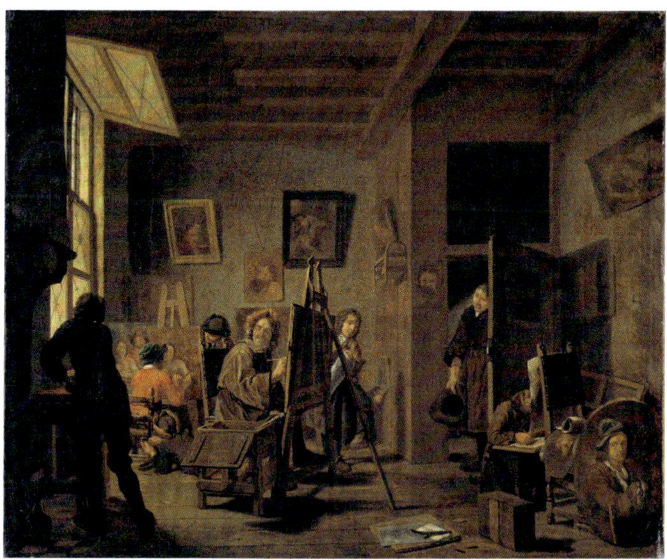

Tiébélé, Burkina Faso

Anonymous, *A Woman Painting the Virgin Mary*, Italian manuscript, c. 1402, Bibliothèque Nationale, Paris

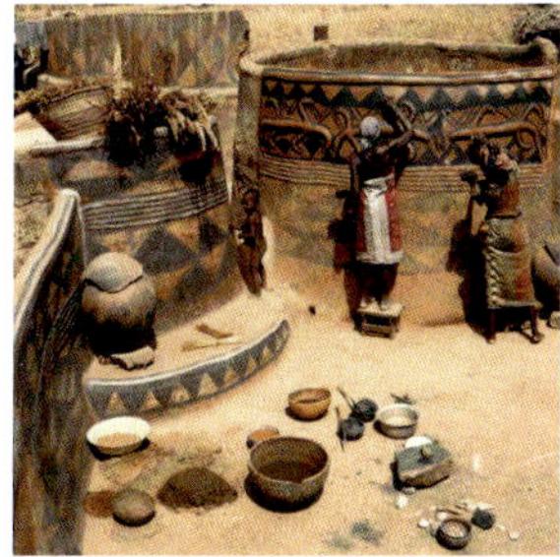

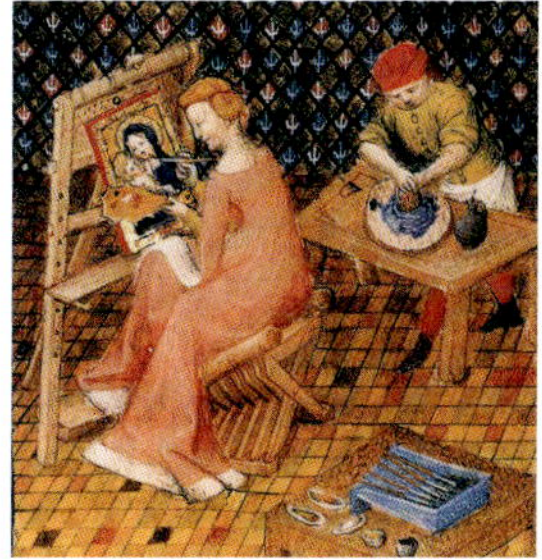

and brush feather, are on the floor in the foreground, beside the box he was sitting on. It is the drawing corner for beginners. A boy lying on the floor (girls are absent) sharpens pens. This shows how the trade was learned. Starting at a young age learning to look and to draw. By copying and being gradually allowed to do more. Eventually, hopefully, gaining recognition as a master and permission to start their own workshop.

Kawanabe Kyōsai, *Students at Work*, 19th cen.

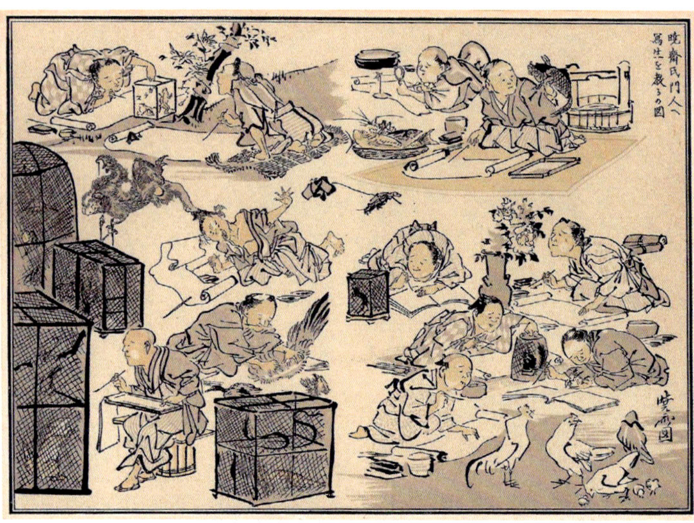

LIFE AFTER THE EASEL AND THE SCULPTING STAND

When an artwork leaves the studio you hope, as creator, it will receive a long and good life. That the new owners will enjoy it, treat it with care, and the materials used will not prove capricious by showing signs of decay. This last is never a certainty. Not historically, nor in the present day. A fast-drying pigment can cause an overlying paint to crack if the first paint layer had insufficient drying time. Some pigments change or lose their original colour, over time, and a fine pigment can seep through other coarser pigments, commonly known as bleeding. There are pigments that dry poorly, or never thoroughly, and combining different types of paint could have disastrous consequences. Ready-to-use factory paint is like a closed book. The formula is kept secret, which makes it difficult to determine the exact composition. Additionally, an error in production may come to light later or after a long period of time. Artworks in museums, whether hanging or standing, also might suffer the aforementioned possibilities. They may, for centuries, have had exposure to fluctuating temperatures, smoke, humidity and draughts prior to their placement within the relatively safe walls of an art institute. Many of these artworks have lost some, or whole sections, of their original appearance. This is not immediately noticeable if you are unfamiliar with these effects. Once aware of the pigments and colours in common use during specific periods, you learn to spot the characteristics.

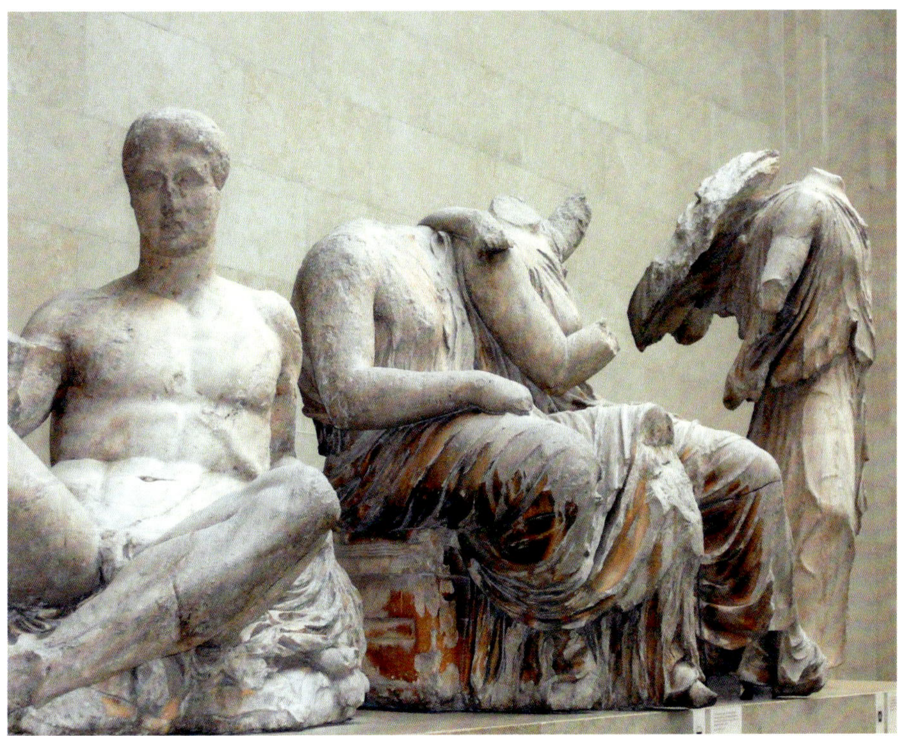

Parthenon Elgin Marbles, detail of the tympanum, Acropolis, British Museum, London

The white marble sculptures from Greek and Roman times, for example, were painted in clearly defined colours to emphasise the status and function of those depicted. Signal colours, which made it possible to immediately recognise, even from a distance, whom or what was presented. Most of these applied paints, with the passing of time, have vanished through weathering or people's actions. Sometimes, you can still discover a remnant of colour in a fold, or on the back of a work, as is the case with the once richly painted Elgin Marbles. The same applies to the wooden sculptures of later times, which were stripped of their paint, especially so during the 19th century. While their form may be more defined without their original colour, it is difficult to recognise who they represent. For a predominantly illiterate population, colour was the essential visual guide.

Paintings can undergo a similar transformation. A part of the composition or a figure might be painted over, or a colour or form that no longer pleases the eye could be modified. The artist may decide to alter something if she or he is no longer pleased with the composition, or an owner of a work could have it adapted to a new trend or a changed circumstance. Murals, by definition, are vulnerable on both exterior and interior walls. They are comparable to the painted walls of a house. Regular repainting is necessary due to discolouring or damage. Paintings on and in public spaces are particularly vulnerable. The number of murals that have disappeared over the centuries is difficult to estimate. In 2012, a well-intentioned repair made international headlines when an 81-year-old resident of Borja, Spain, irreparably 'restored' a damaged mural in her local church.

Elías García Martínez, *Ecce homo*, 1930, and the 'restoration' by Cecilia Giménez, 2012

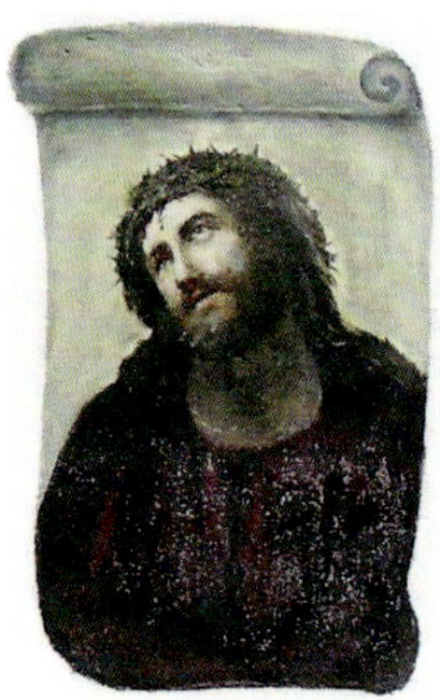

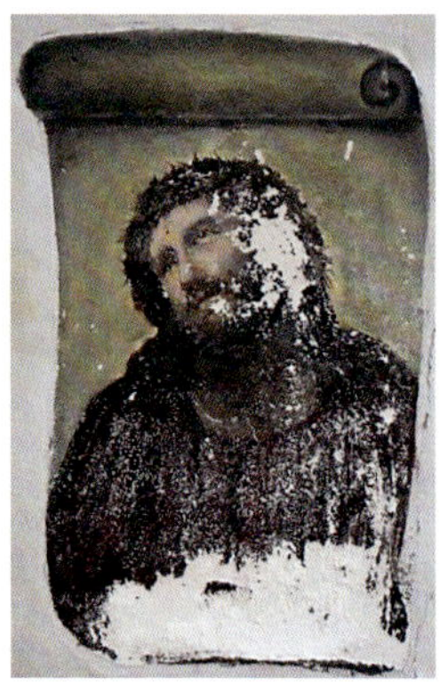

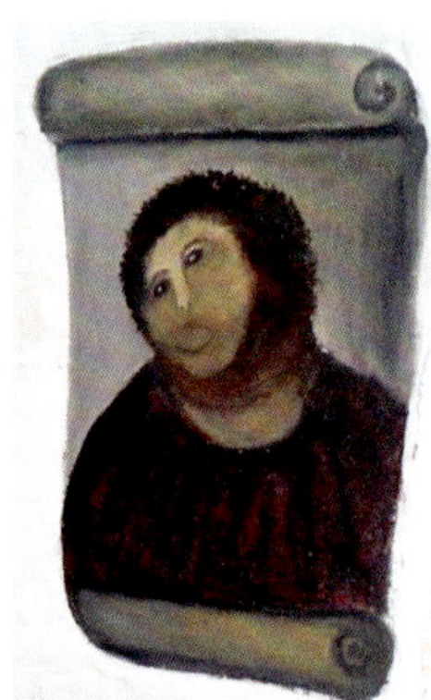

Unfortunately, this is how restoration is often perceived: restoration means repainting. Not so when a restoration is done correctly. Professional restoration involves treating the painting in a manner that protects it from further deterioration. Yellowed old varnish, dirt, and, if necessary, overpainting is removed, and missing sections retouched. Optically adjusted retouching makes it imperceptible.

The starting point is to leave the artist's signature style and palette, and the structure of the paint, as intact as possible. An example of the latter is the restoration of De Heem's *The Dessert* in the Louvre. De Heem's showpiece still life (*Pronkstilleven*) is a sizeable canvas made to flaunt and impress. A status symbol with a display of exclusive objects and food that were, in his time, unattainable for most people. It must have been an explosion of colour, when fresh on his easel, much of which has now become invisible. If you look closely, you can see details that don't actually make sense. The morbidly grey grapes, whitish apples and quinces, the picture-filling, gloomy canopy and the sombre little landscape in the left background, despite a fair-weather cloud having been painted in the sky.

We can see this more clearly now because the thick, dirty, and yellowed varnish has been removed whereby the brownish glow, so characteristic of 'old' art, is dissolved. The faded colours, however, have not been restored.

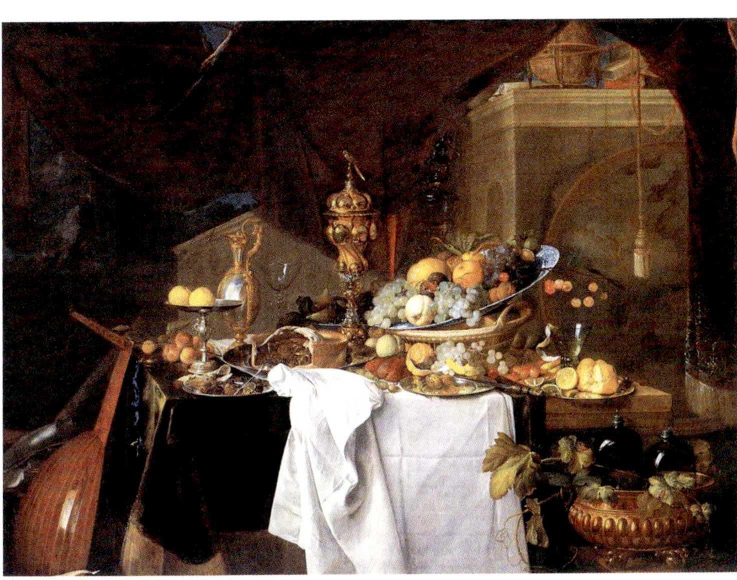

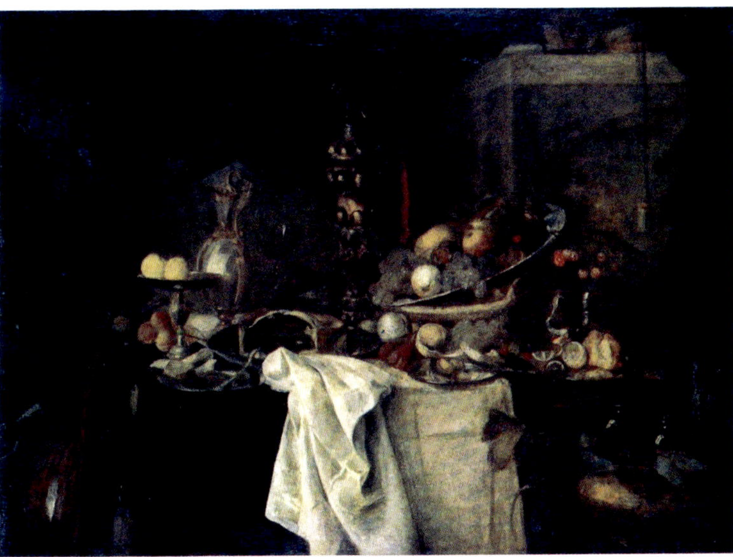

Jan Davidsz de Heem, *The Dessert*, 1640, oil on canvas, 149 x 203 cm, Louvre, Paris

Henri Matisse, *The Dessert*, 1893, 72 x 100 cm, Musée Matisse, Nice

In the late 19th century, Matisse saw this artwork quite differently. Dark and brown, as was believed 17th-century art to have been intended. Like many of his fellow students at the academy, Matisse went to the Louvre to learn the skills of the profession by studying and copying the paintings of old masters. Due to the invisibility of, and the ignorance about, the original colours, it was mainly a case getting a grasp on composition and the distribution of light and dark. About depicting fabrics, the placement of the horizontals, verticals and diagonals, the rhythm. In accordance with the instruction, he correctly painted what he saw, whilst unaware he copied contamination and discolouration.

An example of a restoration project taken to extremity is the 'restoration' of the *Salvator Mundi*. A work which potentially was or was not, or perhaps only a small part, actually painted by Da Vinci, is a painting with a long, eventful history. It became the focus of a number of vested interests. The drastic restoration operation was decided upon due to the imperative of attaching the artist's name. After the removal of several layers of over painting and repairs a heavily damaged and discoloured panel remained. In order to make it into a cohesive whole, large areas had to be repainted.

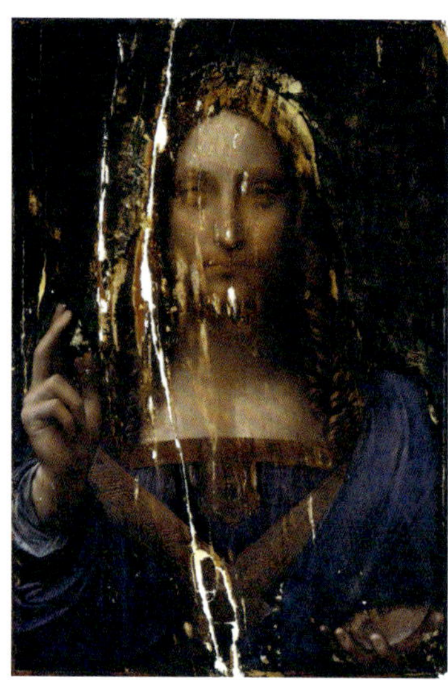

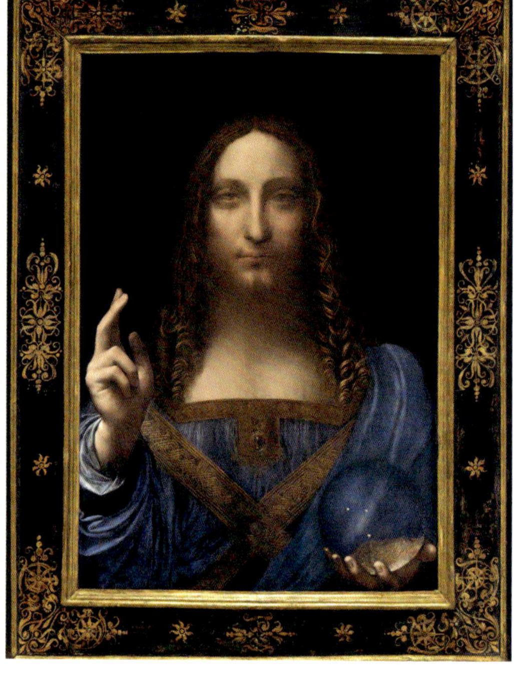

The *Salvator Mundi* in 2007 and at auction at Christie's New York in 2017

The result is an incongruous image where a flat, lifeless figure rises behind a fully realistic hand. The original structure and colours of the paint, the artist's signature style, have all but disappeared. Nonetheless, it was sold at auction for more than 450 million dollars, making it the most expensive painting in the world. What we look at, and what we see, is dependent upon the sum of varied factors. As the chemist and writer Primo Levi so eloquently stated: 'Paints are born, they grow old, and they die like us; and when they're old, they can turn foolish, and even when they're young, they can deceive you, and they're actually capable of telling lies, pretending to be what they aren't; to be sick when they're healthy, and healthy when they're sick.'

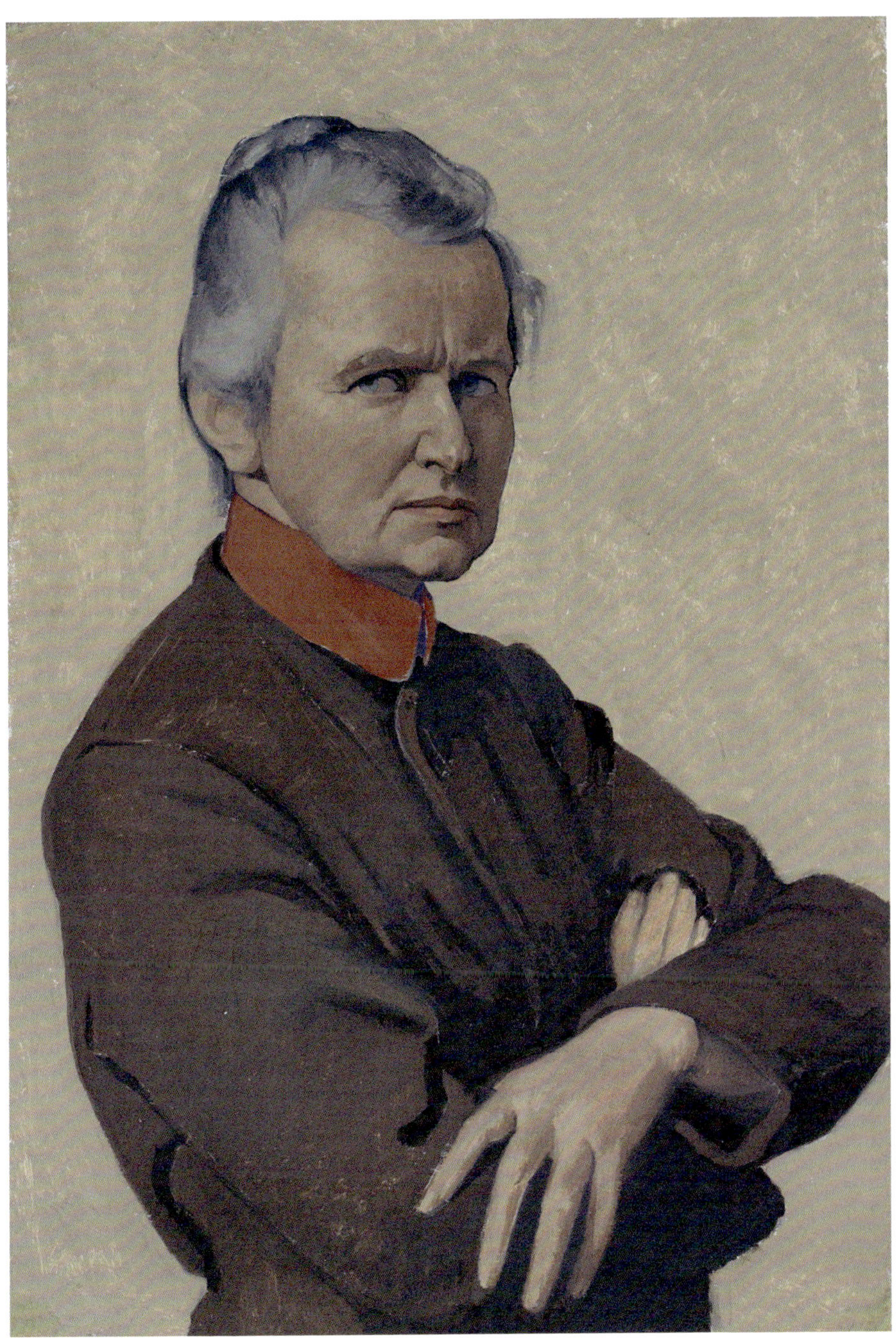

Ottilie Roederstein,
Self-Portrait, 1918,
oil on canvas

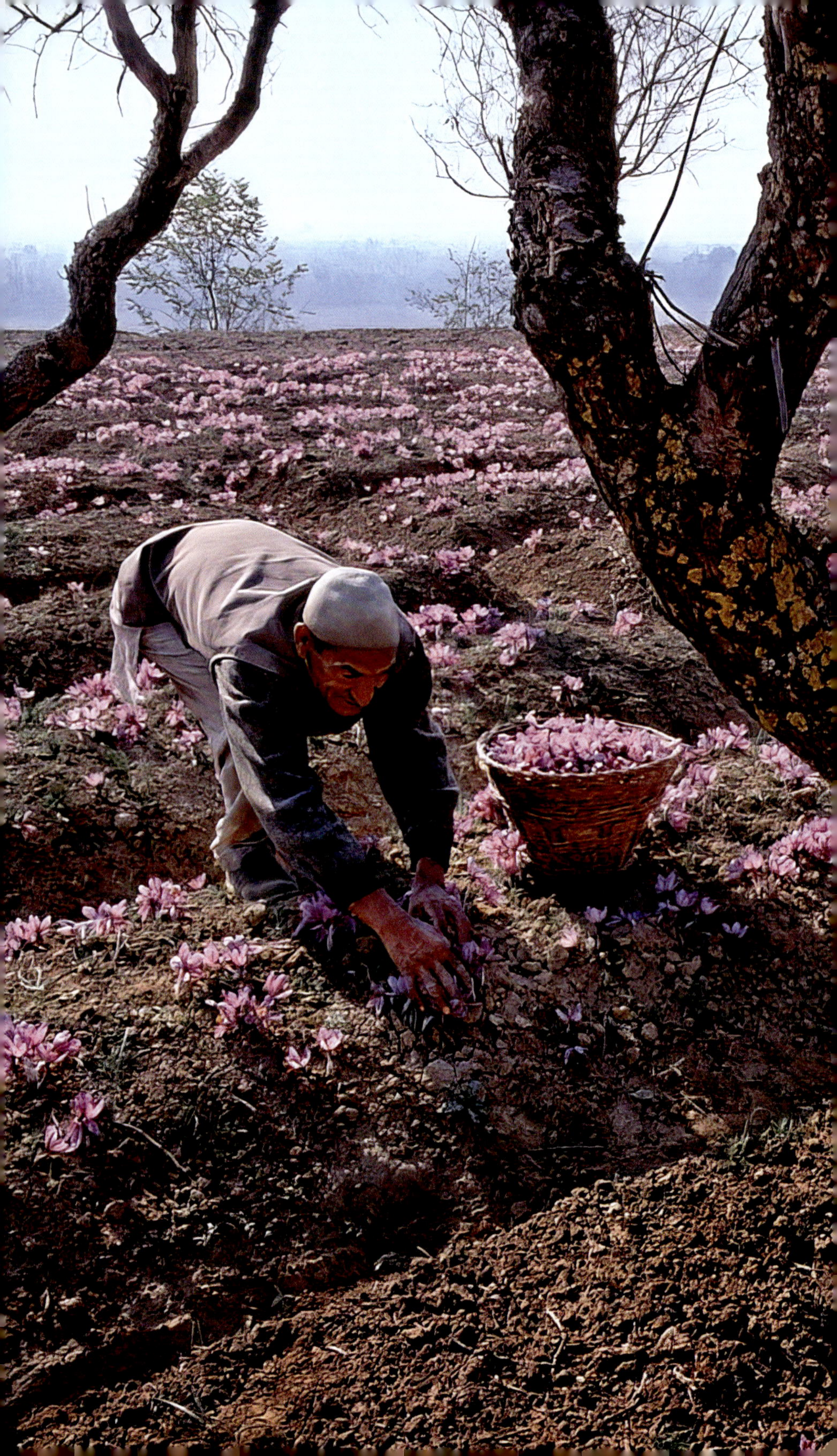

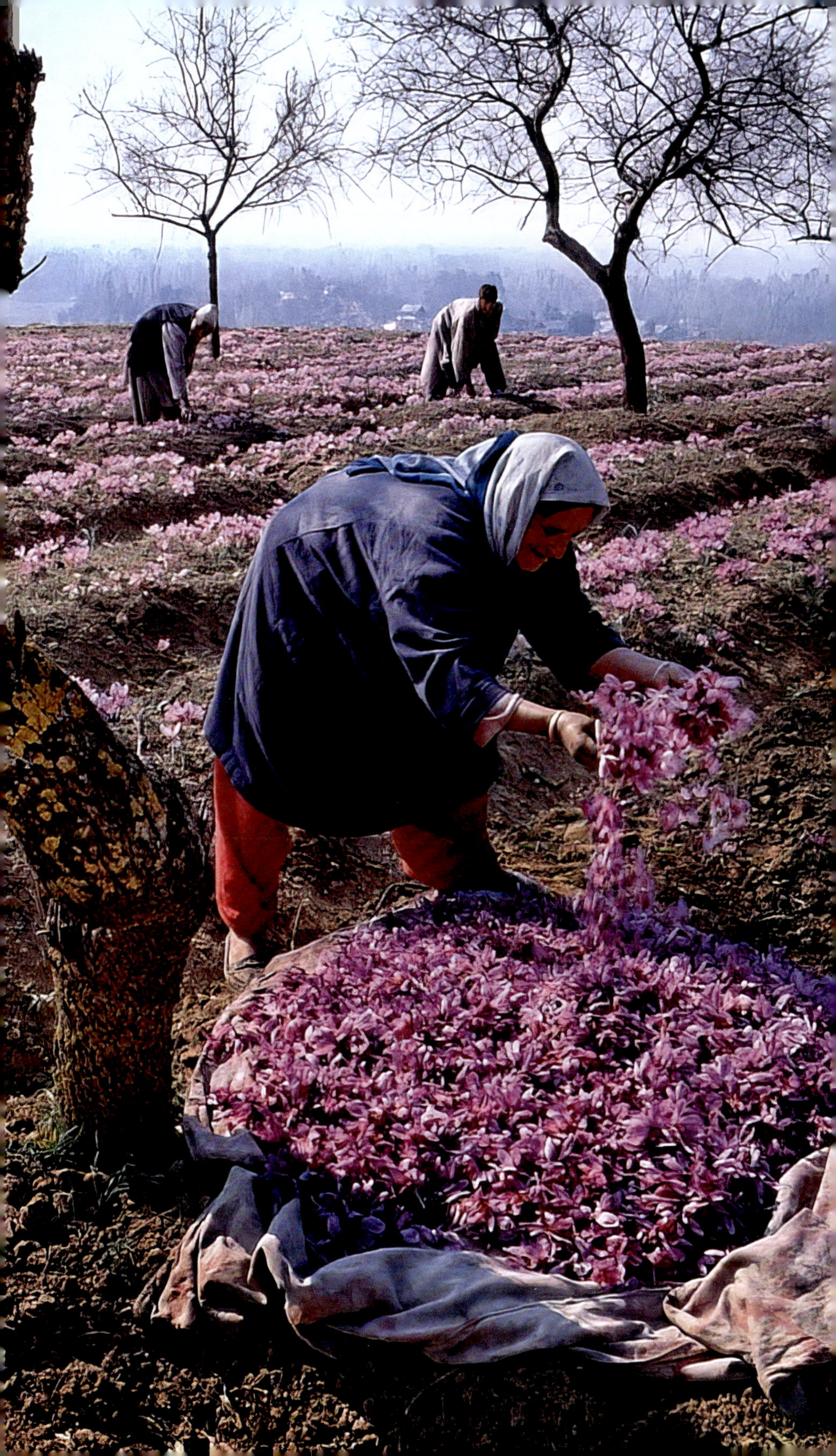

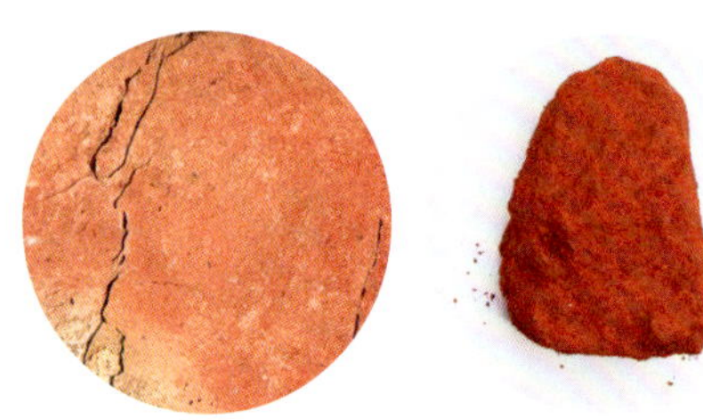

Red Earth

Red earth is the common thread connecting us to the first humans, and to the most diverse cultures, places and times. Earthly red is pivotal in ancient rituals around life, love, birth, initiation, disease, authority, war and death, and was and still is, used everywhere on the colour palette. Due to its magical attributions, red was the first of the colours to be named.

Red earth, wrongly called red ochre, is ferrous clay or sand in which the iron rusts. It is found on all continents, within a spectrum from pale red to dark violet. The robust haematite, from the Ancient Greek *haima* (blood, bloodstone), is the primary mineral building block of red earth. It exists in a red and blackish (iron lustre) form. Haematite is the same material to which the red planet Mars owes its colour and was called *lapis rosso*, the red stone, during the Renaissance. Malleable and plastic types of earth are suitable for ceramics and as bole ground. Pure haematite is easy to cut into shape, making it an ideal tool for the polishing of gold leaf. The gold that in part owes its warm glow to the underlying red bole ground.

Since the beginning of time, red earth has been the colour to adorn and coat the skin of both the living and the dead. It is a signal colour and body paint, with the additional advantage of suppressing body odour

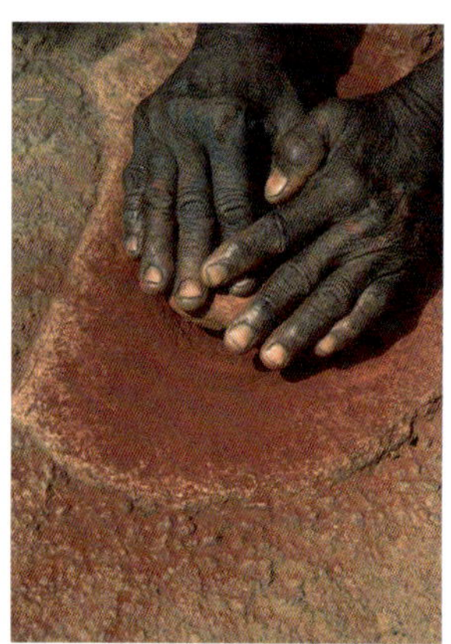

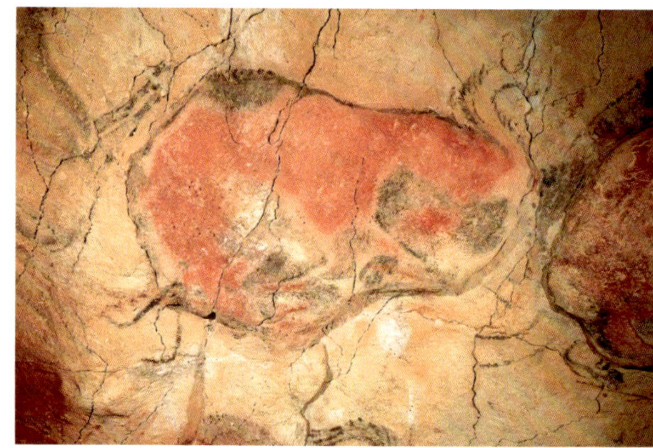

A lump of red earth is rubbed into pigment

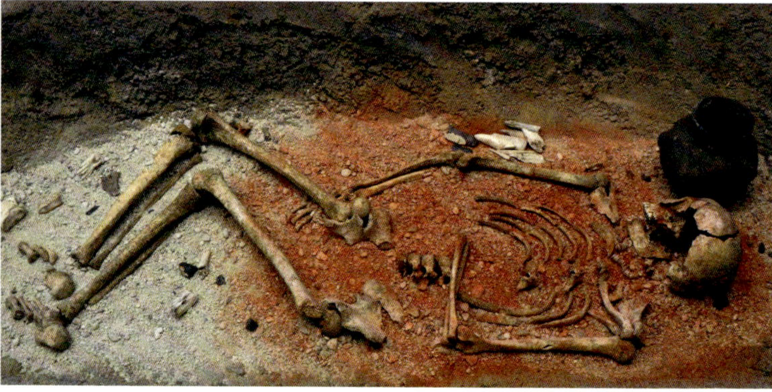

A Neolithic grave of a young man, c. 4500 BC, Musée Remi, Reims

while hunting. A mixture of red earth and fat served, and is still used in various cultures, as an effective protection of skin and hair against the sun, insects and pollution. Metal and timber objects were similarly coated with red earth, to name just a few of its many uses. Red earth has been a universal burial gift from early prehistoric times, as shown in the photo featuring a Neolithic grave from 4500 BC In its fired form, it is called *terracotta*, meaning 'baked earth'. Fattier earth is ideal modelling clay. Therefore, it is the basis of many forms of ceramics and pottery used worldwide for domestic, architectural and industrial purposes, and even special luxury products.

As paint, red earth is a quick dryer and more sparkling than the rather lifeless contemporary synthetic iron oxides. Which, very confusingly, are frequently offered under the same names. Red earth is for the taking in many places and, if necessary, can be purified quite effortlessly before use. Throw a scoop of earth into a bucket of water, stir it vigorously, and let it settle. Once the earth has sunk to the bottom, drain the dirty water. If you want, this can be repeated several times.
Red earth becomes paint by mixing the pigment with water, blood, marrow, lard, milk, fish, hide or bone glue, flour, plant or flower sap, oil, resin, gum, beeswax, honey, manure or saliva. And, nowadays, a synthetic binding medium. We should not overestimate the quantities of paint people were making and using in the past. Little was needed to decorate figurines or to paint the extraordinary animals and symbols in prehistoric caves. The paint is quite thinly applied, as seen in the bison of Altamira, where the bulge of the rock is masterfully incorporated into the shape of the buttocks.

< Painting of a European bison in the Altamira cave, c. 15,000 BC, Spain

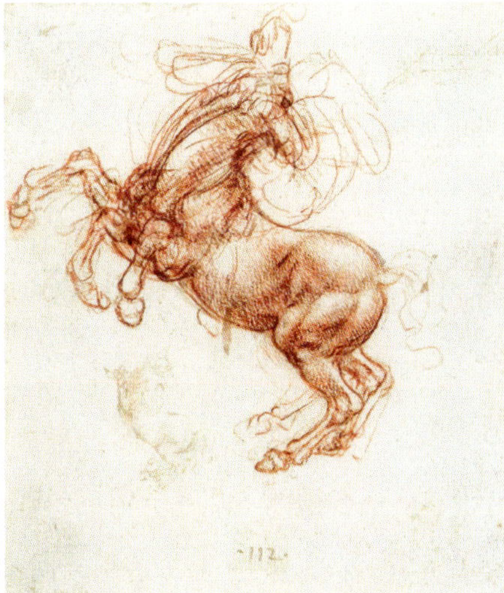

Leonardo da Vinci, *Rearing Horse*, c. 1503

Mural of a fisherman, c. 1650 BC, Aktrori, Santorini

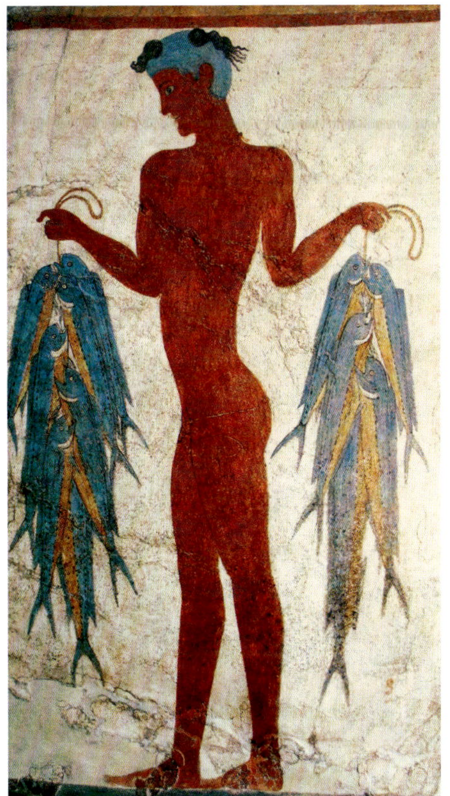

In some of the caves, objects were found where paint was once put on or in, such as the shoulder blade of an animal, an abalone shell, or a flat or hollow stone. Marrow-bones were used as blowpipes to blow pigment on hands and walls.
Red earth is an attractive base colour for painting human figures and animals. It quickly gives the impression of mass, no matter how thinly applied. Moreover, by applying it thicker or thinner on a light surface, it can be used to suggest volume with minimal effort. It is the oldest red used in mixtures for flesh tones, often combined with (yellow) ochre and a white pigment. When mixed with black, the blueish reds are an affordable and easy ingredient to mimic purple.
Red chalk is the solid form of red earth and has been in use since early prehistory. One can be the raw material for the other: a stylus can be ground into pigment. And pigment, combined with a binding medium, can be transformed into a stylus. It requires a direct way of drawing, as can be seen in Da Vinci's sketch. Unlike charcoal, it does not allow any concealing or corrections.

Textiles were (and still are today) dyed with red earth, and probably far more often than we assume. Although textiles are a fragile support, examples from ancient times have survived, such as several haematite-coloured cloths on Egyptian mummies. In Europe, red textile remains of Viking sails from the fifth century were found by chance during the restoration of a small church in Norway. The large sails were surprisingly made of wool, not a very suitable material due to its sensitivity to moisture. However, at a final stage, the woollen pieces of cloth were made water-repellent with red earth

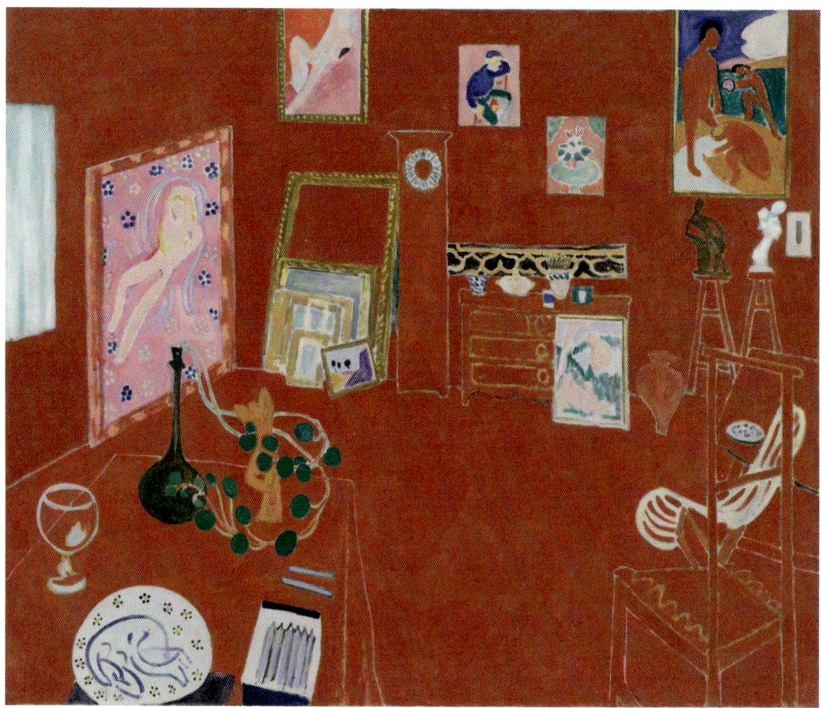

Henri Matisse, *The Red Studio*, 1911, oil on canvas, 162 x 130 cm, MoMa, New York

through *smôrring*, a time-consuming and recently rediscovered process. Another traditional method of dyeing fabric with earth is *bogolan*, from Mali in West Africa. According to legend, this technique was accidentally discovered when a huntsman fell into a mud pool while chasing a rabbit. Back on his feet, he realised he could not remove the mud stains from his clothes. The basis of today's *bogolan* technique is a specific river clay. This clay is fermented for around a year in pots made especially for this purpose, after which it can be used to paint patterns on cotton fabric.

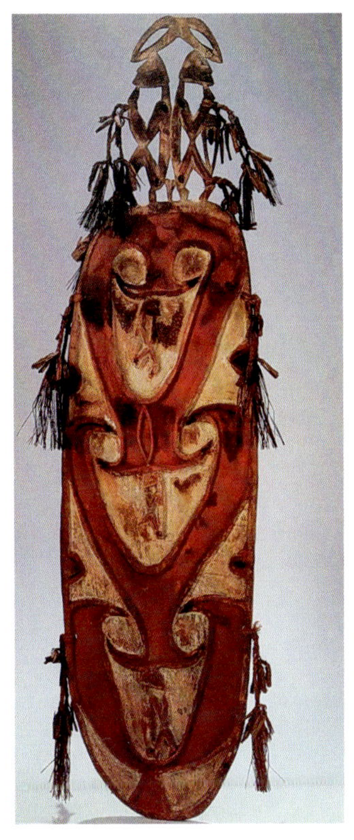

Asmat war shield, h. 139.5 cm, Wereldmuseum, Leiden

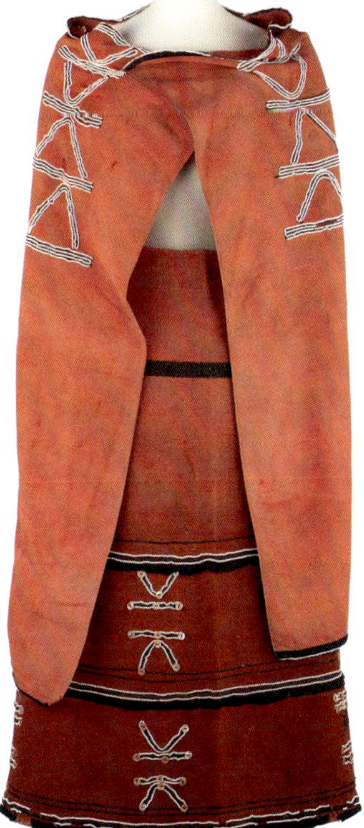

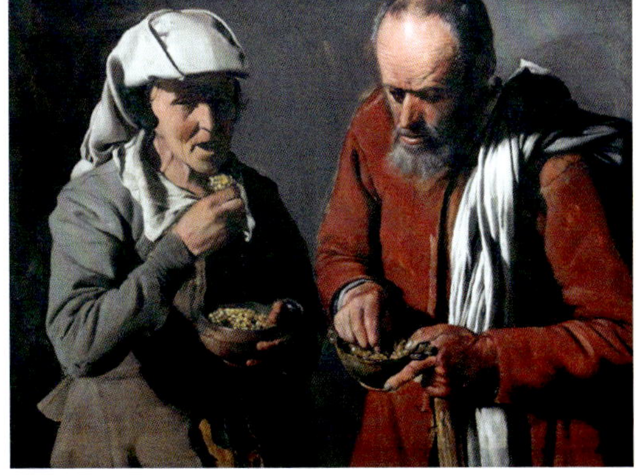

Xhosa women's outfit, 20th cen., cotton dyed with red earth and decorated with glass pearls, mother of pearl and felt, Brighton Museum

Georges de la Tour, *Pea Eaters*, c. 1620, oil on canvas, 74 x 87 cm, Gemäldegalerie, Berlin

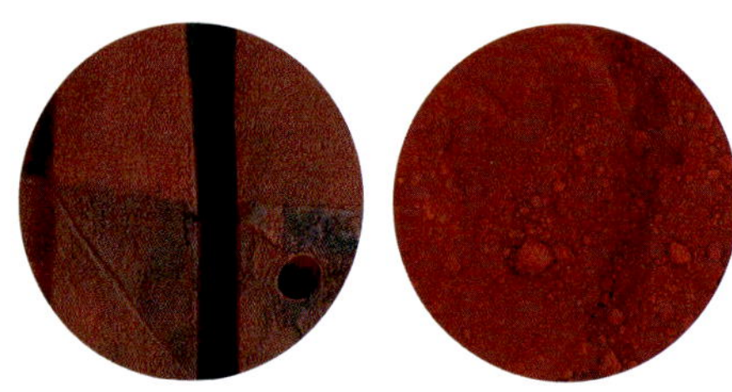

Iron Oxide

Iron is the heart of the oxides, specifically, the man-made variants of earth pigments, the natural, ferrous earth pigments. We may never have an exact timeline for the production of synthetic iron oxides.

Simply allowing a piece of iron to rust or oxidise is a form of production. It can occur spontaneously by chance, or one can create it on purpose, which is the distinction between categorising something as 'production' or not. Either way, by scraping off the rust, it can be transformed into paint by adding a binder. Synthetic oxides are often sold under the same names as their earthly counterparts, the historic pigments. This makes it quite difficult to know which one has in hand, except for Mars Red and Yellow. The term 'Mars' always denotes a synthetic iron oxide. Today, synthetic oxides have all but replaced the natural earth pigments. The stark contrast to a natural earth is their uniformity and enormous opacity. This applies to red oxides as well as the yellow and brown oxides. Ideal for paint manufacturers, but it negatively affects the vibrancy of the colour. These days, synthetic oxides are available in all colours, including blue, bright yellow, green and so on. As an artist, you either love it or hate it.
Iron oxides have long been a defining colour in rural areas with a great deal of

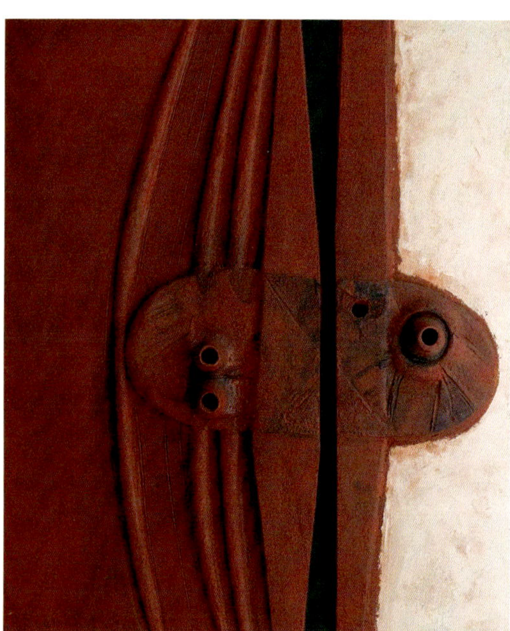

Jaap Wagemaker, *Rust Red*, 1969, mixed media on board, 76 x 66 cm, private collection

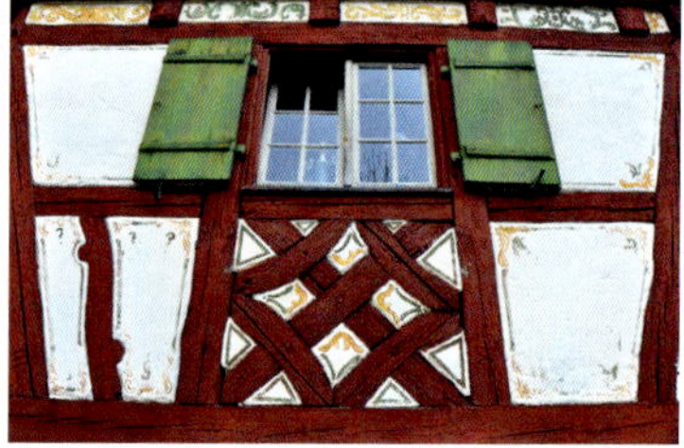

Half-timbered house with treated timbers, Bavaria

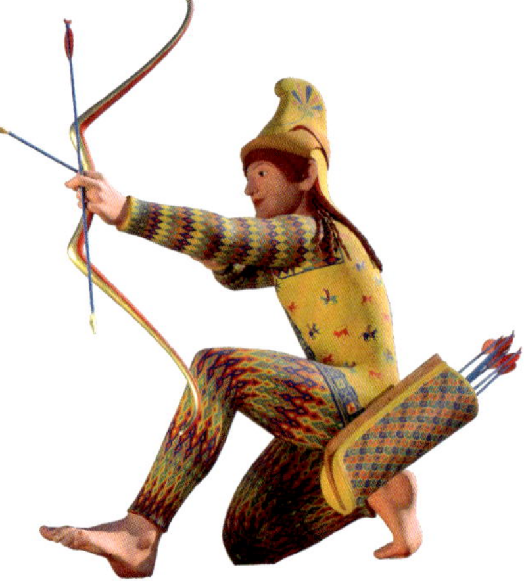

Reconstruction of a Trojan archer, including iron oxides, 2005, Liebieghaus Sculpture Collection, Frankfurt, original: Greece, Aegina, c. 480 BC, Glyptothek, Munich

timber construction. Although not fully water-repellent, the oxides were utilised to protect the wood, with the advantage of the availability of multiple shades. A fine example of such a historic iron oxide is the Scandinavian *Falu*, named after what was once one of Northern Europe's major copper mines. *Falu* is a house paint produced from the waste of iron and copper ore. The resulting pigment powder is tempered with a mixture of water, rye flour and linseed oil, and then boiled. Due to its low cost and being homemade, it was a common paint for exteriors up into the 19th century. Another benefit was that it mimicked the more costly brick. In urban areas with increasing prosperity, it progressively fell out of favour, as timber constructions were replaced by brick and stone. However, in many regions of the Scandinavian countryside and elsewhere, the landscape is still coloured by these traditionally painted timber structures.

Memorial cross, painted ironwork, Bavaria

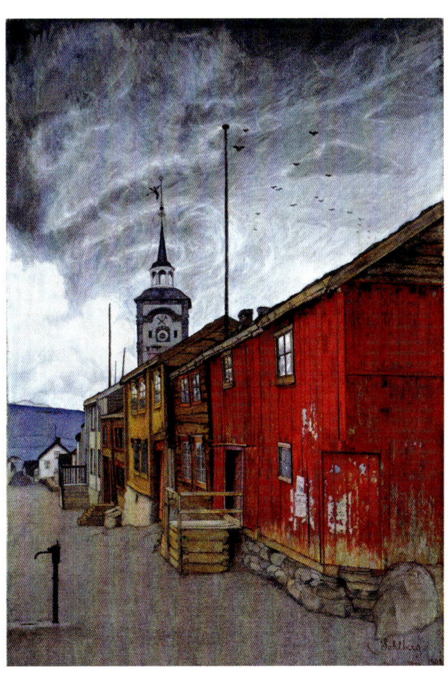

Harald Sohlberg, *Street in Røros*, 1902, oil on canvas, 88 x 60.5 cm, Nasjonalmuseet, Oslo

Box-bed in a Harreveld farmhouse, Nederlands Openluchtmuseum, Arnhem

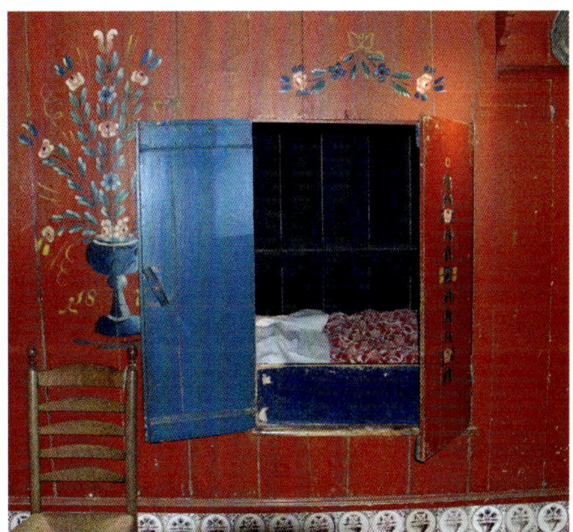

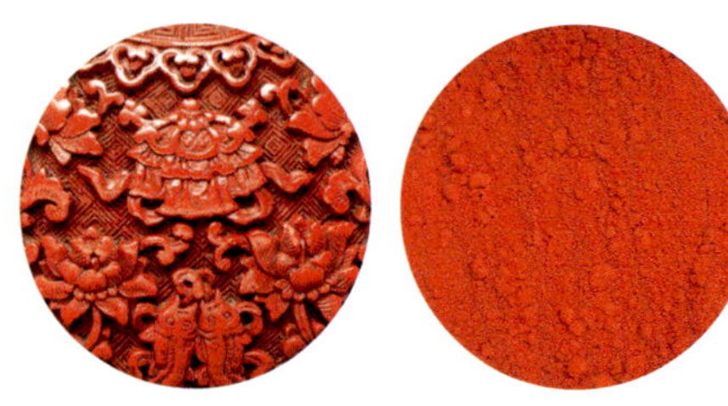

Vermilion

A colour with two guises: the original natural form, officially known as cinnabar, and the man-made version, vermilion.

The natural pigment originated, and can still occasionally be found, in Ephesus (Turkey), Almadén (Spain), Idrija in the Julian Alps (Slovenia), Bohemia (Czech Republic), Hungary, the Urals (Russia), China and Japan. In South America, it was sourced from, among other countries, the pre-Columbian mines in Peru.

Furthermore, there are the more recent mining sites in Australia and in North America, with New Almaden, near San José in California, being the richest. It was after red earth, the most important red in the visual arts until the late 19th century, after which it was replaced by modern substitutes.

Vermilion is a solid, opaque red, ranging from light to darker shades, depending on the quantity of mercury and the size of the pigment particles. And, due to the inclusion of mercury, toxic.

Its toxicity is why true vermilion is rarely offered in the European Union these days, in contrast to Asia, Oceania and America. Moreover, in Asia, it is still in use as medicine, for example, as *Zusha*, against insomnia with the risk of never waking up again. In European paint supply shops, you will mostly find synthetic imitation 'vermilion', recognisable by the word *hue.*

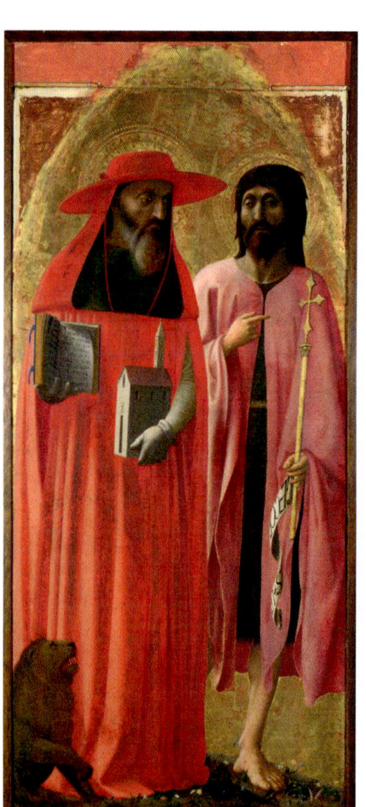

Masaccio, *Saint Jerome and John the Baptist*, c. 1428, tempera on panel, 125 x 58.9 cm, National Portrait Gallery, London

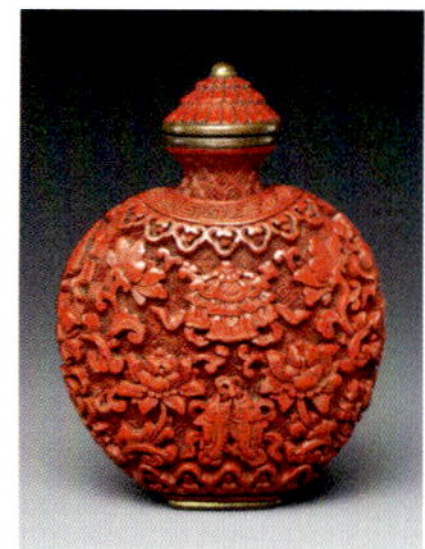

Snuff bottle with Buddhist emblems, 1736-1795, carved red lacquer, h. 7.3 cm, Metropolitan Museum of Art, New York

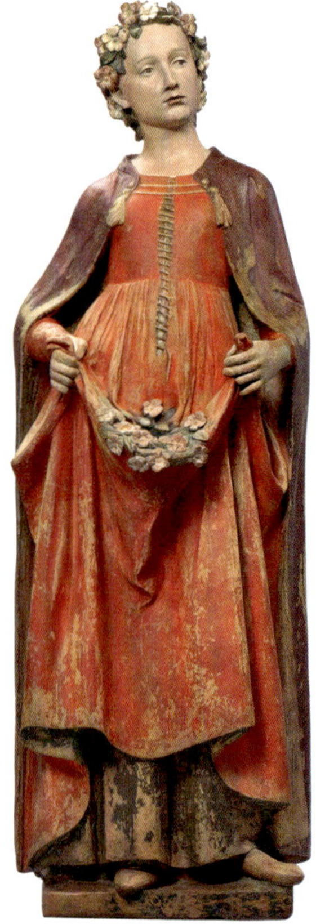

Della Robbia, *Saint Dorothy*, c. 1500, h. 110 cm, SMB, Berlin

From early antiquity, its toxicity has annihilated entire tribes who were in the habit of using this intense red as a body paint. And, over the centuries, masses of women have poisoned themselves by applying it to their lips and cheeks as make-up. Throughout history, vermilion has played an important worldwide role in burial rites. It was most likely used as a status-elevating alternative for the much more common red earth. An extraordinary example is the tomb of the so-called *Reina Roja*, discovered in 1994 in Palenque, Mexico. A vermilion-red Mayan grave from the sixth or seventh century, containing the corpse of an elderly woman, covered in jade and precious, glowing cinnabar. Vermilion is a beautiful and supple, easily processed, pigment. The best quality is more brilliant than even the brightest red earth. In painting, it was, and is, used for skin tones and for inks and (seal) lacquers. It is the defining colour for the renowned Asian red lacquer work. Stradivarius finished his famous violins with a vermilion lacquer. According to tradition, he used it mainly for preservation rather than embellishment.

Pure vermilion is instantly recognisable in a museum. Stroll into a viewing room with older paintings, and it radiates out at you. The cloaks worn by monarchs and saints, women's lavish attire, boiled lobsters, red fruits and flowers, flags, uniforms, luxurious riding saddles, you name it.

If it needs to look costly and luxurious, it is painted with vermilion. A disadvantage, however, is that it may discolour, as can be seen in the murals of Pompeii.

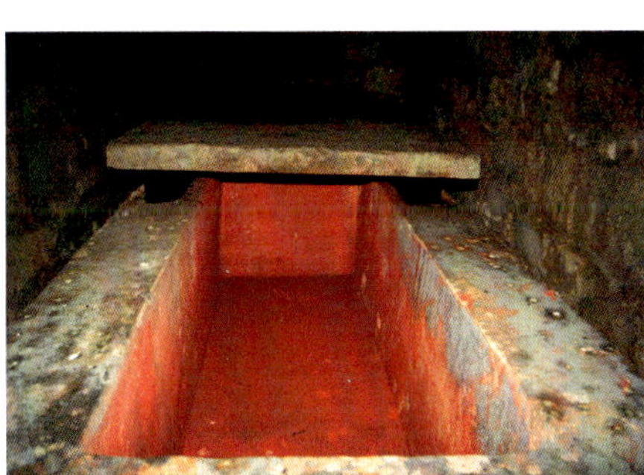

Tomb of Reina Roja, Mayan burial chamber, 6th or 7th cen., covered and painted with vermillion

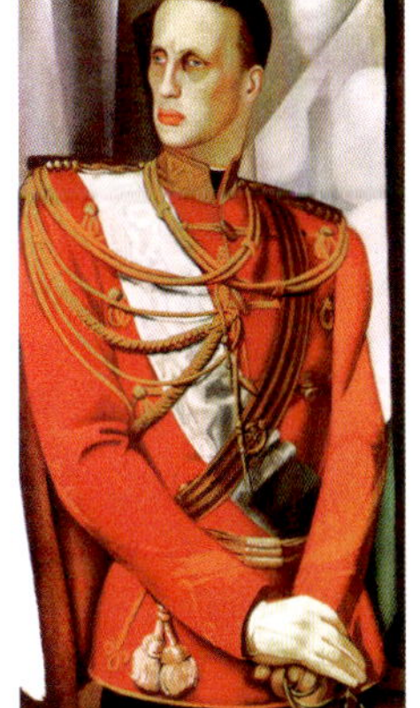

Tamara de Lempicka, *Portrait of S.A.I. le Grand-Duc Gabriel*, 1927, oil on canvas, 116 x 65 cm, private collection

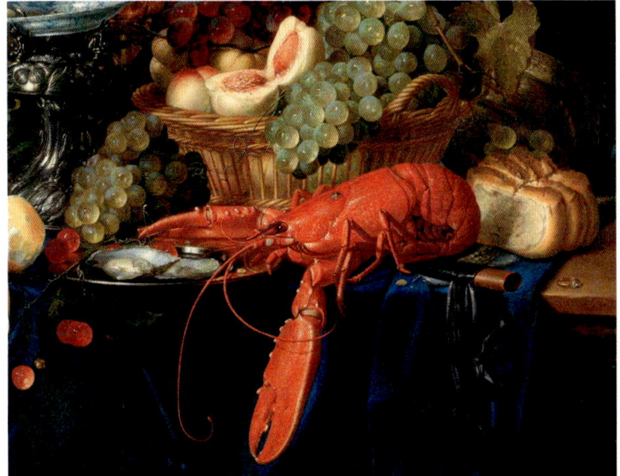

Pieter de Ring, *Still-Life with a Golden Goblet* (detail), oil on canvas, 100 x 80 cm, Rijksmuseum, Amsterdam

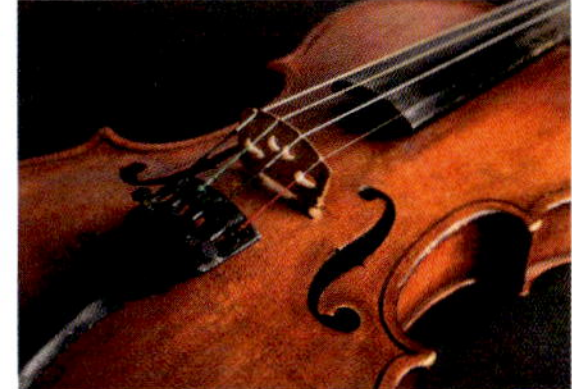

Violin

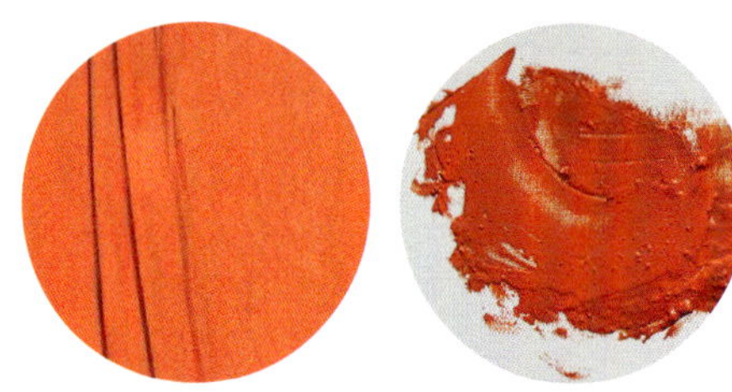

Red Lead

Red lead, also known as minium, belongs to the group of historic, man-made, red pigments. The base is lead white, which turns an orange-red when heated. This, too, is a lovely warm red, opaque like vermilion but softer in tint and much more affordable, as lead is a quite common mineral, worldwide.

Red lead was already known in ancient Mesopotamia, coinciding with the growth of ore smelting in the Near East around 4000 BC Despite its toxicity, lead white and red lead were both popular as make-up and medicine. Thanks to skeletal research, we now know how widespread those uses were on the Eurasian and African continents. In ancient Egypt, for example, it was mixed with kohl for 'eyeliner' as protection against eye infections caused by the many flies.

Red lead is an unstable pigment, meaning it can easily discolour, especially if it is of inferior quality. The quality depends on the lead employed, and the way it is processed. In water paints, for example, it can blacken. When protected from external influences and carefully applied, it remains a radiant orange red. As can be seen in the Persian miniature illustrated here, and the still-bright Fayum-portrait, which looks like it was painted yesterday.

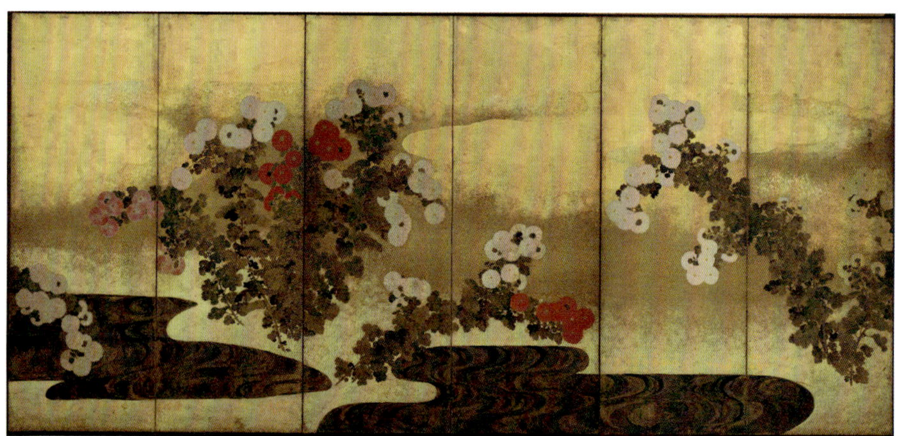

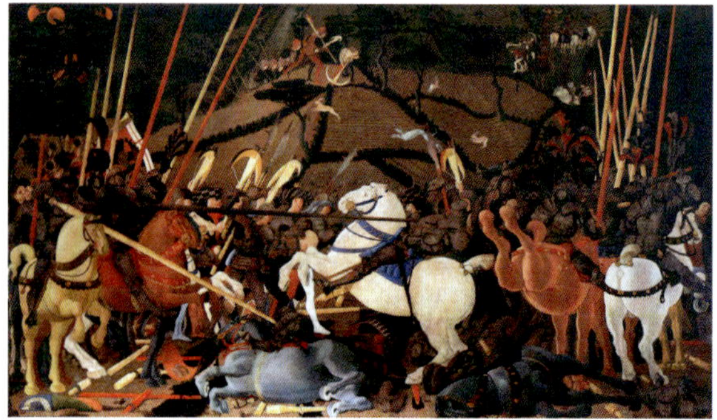

Anonymous, folding screen with 6 panels, 1658-1716, ink, pigments and gold on paper, 174 x 377 cm, Freer Gallery, Washington

Paolo Uccello, *The Battle of San Romano*, 1436-1440, tempera on panel, 327 x 188 cm, Uffizi Gallery, Florence

> *Muzaffar Ali as a Young Prince*, miniature, 16th cen., Persia, Museum of Fine Arts, Boston

Postzegel
niet
nodig

Waanders Uitgevers
Antwoordnummer 2563
8000 VB Zwolle

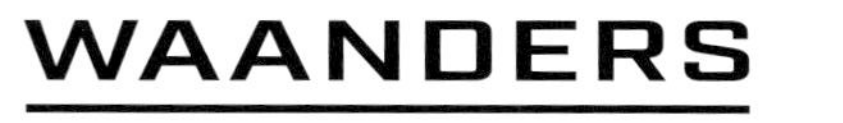

Vul deze kaart in en wij houden u op de hoogte van onze nieuwe uitgaven per e-mail en/of via onze voor- en najaarskranten.

Naam: ______________________________

Adres: ______________________________

Postcode/Woonplaats: ______________________________

E-mail: ______________________________

Telefoonnummer: ______________________________

☐ Ik ga ermee akkoord deze informatie via e-mail te ontvangen.

☐ Ik ontvang graag elk voor- en najaar de nieuwste krant van Waanders Uitgevers.

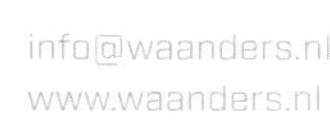

Faradaystraat 19
8013 PH Zwolle
+31 (0)38 460 17 63

info@waanders.nl
www.waanders.nl

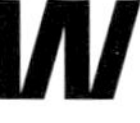

As with vermilion in portrait painting, red lead was part of the so-called incarnates, or flesh tones. The reason why it is regularly mentioned in historical painters' recipes. Moreover, it was a popular spot colour to cut costs on the much more expensive vermilion. That is, the painter first applied the red lead, let it dry properly, and then finished with vermilion, thus needing far less of the expensive pigment. Red lead was found on the painter's palette well into the 19th century, but slowly disappeared once the stronger cadmium, and other synthetic reds, hit the market. If you look closely, you will find lead red, for example, in many of Van Gogh's paintings. In Uccello's large panel, it is almost impossible to miss; it colours the red lances. A fine example of the pigment's versatility – it is still sold in many parts of the world as a protective agent against rot and rust.

In ancient times, people realised that in addition to being a beautiful colour, red lead was also particularly suitable for protecting metal and timber from weathering. Contrary to iron minium primer, it dries in humid conditions, and even under water. This characteristic made it popular in shipbuilding until the end of the last century and is the reason it was used for the treatment of moist wounds.
For thousands of years, these many qualities made red lead one of the most common pigments.

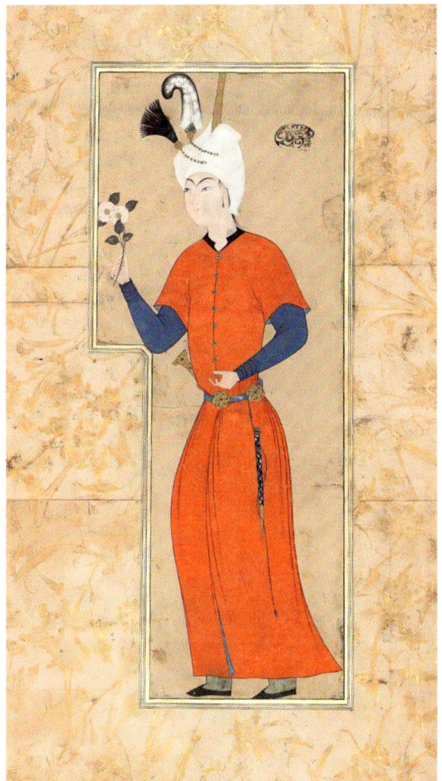

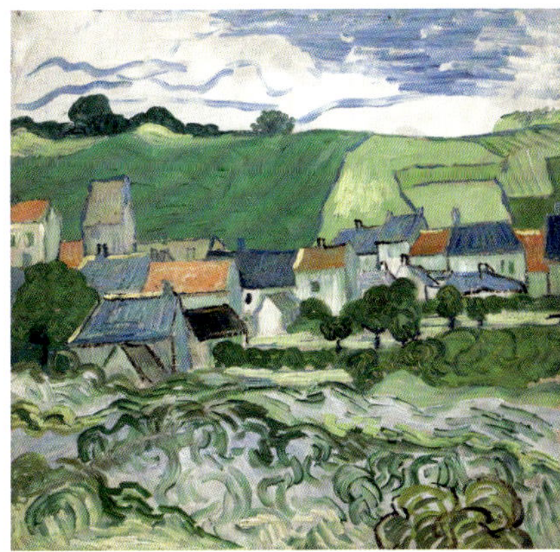

Vincent van Gogh, *View of Auvers*, 1890, oil on canvas, 50 x 52.5 cm, Van Gogh Museum, Amsterdam

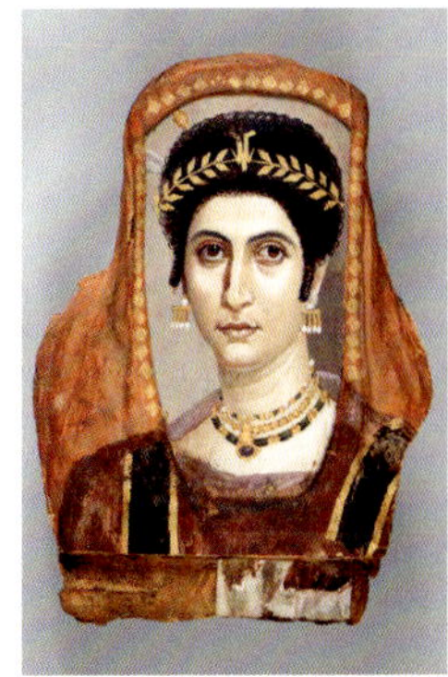

Fayum portrait, c. 100, encaustic on panel, gilt; linen, 48 x 36 x 12,8 cm, J. Paul Getty Museum, Los Angeles

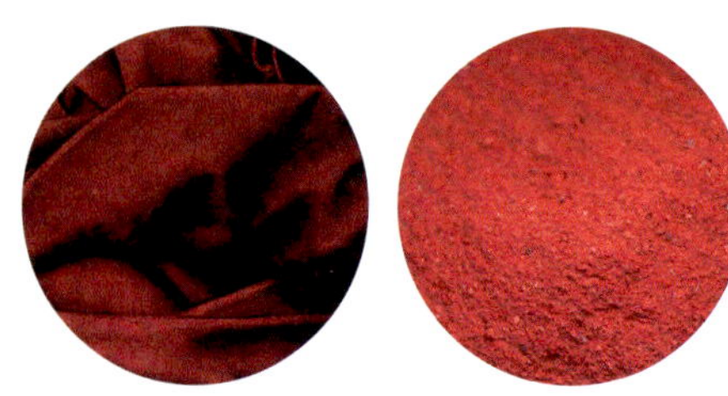

Kermes & Cochineal

The striking red blood of lice, that has been fought over since ancient times. The unappealing mealy and scale insects are the source for one of the most coveted colours in the existence of mankind: carmine.

The two main species are kermes, the scale insects of the Eurasian and African continents, and cochineal of the Americas. Additionally, kermes has long been a medicine. In the *Atharvaveda*, a sacred Hindu text from around 1500 BC, kermes is described as *Laksha*, the 'sister of the Gods', 'the radiant one' and 'healer'.

The species of kermes, used to make the strongest colours, lives in the wild on and around the Mediterranean kermes oak.

A medieval text describes how, by lantern light before dawn, the insects were carefully plucked from the branches by women and children and collected in glazed jars. To ease the harvesting, pickers grew their nails as long as possible before the picking. In a good reaping year, almost a kilogram of kermes could be harvested in a day.

Cochineal was cultivated by the indigenous inhabitants on small cactus fields in Central and South America, long before the Spaniards set foot during the 15th century. The cultivation was concentrated in the Peruvian Andes and in Mixteca,

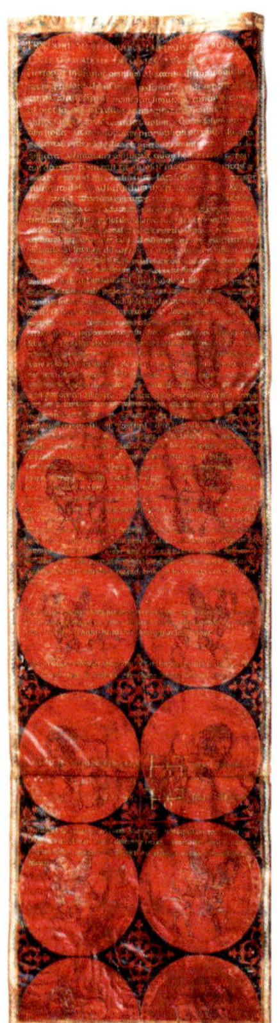

Marriage Charter of Emperor Otto II and Theophanu, 972, vellum, Staatsarchiv Wolfenbüttel

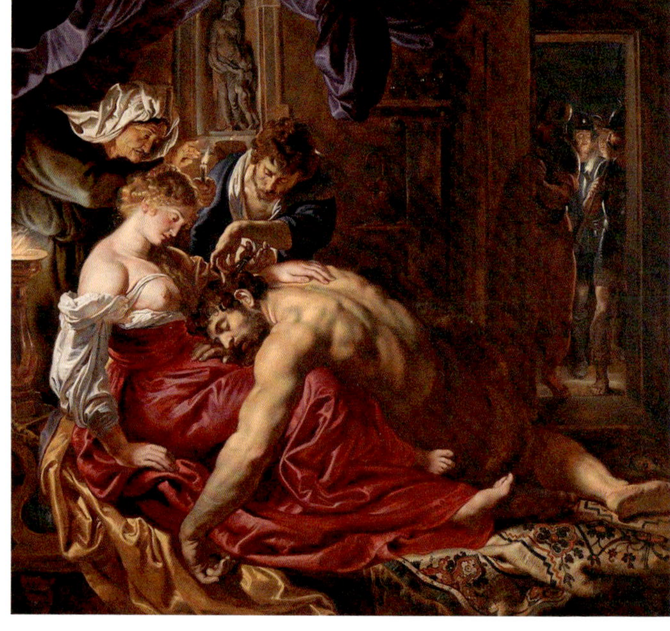

Peter Paul Rubens, *Samson and Delilah*, c. 1609, 50.5 x 52.1 cm, Cincinnati Art Museum

> Jan van Eyck, *Portrait of a Man with a red Turban*, 1433, oil on canvas, 26 x 19 cm, National Gallery, London

present-day Mexico. Cochineal quickly crowned the list of valuable treasures for the conquistadores, followed by gold, silver and pearls. This dye is much more potent and effective than kermes, less of it is needed with better results.

Around 1520, exports to the Spanish port cities of Seville and Cadiz began from what is now Veracruz. From there, the cochineal was shipped to Genoa, Livorno, Venice, Antwerp and several other European ports. From the late 18th century, numerous efforts were made by other nations to halt this profitable monopoly of the Spanish crown by smuggling the live cochineal away from the continent to cultivate the insects elsewhere. The French ultimately succeeded in doing so in Algeria, and the Dutch in Java.

One kilogram of dye requires about 140,000 lice, which highlights the scarcity of the raw material. To turn it into pigment, the transparent red liquid is precipitated on lime, chalk, or another white, absorbent material. The colour can vary from purple-red to bright orange-red by adding varying mordants. The best quality carmine paints were used for glazing, while the less expensive version was applied in the underlying layers. Artists with contacts in the carmine trade, such as Veronese and Rembrandt, were fortunate enough to use the status-enhancing pigment more easily on their palette than their less lucky colleagues, who had to make do with the cheap, vegetable-based, red lakes. Today, cochineal is still used as a pigment in products such as food, lipstick and cosmetic blush.

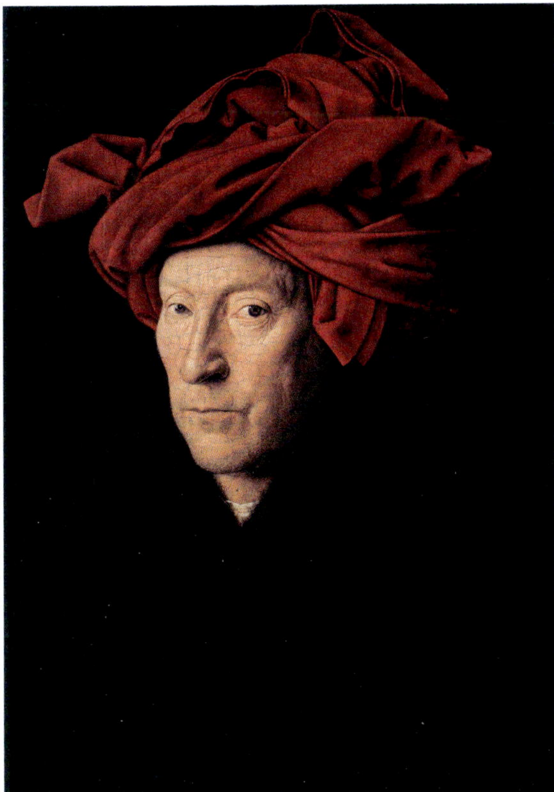

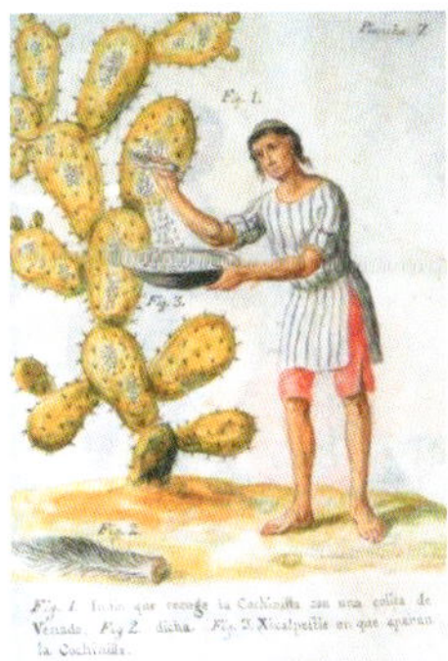

José Antonio de Alzate y Ramíres, *Indigenous American harvesting cochineal*, 1777, Newberry Library, Chicago

Woven fabric decorated with pumas, Peru, 6th-10th cen., alpaca wool and cotton, private collection

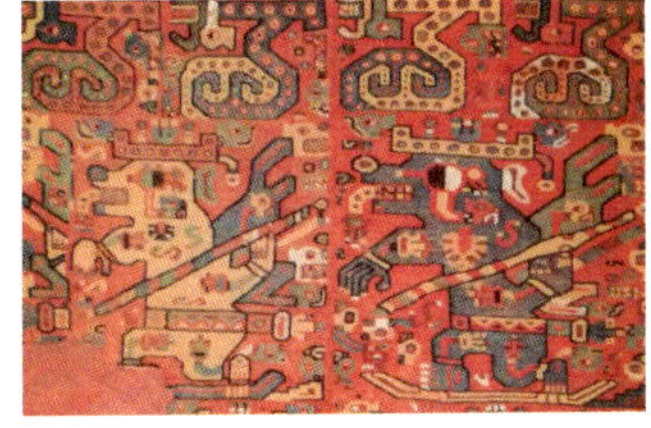

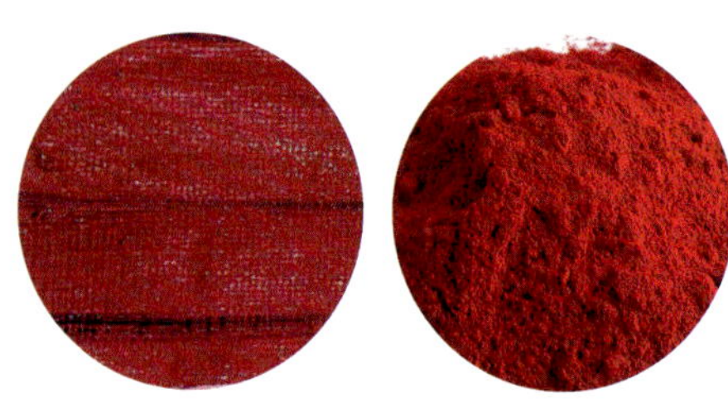

Rose Madder & Alizarin

Rose madder (*krapp-lack*) is the queen of the organic reds. It is literally a global colour and, like so many other pigments, a medicine. For painters and dyers, rose madder is the essential, brilliant and transparent red.

Since antiquity, madder has been the substitute for the invaluable and exclusive Tyrian purple and carmine. The main plants from which rose madder is derived, belong to the *rubiaceae*, with the rose madder (or dyer's madder) *rubia tinctorum*, as the main species.
Alizarin, the name of the synthetic pigment, derives from the Arabic *al-usara* (juice) and refers to the red extracted from its roots. Named *Alizari* in the Mediterranean world, the modern pigment eventually became known as alizarine.
With madder, it's all about the root, and its colour is influenced by the type of soil. For example, madder originating from the humus-rich limestone earths of southern France, produces a bright red, while madder from the clay soil in the Dutch province of Zeeland tends to be more orange. After two or more years of growth, the plants are harvested in autumn when the greens have wilted, and the roots are distributed in drying attics. They are then ground, after which the concentrate is treated with steam and various acids.

Dieric Bouts, *Man of Sorrows*, c. 1470, oil on panel, 365 x 26.7 cm, M Museum, Leuven

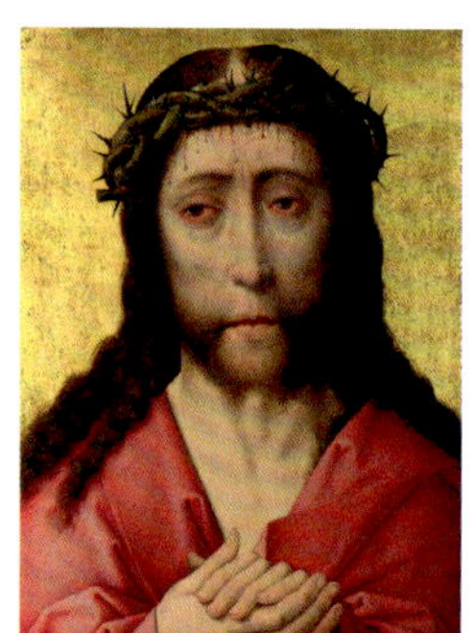

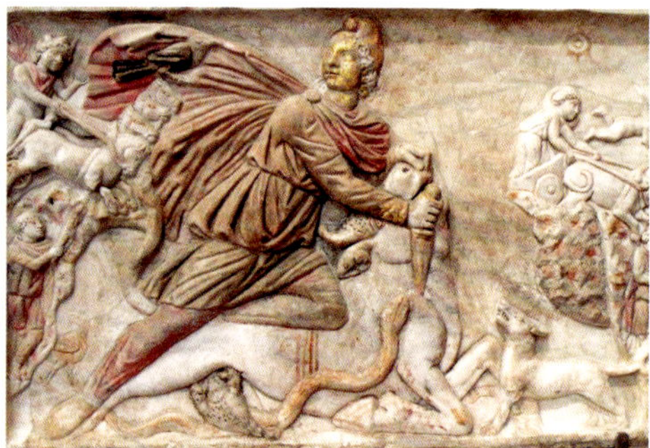

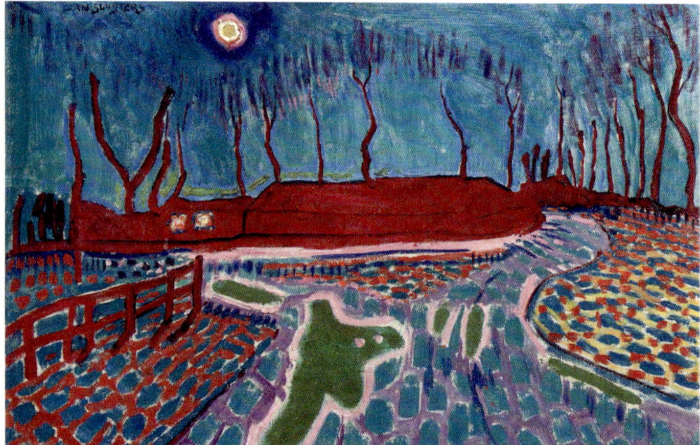

Mithraic relief, 3rd century, Museo Nazionale Romano, Rome

Jan Sluijters, *Moon Night III*, c. 1911, oil on canvas, 32 x 50 cm, private collection

Each acid produces a different shade, ranging from warm to cool, and from a light to dark red.
Rose madder is a striking and versatile colour and is the most common transparent deep red on the artist's palette. It is ideal for mixing purples and for glazes over lighter reds, blues and whites. Glazing gives a stronger result than a blended colour and represents an old technique widely used by, for example, the Flemish Primitives. Most of the luxurious red costumes, fabrics, carpets, draperies and curtains we see in state portraits, are dyed (as fabric) and painted (as paint) with rose madder. In the illustrations here, you can see rose madder as the dye for the kimono, and as the paint for Mithras' costume.
Rose madder has the tendency to discolour over time and even optically disappear, as can regularly be observed in tapestries. William Turner is one of many painters whose work suffered gravely from the fading of madder reds. He was a great enthusiast, and carried around a dozen different madder lakes in his paint box, ranging from brownish red through violet, to purple red.
From the 1870s, rose madder was rapidly replaced by the synthetic alternative alizarin, with the commercial cultivation of madder disappearing from view.

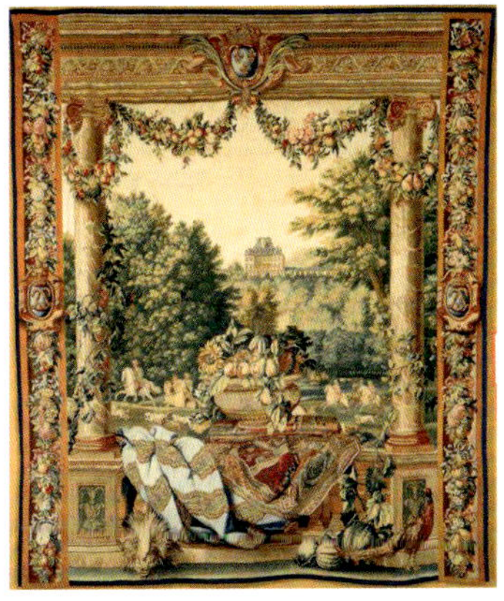

Charles le Brun, *Les Maisons royales: Marimont*, c. 1680, tapestry, Pau Castle

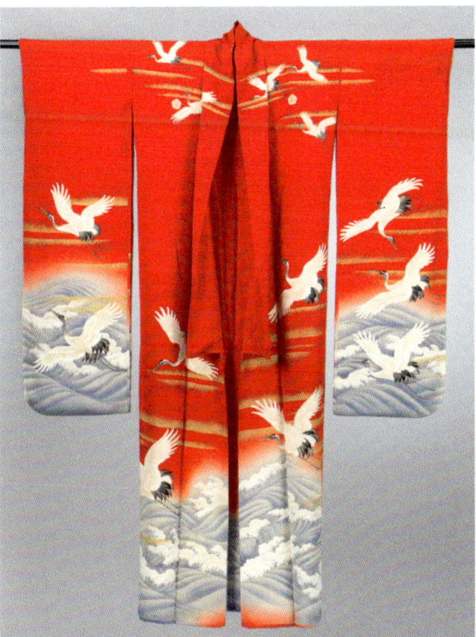

Anonymous, Kimono for an unmarried woman, 1920-1940, Rijksmuseum, Amsterdam

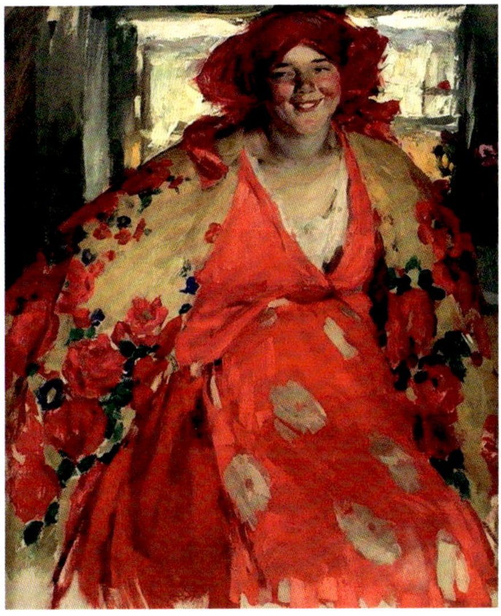

Abram Archipov, *Smiling Girl*, c. 1920, oil on canvas, Belarusian National Arts Museum, Minsk

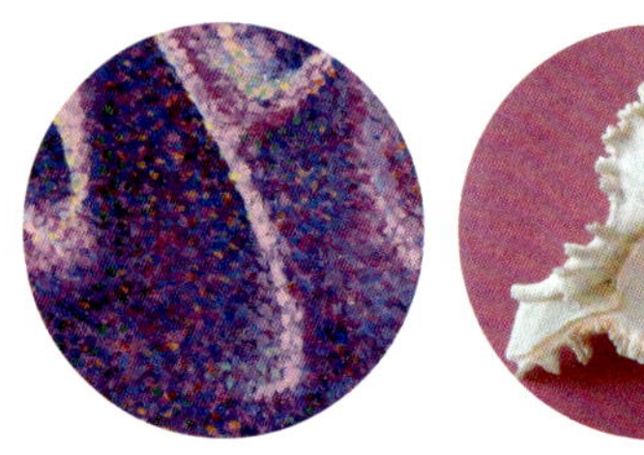

Purple & Mauve

Tyrian purple is a mythical colour entwined with the worship of blood as the source of life. For millennia, it has symbolised the power over life and death worldwide.

Purple textiles have been found in ancient Egyptian and Greek tombs, a Roman tomb in Germany, and Inca graves in South America. Tyrian purple was used as paint in some mummy-portraits excavated in Fayoum, and in precious manuscripts from all over the Old World.

It is as exclusive today as it was then. Currently, the price continues to rise as climate-change, overfishing and pollution of habitats cause the number of purple snails everywhere to decline.

Tyrian purple is produced using mucus secreted from glands of predatory sea snails, and varies from dark red to purple, to blue. The snail's secreted glandular fluid is naturally colourless, but early on someone, somewhere, discovered that it changes colour through oxidation; from colourless to blue-violet and, in some species, to a deep red.

The oldest known remnants of purple dyeing date from 1800-1600 BC and were discovered on the Greek island of Crete and its surrounding islands. The Phoenicians, from the Greek *phoinos* meaning purple (the people of purple), plundered the Mediterranean Sea as far as the Atlantic coast of northern Africa in their hunt for

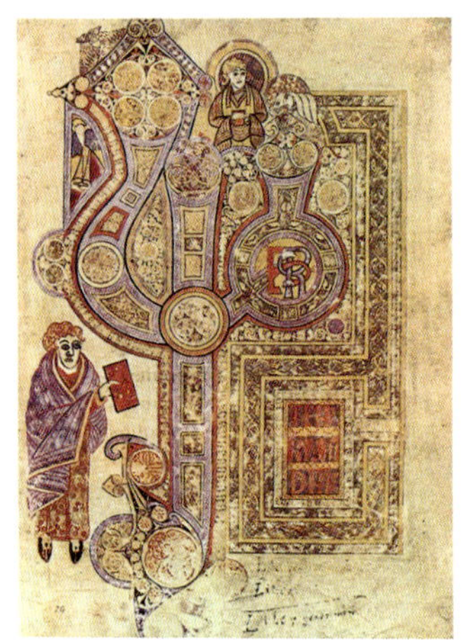

The Opening Page Of The Book Of Matthew, Book of Kells, c. 800, 33 x 25.5 cm, ink on vellum, Trinity College Library, Dublin

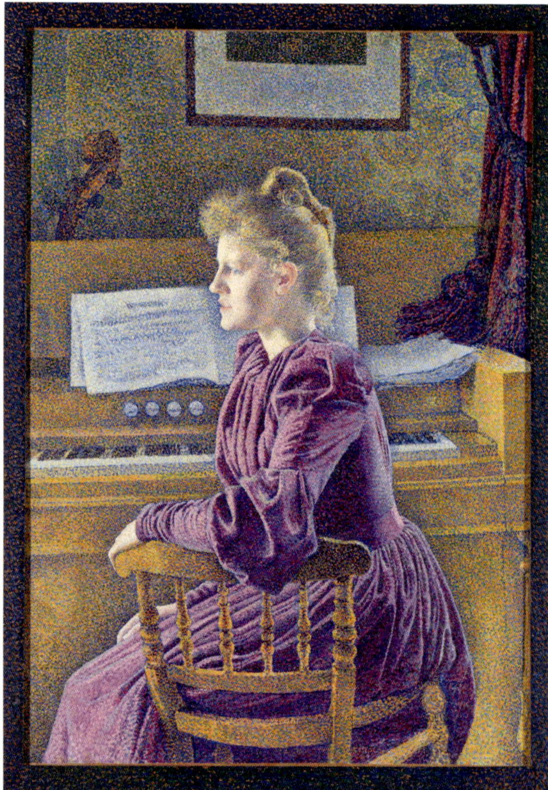

Theo Van Rysselberghe, *Maria Sèthe*, the future Mrs Henry Van de Velde, 1891, oil on canvas, 120 x 86 cm, Royal Arts Museum Antwerp

the various sea snails. Dispersed along their routes, they established Tyrian purple production workshops, once easily perceptible by the heaps of decomposing, stinking snail shells.
The Eurasian and native American regions are fundamentally divergent in their use of the snails. The latter kept the gastropods alive. In Oaxaca, the animals were 'milked' once a month from October to May to avoid interfering with its reproduction and renewal of the mucus secretion. The dyers can harvest the snails off the rocks for around three hours daily, when the tide is low enough. Their yield is sufficient to dye approximately 250 grams of cotton, roughly one skein per gathering session, per person. In the 1950s, about three skeins were dyed daily, sometimes multiple times to deepen the colour. But here, too, the extinction of a tradition is looming because of overfishing. The initial threat began in the 1980s due to Japan's production of Imperial Purple, which led to the snails being processed on an industrial scale. Today, production is dangerously at risk due to the ever-increasing popularity of ceviche. Meeting the demand leads to the depletion of the sea snails and their prey.
It took until the 19th century to find a synthetic alternative, aniline purple, named 'mauve'. It was discovered by chance in 1856 by the young chemist William Henry Perkin, and completely revolutionised the fashion industry. New, affordable, aniline-based dyes became widely available and triggered unprecedented changes in the everyday colour spectrum. It marked the beginning of our now, virtually unlimited, plethora of colours. The portrait by Van Rysselberghe is a fine example of the effect of the new mauve in fashion, and on the artist's palette.

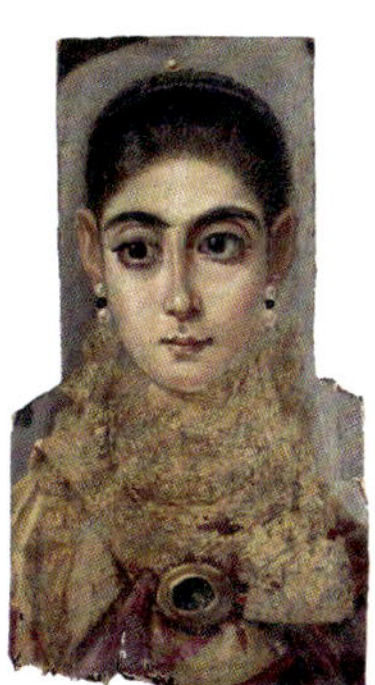

Portrait of a woman, known as 'L'Européenne', 117-138, encaustic on panel, 42.5 x 24 cm, Louvre, Paris

The Virgin Mary, Antequera

A replica of the Augustus of Prima Porta statue with a reconstruction of the original colouring, Ashmolean Musem, Oxford, original: 1st cen., h. 208 cm, Vatican Museums

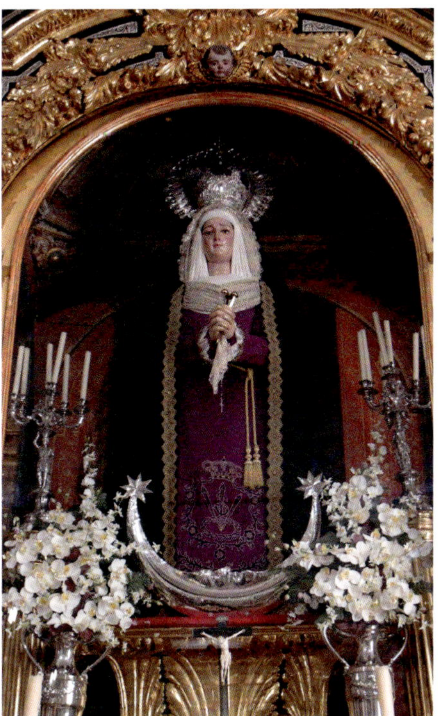

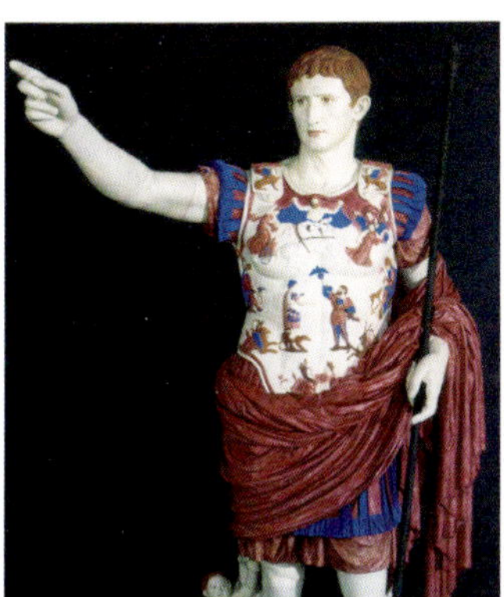

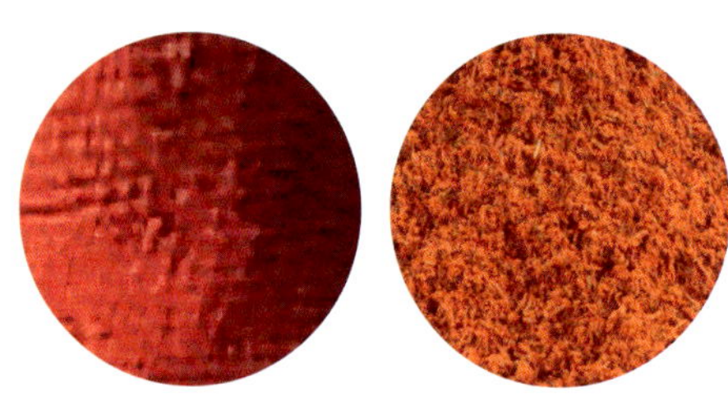

Organic Reds

The reds that are extracted from trees, plants, flowers, seeds and fruits. Already in earliest prehistory, humans were aware that the flora of their immediate environment is a living paint box, free of cost, and each passing year restocked by nature. Downside to this advantage: plant colours are rarely lightfast.

Awareness of the colour and healing power of plants and minerals used to be a natural and necessary part of existence. It formed the basis for the preparation of paints and medicines, knowing what nature and the season have to offer.
One has long known, for instance, that plants with a high tannin concentration, such as pomegranate, prevent fungus and bacteria. Equally important, indigo and madder protect against UV radiation. Information that has been forgotten in our urbanised world, as fewer and fewer people live in the countryside. Thus, we often have no insight into the origin of most of the products we buy. Comparable to children who believe chocolate milk comes from brown cows.
The variety of plants that were, and still are, used as sources of red pigment, is enormous. Red and orangåe flowers, such as safflower, are fine examples. Harunobu used it to create the orange-red in his prints. The Orlean tree, the *Urucu*, originally from South America, is now

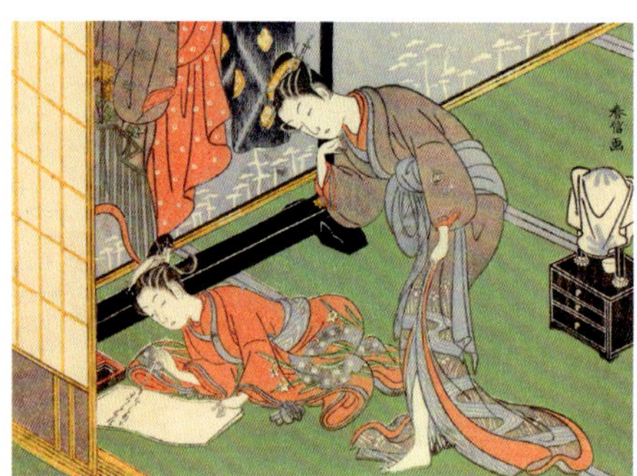

Suzuki Harunobu, wood cut from the book *Haikai iro no minato*, 1765-1770, 15.4 x 21.6 cm, British Museum, London

Jeanne Laporte-Fromage, woollen robe, 1938-1948, Musée LaM, Villeneuve d'Ascq

Henna decoration

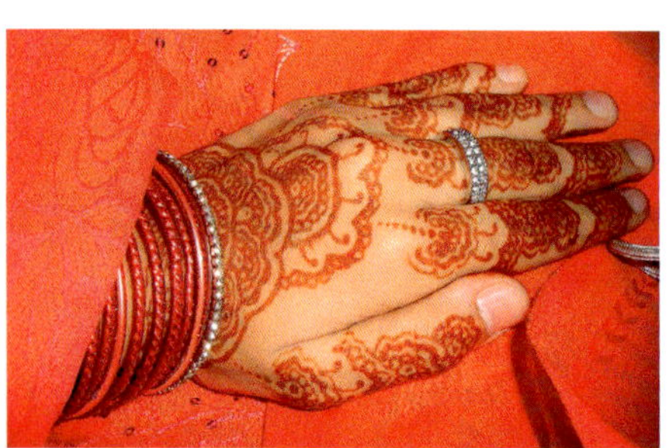

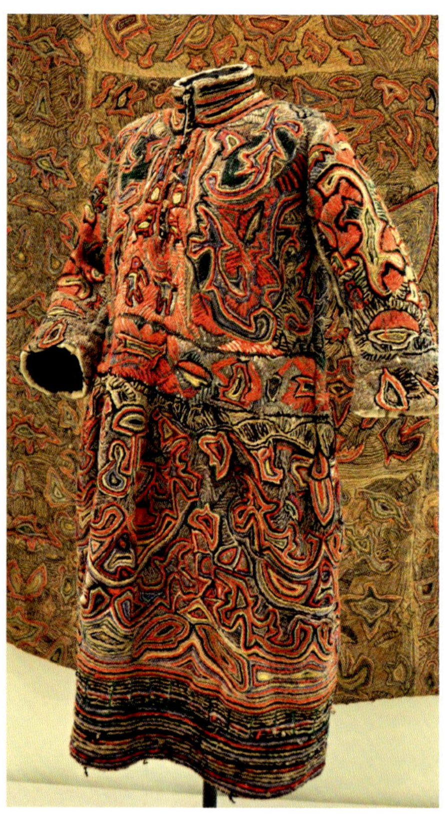

found worldwide. Its fruit is the raw material for the red body paint of the Yanomami of the Amazon, and communities in Southeast Asia.

Probably the most renowned organic red, after madder, is brazilwood. *Brazil* is the general name for redwood, originating from the Portuguese *brasa*, meaning red-hot. Long before the Europeans landed in Brazil, with its countless redwoods, *brasil* was the name for wood from what is now Indonesia and Malaysia. It is a fine and exceptionally affordable substitute for the pricey red of lice. From the 12th century, it was shipped to Europe as a foundation for red lakes and inks. The South American nation Brazil was given the name due to the abundance of redwood found there by the Portuguese in 1500. Brazilian redwood is an undemanding material as, unlike other redwoods, it can easily be dissolved in cold water. After removing its bark, the solid heartwood needs to be grated into shreds. In the Netherlandish countries, from the 16th century onwards, this was primarily carried out by detainees in the so-called *rasphuizen* (rasp houses), the notorious disciplinary houses for men. It was not until 1770 that the production was taken over by windmills.

The only, still operational, paint-mill, is in the Netherlands: 'Verfmolen De Kat' on the Zaanse Schans.

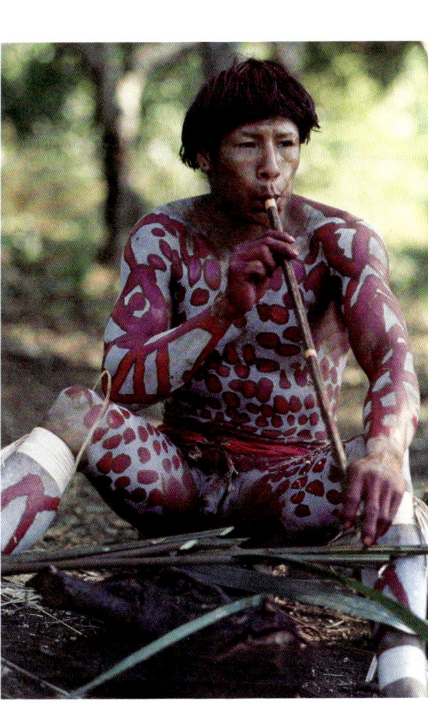

Waurá, Brazil, Red Urukú body painting

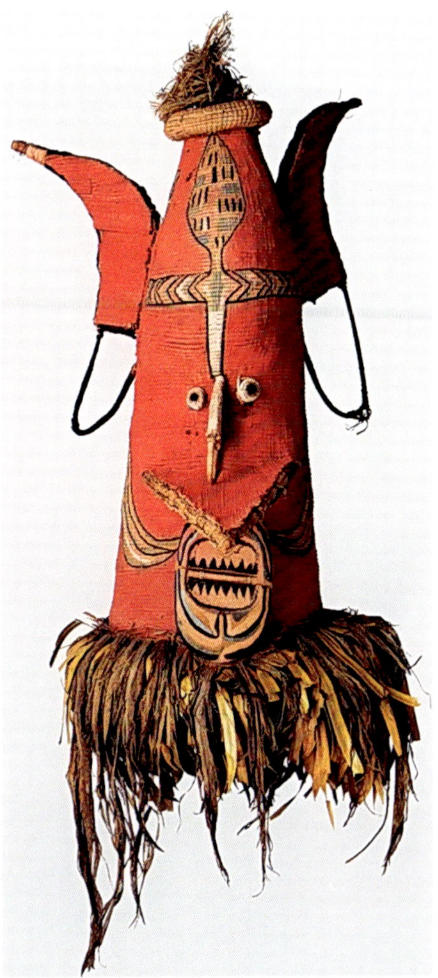

Sulka, *Sisiu Mask*, h. 100 cm, Museum am Rothenbaum, Hamburg

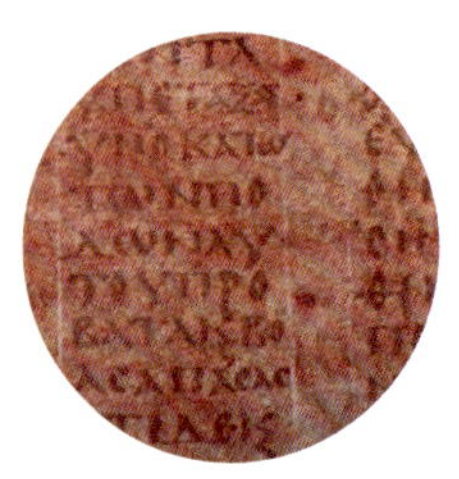

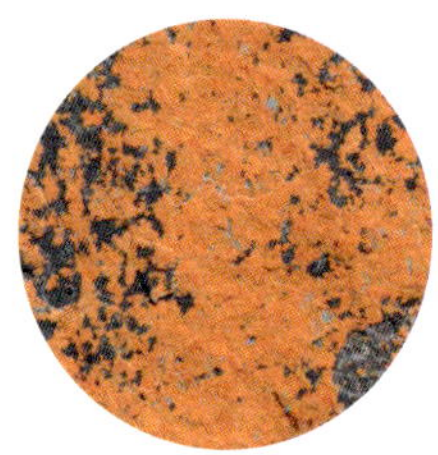

Lichens & Fungi

Colours extracted from lichens and mushrooms are considered 'the great unknown'. Lichens and mushrooms are both fungi. The distinction is that lichen is more than just a fungus; it is a symbiosis of a fungus and an alga. A collaboration from which they mutually benefit.

Ancient dyes based on lichens and fungi disappeared from common use after industrialisation and are only now slowly being rediscovered. As there are still many uncertainties, I categorise lichen and fungi under 'prehistory/ antiquity'.

They were used to suggest exclusive colours by both textile dyers and illuminators of manuscripts. One can indeed make exquisite and striking colours with them, as one can see from the images.

The unpretentious lichens belong to the group of oldest living organisms, yet they are seldom noticed. They flourish on stones, boulders and timber and can be found all around us on undisturbed surfaces. Their colours range from silky whites and cool and warm greys to greens, oranges and reds.

It is perhaps fortunate that the lichen is a forgotten lot, as they are extremely fragile. They sometimes grow barely a millimetre a year.

James Sowerby, *Coloured figures of English Fungi or Mushrooms*, 1797, p. 43

Lichen

The entry of Jesus into Jerusalem, from the Codex Purpureus Rossanensis, 5th-6th cen., Diocesan Museum, Rossano

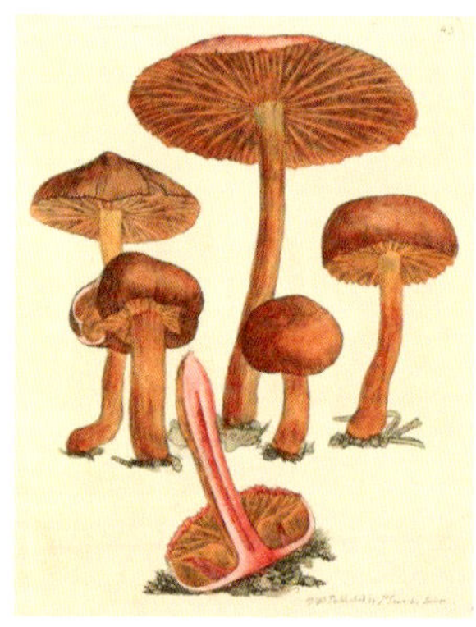

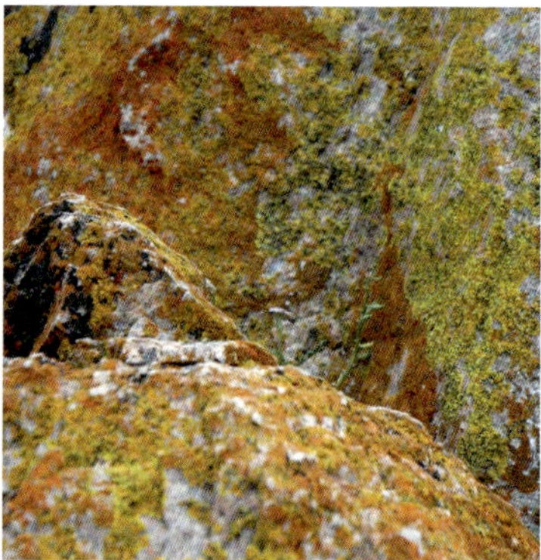

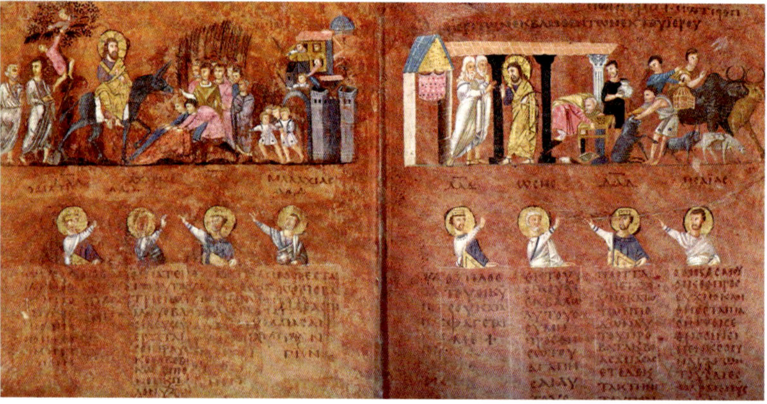

An unassuming moss can easily be a hundred years of age. When foraging for use as a dye, it is advised to gather only loose samples.

In Europe, Orseille (or Orchil) is likely the best-known of the mosses. It originated predominantly from the Canary Islands and the Portuguese coast. Dyers used it as an individual colour or as an enhancer for more costly ingredients, such as indigo, kermes or cochineal. Orseille was nicknamed the 'purple of the poor'.

The third-century *Papyrus Graecus Holmiensis* features several formulas with Orseille as a basis for purple colour imitations. Unlike true Tyrian purple, their lightfastness is poor. Nonetheless, in the 19th century, lichen purple was still listed as a usable violet pigment for the painter.

A fine example of the abundant use of this imitation purple is the sixth-century Byzantine *Codex Rossanensis*. Since the discovery of this codex in 1879, it was presumed that it was made with precious Tyrian purple, but nothing could be further from the truth. The purple-coloured parchment pages were, in fact, dyed with lichen.

The earliest references to the use of mushrooms in Europe were discovered in 15th-century formulas for dyeing silk and velvet. It took researchers some time to learn that they contained an ingredient previously unknown to them: fungi. One can therefore assume that fungi have been used for much longer and belong to the group of ancient common dyes.

As far as we can determine, lichens and fungi have been known and used as (under-) earthly pigments in Europe, Africa, Asia and North America since the beginning of time. As the title of one of fungi expert Arleen Rainis Bessette's books so eloquently states, 'The rainbow under our feet'.

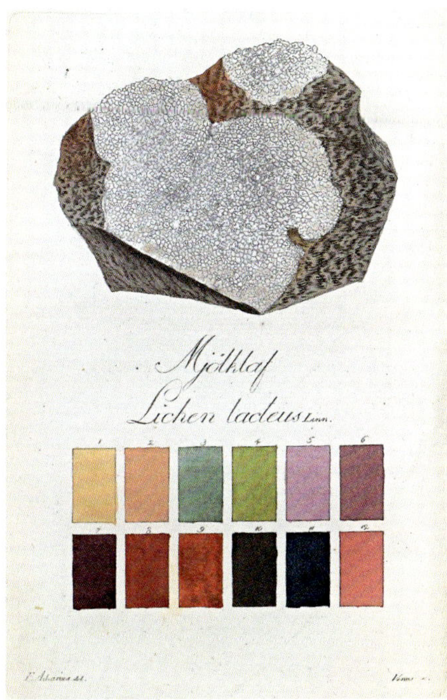

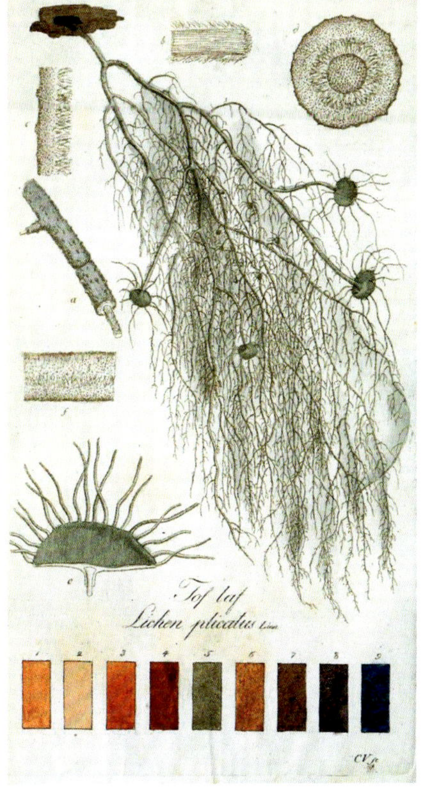

Johan Peter Westring, two lichen colour charts, from *Svensk Lafvarnas Farghistoria*, 1805-1809, Bohusläns museum, Uddevalla

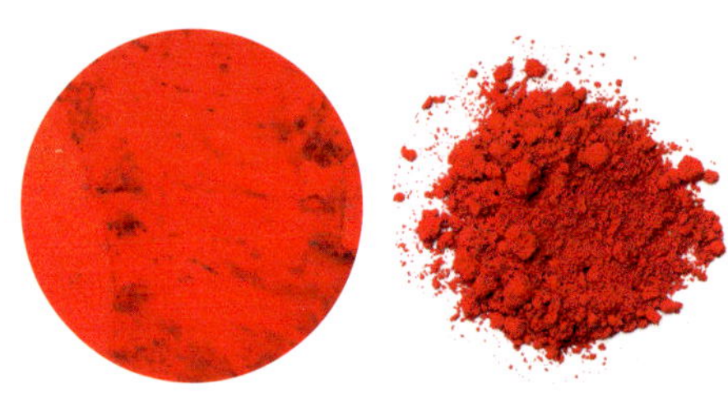

Cadmium Red

A member of the cadmium family, cadmium red is derived from the older cadmium yellow, another pigment discovered by chance.

Around 1930, cadmium surpassed the old minium and vermilion as the leading red, not only in oil paint but also in water and glue paints and pastels. It is an elusive red, which (I believe), has not yet been matched by any state-of-the-art substitute. I was once overwhelmed by a red triptych by Bacon from the collection of José Capelo; in a private collection, hence no available image. From just one glance, it was obvious that such an overpowering red could have only been made with cadmium. This same red figures prominently in the work of Mondrian and his contemporaries.

It is an expensive pigment. Finding it for a bargain is impossible. It is toxic, limiting its sale in Europe since the beginning of this century. Fortunately, it is still available from a few manufacturers as an artists' paint, sometimes with the clear warning label: 'Poison'. It can be used without worry if care is taken not to get it on your skin or in your mouth, the studio is well-ventilated, and the rinse water from the brushes is treated as chemical waste.

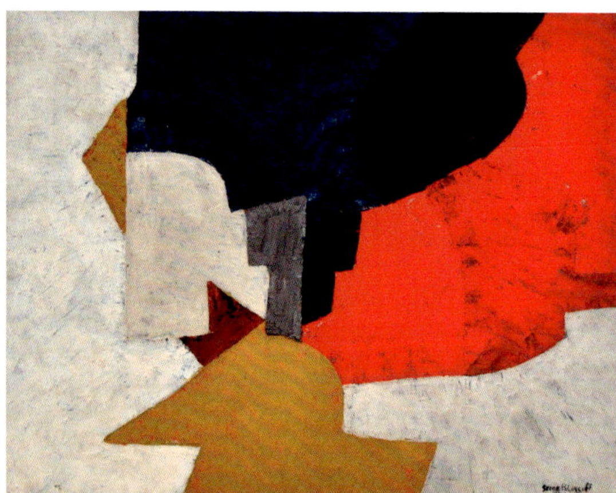

Serge Poliakoff, *Composition*, 1954, oil on canvas, 89 x 116 cm, Palais des Beaux Arts, Lille

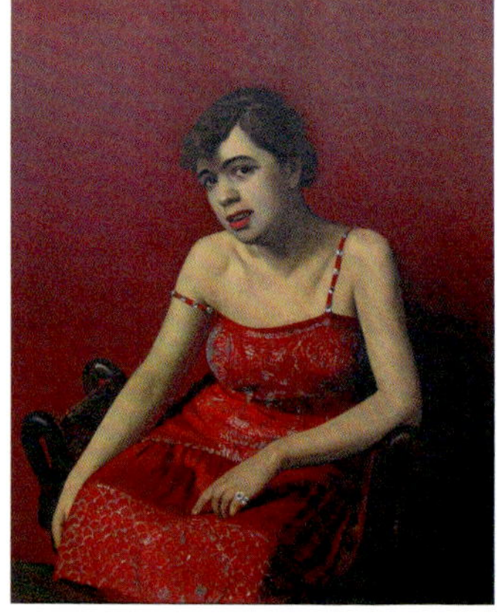

Félix Vallotton, *Romanian Woman in a Red Dress*, 1925, oil on canvas, 105 x 81 cm, Centre Pompidou, Paris

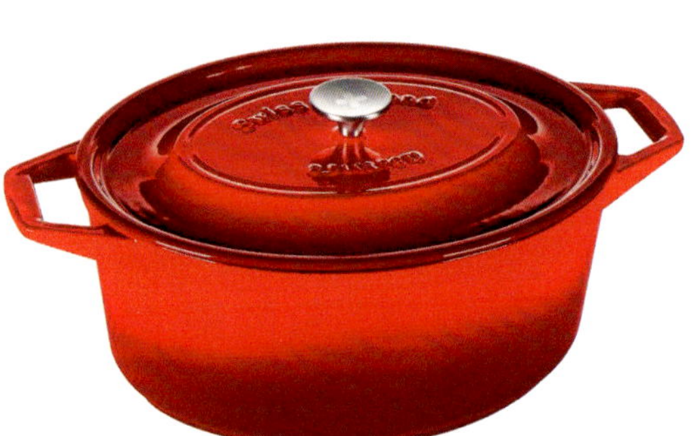

Casserole

> Piet Mondriaan, *Mill in Sunlight*, 1908, oil on canvas, 114.8 x 87 cm, Kunstmuseum, The Hague

For artists, this red must have been quite a revelation, familiar as they would have been with the weaker chrome paints, vermilions and red leads. Cadmium reds are versatile reds, with strong coverage, clear, heat-resistant and stable. Its resistance to heat makes it an excellent pigment for the glass and metal industries, allowing it to be found on objects as basic as pans. However, it is also used in costume jewellery and toys, which is not beneficial to health.

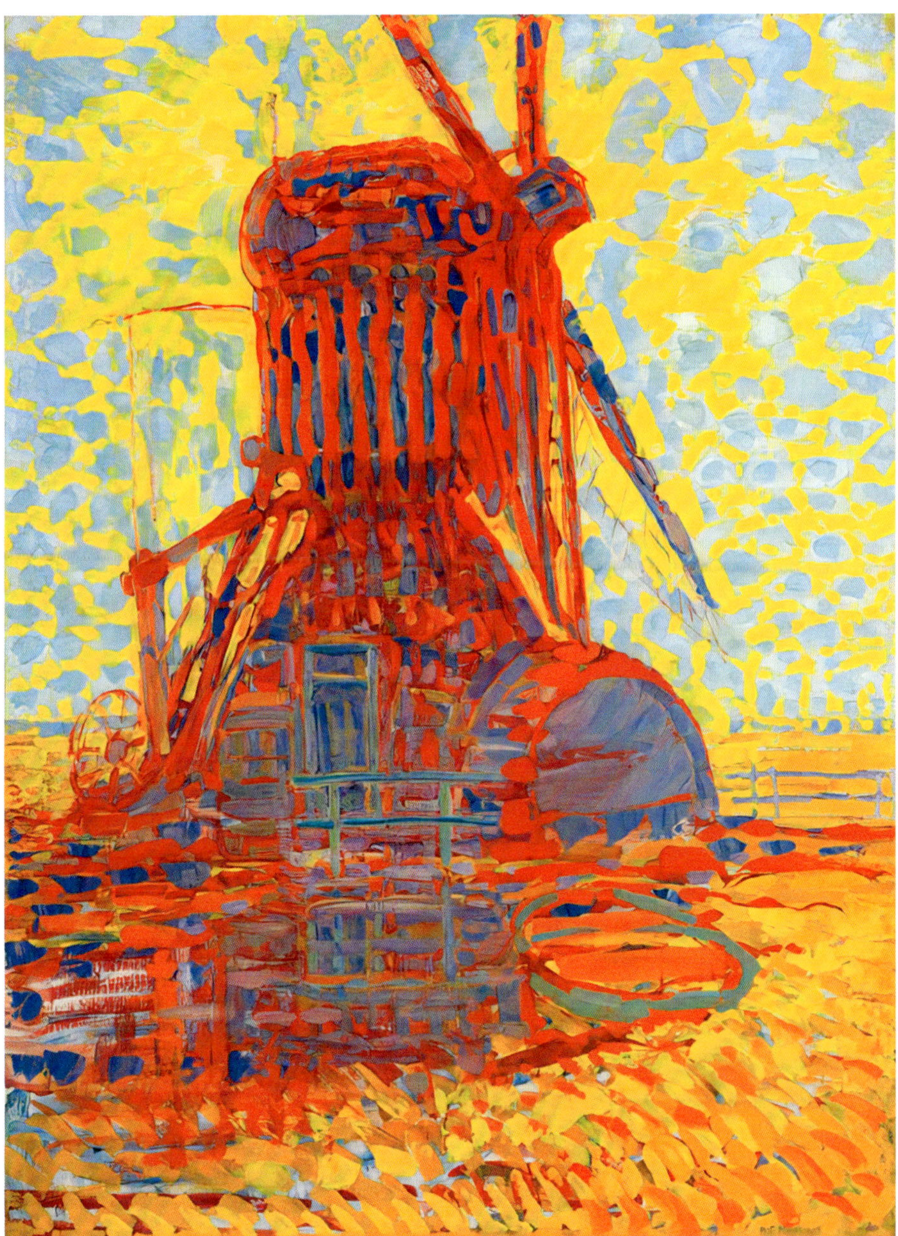

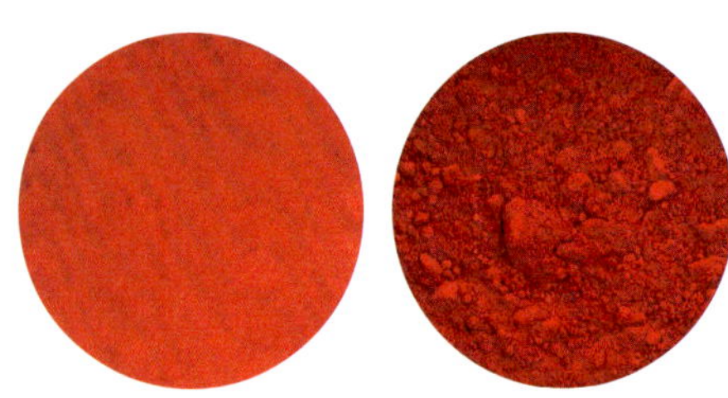

Naphthol Red & Quinacridone Red

Two different shades of red that are iconic in the modern street scene. Easy to use and far less toxic than historical reds such as vermilion and cadmium, they are both substitutes for diverse historical pigments.

Naphthol red is a genuine azo pigment. The word azo derives from the French *azote*, the historical name for nitrogen (which it contains), and literally means no (*a*) life (*zoe*). It is a member of a large group of organic pigments including browns, blacks, blues, yellows and reds, that defines much of the current artist's palette. Naphthol red is yet another pigment developed in the 19th century. As an artist's paint, it is principally used as an alternative for cadmium. While it comes close, it lacks cadmium's tinting strength. This is evident in its name, 'Cadmium Red Hue', with *hue* indicating its role as an imitation of, rather than a replacement for, the original. My own red *Summer Ocean* is built up out of circa 12 layers of paint, for which I used two differing naphthol reds, supplemented by a quinacridone to depict the seawater. Azo pigments are broadly used for numerous products, from foodstuffs and medicine to paints, inks and textiles. Worldwide, they make up about 70 per cent of all dyes.

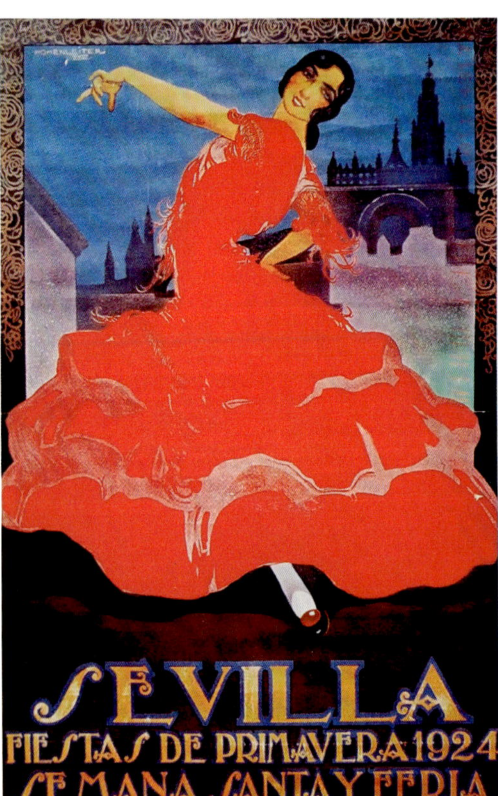

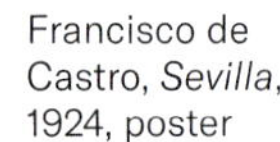

Francisco de Castro, *Sevilla*, 1924, poster

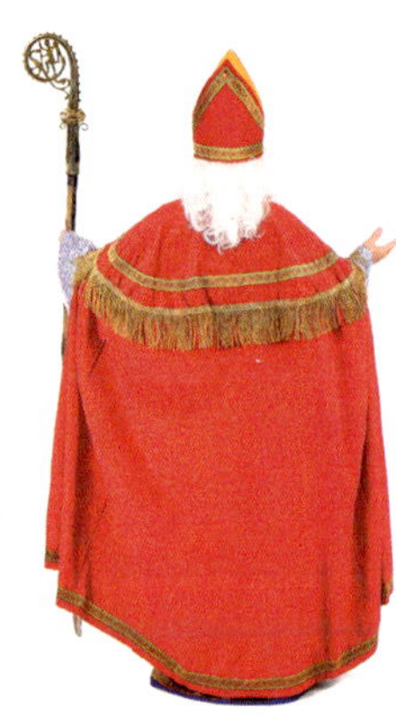

Saint Nicholas costume

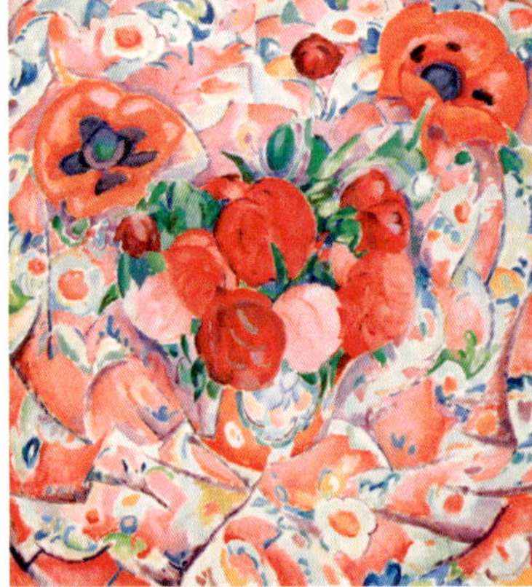

Leo Gestel, *Pionees*, 1912, oil on canvas, 100.5 x 90.5 cm, Kunstmuseum, The Hague

Quinacridone red likewise has its roots in the 19th century but was not marketed as a paint pigment until 1958. An exquisite, transparent red, it forms the modern-day replacement for carmine and madder and is lightfast, in contrast to its historical forerunners. A bit more expensive, but its capacity to preserve colour intensity should negate any objection to the higher costs.
Like rose madder and alizarin, it covers a wide colour spectrum: from deep magenta to violet to brownish red. Quinacridone's cool, bluish undertone makes it perfectly suitable for the making of purples and violets.

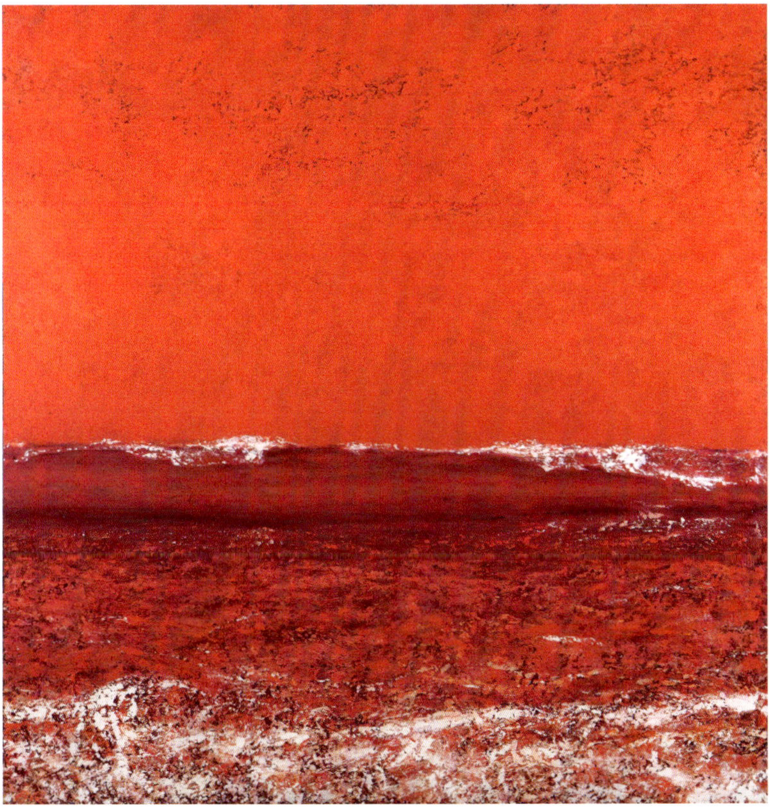

monica rotgans, *Summer Ocean*, oil on canvas, 180 x 180 cm, artist's collection

Pierre Alechinsky, *Octave*, 1983, private collection

Maurice Wyckaert, *Composition*, 1979, oil on canvas, 80 x 70 cm, private collection

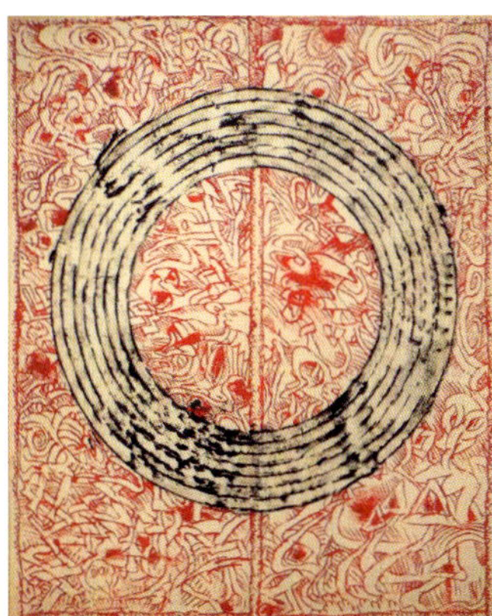

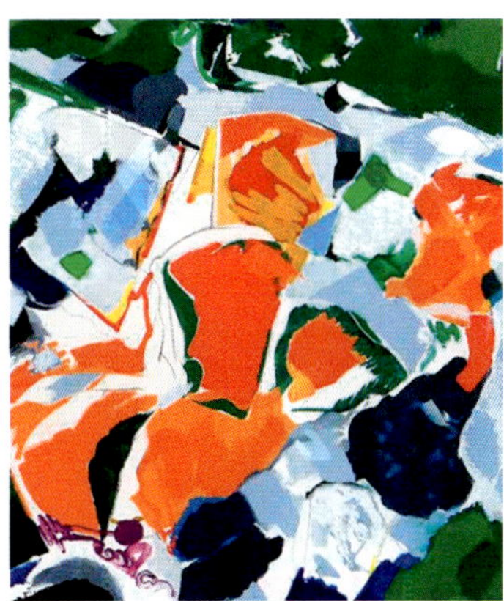

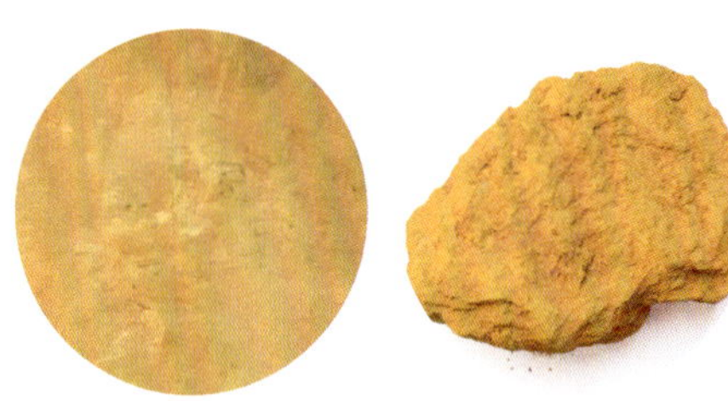

Yellow Earth & Sienna

The colour of ripe nature. In everyday life, it is called 'yellow ochre', which is actually redundant as the word 'ochre' derives from the ancient Greek ὤχρα (*ộkhros*), meaning (bright) yellow. To complicate things further, natural red earths are also called ochre. Therefore, one can never be sure which exact colour is meant in a text if it does not explicitly mentions 'yellow' or 'red'.

Like most other ancient pigments, it is still commonly used as medicine worldwide. In China, it is known as *Fu Long Gan*, a remedy to halt haemorrhages.
Until the late 19th century, ochres on the palette were natural products and often collected in situ by the painters. With just a little attention, you can find raw ochre under your feet in countless places on every continent. I have been collecting it for years and thus have a wide range of earthy yellow at my disposal that no paint manufacturer can match.
One of the few remaining ochre mines still functioning in Europe is in France's Luberon region. Near the town of Apt, an old quarry, including the workshop, has been restored to its former glory, and the entire production process, from raw earth to pigment, can be observed.
What is now sold as ochre paints are mainly synthetic varieties, less expensive

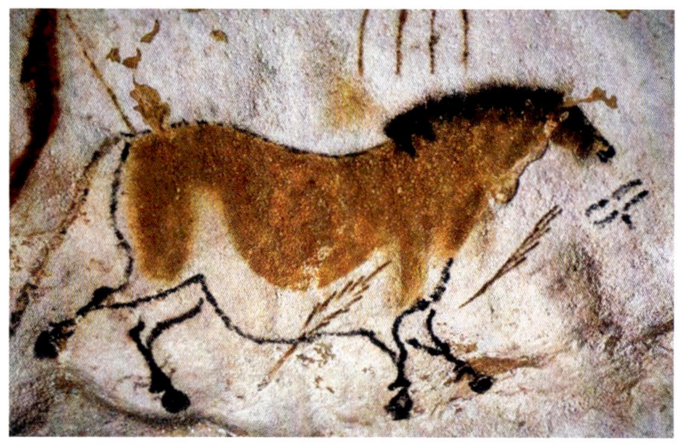

Cave painting of a horse in the caves of Lascaux, 15,000-10,000 BC

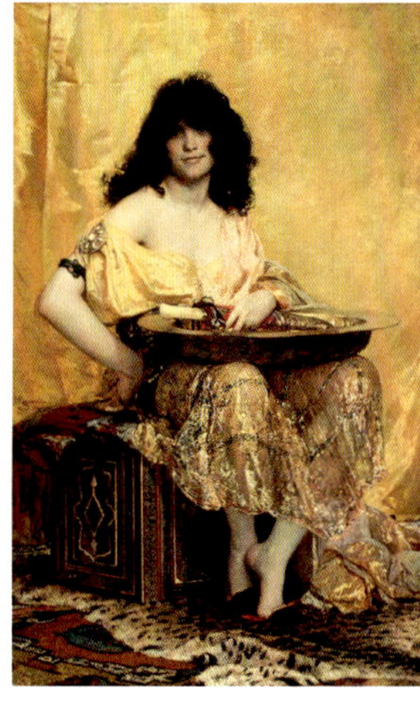

Henri Regnault, *Salomé*, 1870, oil on canvas, 160 x 102.9 cm, Metropolitan Museum of Art, New York

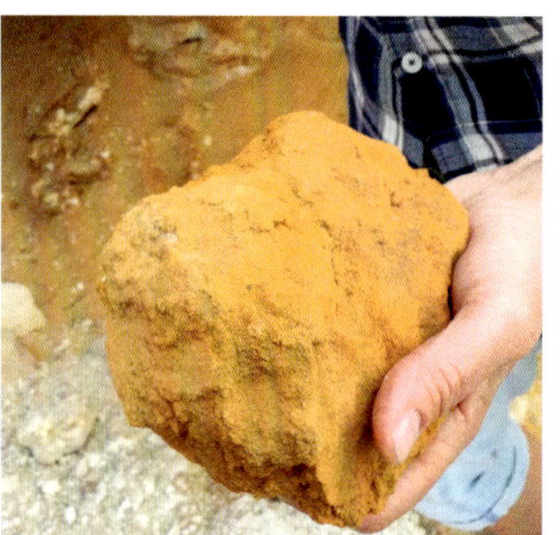

Fresh ochre, Australia

and consistent. Not everyone will love them because, like red iron oxides, these uniform yellows lack the energy of natural earths. Unfortunately, with every ochre quarry shut down, an often centuries-old colour disappears.

Ochre is an opaque and stable pigment, cheap and efficient. A perfect alternative to suggest gold, unattainable to many, hence the term gold ochre for certain hues. Easy to mix with other colours, it is, in short, the perfect partner. The plastic types have a long history as the foundation for all sorts of pottery and as building materials. Because it is such a common and versatile pigment, little has been written about it, with the idea that 'good wine needs no bush'. But, if you start paying attention, one can see how it has served as a colour and a paint for thousands of years, not only in easel painting but also as wall paint, in decorations and on furniture. It is, for example, easy to recognise in Egyptian hieroglyphics and paintings where, for a time, it distinguished women from men, with an ochre-yellow for the female and red for the male's skin. It was on the palettes of Fayum painters as a mixing colour for skin tones. A function it has held to this day. Innumerable buildings were painted with it, such as the still-existent birthplace of the Spanish painter Velázquez in Seville. An avid user of yellow earth, he incorporated it into the priming of his canvases for many years.

Ochre was the principal colour in summer landscapes with cornfields, and for the suggestion of gold or leather attire until the 19th century, when chrome yellows took the stage, followed soon after by the cadmiums.

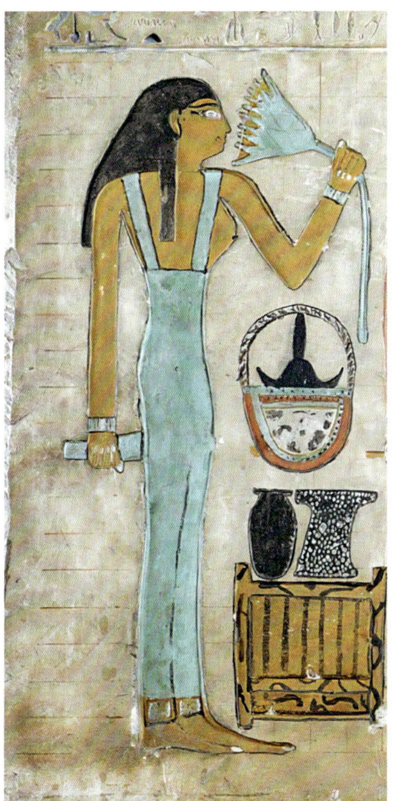

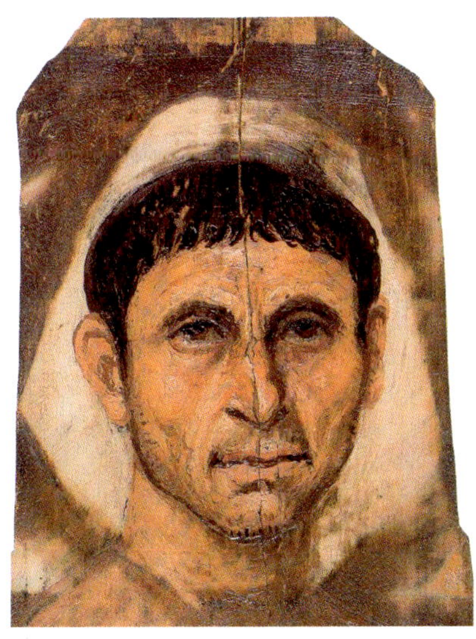

Fayum portrait, encaustic on panel, 1st cen. AD, h. 42 cm, British Museum, London

< Grave relief of the Cheti, c. 1980 BC, Kunsthistorisches Museum, Vienna

Looking at self-portraits of artists with their palettes can provide insight into the universality of yellow ochre (see the Conclusion). From the earliest depictions of Egyptian writers to those of contemporary artists, it is rarely absent.
The renowned raw sienna, or Italian ochre, is rich in silica and has a high iron content, making it more transparent than regular ochres. It is named after the historical, but now depleted, deposits near Siena, Italy. The natural sienna offered today originate from other regions. Like the opaque ochre, sienna covers a range from yellow to brown hues. And just like ochre, you can treat it with heat, turning it into burnt sienna. Depending on the basic pigment, at times a vibrant brown, ideal for painting

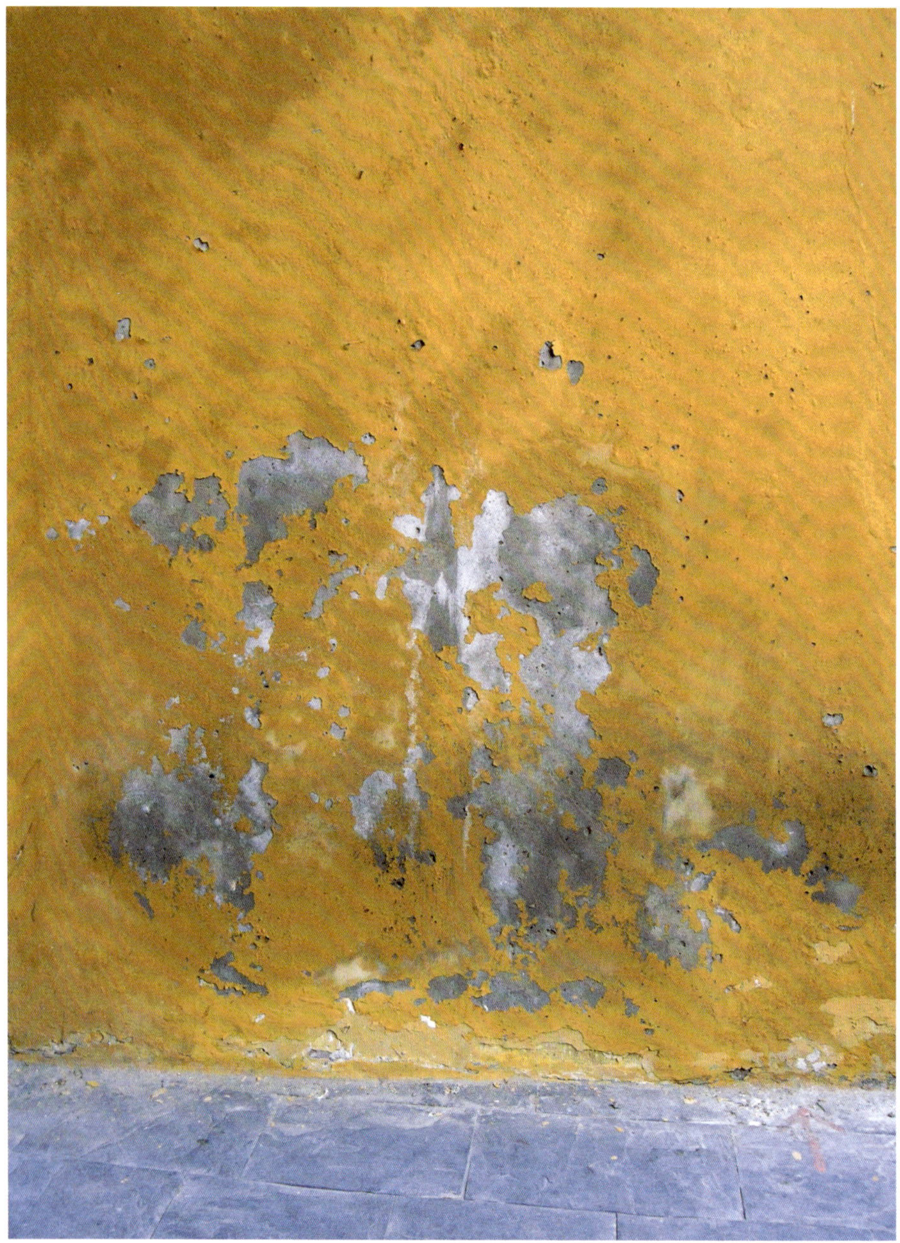

coats and hair and for imitating wood. Today's burnt sienna is usually made from a mixture with synthetic red iron oxide. It does not truly replicate the original natural pigments, and each manufacturer chooses its own specific colour temperature. Sienna's transparency makes it very suitable for watercolours and glazes. As a watercolour, it retains its vibrancy well, but in oil paint, it darkens significantly – much more than ochre, as it requires almost 100 per cent oil. In lithography, this was called the 'growing' of a colour, resulting in dominating the others. It dries fast, which can easily cause *craquelure* when applied over a slower-drying pigment.

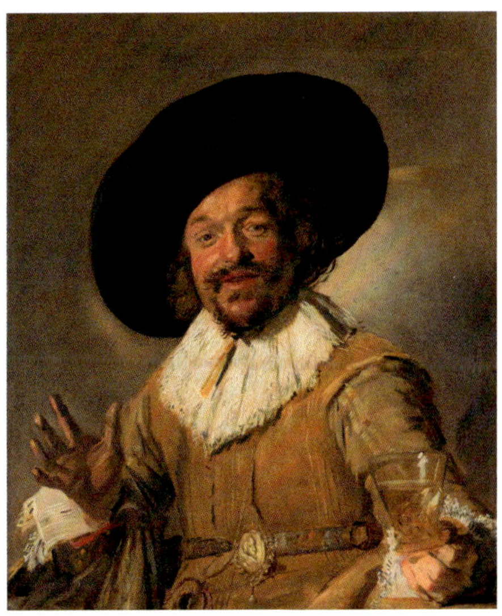

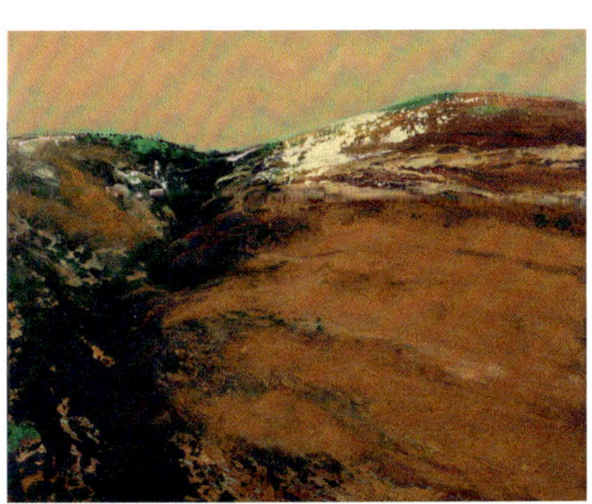

< Peeling ochre, Cordoba

monica rotgans, *Mute Land*, 2019, ochres and acrylic paint on panel, 51 x 40 cm, artist's collection

Frans Hals, *The Merry Drinker*, c. 1630, oil on canvas, 81 x 66.5 cm, Rijksmuseum, Amsterdam

Pieter Bruegel the Elder, *The Harvesters*, 1565, oil on panel, 166.5 x 159.5 cm, Metropolitan Museum of Art, New York

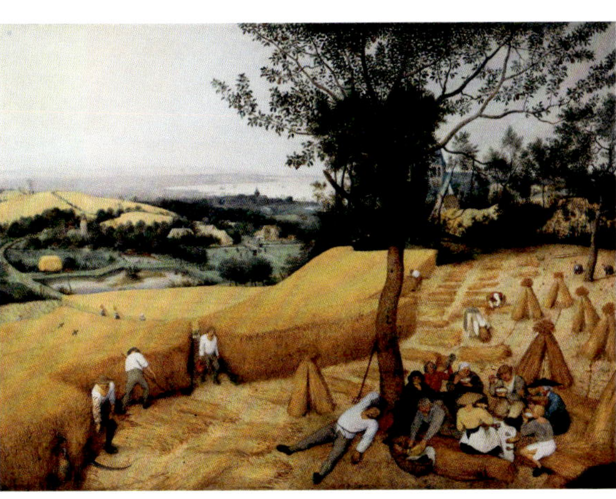

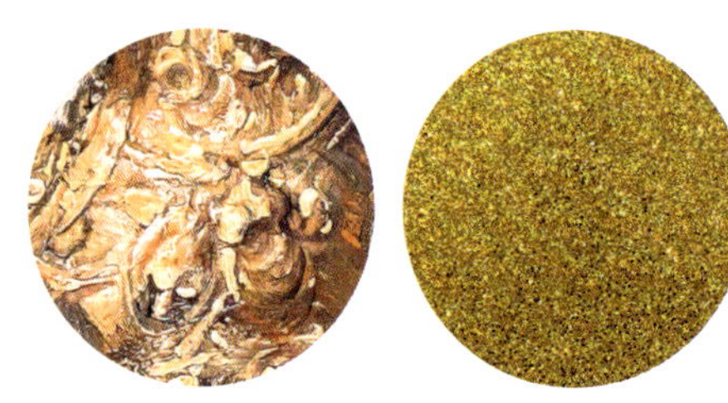

Gold

The substitute for the sun on Earth. The eternal, indestructible and immortal, the body of the gods, which is how ancient cultures perceived it. Worldwide, gold has long been considered the 'Emperor of Metals', a reputation it owes to the fact that it never rusts and will always retain its lustre and value.

Gold can still be found all over the earth but rarely in profitable quantities. Since antiquity, Africa has been Europe and Asia's main source of gold. Painters had to learn to imitate all forms of gold in paintings and decorations as one of their basic skills. Rembrandt's *The Man with the Golden Helmet* is a good example, showing how 'gold' is built up with basic yellow ochre. Adding a miniscule amount of gold into liquid glass, studios produced striking ruby-red glass, which played a prominent role in church windows and luxury glassware.
Countless large and small objects and buildings were, and are, given status thanks to gold. Crowns, temples, palaces, works of art, sculptures of gods, monarchs and saints: in gold, they are deemed most exclusive. Golden awards, medals and trophies have represented the highest achievements since time immemorial, with yellow fabrics, such as the yellow jersey of the Tour de France, as symbolic substitutes. Even mundane items, for example cutlery, teeth, face masks, faucets

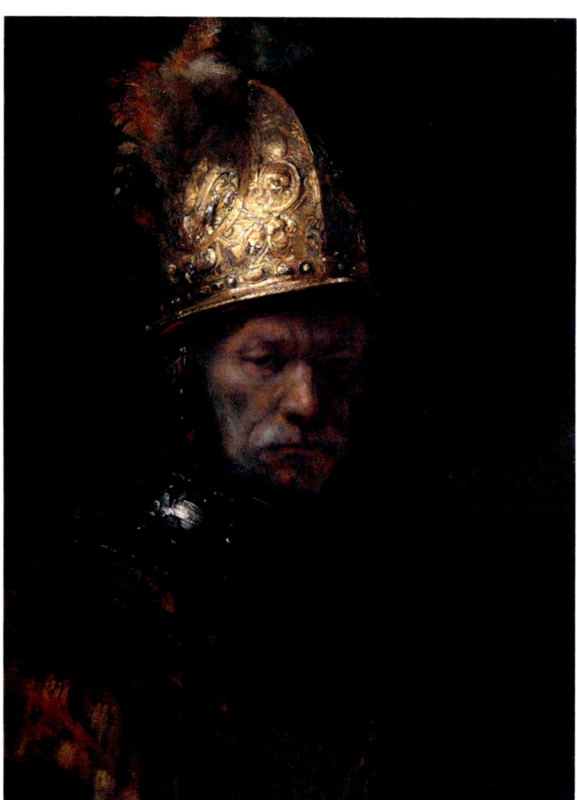

Rembrandt (Studio), *The Man with the Golden Helmet*, c. 1650, oil on canvas, 67.5 x 50.7 cm, Gemäldegalerie, Berlin

Matthäus Baur II, spice container, glass, copper, enamel and gilt, 1690-1694, National Museum, Warsaw

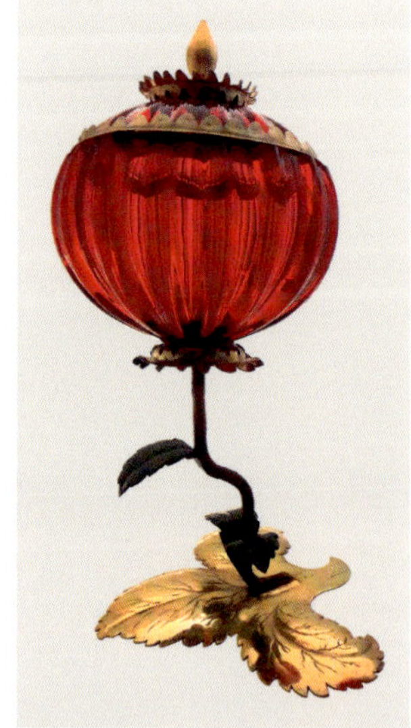

and toilets, can be purchased in gold to quench the desire for distinction. Worldwide, gold was an exclusive funerary element for the elite, with the most famous example being Tutankhamun, I suspect. Without question, the abundance of gleaming gold found in his tomb contributed to the hype surrounding the pharaoh, who died at a young age and was insignificant in his own time. With this knowledge, one can only imagine the colossal scale and grandeur of the burial of an aged and influential ruler such as Ramses II. It will have to remain speculation, as the looting of his final resting place, the imposing tomb in the Valley of the Kings, had already begun in antiquity. The amount of gold objects stolen, confiscated, hauled between continents, and melted down over thousands of years, is unfathomable. Well-known examples are the 16th-century raids by the Spanish in Central and South America, in which shiploads of gold were dispatched to Europe and repurposed – a prime example of this being the gigantic *Reredos* in the Cathedral of Seville.

Earlier, during the Middle Ages and early Renaissance, gold dictated the Eurasian arts. In portraits, monarchs and saints were 'mummified' in gold until a more realistic depiction took over in painting. Gold gained prominence once again in the Art Deco era, with probably the most famous example being the works of Gustav Klimt.

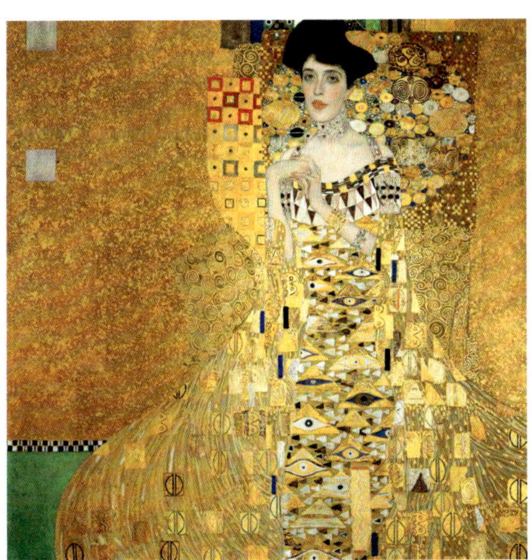

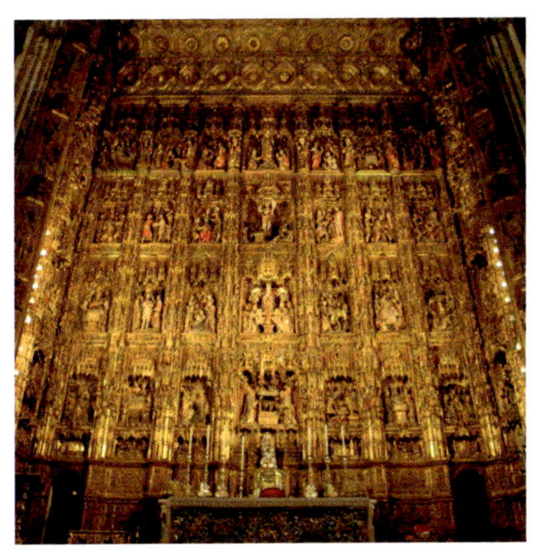

Pierre Dancart, Reredos of the Cathedral of Seville, 1482-1564

Gustav Klimt, *Portrait of Adèle Bloch-Bauer I*, 1904-1907, oil on canvas, 138 x 138 cm, Neue Galerie, New York

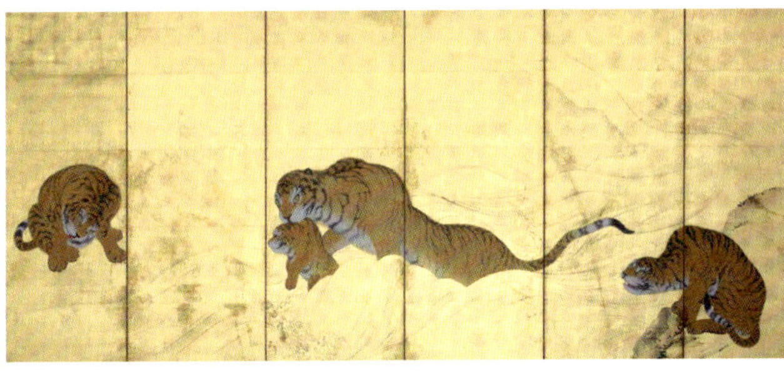

Maruyama Okyo, *Tigers Crossing a River*, folding screen, c. 1781, 153.5 cm x 352.8 cm, British Museum, London

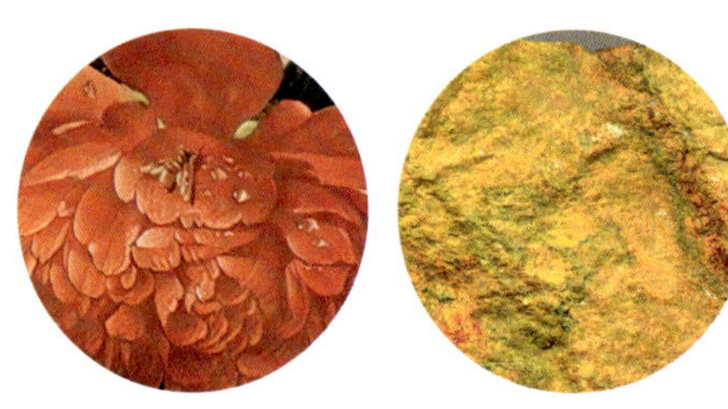

Orpiment & Realgar

Orpiment and Realgar are a life-threatening couple, due to the arsenic they contain. Nevertheless, the beauty of their colours has kept them on palettes for thousands of years worldwide.

They are still used as resource for cosmetics and medicines and were crucial ingredients for historic pharmacies to treat syphilis, fistulas, acne and open wounds. In the Victorian age, women consumed these kinds of arsenic-containing substances, regardless of the consequences, for whiter skin to emphasize a higher status. They are also well-known preservatives, pesticides and fungicides. And, last but not least, effective poisons to eliminate unfavourable fellow humans, which earned them the moniker 'the Poison of Kings'.

Orpiment has a long history as the only true bright and opaque yellow, more vigorous than even the strongest yellow ochre. It can be found in manuscripts and paintings, as well as on sculptures and statues, of the most diverse cultures.

It was used in Egyptian wall painting and, additionally, on sarcophagi and papyri. The tomb of Tutankhamun contained a small pot of orpiment for use in the afterlife. In India, orpiment was found on the walls of the 17th-century Taj Mahal, and it colours the traditional lacquer-work of Southeast

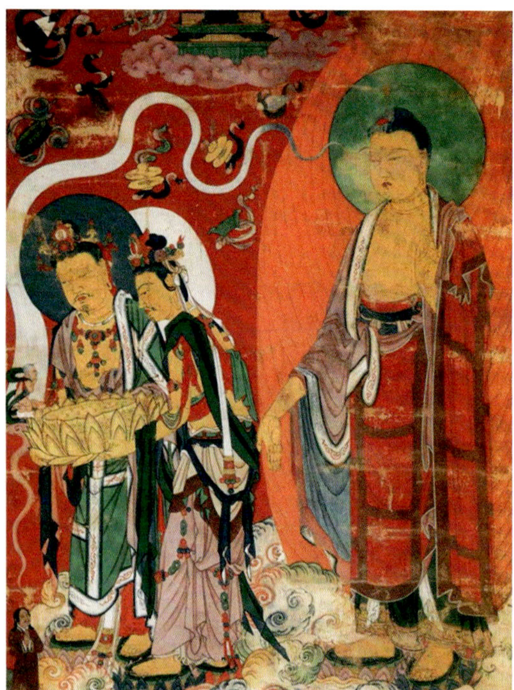

Anonymous, *Greeting of the Righteous Man on the Way to the Pure Land of Buddha Amitabha*, Kara Khoto (982-1227), Hermitage, St. Petersburg

Mu'in Musavvir, *Shahnama (Book of Kings) of Firdausi*, c. 1660, ink, opaque watercolour, gold, and silver on paper ink, Metropolitan Museum of Art, New York

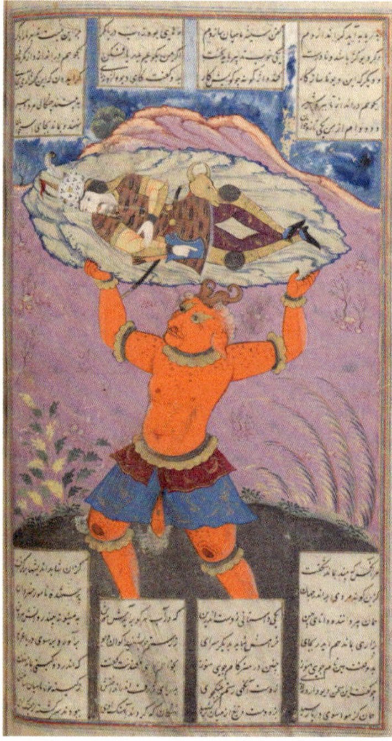

Asia. The yellow ink on black paper in classical Thai painting was made with orpiment. In Chile, it was found as a funerary offering in a pre-Columbian burial site and later appeared in the murals of churches and monasteries.
However, orpiment can lose its colour, turning into a leaden brown. This clarifies the appearance of peculiar, dead flowers in many sumptuous, ornate old master still-life paintings (*pronkstilleven*) which once showed a bright orpiment yellow.

Realgar is a beautiful orange-red colour. Until chrome orange was invented, it was the only pure and robust orange, with the duller lead red and the lightest variant of vermilion. It is a colour that cannot be matched by mixing red and yellow, widely considered a weaker alternative. This is especially evident in the still-bright colours of the Mummy Mask of Khonsu.
This incomparable vibrancy is why realgar, like orpiment, was such a coveted pigment across cultures and countries.
The 16th-century painter Giovanni Paolo Lomazzo even proclaimed 'burnt orpiment' (realgar) to be 'the alchemy of the Venetians.' Realgar remained on artists' palettes well into the late 19th century, only to quickly disappear from Western art.
China still produces it as a painting pigment and a medicine, just like orpiment. In 2004, the Netherlands Food and Consumer Product Safety Authority issued an urgent warning against using products containing the ingredient *Xiong Huang*, realgar, in Ayurveda, the Indian alternative herbal medicines system, and other oriental preparations.

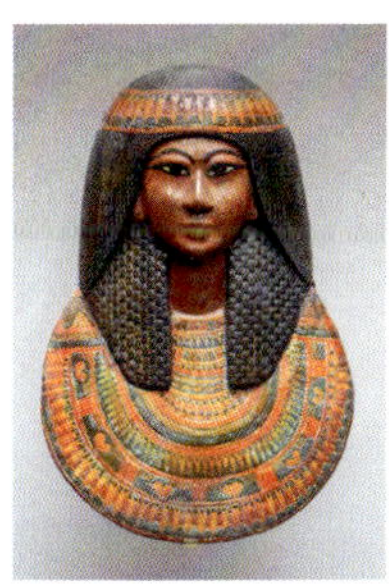

Anonymous, *Mummy Mask of Khonsu*, c. 1279-1213 BC, painted wood and cartonnage, h. 48 cm, Metropolitan Museum of Art, New York

Abraham Mignon, *Flowers in a Glass Vase*, 1670, oil on canvas, 90 x 72.5 cm, Mauritshuis, The Hague

Raphael, *The Sistine Madonna*, 1512-1513, oil on canvas, 269.5 x 201 cm, Gemäldegalerie Alte Meister, Dresden

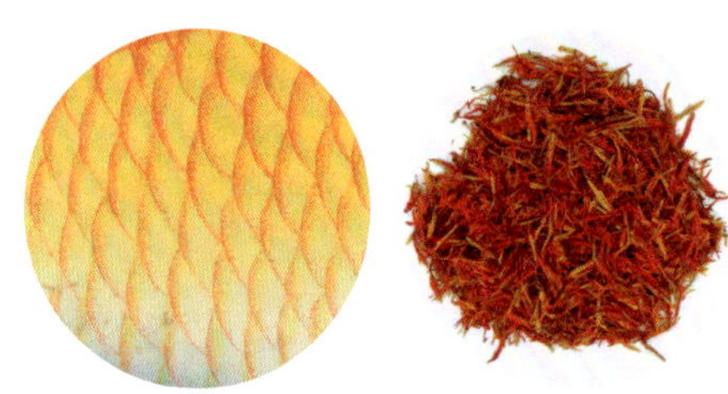

Stil de Grain Yellow & Weld

The biggest problem when discussing the pigment stil de grain yellow (*Schietgeel* or *schijtgeel* in Dutch) as a historical paint is that it is rarely visible. This explains the numerous unnaturally blueish-green landscapes in works of art, such as the iconic, but severely discoloured, *Mona Lisa*.

We can, however, still see how spectacular this renowned yellow was in preserved watercolours, and the graphic works of manuscripts and other printed matter. The bound book, cut off from light and air, allows Stil de grain yellow to retain its original brilliance. Stil de grain yellow was commonly made from ripe and unripe berries and bark of the buckthorn, *Rhamnus cathartics*. The dye could be enhanced with weld, yellowwood and other organic yellows. Of these, weld plays the most important role as the plant from which it is extracted, *reseda luteola* (or dyer's rocket), is so common that it can even be found in urban areas.

The Tuscan artist Cennini, born around 1360 and author of one of the most fundamental painting manuals from the Middle Ages, uses the term yellow lake only as a reference to weld, which he then describes as a product of alchemy. In any case, Stil de grain yellow is frequently mentioned in historical discourses featuring recipes for the practice of painting. However, it remains unclear how

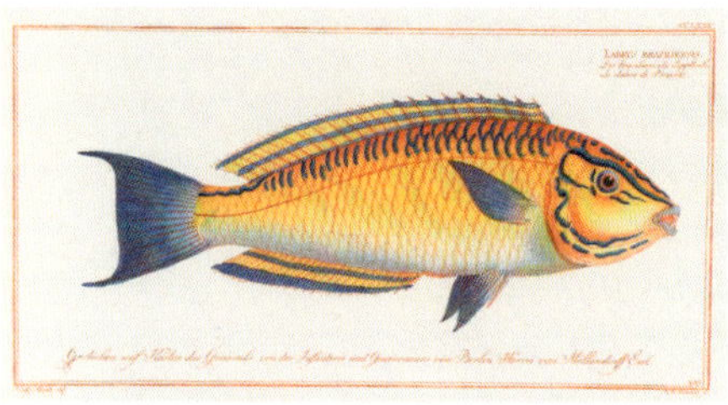

J.F. Hennig, *Brazilian Wrasse*, coloured copper engraving, from Allgemeine Naturgeschichte der Fische, Marcus Bloch, Berlin, 1795-1797, plate 280

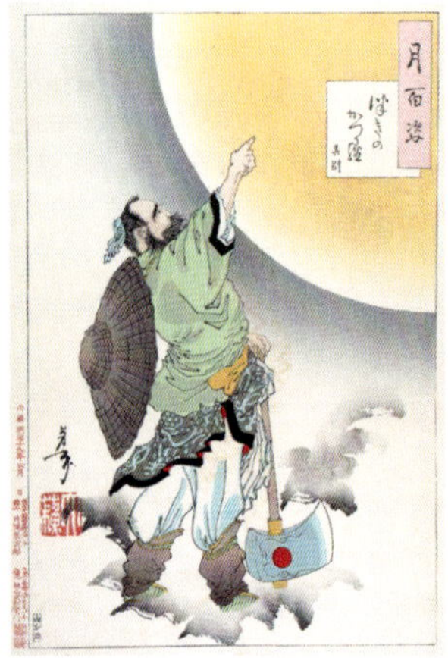

Tsukioka Yoshitoshi, *Casia-tree moon*, 1886, ukiyo-e, 39 x 26 cm, Art Gallery of NSW, Sydney

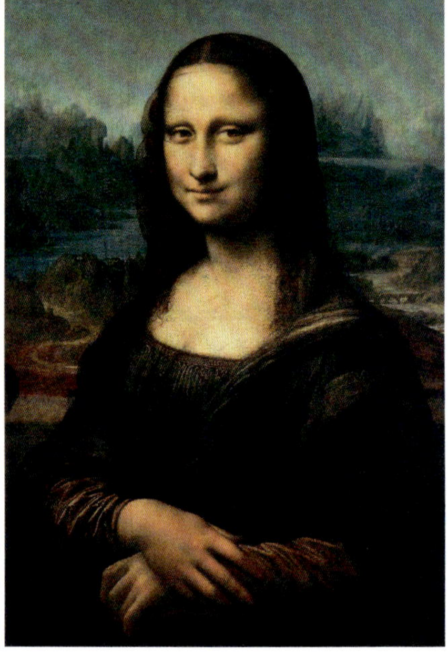

Leonardo da Vinci, *Mona Lisa*, c. 1503, oil on canvas, 77 x 53 cm, Louvre, Paris

long it has been part of the artist's palette. Its use may be substantially older than alluded to in the records known to us because, like other organic pigments, it was a common ingredient for the dyeing of fabrics. It has been suggested that its peculiar name in Dutch – *schietgeel* or *schijtgeel* – stems from the pharmacological properties of buckthorn berries as an effective laxative. Be that as it may, a more appropriate interpretation of the term is the association with the paint consistently fading and disappearing. De Mayerne (1573-1655), Royal Physician to several succeeding kings at the French and English courts, writes: 'This colour (...) tolerates neither light nor rain; it is fleeting, it turns white, it disappears.' Because it quickly loses its brilliance, even the most conservative cleaning may give the remaining yellow the final fatal blow. Another consequence is that within a few years of their execution, many faded pieces were either adjusted or painted over upon the request of their owners, often by a different painter than the original artist. However, painters had little to choose from due to the continuing, and not to be underestimated, scarcity of warm yellows and greens. Stil de grain yellow and the other organic yellow pigments remained on the artist's palette. They were applied as glazes over blues to create greens, added as glaze over, or mixed with the common muted yellows, like lead-tin yellow and ochre, to enhance their brilliance. Many of the now blue landscapes and vegetation depicted in old paintings were originally a warm, natural green. Therefore, the short-lived, but once indispensable Stil de grain, profoundly influences what we see today when we look at, for example, a 17th-century flower arrangement. The artist neither painted, nor intended it to appear, as it currently does.

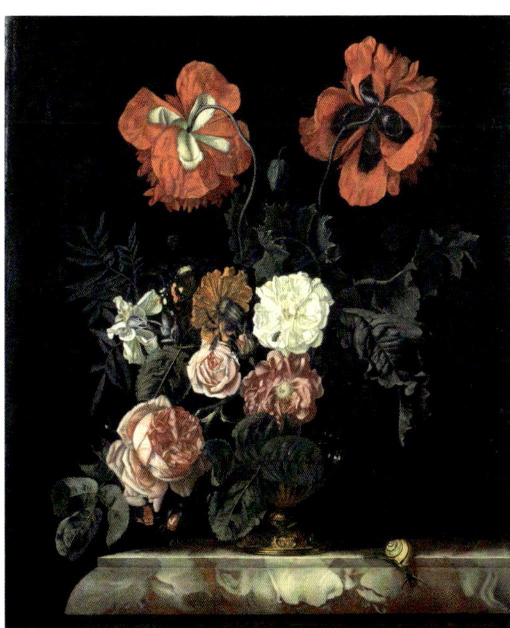

Nicolaes Lachtropius, *Still-Life with Flowers*, 1667, oil on canvas, 63 x 52 cm, Rijksmuseum, Amsterdam

Maria Sibylla Merian, *Pineapple and a caterpillar, chrysalises, two Scarce Bamboo Pages and a cactus beetle, depicting the life cycles of the insects*, c. 1701, watercolour and gouache on vellum on paper, 41.5 x 27.9 cm, British Museum, London

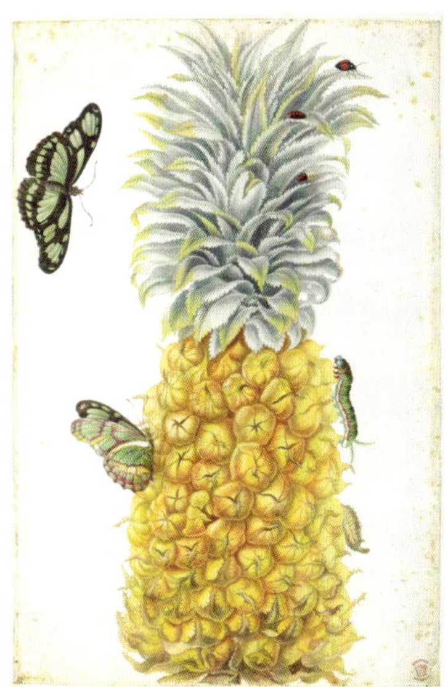

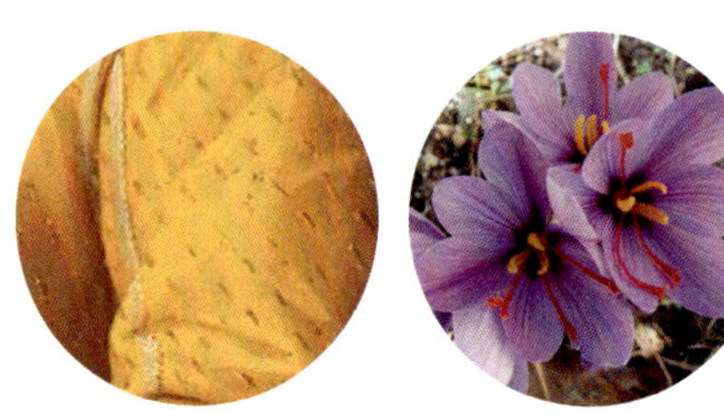

Saffron

The name saffron derives from the Latin *saffranum*, with roots in the Persian Arabic *za' farân*, meaning 'yellow colour'.

Saffron is the most important and precious organic yellow. It is extracted from the three tiny stigmas of the *Crocus sativus*, a direct relative of the woodland crocus that originally flourished around the eastern Mediterranean.
One kilogram of dried saffron (equivalent to five kilograms of freshly harvested saffron) requires the hand-picked stigmas of 120,000 to 200,000 flowers. Used as a dye and pharmaceutical since early antiquity, it was cultivated in countless varieties and places. From Persia, present-day Iran, it was exported to Mesopotamia, now Iraq, and later used by the Greeks and the Romans in cosmetics and perfumes. Sex workers dyed their hair with saffron, inspired by the golden hair of Aphrodite, the goddess of love. As they advanced towards the West, the Arabs first transferred their saffron cultivation to northern Africa, and in the ninth century to the Iberian Peninsula.
Saffron from France's Gâtinais and Austria's Krems and Melk was long regarded as the finest. Today, most comes from Iran and Spain. As with purple and pure ultramarine, the dye was frequently more expensive than gold. It was second only to Tyrian purple in its exclusiveness.

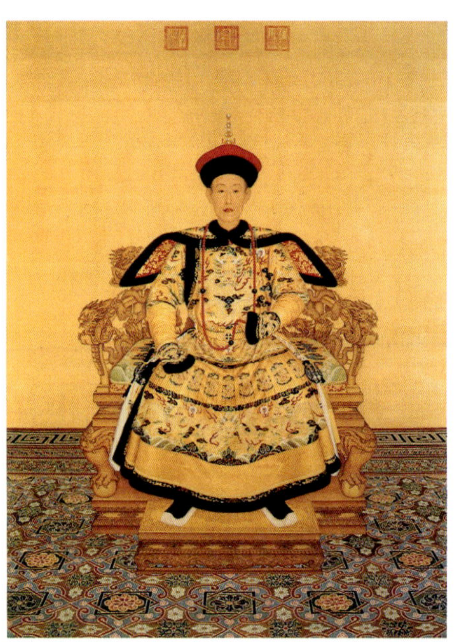

Emperor Qianlong, scroll painting on silk, 271 x 142 cm, The Palace Museum, Beijing

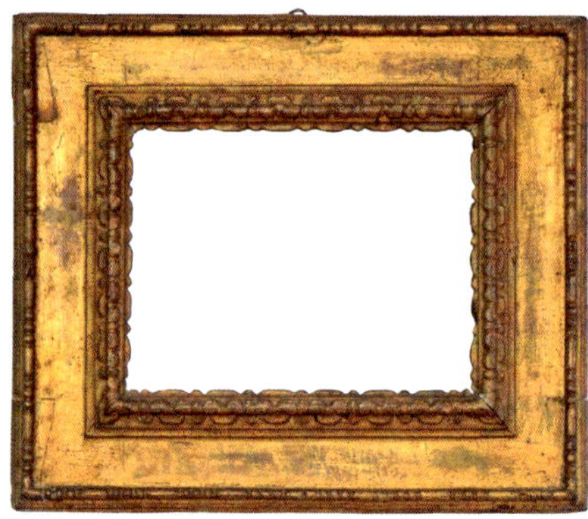

Frame, early 17th-cen., gold leaf, possibly with saffron

Gerrit W. Dijsselhof, book cover, lithograph, 1897, Museum of Fine Arts, Boston

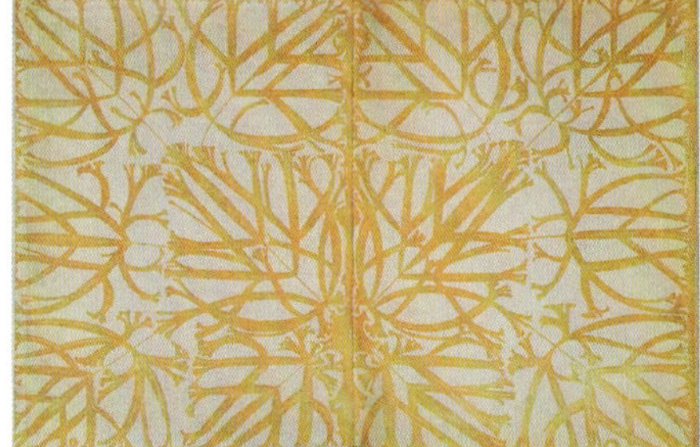

This unavoidably led to inferior imitations; lily stigmas and mixtures of pulverised fungus with chalk were offered as saffron yellow. During the late Middle Ages, an institute was founded in Nuremberg, Germany, to tackle the lucrative illegal trade in counterfeit saffron. It had the extreme jurisdiction to fine, exile, burn or bury alive, rogue traders.
Only the finest and whitest silk will produce a brilliant golden yellow with saffron, making it one of the most exclusive fabrics and a much-coveted status symbol. All other textiles treated with the precious dye will turn a drab and lifeless yellow.
In China, saffron fulfilled the role that purple has long held in the Western world. Upon penalty of death, it was solely the sartorial privilege of the emperor, his court, and Buddhist monks.

Saffron is an ancient raw material for inks. From the Middle Ages on, it was consistently listed in recipes to intensify yellows by producing an egg-white based varnish. The 1596 painting manual *Book of Secrets* recommends mixing saffron with egg-yolk to make a glossy and brilliant deep yellow. In 1773, Jean Félix Watin, in his book *L'art du peintre, doreur, vernisseur*, advised saffron for the reddish varnish that gives gold that extra radiance. As recently as the 19th century, saffron-coloured varnishes were used to give paintings a 'golden glow' and to enliven the greens. An effect similar to Stil de grain.

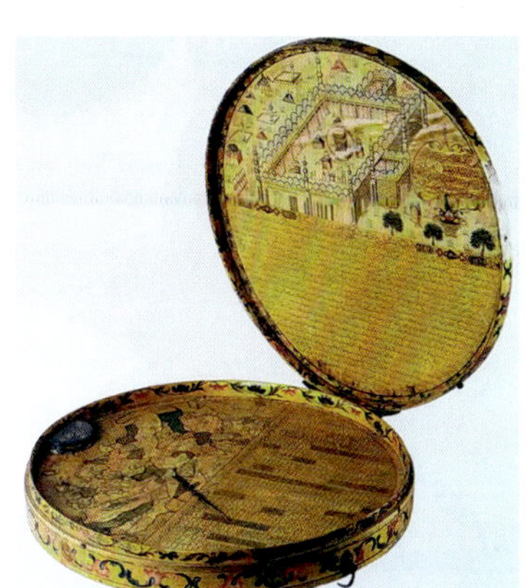

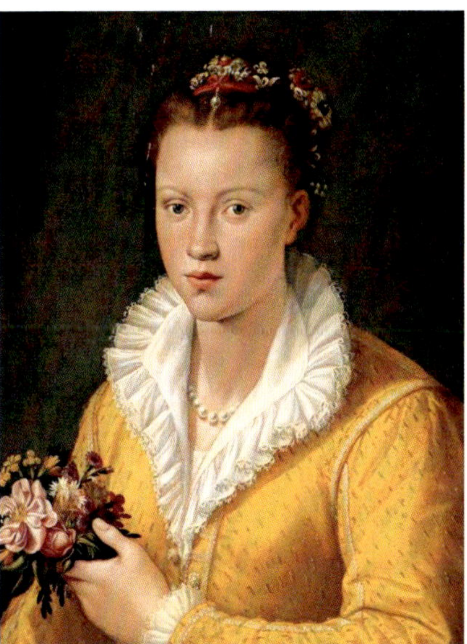

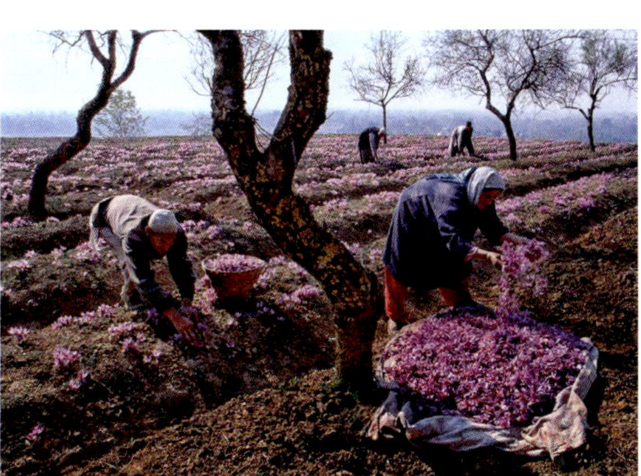

Compass, painted wood lacquered with gold, diam. 30 cm, Museum of Islamic Art, Cairo

Santi di Tito, *Portrait of a Girl*, c. 1550, oil on panel, 59 x 45 cm, private collection

Saffron harvest in Kashmir

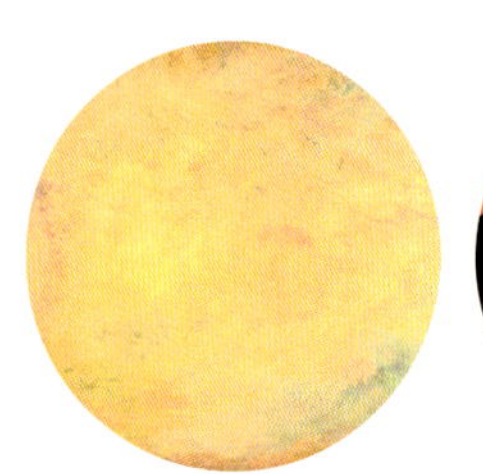

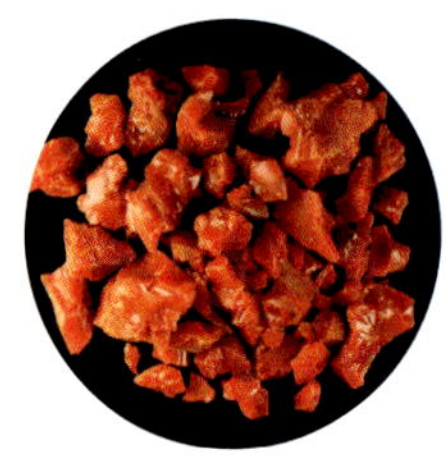

Yellowwood & Gamboge

Every continent has unique tree species whose timber or saps can be used to create yellow pigments. Over time, this knowledge has faded into oblivion, and we only have ourselves to blame for allowing the industry to get such a firm grip on us.

We have become so accustomed to ready-made dyes and pigments, that we have no idea what our immediate surroundings have to offer. For example, common yellowwood.

Yellowwood is the collective name for the various yellow timber species found in Europe, Asia and the Americas. In Europe, the wood of its native wild and cultivated apple tree, the *genus malus*, as well as the European smoke tree were traditionally used, until they were replaced by imported wood.

The apple tree as a supplier of colour takes some getting used to, but it was listed as an ingredient in formulas for painters and dyers as early as the Middle Ages. The word *malus* in the Latin name *Malus domestica* refers to the detrimental reputation the apple had in Christianity, as an accomplice to the *Fall* in *Paradise Lost*.

With the beginnings of the colonisation of the Americas and the subsequent increasing exports to Europe, the native trees disappeared from both view and use.

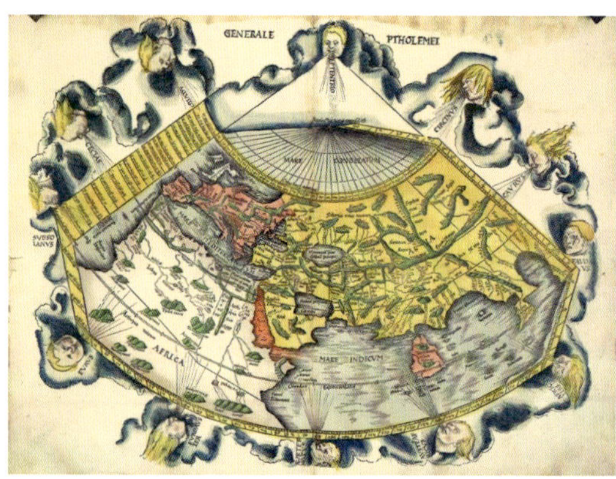

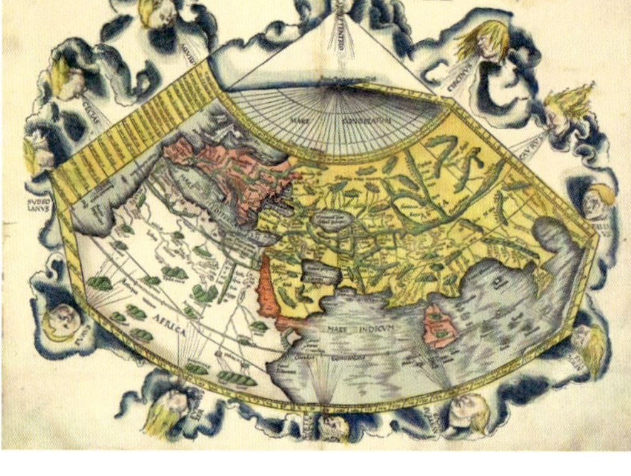

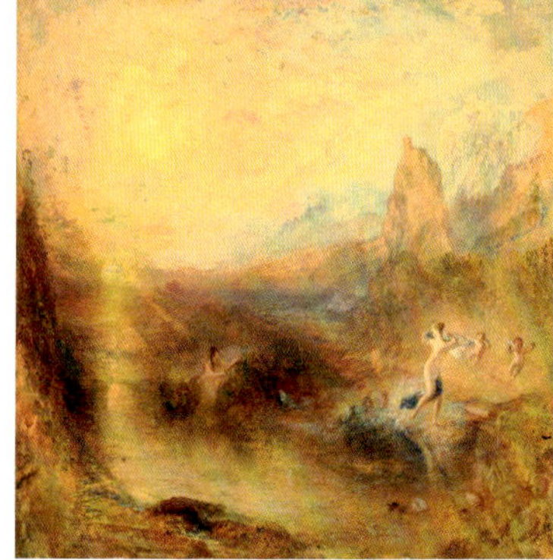

Martin Waldseemüller, *Generale Ptholomei*, 1520, coloured woodcut

Joseph Mallord William Turner, *Glaucus and Scylla*, 1841, oil on panel, 78.3 x 77.5 cm, Kimbell Art Museum, Fort Worth

Léon Spilliaert, *The Bridge at Zandvoorde*, 1930, watercolour on paper, 48 x 60 cm, Art Center Hugo Voeten, Herentals

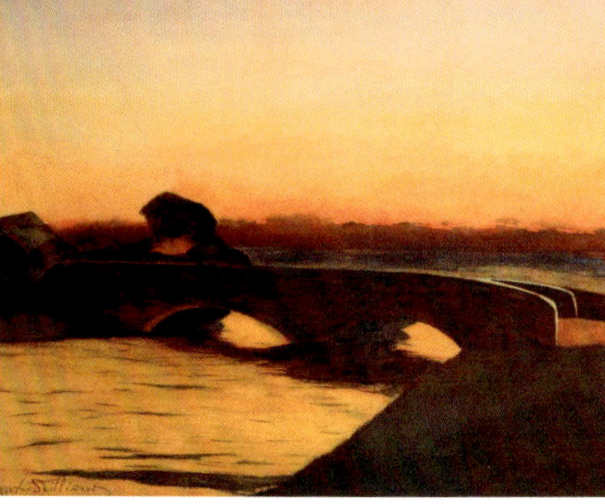

From the early 16th century, the heartwood of the dyer's mulberry from Central and South America steadily became the primary yellowwood. Like redwood, this species was processed by men in the grating houses into ready-for-use material. In the 18th century, the dyer's mulberry was replaced by the stronger colour of the American Dyer's oak, which in turn had to give way in the 19th century to new synthetic dyes. A well-known contemporary colour, originating from the old yellowwood pigment, is khaki.
Gamboge (Gutta Gum or Goma Gutta) is an ancient sap yellow from the East. It first captured the European market during the 16th century and was introduced in America in the 18th century. Gamboge was named after one of the Asian countries of origin: Cambodia, or as Cambodians call their country, Kampuchea.

Stunningly brilliant, warm, and golden yellow, gamboge is best known in the West as a watercolour pigment and a glaze in oil paints. It was used in Chinese and Japanese prints as early as the eighth century and probably much longer as medicine. It was sold as a cure for ailments such as high blood pressure and fevers and used as a purgative cleanser. However, even a small dosage (circa 7 grams) could be lethal. Quite a risk for paint makers as they had to handle the dried resin (gum) to turn it into pigment.
The raw material is the gum resin excreted by Southeast Asian evergreen tree species, including the *Garcinia gummi-gutta* and the *Garcinia hanburyi*. Only when the trees are at least ten years old, the bark is incised to activate the 'bleeding' of the gum. When the fluid emerges, it is collected drop by drop in bamboo sticks. Once the gum has dried, the sticks are peeled off.

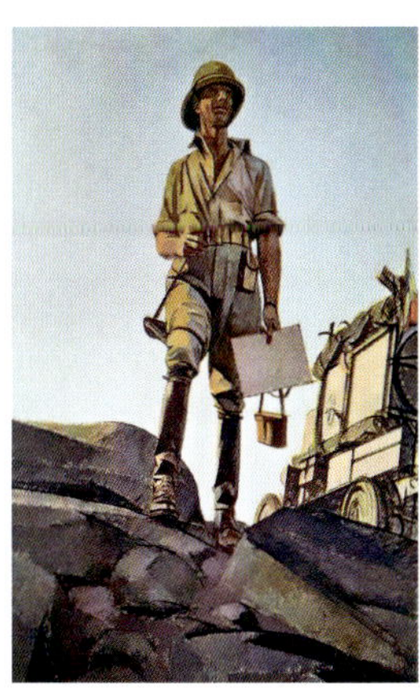

Bernard Boutet de Monvel, *Portrait of Georges-Marie Haardt*, 1926, oil on canvas, 104 x 75 cm, Musée du Quai Branly, Paris

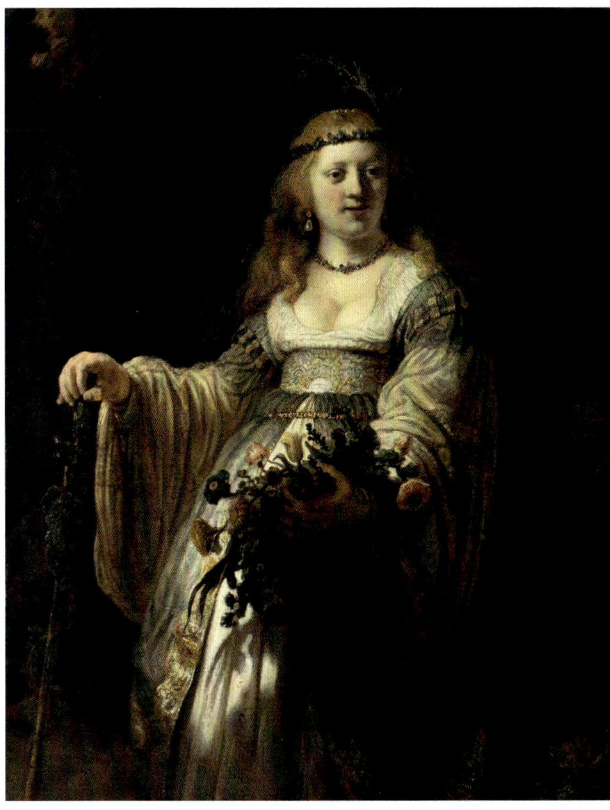

Rembrandt, *Saskia as Flora*, 1635, oil on canvas, 123.5 x 97.5 cm, National Gallery, London

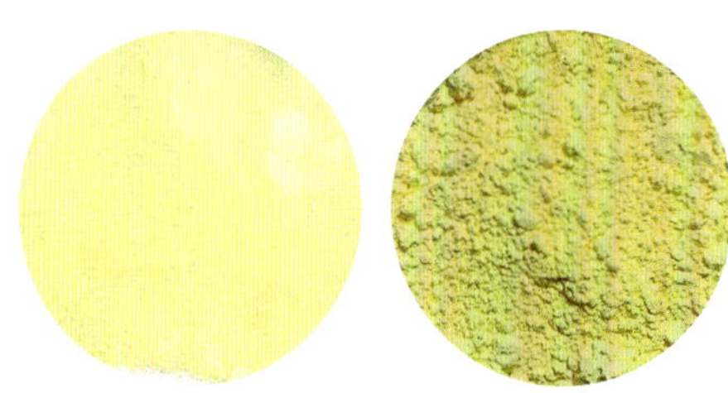

Lead-Tin Yellow & Massicot

Lead-tin yellow is also called the 'yellow of old masters', as the word is a 20th-century invention. It was given the nickname because, when it was rediscovered through research in the last century, it was found in a significant number of historic works of art. It is, as the name suggests, a lead and tin-based, hence toxic yellow.

Why the pigment vanished so ingloriously remains a mystery. It was affordable, lightfast and more consistent than its successor, Naples Yellow. Moreover, the two are very similar.

Nevertheless, it disappeared from painters' studios around 1750 and then quickly from the collective memory. It was not until 1938 that Richard Jacobi of the Doerner Institute in Germany rediscovered it. Lead tin-yellow is the default translation of the term he introduced: *Bleizinngelb.*

An attempt at reconstructing its history is not made any easier by, once again, the randomness of its name in historical recipes. The variety of original and forgotten names could not be more different: in German, it was *Plygall*; in Spanish, it was *genuli*, *giallorino* in Italian; in Portuguese, *mecchim*; and English, *general.*

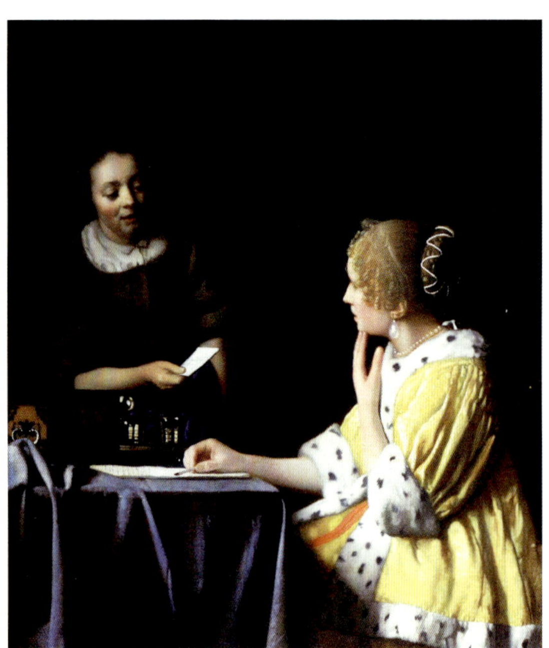

Johannes Vermeer, *Mistress and Maid*, ca. 1666, oil on canvas, 90.2 x 78.4 cm, The Frick Collection, New York

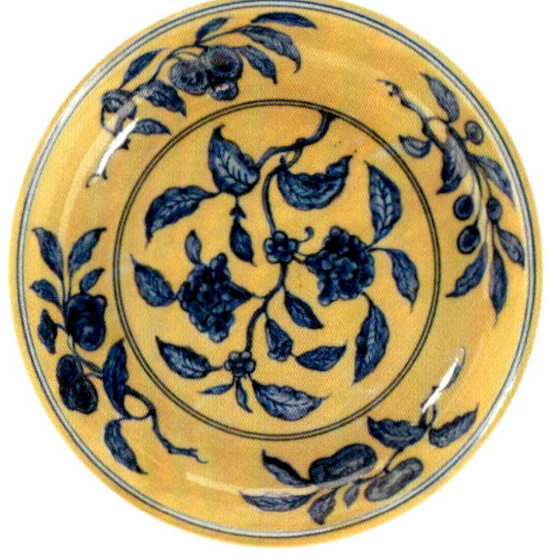

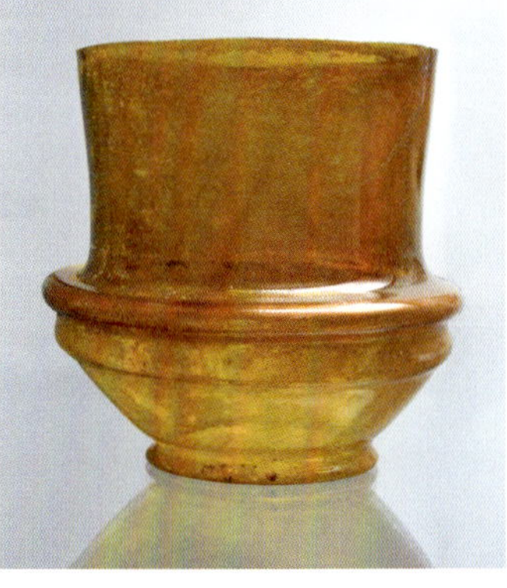

The Munich Cup, Roman glassware, 3rd-2nd cen. BC, Staatliche Antikensammlung, Munich

Because they are so difficult to tell apart, massicot, Naples yellow and what is now called lead-tin yellow were habitually mixed up.

Lead-tin yellow is a convenient and practical colour for painting. It is not obtrusive and very suitable for depicting a warm glow of light. It colours the light-catching chamber coats in Vermeer's paintings. When one sees an opaque, unblended and calm light yellow, there is a good chance it is the 'yellow of the old masters'. And this applies to both easel and wall painting.

The very closely related massicot is as old as lead white, but unlike its kin lead-tin yellow, a pure lead yellow. It is crafted by heating lead white until it turns yellow. It is not a particularly favourable or robust colour on the painter's palette, but quite suitable for glazes and colouring glass, resulting in a striking golden yellow in the latter.

So far, massicot has been found as pigment in, among others, Pompeian wall paintings and as a glaze on ancient Egyptian pottery.

Neither pigment is suited for making strong mixed colours. They will sooner dull those. A vivid green or orange cannot be made with them.

< Anonymous, dish with pomegranate blossom and sprigs of fruit, c. 1506-1521, porcelain, Rijksmuseum, Amsterdam

Giotto, *The Last Supper*, c. 1305, fresco, 200 x 185 cm, Cappella degli Scrovegni, Padua

Jan Davidsz de Heem, *Still-Life with a Glass and Oysters*, c. 1640, oil on panel, 25.1 x 19.1 cm, Metropolitan Museum of Art, New York

Diego Velázquez, *Apollo in Vulcan's Forge*, 1630, oil on canvas, 223 x 290 cm, Prado, Madrid

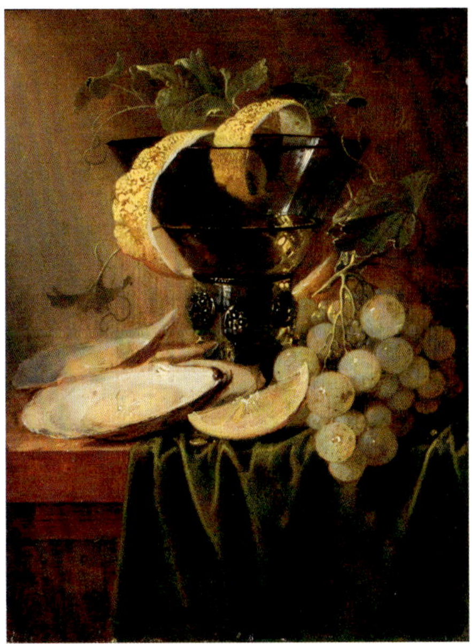

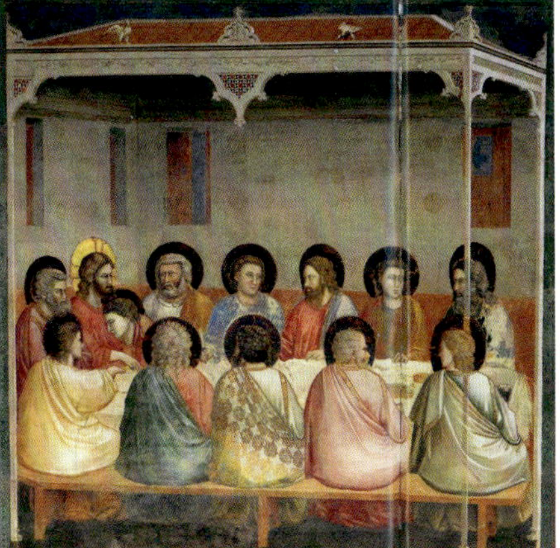

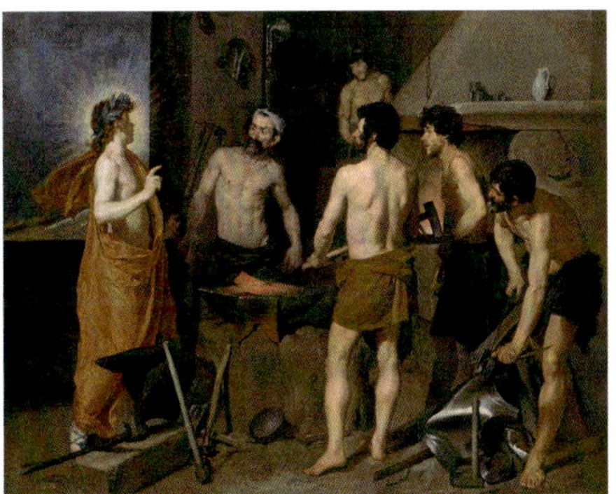

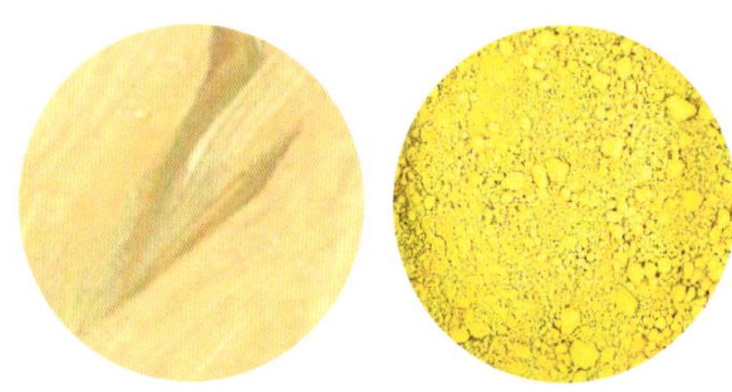

Naples Yellow

Very similar to lead-tin yellow, Naples yellow is a pigment with multiple lives. It was forgotten and rediscovered and is far older than its current name.

Research has revealed that a pigment with virtually the same composition was made as early as the 16th century BC. However, there is still no explanation as to where the name Naples yellow comes from, since the natural yellow found in the flanks of the Vesuvius near Naples is orpiment.

Naples yellow is an opaque matte yellow, ranging from a light, medium yellow to a lemony tone. The reddish variant is supplemented with a red pigment. Together with Egyptian blue, it belongs to the group of early synthetic pigments. It is a cross-cultural pigment, as recent discoveries show. From the second millennium BC onwards, it played a major role in the production of glass and ceramics in a greater part of the Middle East and northern Africa. And, considering the widespread trade routes of the time, it will undoubtedly have travelled across much of the Eurasian continent.
With the fall of the Roman Empire around 400, the pigment faded from view, comparable to the disappearance around the same time of the equally practical Egyptian blue. It was seemingly rediscovered some 600 years later when

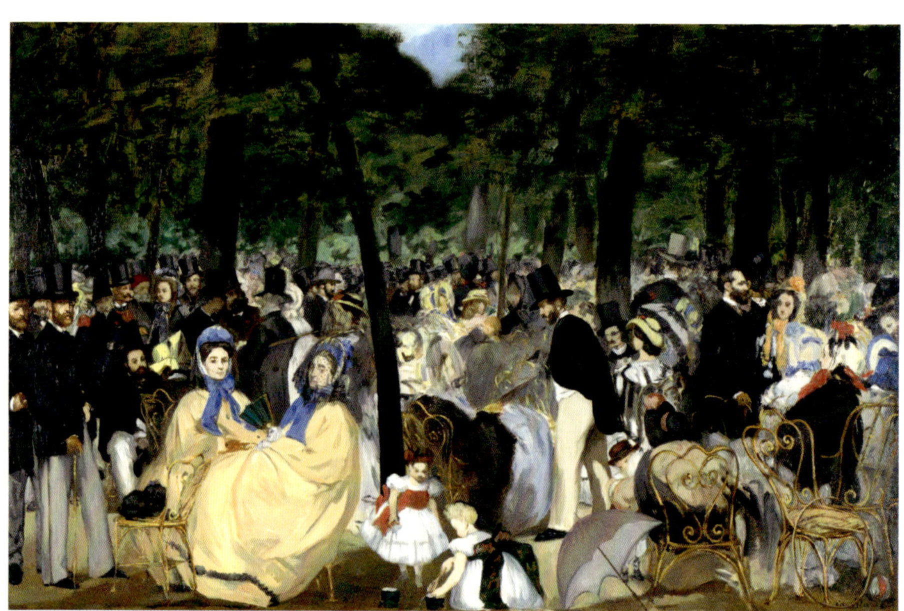

Edouard Manet, *Music in the Tuileries Gardens*, 1862, oil on canvas, 76 x 118 cm, National Gallery, London

> Dish, *Cupid with Bow*, Castel Durante, c. 1550-1570, Musée des Beaux-Arts, Lille

it resurfaced as a glaze in Asia, after which it re-emerged in Europe. Manet used it in the same manner Vermeer applied the related lead-tin yellow. It catches both the eye and light in his jam-packed canvas of the Tuileries. An easy and uncomplicated colour for landscapes, it quickly ties a composition together.

When applied over a brown underlayer, Napless yellow takes on a white hue, an effect that the French painter Prud'hon exploited when painting skin. Not only was Naples yellow popular with artists, but the pigment was also an equally sought-after house and decorative paint. Moreover, although this yellow was rather weak, numerous greens were mixed with it during the 18th and 19th centuries, recognisable by their slightly cool and flat tone. What is now being sold under the name Naples yellow is a mixture of less toxic pigments, based on the colour nuances of the original pigment.

Pierre-Paul Prud'hon, *The Zephyr*, 1814, oil on paper on canvas, 21.4 x 16 cm, The Wallace Collection, London

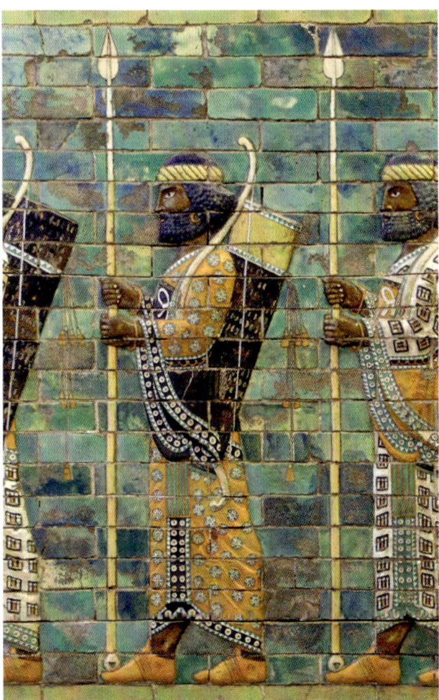

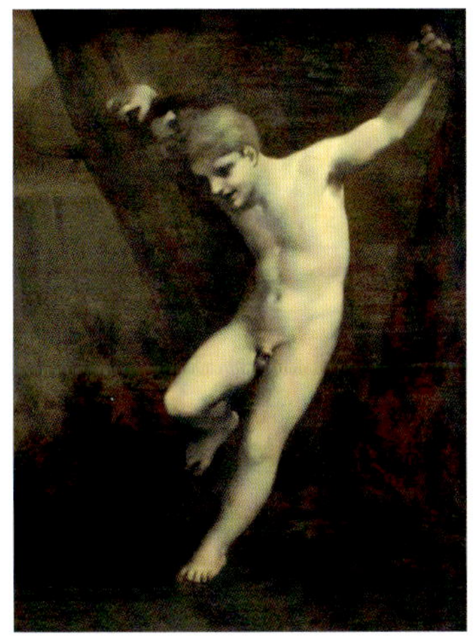

Ishtar Gate, detail, relief tiles, Pergamon Museum, Berlin

Ferdinand Kobell, *Landscape with Travelers*, second half 18th cen., oil on canvas, Busch-Reisinger Museum, Cambridge

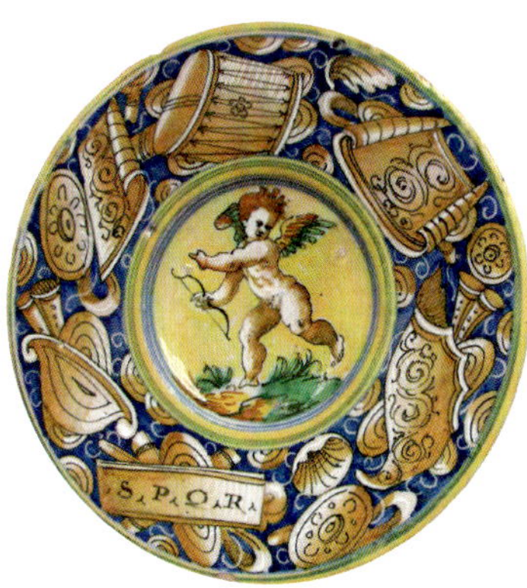

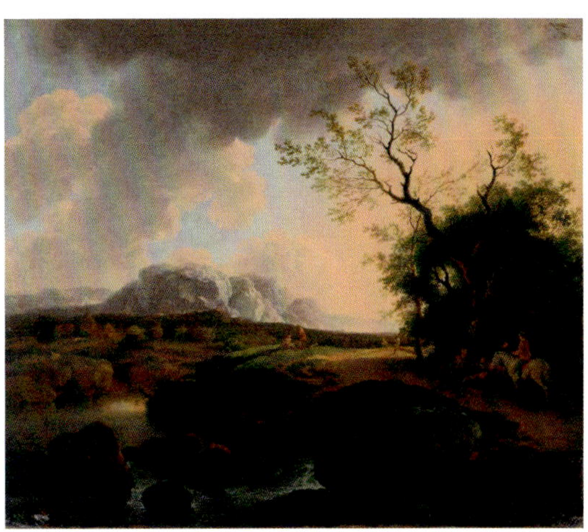

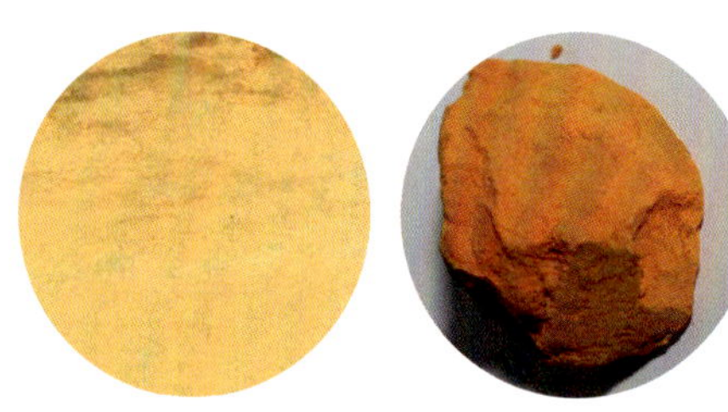

Indian Yellow

Swallow a vitamin B supplement, and your urine will turn an intense, bright yellow. The mango leaf has the same effect but is not edible. However, around the 15th century, it was discovered in Asia that feeding mango leaves to cattle produces the same result. This tremendously unhealthy diet, with a minimum of regular feed, slowly destroyed the kidneys of the livestock (most likely the less profitable bulls), causing them to suffer ever-increasing pain as a result. They rarely lived beyond two years of age.

Three litres of urine yielded about 35 grams of pigment. The urine was collected in earthenware crocks and boiled overnight, after which the sediment, or *piuri*, was rolled with earth into a ball and baked over a fire.

The nugget-like lumps were then placed in the sun to dry further. The 'production' was banned in 1908, and the pigment disappeared from the market within a decade.

In India, the pigment was widely used for the (re)painting of walls and balustrades. European painters had it on their palettes as early as the 17th century. For artists like Rembrandt, living in an international port city, Indian yellow was a favourable alternative to the perpetual lack of a strong, luminous yellow.

Even Turner's golden landscapes partly owe their glow to this yellow from the East.

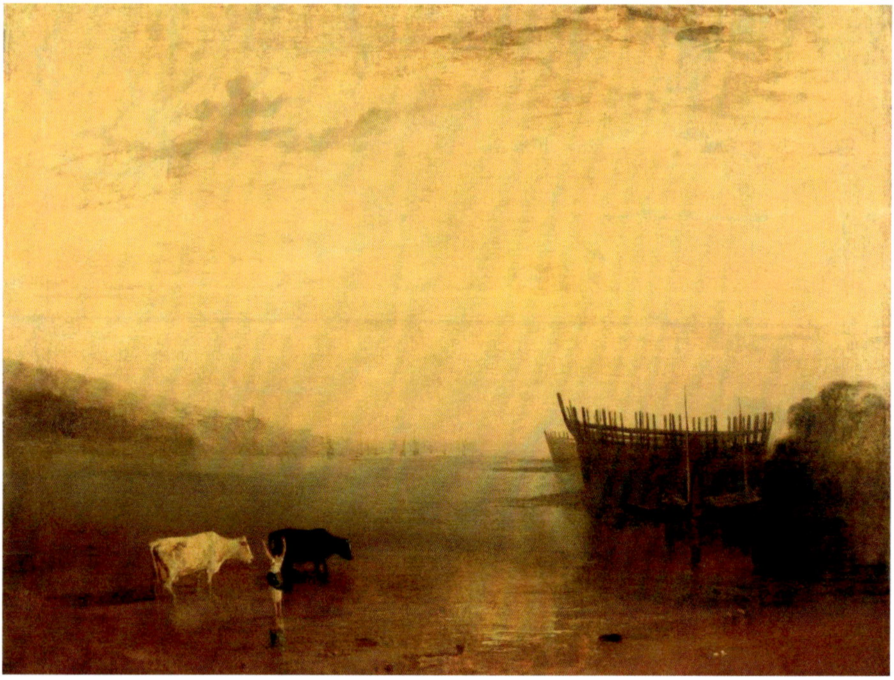

Joseph Mallord William Turner, *Teignmouth Harbour*, 1812, oil on canvas, 90 x 120.5 cm, Tate Gallery, London

A modern variation is Andy Warhol's series of *Piss Paintings*. These works were made in 1977-78 using his own uncondensed urine and, therefore, not nearly as colourful.

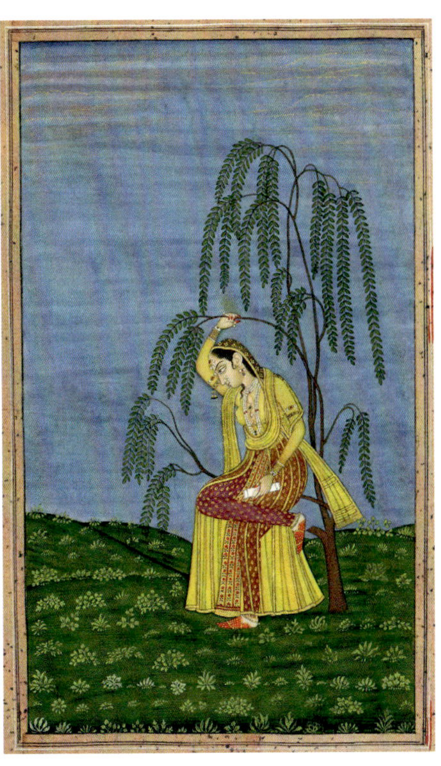

Anoniem, *A Female Flagellant Leaning Against a Willow Tree*, 18th cen., ink on paper, British Museum, London

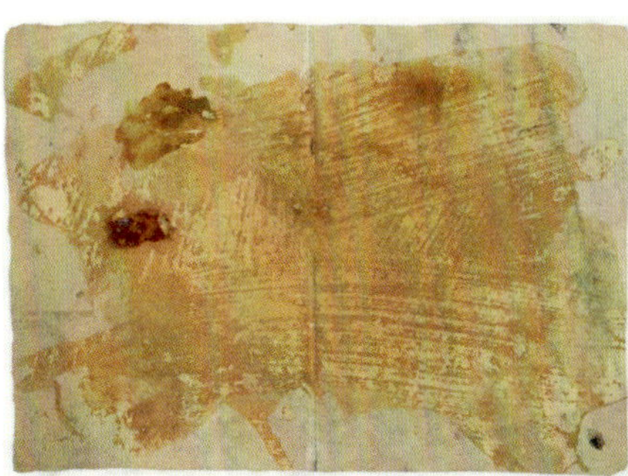

Joseph Mallord William Turner, sketchbook page with stains in Indian yellow, c. 1798, Tate Gallery, London

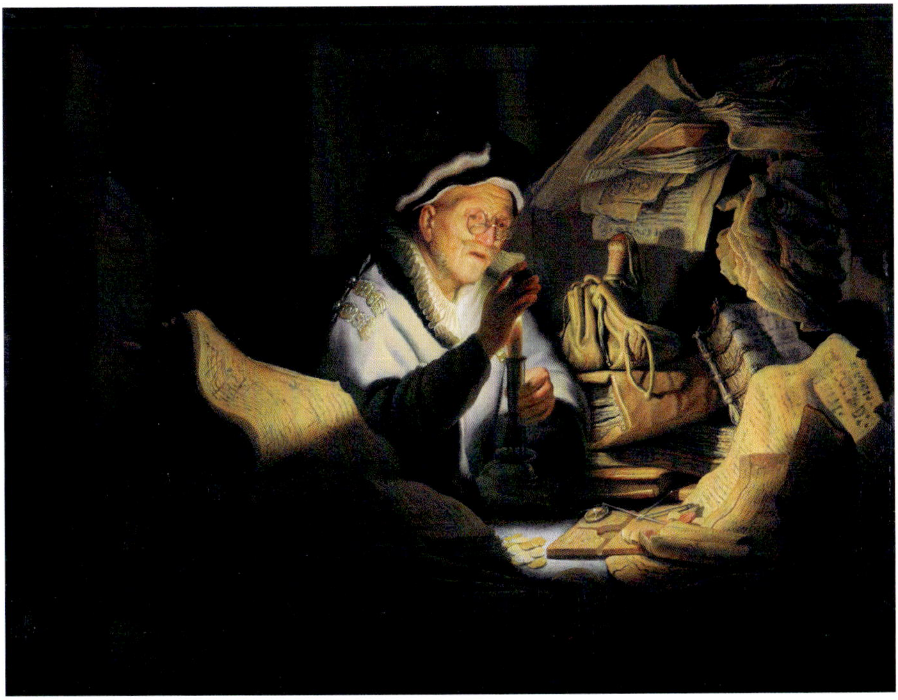

Rembrandt, *The Parable of the Rich Fool*, 1627, oil on panel, 42.5 x 319 cm, Gemäldegalerie, Berlin

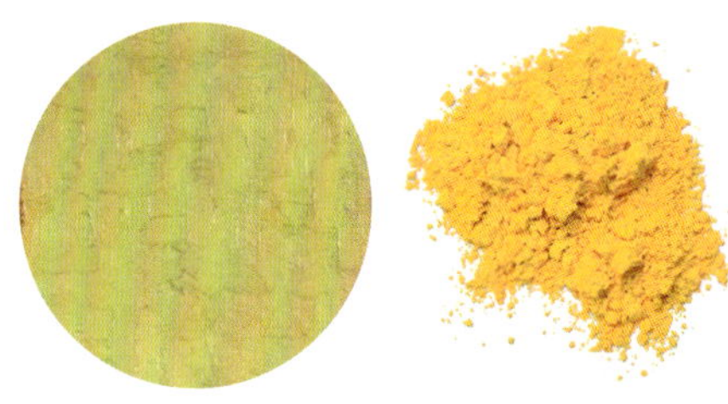

Chrome Yellow & Chrome Orange

Another pigment invented by the French chemist Nicolas-Louis Vauquelin, after he successfully isolated the element chromium from the mineral crocoite in 1797. For its name, he chose the word chromium, after the Greek *khroma* (colour), because of the different nuances that could be made with it.

Due to the presence of lead, chromium is categorised as a toxic pigment. So, again, beware when using. Avoid contact with and inhalation of the dry or sanded pigments.

The chrome pigments were a much-welcomed addition to the historical palette, which barely had any strong, warm or cool yellows and oranges. Orpiment, realgar and mixtures with ochre, yellow and red lacquers all had their specific shortcomings, and cannot compete with this strong, ready-made product.

From 1818, the production of both water-based and oil-based paints soared for decorative and industrial use. Yellow and orange cookware appeared in kitchens, and in the streets brightly coloured carriages, façades, and commercial placards. For a period, these light and dark yellows were even trendy in the textile industry. During the 19th century, the fabric for the British Indian uniform was dyed with it.

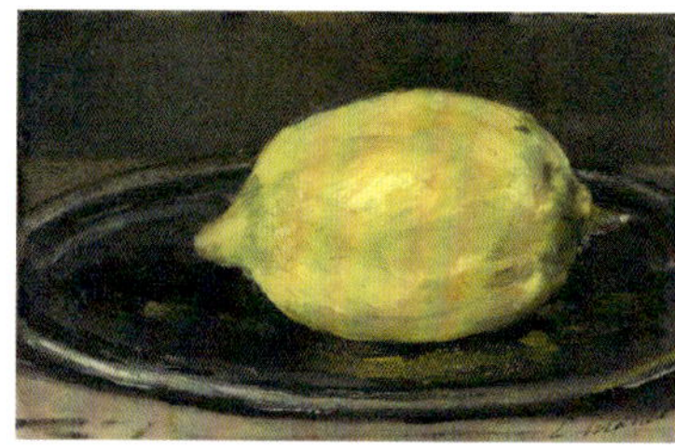

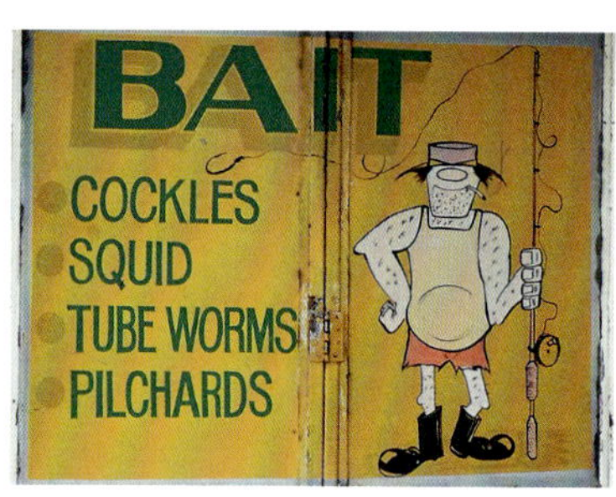

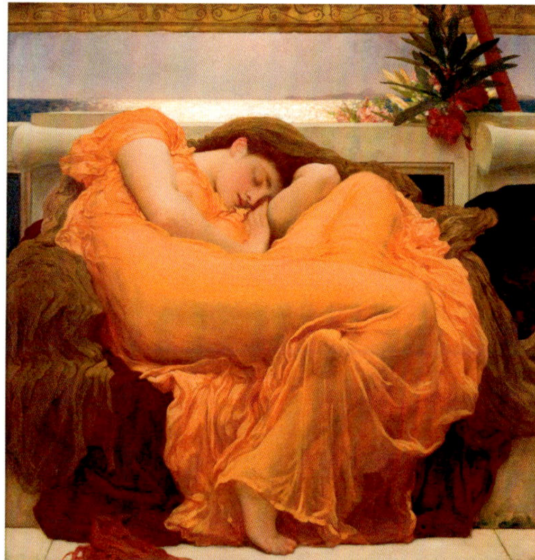

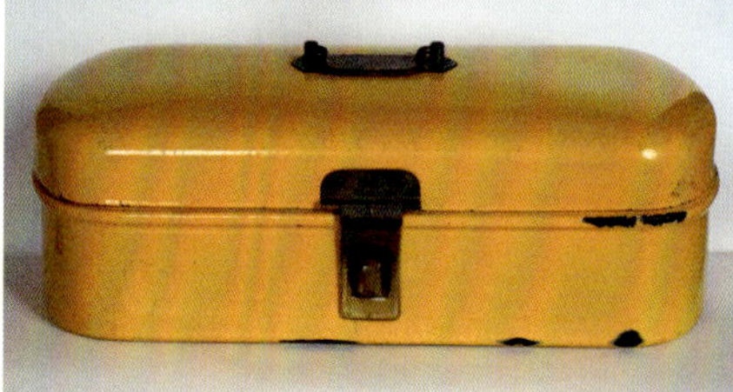

Edouard Manet, *The Lemon*, 1880, oil on canvas, 14 x 22 cm, Musée d'Orsay, Paris

Bait, advertising sign, Australia

Frederic Leighton, *Flaming June*, 1895, oil on canvas, 120.6 x 120.6 cm, Museo de Arte de Ponce

Enamelled bread box

The new colours had an immediate impact on painting despite their high price. Compare a summer landscape by Pieter Breughel, painted with ochre, with that of a French Impressionist, which has a colour strength many times higher thanks to chrome yellow. Yet, every good thing has its flaws. In painting, the early pigment variants left their marks in a negative manner. They are unstable and darken, having a significant impact on the painted image. This process can be visible within just a few years.

The most famous victim of the short-comings of the many new industrial pigments introduced during the 19th century, is Van Gogh. As a fervent user of chrome yellows, he thought they were perfect for his colour-schemes because of the cool and warm variants. He knew that 'colours wilt like the flowers do', but he would have never been able to foresee the disastrous browning of his once so radiant yellows. Van Gogh's *Sunflowers*, now displayed in London and Amsterdam, are a discoloured bouquet of joyless and tragic browns, whose positive image is upheld thanks to printed words and colour-edited illustrations.

Today, chrome pigments are more or less banned in artist's paints in Europe. This is not the greatest loss, as the modern versions are still unstable.

Chrome paints employed for industrial purposes regularly make the headlines negatively. They have not yet been prohibited from the paint industry, nor is there a general product ban. Moreover, it appears that exemptions will always be granted for specific industries, such as aviation and aerospace. Chrome pigments are simply too versatile to be outlawed.

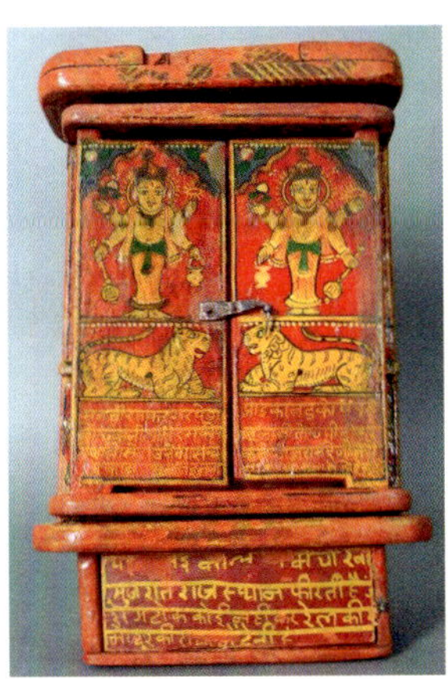

Kaavad, portable wooden temple, Rajasthan, India, Museum of Archaeology and Ethnology, Berlin

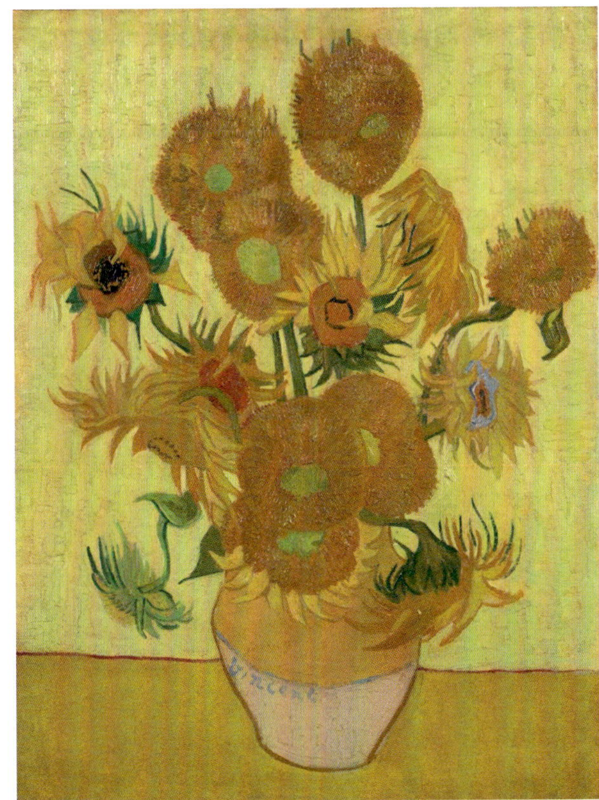

Vincent van Gogh, *Sunflowers*, 1889, oil on canvas, 95 x 73 cm, Van Gogh Museum, Amsterdam

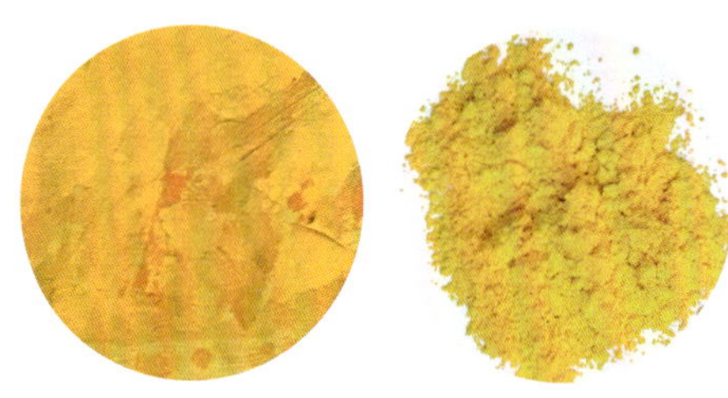

Cadmium Yellow & Cadmium Orange

Finally! The ultimate whopping yellow and orange that was so missed for so long! Interestingly, it is another product rooted in the 19th century. Cadmium pigments came on the market in 1840 and have been the most important strong opaque yellow and orange since the origin of painting. They are more stable and powerful than the chrome yellows and oranges created that same century.

This significant and essential expansion of the artist's palette was developed by two German chemists, Friedrich Stromeyer and Carl Samuel Hermann, who each independently *and* unknowingly discovered the element cadmium in 1817. Stromeyer found cadmium during a stock inspection at an apothecary. While heating contaminated zinc carbonate, he noticed an unknown yellow substance emerge. Hermann, the founder of the firm Hermania, which specialised in the production of salts and hydrochloric acid, also discovered cadmium by coincidence when researching zinc oxide. For almost a century, the findings provided Germany with a lucrative monopoly on the production of cadmiums.

As an artist's paint, cadmium yellow is available in four shades: lemon yellow, cadmium light, medium and orange. This offers the artist a spectrum from cool to

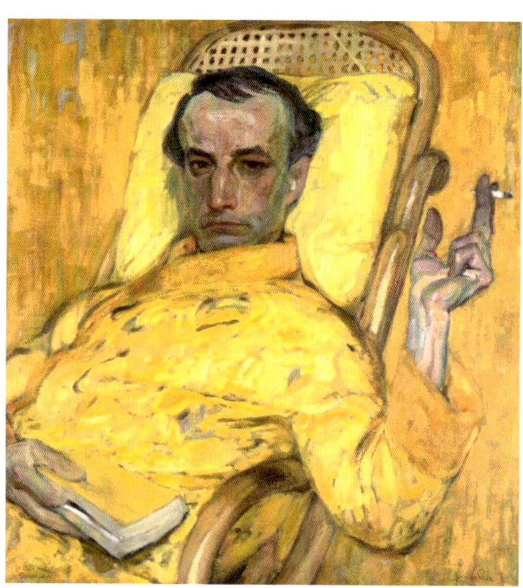

František Kupka, *The Yellow Scale*, c. 1907, oil on canvas, 78.7 x 74.3 cm, The Museum of Fine Arts, Boston

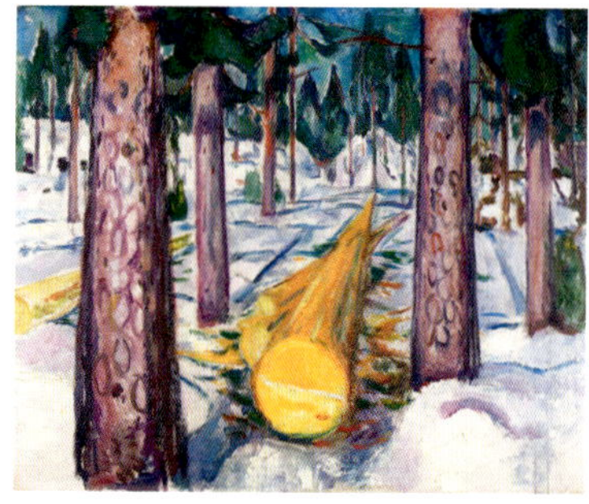

Edvard Munch, *The Yellow Log*, 1912, oil on canvas, 129.5 x 159.5 cm, Munch Museum, Oslo

Kees van Dongen, *Haystacks*, 1904-1905, oil on canvas, 50 x 65 cm, Virginia Museum of Fine Arts

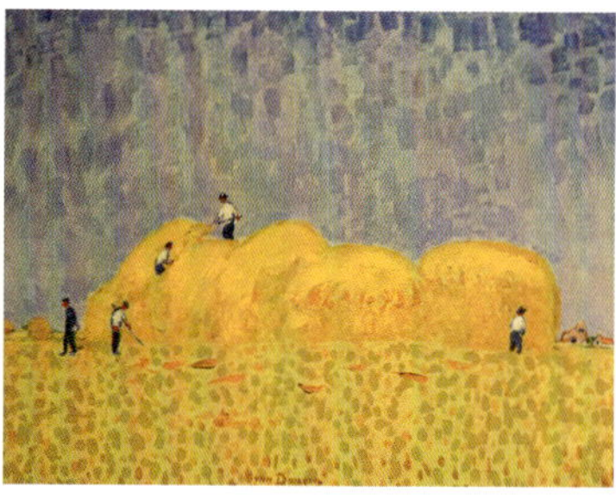

warm and a wide base for various strong mixed colours. Moreover, cadmiums are generally more stable and permanent than chrome yellows, as can still be seen in the ever-glowing portrait of Kupka. Within the impressionist colour scheme, the cadmium yellows are the ideal counterpart to purples and violet and play an image-defining role in vibrantly colourful Expressionism. Additionally, the colours' lustre proved to be a much-welcome addition to the production of toys, jewellery, plastics, ceramics, industrial glass and paints. Items hit the market in hitherto unseen brightness in colours. It later became clear that cadmium has deleterious effects on consumer health and the environment due to its high toxicity. It has been prohibited from plastics in the EU since 1991 and in opaque materials such as varnishes and house paints since 1996. So far, a ban on the pigment in artists' paints has failed to be enforced. The modern alternatives, recognisable by the word 'hue' in their labelling, still cannot match the tinting strength of the original, and their removal from the market would seriously affect the colour palette of painters and printers.

For professionals, cadmium is a wonderful pigment to work with, but only when handled with care –ensuring no skin contact and the dry powder is not inhaled. Recently, some manufacturers have begun labelling these paint tubes with the unmissable 'POISON'. It is a good idea to assume that by no means everyone is aware of the possible negative properties of the colours that end up on the palette.

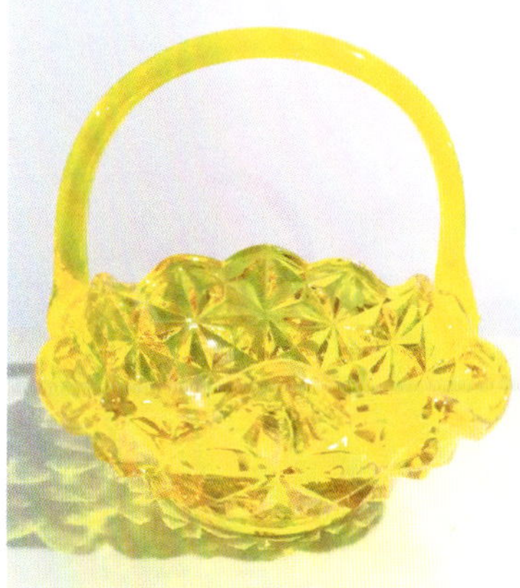

Cadmium yellow glass bowl

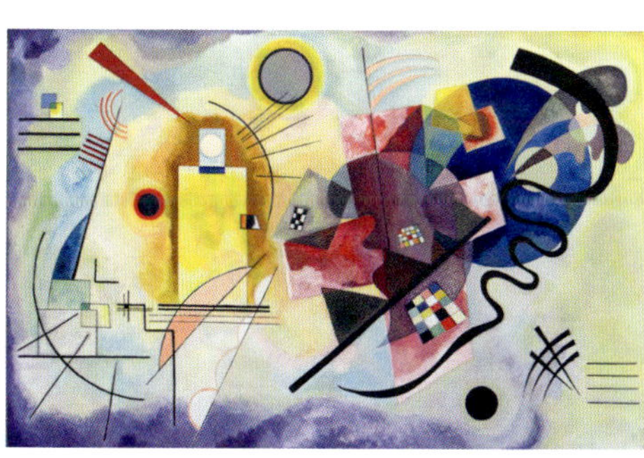

Wassily Kandinsky, *Yellow-Red-Blue*, 1925, oil on canvas, 127 x 200 cm, Centre Pompidou, Paris

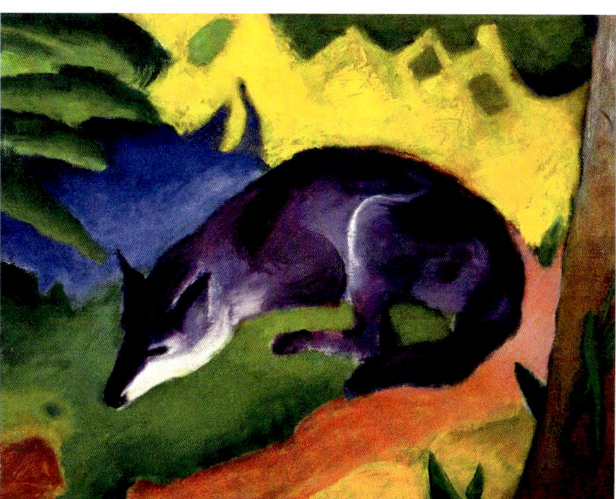

Franz Marc, *Fox*, 1911, oil on canvas, 50 x 63.5 cm, Von der Heydt Museum, Wuppertal

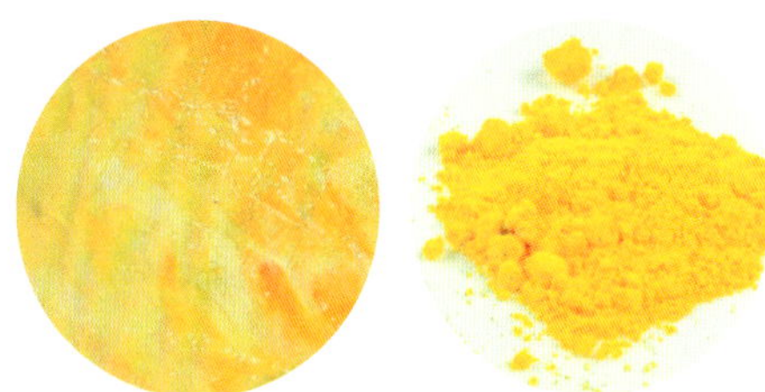

Hansa Yellow

Hansa yellows belong to the large synthetic, organic Azo pigment family. Formerly known as aniline and coal tar yellows. It is the bright yellow of *Les Gilets jaunes*, lanterns, clothes, shoes – you name it.

Hansa yellow is a strong, semi-transparent pigment with a high tinting strength. It retains its colour when mixed or diluted with the common fillers. Moreover, it is strongly recommended to not use it in its pure form.

It is used as a replacement in all paints for the historical strong yellows. And, with seven hues, the range to choose from is far more extensive than the yellow cadmiums and chrome yellows, for which Hansa is increasingly used as a substitute. They are easy yellows and the variety in

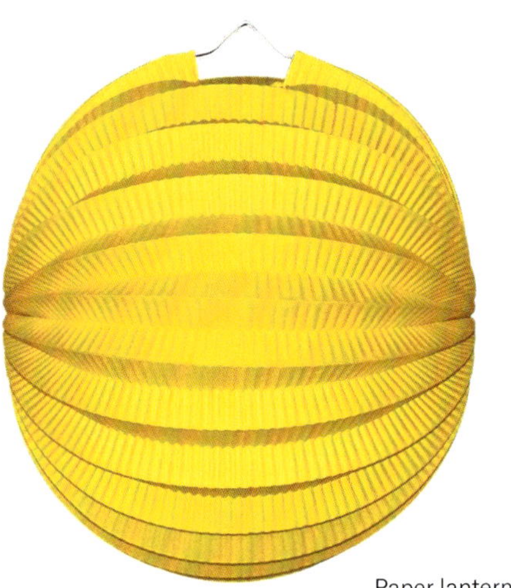

Paper lantern

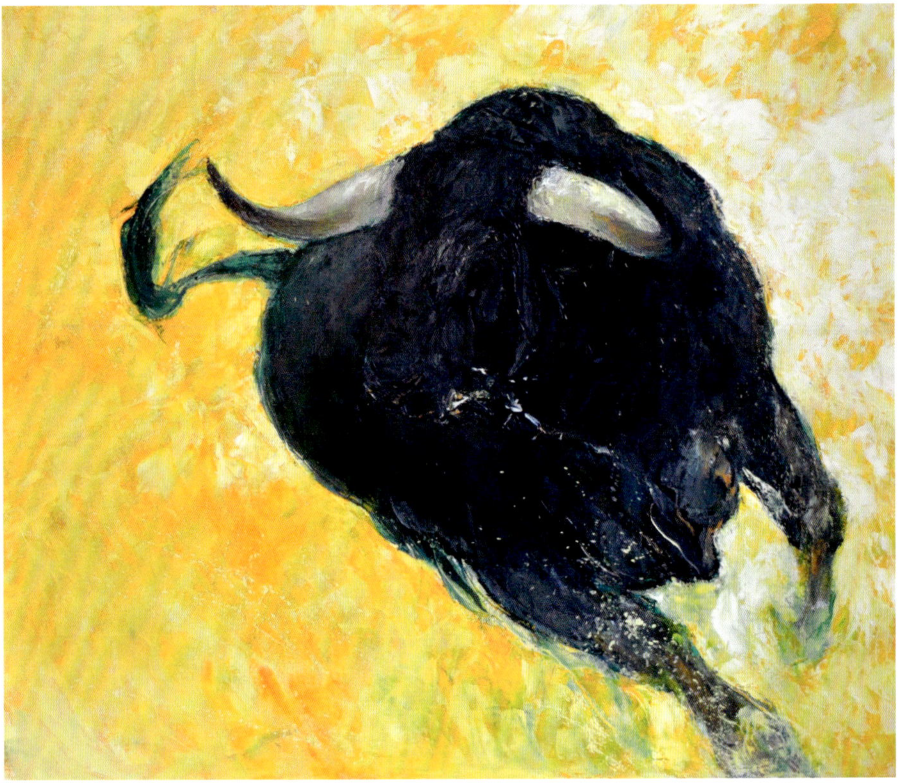

colour temperature makes them ideal for mixing deep oranges and luminous greens. For my bull, Toro Negro, I created a vivid green by mixing it with ivory black.
Hansa yellow was developed around 1900. The predecessor of the German chemical concern, Hoechst, patented the first version in 1909, and the modified, more lightfast variants entered the market in 1949.
Nonetheless, painter's manuals from the 1940s still warned of its poor durability. Today, it is a popular and relatively reliable pigment and considerably more affordable than the cadmiums. It is a multi-purpose and versatile pigment. In addition to artist's materials, it can be found in inks, industrial paints and plastics.
Paint manufacturers are always keen to come up with names to make clear how extraordinarily wonderful their product is; hence, the trade names 'Real Yellow' and 'Permanent Yellow'. The variants, Py74 and Py151, are frequently offered on the market as if they are unique paints created by the seller's factory, such as Winsor Yellow, Scheveningen Yellow and Royal Talens Yellow.

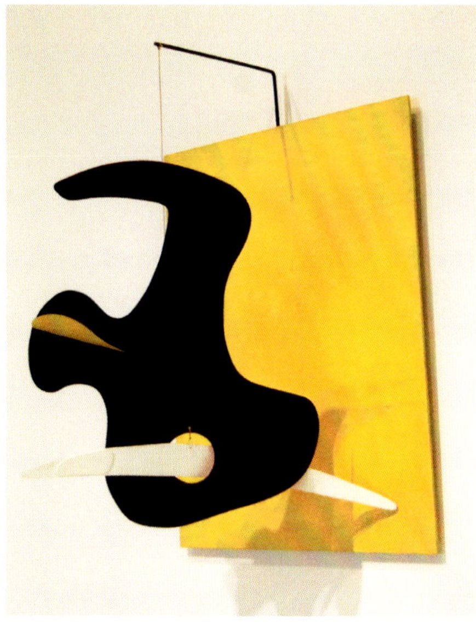

Alexander Calder, *Form Against Yellow*, 1936, oil on metal, Hirshhorn Museum, Washington

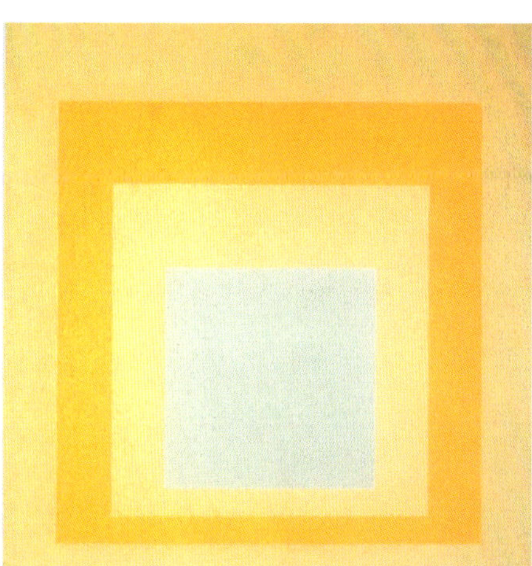

Josef Albers, *Homage to the Square*, 1959, oil op masonite, 122 x 122 cm, Metropolitan Museum of Art, New York

< monica rotgans, *Toro negro*, 2016, oil on canvas, 100 x 120 cm, private collection

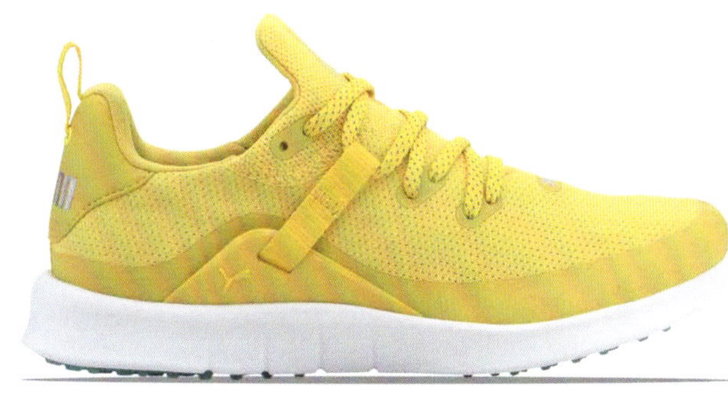

Sneaker in Hansa yellow

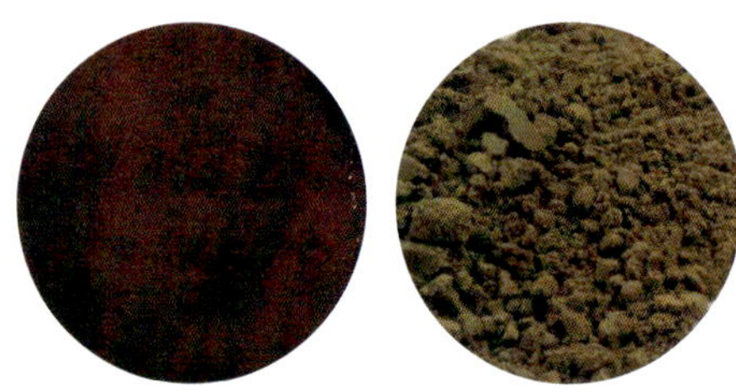

Umber

Umbers belong to the family of historical earth pigments. They can be found, along with red, yellow and burnt earth, as the browner shades in prehistoric cave paintings.

I use the plural 'umbers' because the pigment cannot be classified as a specific brown. Like all natural earth colours, umber can be found all over the world in a variety of hues ranging from a greenish to a greyish brown. The finest, best-known, and most sought-after is the cool, greenish, raw umber of Cyprus. Other historical sites are in Germany, with grey umber, in Britain, Italy's Umbria and its island Sicily. It is thought the pigment's name originated in Umbria. Another theory links it with the Latin *umbra*, shadow, for which it was commonly used in painting.

Umber is very suitable for emphasising the lack or absence of colour. It is employed to represent poverty, consciously or unconsciously, as evidenced in Giotto's *St Francis* and Pelez's downtrodden young street urchins.

The reputation of European oil painting as predominantly brown is partly due to the substantial use of umber after a more realistic manner of representation came into fashion. Artists like Caravaggio and his followers took *chiaroscuro* – the pictorial suggestion of three-dimensionality through light and dark – to great

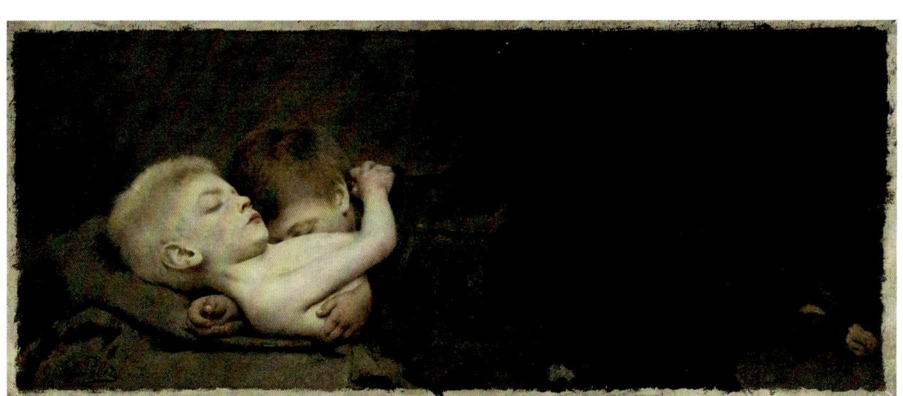

Fernand Pelez, *A Nest of Misery*, 1887, oil on canvas, 58.5 x 133 cm, Musée des Beaux-Arts de la ville de Paris

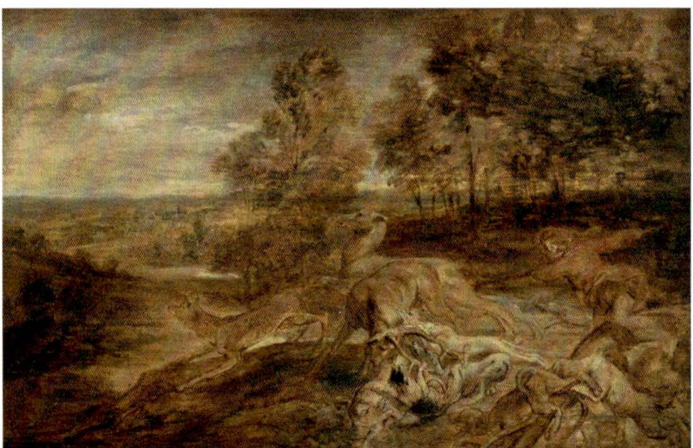

Peter Paul Rubens, *The Deer Hunt*, oil on panel, 41 x 63 cm, Royal Arts Museum Antwerp

heights. Furthermore, Rubens showed that it is an excellent colour for creating a landscape with minimal paint.
In the mid-19th century, however, the Impressionists declared umber and its earthy family an undesirable matter. They effectively returned to the bright and translucent Medieval palette, where browns often consisted of mixtures including reds, yellows and blacks. Rejecting 'The Browns' created a dichotomy in painting. The academies of the visual arts firmly held on to tradition in what came to be called the classical palette, with earth colours as its foundation – a palette that also young Mondrian used for his early landscapes.
Umber contains an additional element, manganese, clearly setting its colour apart from the other earth pigments. And, thanks to this manganese, it is a fast dryer in oil paints. Its great disadvantage, however, is that this naturally fine pigment requires a great deal of oil, causing the paint to darken considerably after application. If employed incorrectly, it can affect the other colours and, as an underlying layer, it can 'bleed' through. An abundance of examples of this drawback can be found in museums worldwide.
Like the other earth colours, raw umber can be heated. Burnt umber takes on a red glow, making it a warmer colour. An additional benefit is that burnt umber requires less oil and will not darken as much as the original pigment.

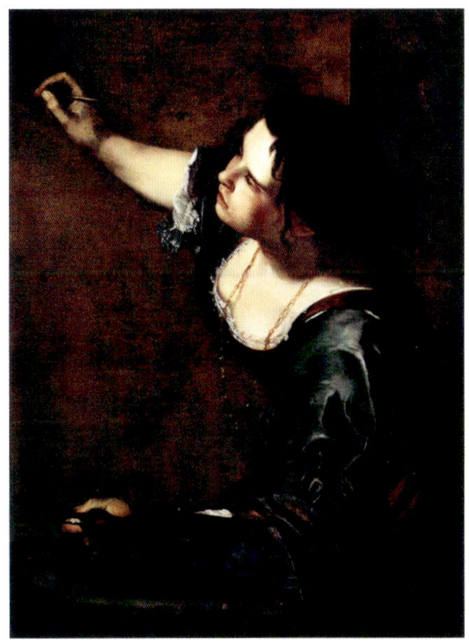

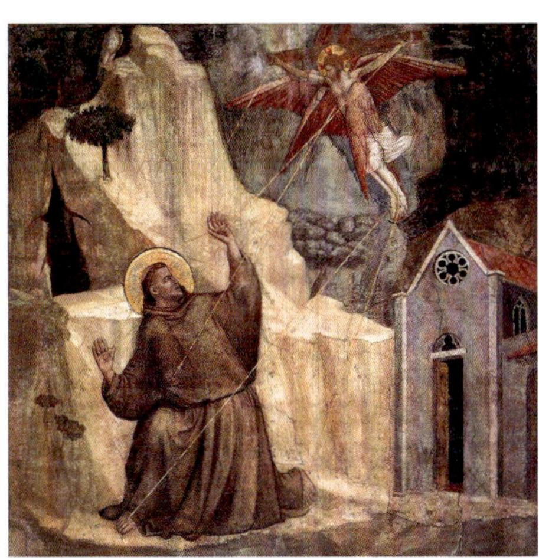

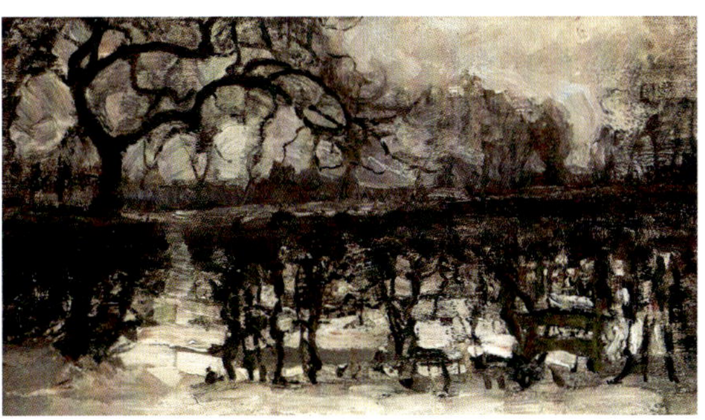

Giotto, *The Stigmatisation of St. Francis*, 1320-1330, fresco, Bardi Chapel, Santa Croce

Artemisia Gentileschi, *Self-Portrait as the Allegory of Painting*, 1638, oil on canvas, 98.6 x 75.2 cm, Royal Collection Trust, London

Piet Mondriaan, *Landscape with Apple Trees*, c. 1907, oil on canvas, 35.5 x 61.5 cm, private collection

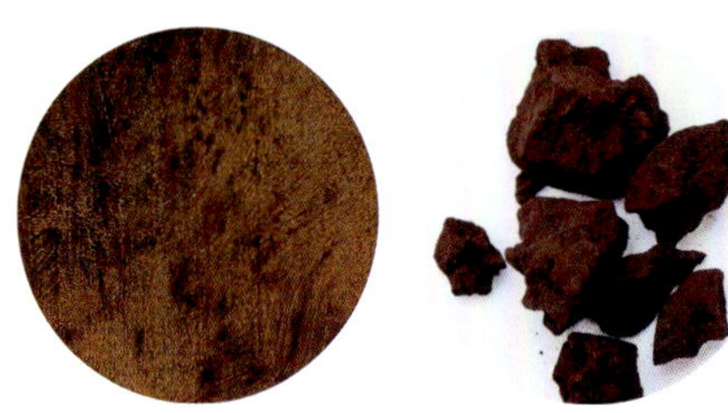

Cassel Brown

A brown named after the German city of Cassel, spelled as Kassel until 1928. Another name for the pigment is Cologne brown, signifying the importance of these historical sites for painting.

Cassel brown is an appealing, warm and transparent dark brown. This pigment, as well, should be treated cautiously because of the risks of bleeding and greying. Nevertheless, great masters like Velázquez, Rubens, Van Dyck and Rembrandt are associated with it. They, and many other artists like them, had it on the palette specifically because of its glowing transparency.

It is wonderful to work with as both a glaze and a pure colour. It is particularly suitable for deepening shadows without dulling them, contributing to its popularity. In old recipes, several names, such as Van Dyck's brown, Cassel earth and Cologne earth, were used to refer to the different shades. The modern 'Cassel brown' (or featuring the name of one of the great masters) is usually a mixture of the stable Burnt Sienna with a black pigment. Manufacturers committed to quality will list the numerical codes of the pigments used as alternatives on the canister or tube. However, the original earth pigment is still available, and if you know where to look, you can find the raw organic material in nature.

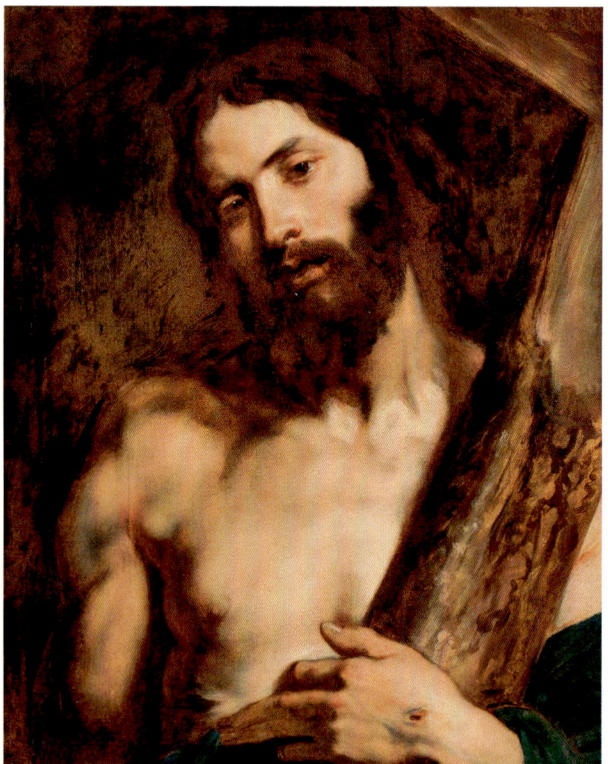

Anthony van Dyck, *Christ Carrying the Cross*, first half 17th cen., oil on canvas, Musei di Strada Nuova, Genoa

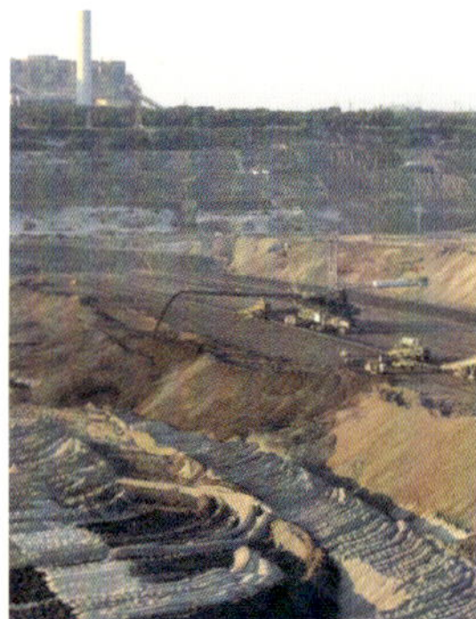

Lignite mine, Germany

> Jacques-Louis David, oil sketch for the *The Tennis Court Oath*, 1791-1792, oil on canvas, 358 x 648 cm, Musée National de Versailles

The original Cassel brown, or lignite or brown coal, is a largely organic substance, better known in its soft and younger form as turf or peat. It is formed by old plant remains, which over time have been turned into lignite deep underground. In the 19th century, lignite mining steadily increased due to the growing demand for fuelling the rising number of steam engines. Today, it is an extremely controversial fuel used for power plants. Like all mining sites, lignite quarries have a disastrous effect on the surrounding area by destroying the natural landscape and disrupting or polluting its water management. Furthermore, the population of entire villages are frequently forced to move when an expansion of a quarry is required.
In comparison, the amount that was, and is still, made into paint as a pigment is simply inconsequential.

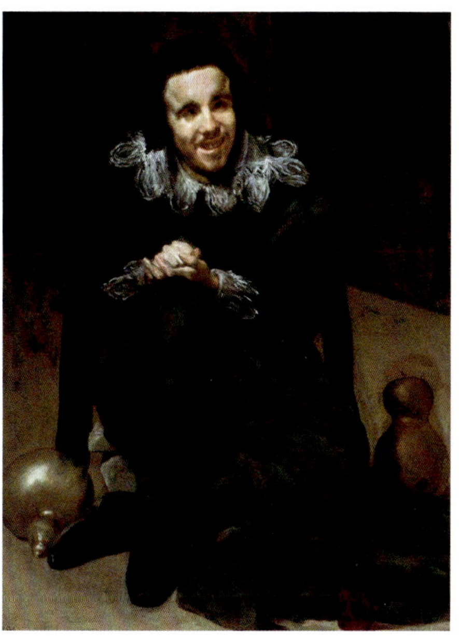

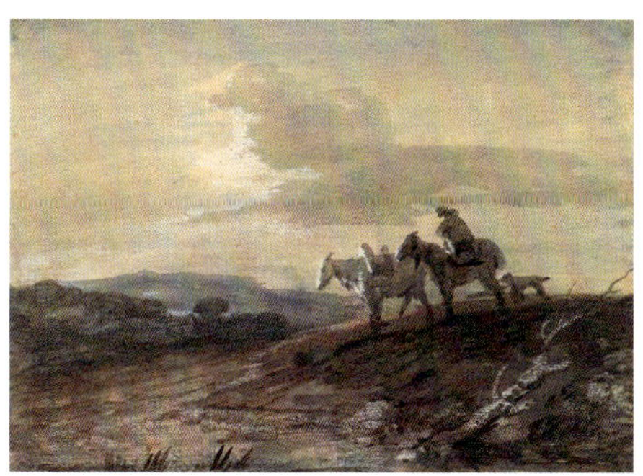

Thomas Gainsborough, *An Open Landscape at Dusk*, watercolour, heightened with white chalk, 21 x 30 cm, private collection

Diego Velázquez, *The Jester Calabacillas*, c. 1635, oil on canvas, 106 x 83 cm, Padro, Madrid

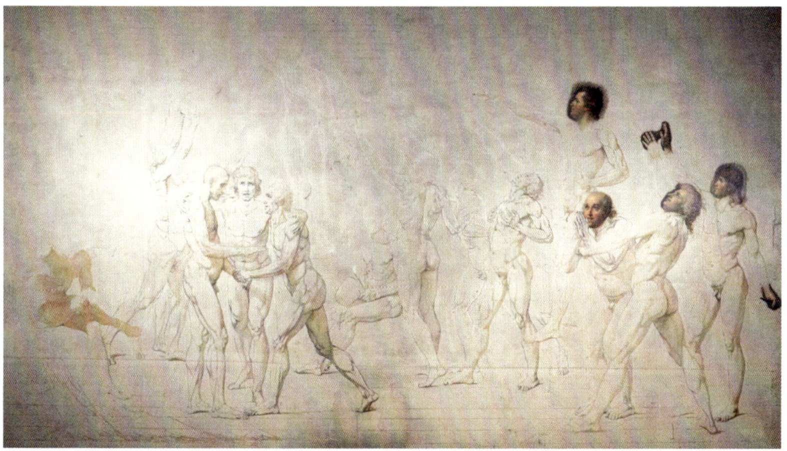

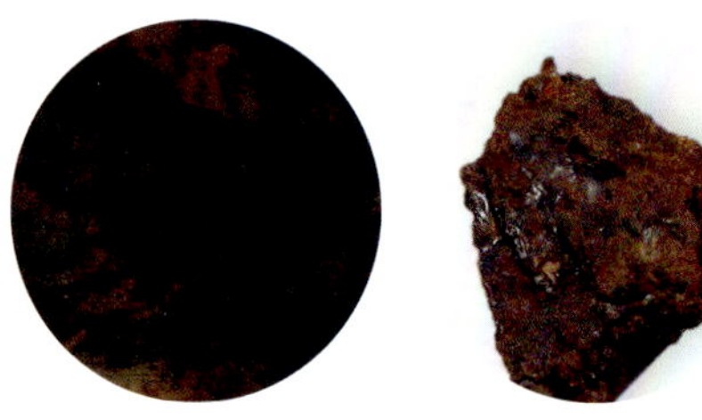

Asphalt & Mummy

The word 'mummy' often triggers thoughts of horror, but for many centuries, the substance prepared from mummy tissue was an accepted medicine and pigment. Asphalt and mummy are treated together in this text because, in the south-eastern Mediterranean, the dead were covered with resins, fats, and herbs and occasionally embalmed with bandages prepared with asphalt. Both are warm browns.

As unimaginable as it may be to paint with parts of human corpses or dead animal carcasses ground into powder, this pigment was commonly available in shops until around 1925. And so was asphalt, also known as bitumen. These days, it is best known as a road surface. The liquid form is known as petroleum and, in the graphic arts, as etching ground. Doctors recommended asphalt for ailments ranging from gout to leprosy and everything in between. A remnant of this practice is the still-existent topical tar cream.

The word asphalt presumably comes from the Greek *a-sphallein*, meaning 'not able to be thrown down'. Bitumen is the Latin version from which the Dutch word for concrete, *beton*, stems. Both refer to the role it has held since prehistoric times: a sealant for joining materials, and a binding agent for keeping human remains together.

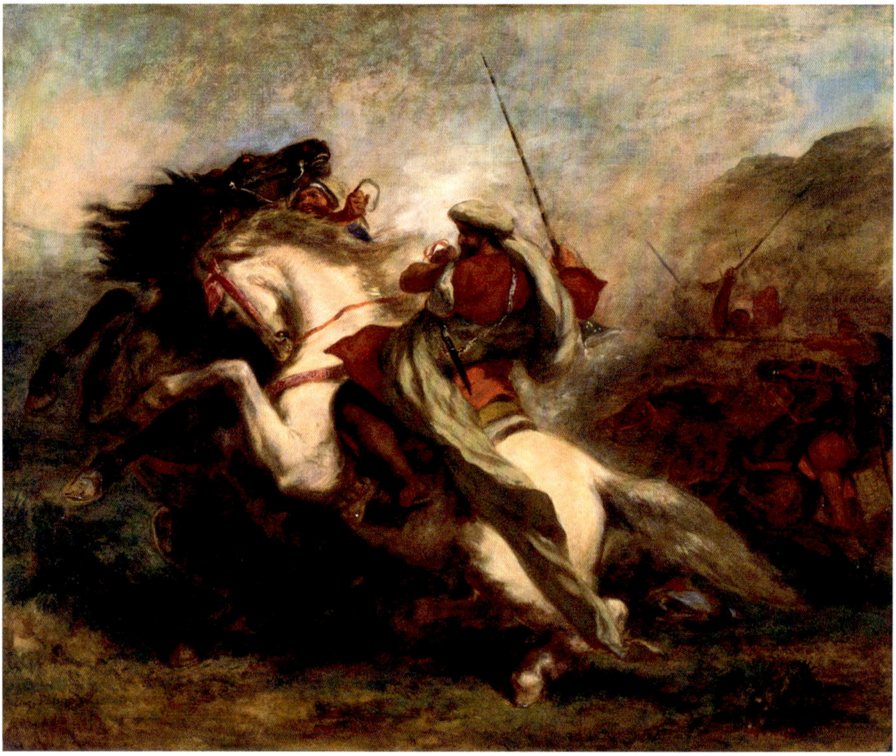

Since at least the second millennium BC, ceramics have been decorated with asphalt-*stylos*, with here a Cretan jar as an example. When applied to a heated surface, the naturally pulpous asphalt paint stick melts a little and attaches to stoneware like oil pastel. Comparable to a heat-softened tarred road surface sticking to tyres or shoes.

The Old Testament mentions asphalt's extraordinary suitability for tarring vulnerable or exposed materials such as ship timber to protect against moisture, for glueing and waterproofing ceramics, and for painting.

However, due to precisely these thermally related properties, asphalt is completely unsuitable as an artist's paint: it does not dry, is unstable, bleeds through other layers, et cetera. Yet, this has seldom prevented artists from including it in their palette. As Van Gogh wrote in a letter to his brother Theo in 1884: '...some of the painters nowadays are taking from us the bistre and the bitumen with which, after all, so many magnificent things were painted, which – properly used, make the colouration lush and tender and generous, and at the same time so dignified.'

The demand for mummy was already so high in the Middle Ages that merchants collected the corpses of executed people. They were prepared, laid out in the desert sun to dry and sold off as original, ancient mummies.

Commercially labelled 'Egyptian brown', mummy most likely became a common pigment for painting from the 16th century onwards. It remained in stock for a long time due to the continuous mass looting of newly discovered burial grounds. And nearly every self-respecting 19th-century upper-class world traveller was adamant about bringing at least one such 'mummy' home, as a souvenir.

< Eugène Delacroix, *The Collision of Two Horsemen*, 1843, oil on canvas, 32 x 39 cm, The Walters Art Museum, Baltimore

Anonymous, *Osiris*, bitumen-coated wood, 18th Dynasty, Egypt, British Museum, London

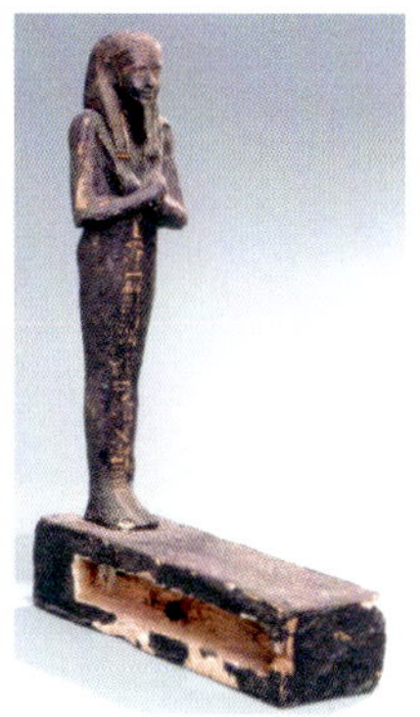

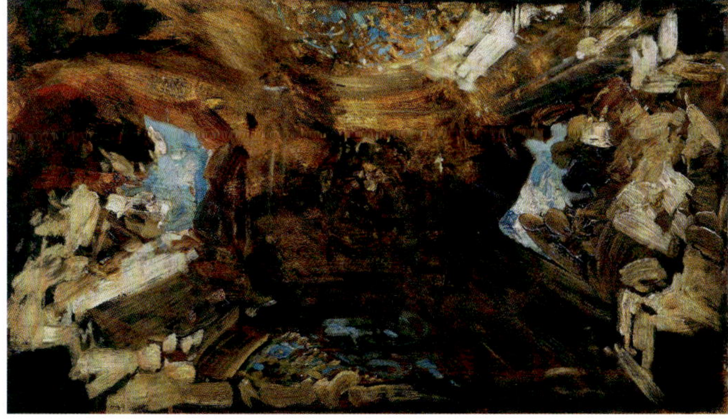

Hans Makart, *The Four Continents*, oil sketch, c. 1870, 41.5 x 73.5 cm, Österreichische Galerie Belvedere, Vienna

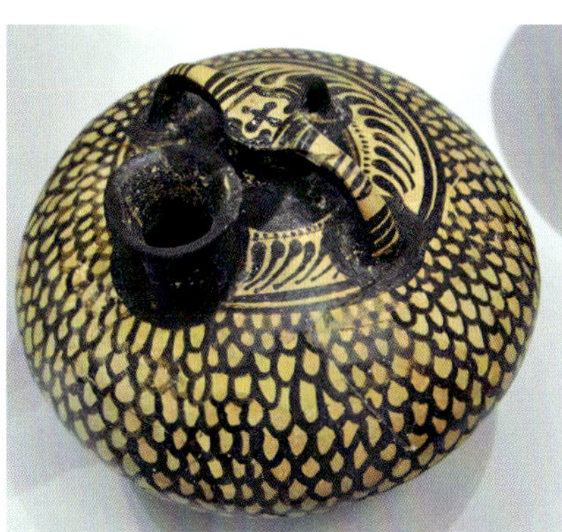

Jug, c. 1500 BC, Crete, Heraklion Archaeological Museum, Heraklion

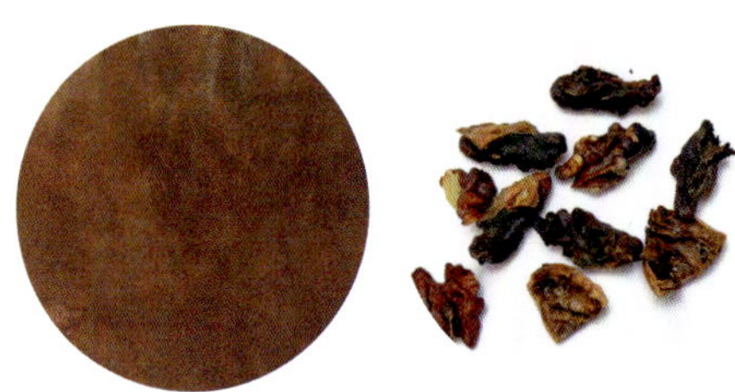

Organic Brown

The palette of autumn. The many shades of fallen leaves. Of nuts, mushrooms and decomposed plants in empty fields. Colour.

In principle, paint can be made from all these organic materials, as has been done since prehistoric times. In addition to nuts, the list includes berries, seeds, bark, leaves, tubers, insects, and so on. It is enough for a complete colour chart. The drawback is, that most are unstable colours. They can start fading after just a couple of hours.

Nonetheless, some have served as a raw material for dyes for thousands of years. The first known inks were made at around the same time in ancient Egypt and China. Essentially, ink and paint are virtually the same thing. Ink is a mixture of a dye with a gum arabic or resin, also the original ingredients for watercolours. When gum is replaced with starch, oil, egg or a contemporary acrylic binding medium, you have what we call 'authentic' paint.

The best-known historical brown inks were created with gallnuts, molluscs such as octopus and squid, and soot from burned (nut) wood. These inks were ideal not only for scripture and drawing but also for use in watercolours, a perfect tool for modelling a broad range of light-to-dark contrasts. Since the advance of the chemical industry, the number of coloured inks has become extensive, the most significant being the aniline inks.

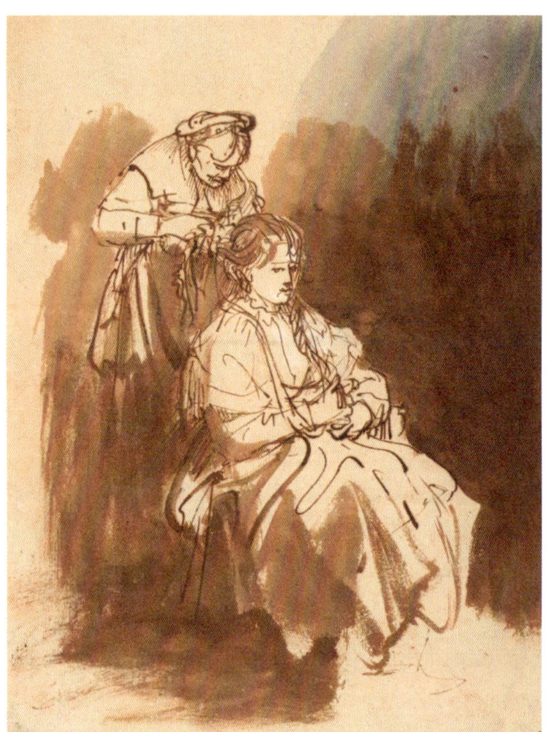

Rembrandt, *A Young Woman Having Her Hair Braided*, c. 1635, Albertina, Vienna

Nick Neddo, *Looking up a Walnut Tree*, 2013, walnut ink

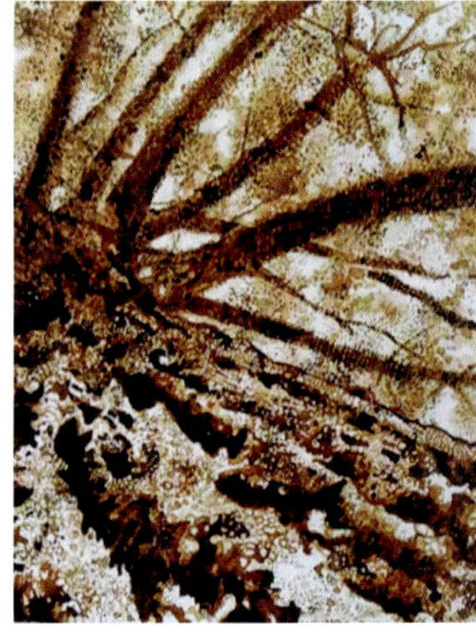

Gallnuts, or gall apples, are not fruits, but rather nutlike growths on plants caused by chemicals injected by insects or parasites. They are the nurseries for the larvae of various insects, of which a variety of circa 15,000 species are known around the world. The gallnut mainly grows on oak trees and was mentioned as early as 400 AD as a raw material for inks in the Talmud. For example, gall ink can be found on *papyri* from around 2500 BC.
Into the 1950s and 1960s, students' ink-wells in primary schools in the Netherlands were still filled with gall ink from large bottles, a now-vanished link to a distant past.
Another old and familiar ink is sepia, named after the *sepia officinalis*, or the common cuttlefish. This animal is native to the North Sea, the Mediterranean Sea and Africa's west coast. What we call sepia, is the dark fluid defensively secreted with great force by cuttlefish as an escape mechanism to hide from the view of predators. To change the fluid into artist ink, the ink sac must be removed immediately after the catch. It is then dried, finely ground, and processed.
Sepia is a fine ink with which to work. A magnificent, transparent and supple dark to black brown, and quite suitable for brush, (reed) pen and less conventional means such as twigs and feathers. In painting, it can only be used on paper in watercolour.

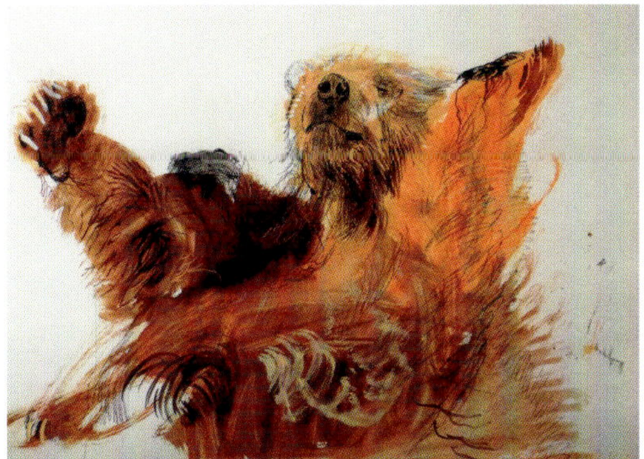

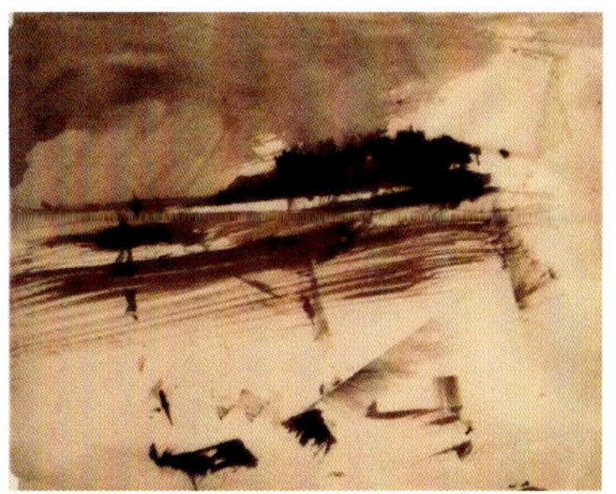

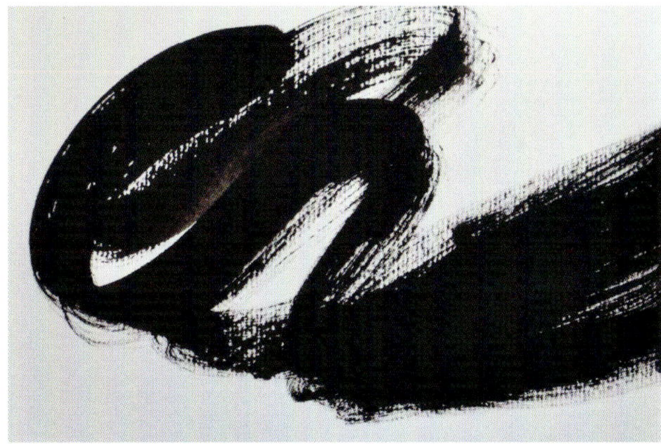

Erik Andriesse, *Brown Bear*, 1992, mixed media on paper, 73 x 110 cm, Teylers Museum, Haarlem

Victor Hugo, *Evacuation from an Island*, 1870, ink on paper, Scharf-Gerstenberg Collection, Berlin

A proof of untreated, still black, ink fresh from the squid, monica rotgans

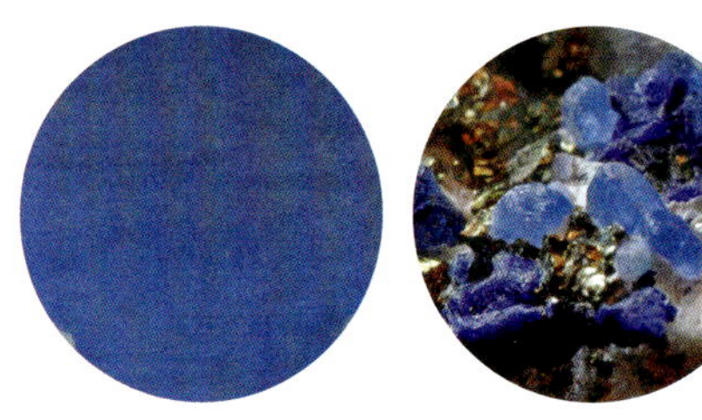

Lapis lazuli

The miracle stone, the sky-blue throne of the gods and the colour of the afterlife. Lapis lazuli, literally 'stone (of) blue', is the raw material for natural ultramarine. The only warm blue that approximates the colour of the sky, and the seventh colour of the rainbow.

For thousands of years, it was more precious than gold and, therefore, reserved for Eurasia and Africa's religious and secular elite.

In painting, it was a scarce commodity. With the exception of illuminators (image-makers of manuscripts) and miniature painters, due to the minimal quantities they needed.

In a museum, it is immediately obvious when this ultramarine was used: it is that unmissable, glowing, blue. Note the Titian, where the ultramarine regained its original power after the removal of discoloured varnish. It instantly shows the advantage of working in the heart of the European lapis trade of the time and having wealthy patrons. This access allowed the Venetians to have a relatively large amount of ultramarine at their disposal.

There are three historical sites for lapis lazuli: the Hindu Kush, west of the Himalayas in Badakhshan province, the vicinity of Irkutsk in Siberia, and on the other side of the world in the Chilean

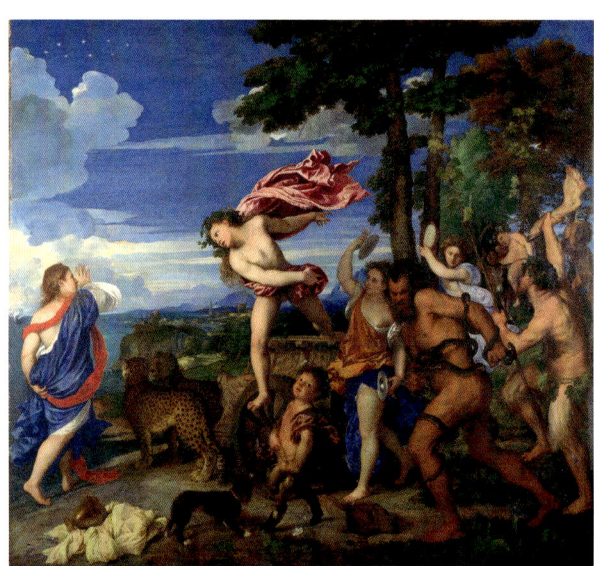

Titiaan, *Bacchus and Ariadne*, 1523, oil on canvas, 175 x 190 cm, National Gallery, London

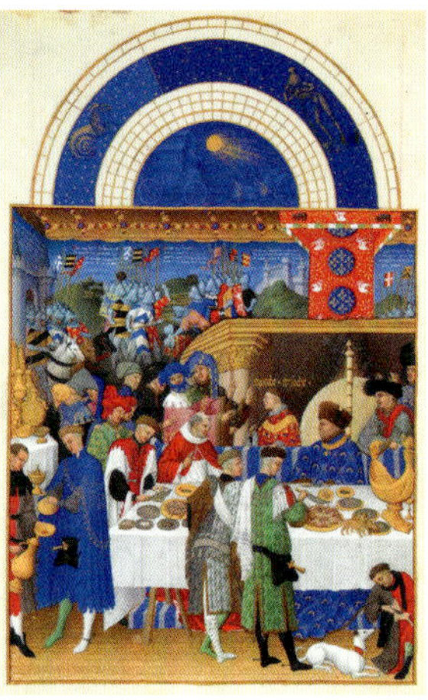

Limbourg Brothers, *January*, from *Les Très riches heures du Duc de Berry*, c. 1411-1416, tempera on vellum, 29 x 21 cm, Musée Condé, Chantilly

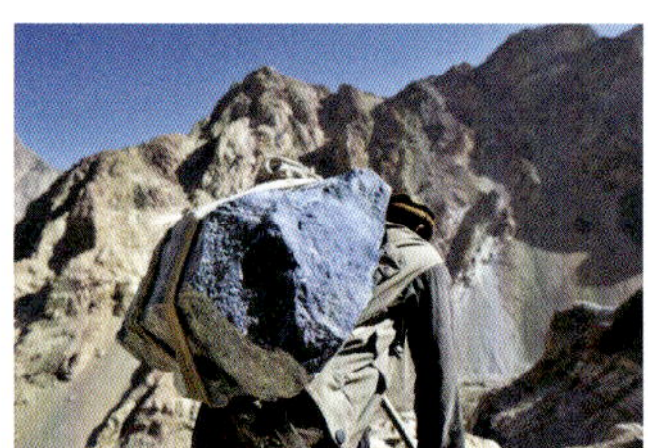

A chunk of lapis lazuli on the way to passable terrain

Andes. For centuries, almost everything written about lapis lazuli refers to the so-called Badakshi-lapis from present-day Afghanistan. From the inaccessible mountains, where the harsh climate barely allows three months a year of work, the rough stone found its way by land and sea (*ultra-mare*) into the most diverse cultures. This is extraordinary, considering that the stone was first transported by humans, followed by a beast of burden, and onward by caravan or ship, before it reached an artist's hands.

Traditionally, the people of Badakhshan distinguished at least nine varieties of lapis, based on colour properties and quality. The fakes and substitutes are almost as old, and often based on cobalt.

We will never know where and when someone came up with the idea to add a binder to pulverised lapis lazuli. It could have been a by-product of the manufacture of figurines and amulets, in which a paste was made from the precious waste, which was given a new life as paint, medicine or make-up.

While its use as a paint is much older, the recipe in various manuscripts for the complicated and time-consuming purification of lapis lazuli into the dazzling blue pigment dates to the 12th century and appears almost simultaneously in both the Islamic and Christian worlds.

The astronomical sums required to purchase ultramarine made it the status symbol for both client and craftsman. After the introduction of inexpensive synthetic ultramarine in the 19th century, the colour of the gods toppled from its throne.

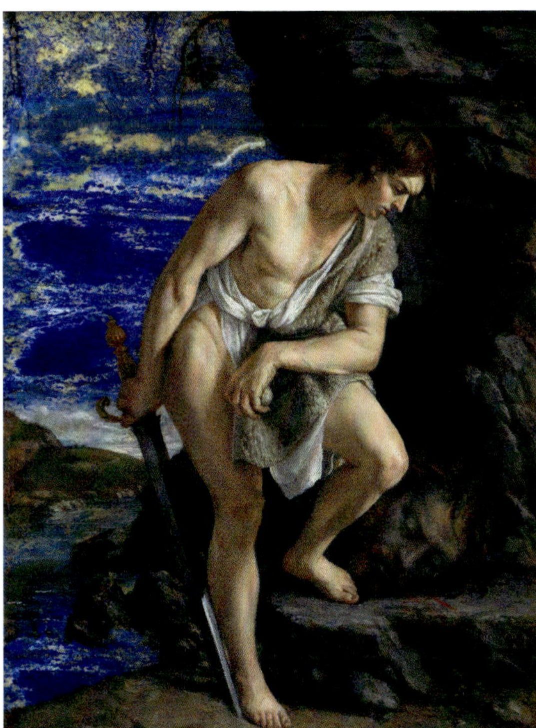

Orazio Gentileschi, *David contemplating the Head of Goliath*, c. 1612, oil on lapis lazuli, 25 x 19 cm, private collection

Mir 'Ali Haravi, Shamsa bearing the name and title of Emperor Aurangzeb, folio from the Shah Jahan Album, c. 1648, ink, tempera and gold on paper, Metropolitan Museum of Art, New York

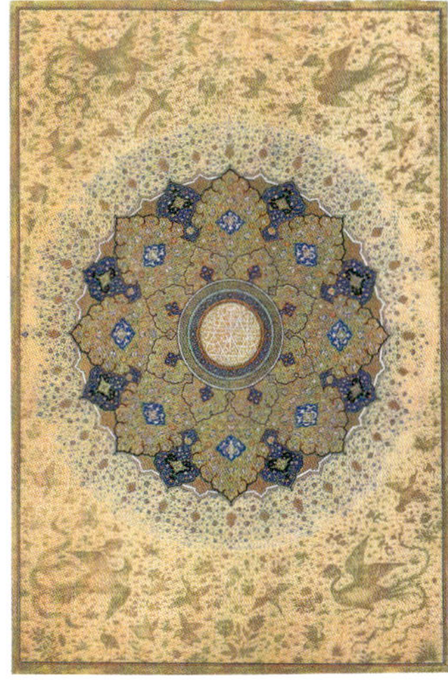

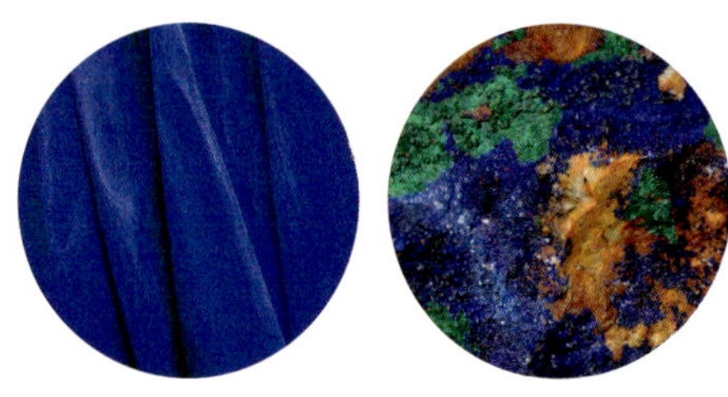

Azurite

Clear copper blue, and the oldest mineral blue pigment. Azurite is the twin brother of that other historic copper pigment, malachite, and they are often found together.

Since prehistoric times, it has been made into paint and medicine, mainly because it is found in so many places. The highest quality is an intense, clean blue. It just lacks the deep, warm blue of lapis lazuli, and one can easily spot that typical greenish tinge of copper in the inferior varieties.

Like lapis lazuli, azurite is a multicultural pigment. It has been used in Buddhist paintings, Egyptian temples, on Greek and Roman statues, the ceilings of cathedrals, in mosques, in manuscripts, and on the masks and murals of the indigenous Americans. And, across the full range of painting. Innumerable holy figures and monarchs are depicted in robes painted with azurite. Azurite was the main affordable and local substitute for the more expensive, natural, ultramarine. For artists such as Dürer and Cranach the Elder, its source could be the nearby mines of Goldberg and Wallerfangen.
In the 15th century, the annual yield in Wallerfangen was around 700 pounds. By comparison, this is the amount of azurite Giotto needed, two centuries earlier, just to paint the Scrovegni chapel.
Azurite was a part of the standard colour scheme in the Americas as well. It has been

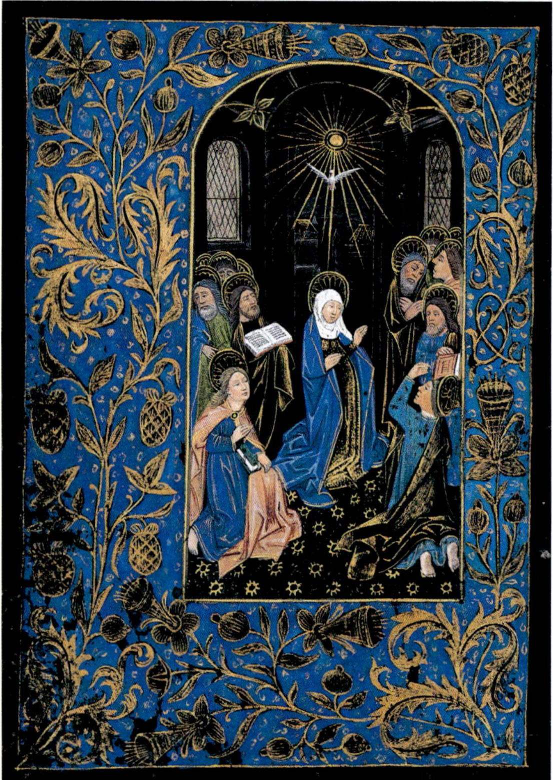

Pentecost, folio from the *Black Hours*, c. 1480, c. 12.2 x 8.5 cm, tempera and gold leaf on parchment, Pierpont Morgan Library, New York

Albrecht Dürer, *Dead European Roller*, c. 1500, tempera op parchment, 27.4 x 19.8 cm, Albertina Museum, Vienna

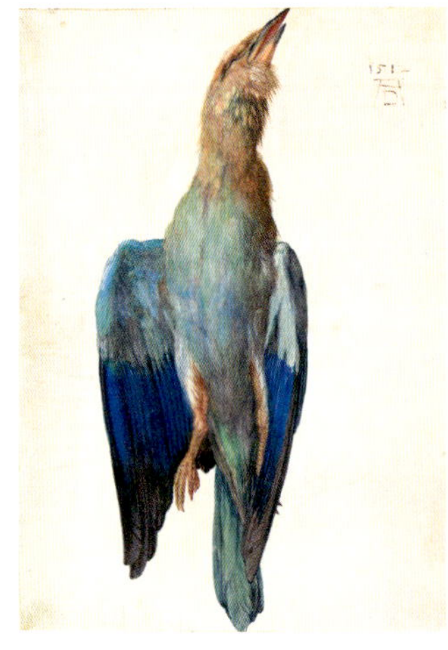

found in the mural paintings of the ancient Maya archaeological site in Bonampak, and in pueblos in the southwestern United States. From the 16th century, the Spanish conquistadors shipped enormous quantities of so-called *Azul de Santo Domingo* to their motherland.

In the 13th century, Marco Polo describes how, in the garden of his winter palace, the Khan had a hill half covered with a blue powder, most likely, azurite.

The combination of azurite and malachite in the so-called blue-green (*qinglu*) landscape paintings later even acquired a special status in Chinese culture as a reference to paradise, free from earthly woes.

The amount of azurite employed in European painting diminished for no apparent reason in the late 17th century. For a large group of painters this meant the end of a familiar colour. They had no other choice but to switch to the costly ultramarine, the cooler indigo, or the unreliable smalt and unstable vivianite. The typical artist had to make do with these inferior pigments, until the discovery of Prussian blue in the 18th century.

Azurite blue is fairly easy to produce. Take a stone of good quality, smash it into increasingly smaller pieces, and grind and sieve the grit until the desired purity, grain size and colour are achieved. Add a binder and you have paint.

A coarse grind produces the deepest blue, a finer grind will give a lighter to dull blue. The different grinds of azurite are still available at specialist shops.

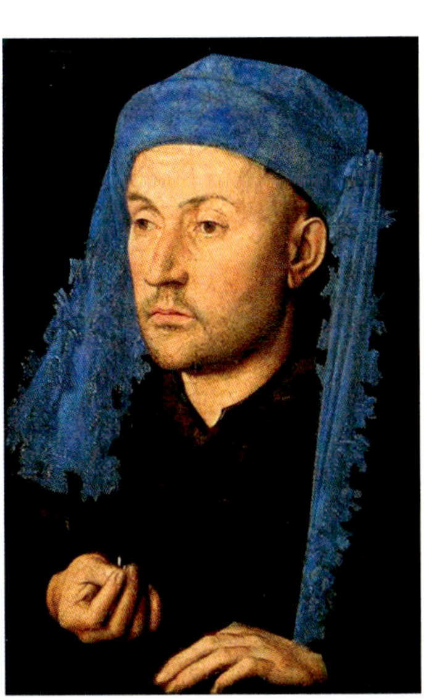

Jan van Eyck, *Portrait of a Jeweller*, c. 1430, oil on panel, 16.6 x 13 cm, Brukenthal National Museum, Sibiu

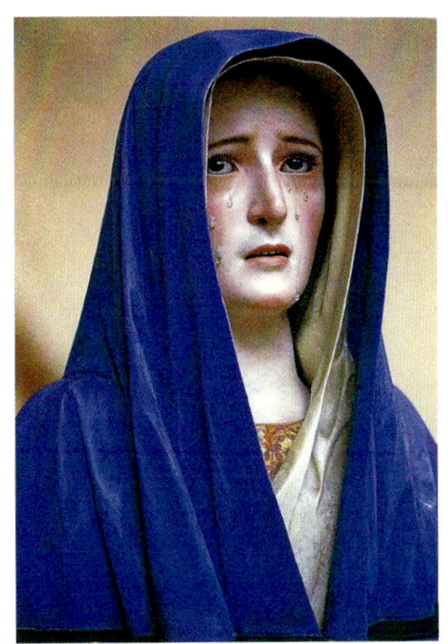

Anonymous, *Virgin of Sorrows (Mater Dolorosa*, polychromed wood, Antequera

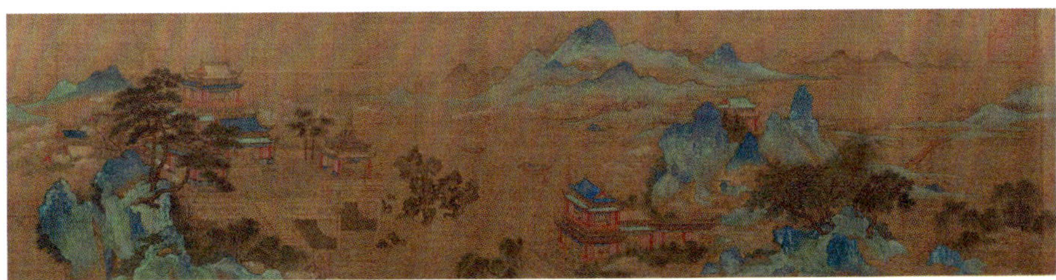

Anonymous, *Spring Morning at the Palace of the Han Emperors*, 17th cen., ink and paint on silk, 16.2 x 87.6 cm, Metropolitan Museum of Art, New York

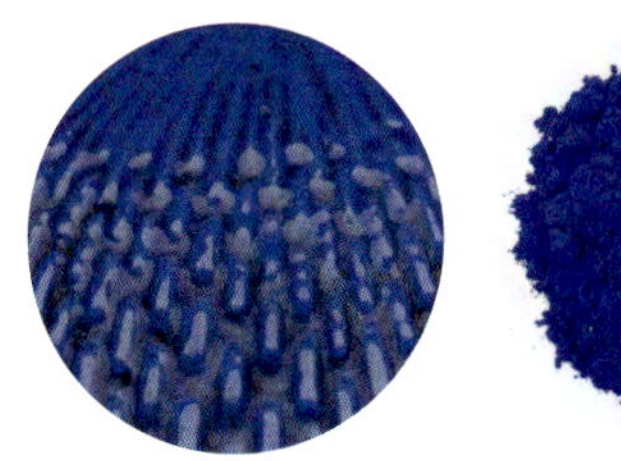

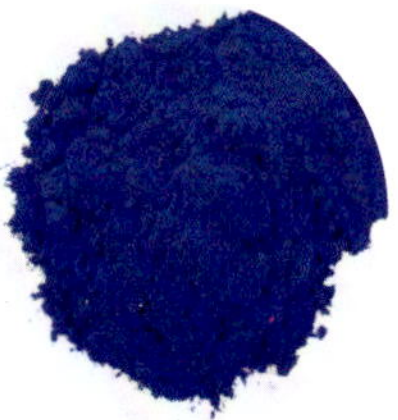

Smalt

Smalt is ground, blue cobalt glass. For thousands of years, it has been used as a raw material for paint, ceramics, enamel and decorative glass. For Abbot Suger, who was responsible for the reconstruction of the monastery of Saint-Denis in the 12th century, and thus the founder of Gothic architecture, it was nothing less than the symbolic representation of '...the inaccessible light in which God exists.'

Glass production emerged in Mesopotamia over five thousand years ago with a primitive form of glass casting, which soon dispersed into the Mediterranean world. In virtually all ancient cultures, objects were cast in glass. It was made into jewellery, used for statues (details such as eyes and hair), furniture, reliefs and a wide range of other items. In this aspect, blue cobalt glass was primarily a substitute for the precious lapis lazuli. With increasing demand, the production and trade of glass grew, but so did the need for firewood for the ravenous blazing ovens. These wood consumers are now viewed as partly responsible for the large-scale deforestation in antiquity. Between the 12th and 18th centuries, the Ore Mountains, *Erzgebirge*, in Germany were the most important source of cobalt in Europe and part of western Asia. Vast quantities of silver, tin, nickel and cobalt

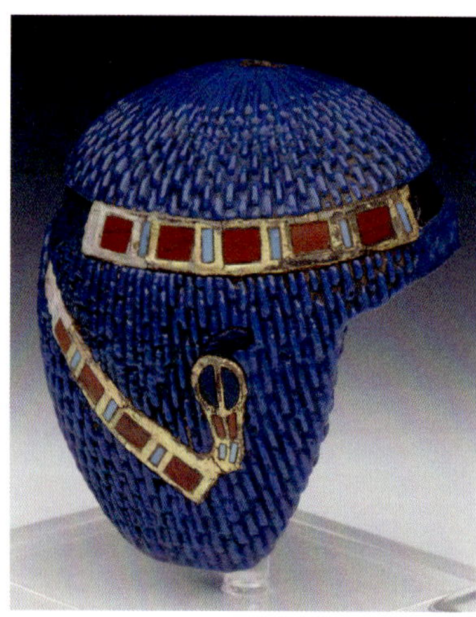

Composition wig from royal statue, Egypt, 19th-18th Dynasty, British Museum, London

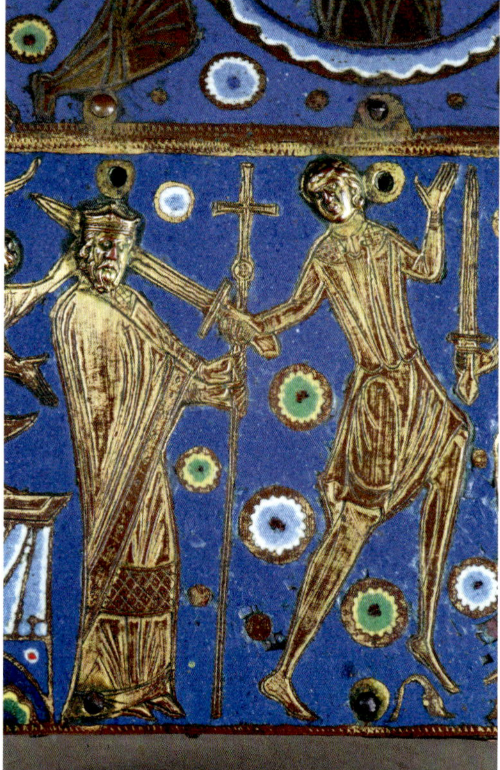

Anonymous, Reliquary of Thomas Becket with detail of a scene of his Martyrdom, 1200-1209, originally from Maashees, Catharijneconvent, Utrecht

ore were once mined here, but little remains today. The cobalt ore became the raw material for smalt pigment. Affordable, beautiful in colour and warmer than azurite. Comparable with ultramarine, various hues were produced in different grades, the highest of which was intended as an alternative to Fra Angelico blue, the purest and deepest ultramarine.
Smalt was prominent on the palettes of European painters for some four hundred years. It became the replacement of natural ultramarine, especially when there was a shortage of supply due to wars or epidemics. Additionally, smalt was a coveted siccative, a drying agent that accelerated oil paint's often slow drying. As the Low Countries (present-day Flanders and the Netherlands) were the main producers of ready-to-use smalt for several centuries, it was easy for local artists to acquire. Yet this is hardly noticeable today. Research has shown that the pigment was quite prominent on the palette, but over time, the once brilliant smalt in paintings has turned into an indefinable greyish brown. Take a look at Treck's still-life, for example. At first glance, it is an intact 17th-century still-life. But when the painter put down his brush, the exquisite tablecloth was blue, with the two exotic blue-white Ming dishes set against a blue background. Luxury and status. All of this is no longer visible in today's greyish-brown version. The crystal-like smalt was a common painting pigment and siccative until the mid-18th century. House painters even employed it until the middle of the last century, especially for decorative work.

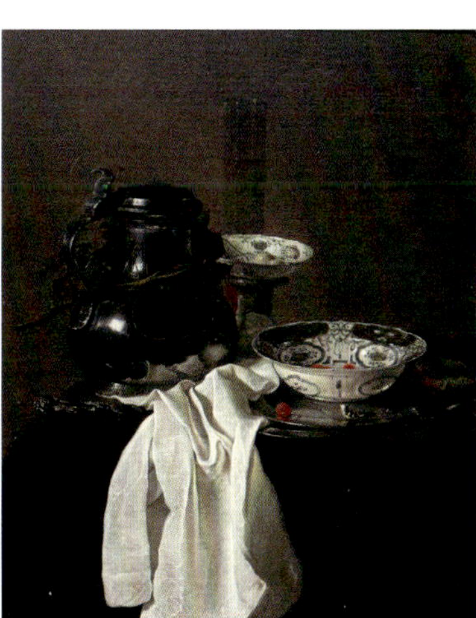

Jan Treck, *Still-Life with a Pewter Flagon and Two Ming Bowls*, 1651, oil on canvas, 76.5 x 63.8 cm, National Gallery, London

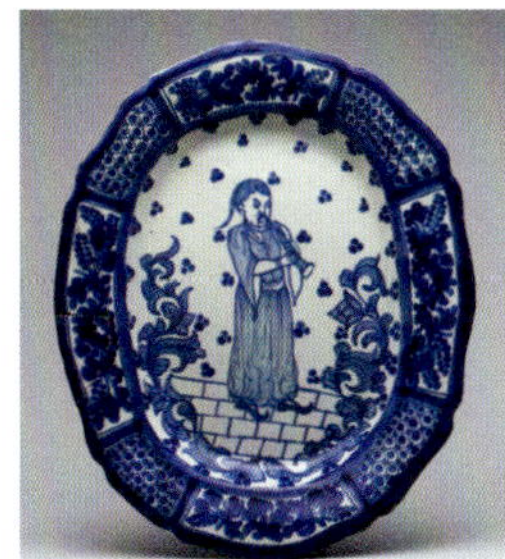

Mexican dish, c. 1830, majolica earthenware, h. 18 cm, Metropolitan Museum of Art, New York

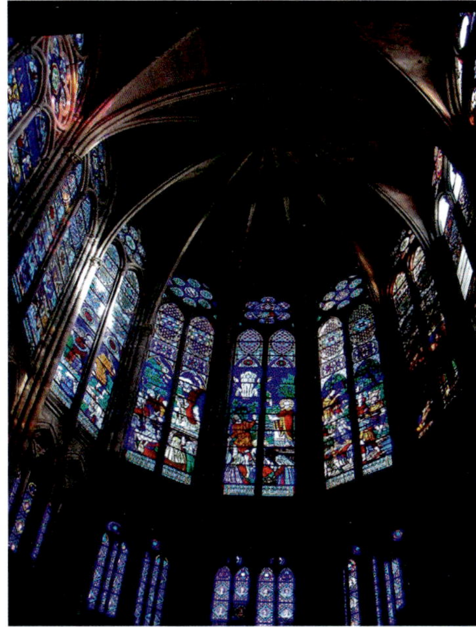

Stained glass windows of the choir in the Basilica of Saint-Denis, c. 1140

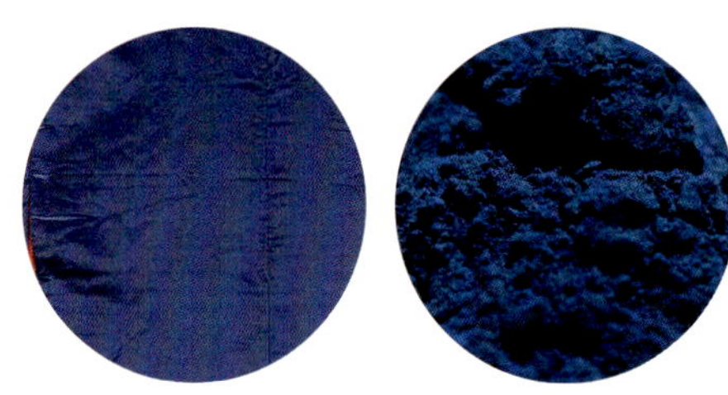

Indigo & Woad

Indigo is born and dies, to be born again. Essentially, this means the metamorphosis from plant to colour, where the basic indigo-white changes from green into a deep blue. In many cultures, it is seen as the representation of the spiritual growth in a human life.

Indigo and woad have become practically synonymous, even though they are members of distinctive plant families from different geographical regions. The common denominator is that both belong to the group of historical blue-dyeing plants. And, as with purple, contact with oxygen causes their fairly colourless fluids to turn blue. Indigo blue signified power and might – supremacy in religious, social and political fields. This was presented, for example, in the form of innovative textiles or embroidery, a body painting, a tattoo, or an exclusive fabric – the more exquisite the fabric, the purer and richer the colour. In the sixth century BC, the prophet Ezekiel describes the beautiful blue attire and embroideries of the wealthy merchants of Seba, present-day Yemen. Indigo derives from the ancient Greek *indikon*, meaning 'from India'. In the fourth century BC, India formed the eastern border of the greater Greek Empire. It also refers to the raw material originating from this region (present-day Pakistan and northwest India), dried indigo pulp, which the Greeks highly valued.

Sian Bowen, *Gaze*, 2006, drawing, laser-cut indigo painted blue paper and applied silver line, 66.4 x 48.8 cm, artist's collection

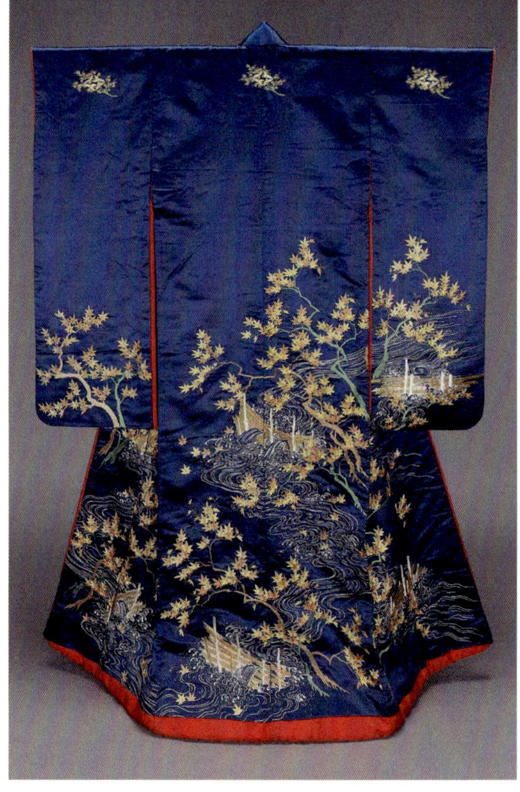

Kimono (*furisode*), Japan, c. 1900, satin and embroidery with gilt-metallic yarns on silk, 173.4 x 125.1 cm, Museum of Fine Arts, Boston

Until the opening of sea routes to Asia via the Cape of Good Hope, indigo was known in Europe as Baghdad blue. Named after the city selling the best qualities and which, for centuries, was the bustling crossroads for transhipment goods from Asia, Europe and Africa, giving it a mythical reputation. Indigo blue – we are all familiar with it. The original colour of denim jeans, conquering the world from the United States, is a cool blue with a greenish or black nuance. In everything the counterpart of the shimmering ultramarine.
Indigo-based inks and paints have been around for thousands of years, as the pigment combines well with traditional binders such as egg, hide glue, honey and resin. It is a versatile multi-purpose colour. Unfortunately, when mixed with linseed oil, the paint darkens to a blackish blue, which can be resolved by adding a white pigment.

In Europe, indigo blue was employed as an oil paint in Scandinavian panels as early as the 13th century, which shows how widely branched international trade was. With a growing supply by the various East India Companies, indigo became more common and affordable, and a more prominent colour on the painter's palette.
At the start of the 17th century, the port of Antwerp handled forty percent of the world trade, making it an important transhipment point for the Portuguese indigo from Asia. Hals visited his native Antwerp in 1616 and, from then on, included indigo in his palette. He thus starts a trend in the northern Netherlands. First with colleagues in his hometown of Haarlem, followed by others such as Vermeer in Delft, and Steen in Leiden.

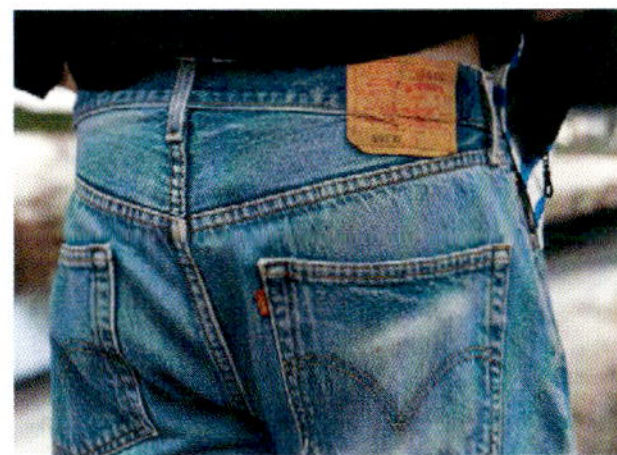

Levi's-jeans

A Tuareg with a litham

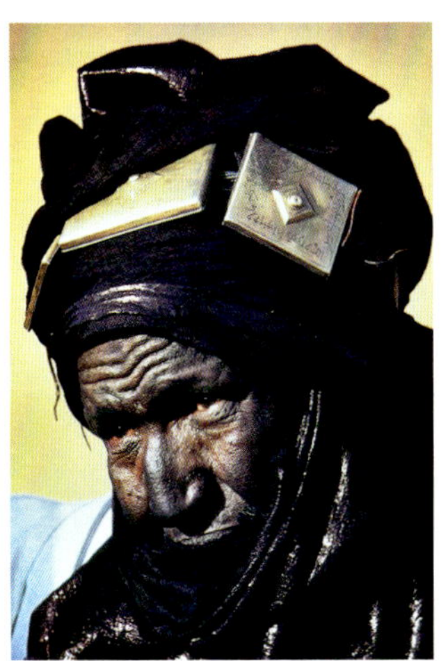

Johannes Verspronck, *Andries Stilte as a Standard Bearer*, 1640, oil on canvas, 104 x 78.5 cm, National Gallery of Art, Washington D.C.

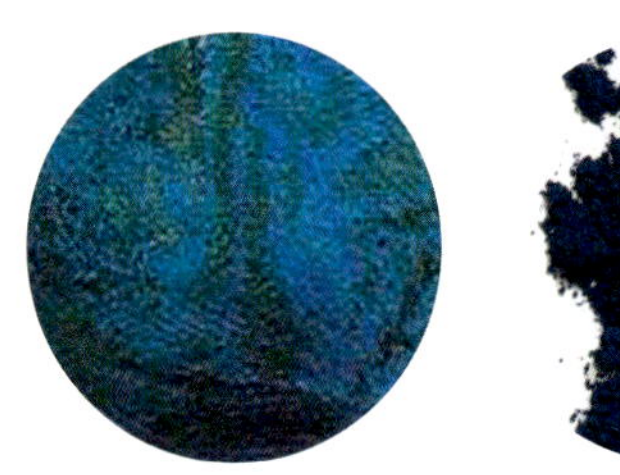

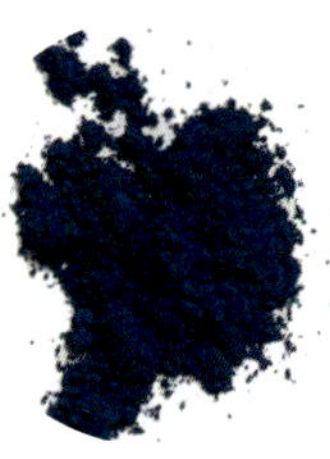

Mayan Blue

Indigo, but different. The exact details of how this paint was developed may always remain unclear, but it is most likely linked to local, indigenous indigo dyeing.

In what is now called Guatemala, blue dyeing traditionally involved carving out tub-shaped pits in the ground, which were made waterproof by sealing them with a layer of fine *palygorskite* clay. After the indigo dye had worn off, the remaining liquid was left in the sun to evaporate and stuck to the clay. As the pits were used multiple times, a blue crust gradually grew on the inside.

When the pit was eventually written off, the hardened clay crust was removed and pulverised. The start of a second life as paint with a binder, such as gum. Because of the clay's purity, Maya blue is a magnificent, opaque, light blue, comparable to a gouache or poster paint.

It was overlooked for several centuries, despite being common in many locations in the former Spanish colonies. For example, it was used in the many temples of the Mayas and Aztecs and on innumerable figurines, statues and sculptures. The role of this blue was no longer recognised after it became part of the colonial palette. Its pre-Columbian origins were forgotten or ignored after the Spanish conquest and occupation, when indigenous painters and their materials were employed to decorate

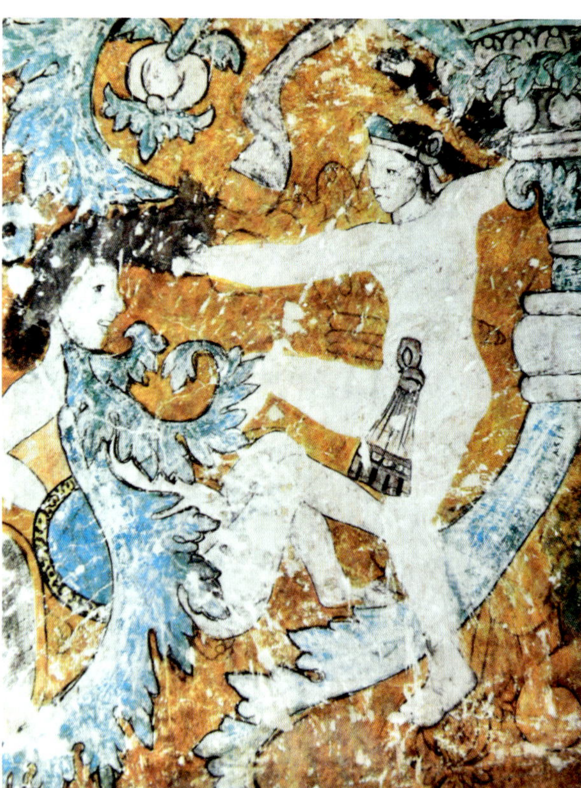

The Centaurs of Ixmiquilpan, c. 1550-1570, fresco, church of San Miguel, Ixmiquilpan, Mexico

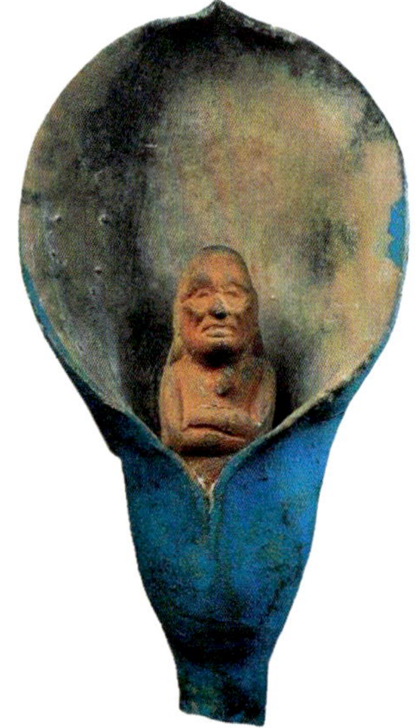

Maya Anthropomorphic Figurine, 1000-1524, Jaina, Campêche, Museo Nacional de Antropología, Mexico City

the newly built churches and monasteries with biblical paintings, in which they combined ancient techniques with the new forms.
It took until the middle of the 20th century to rediscover the ruins of Bonampak, with the aid of the indigenous people. Finally raising awareness of the beauty of the original colours and art, for centuries protected by the dense jungle. Saving the indigenous skill and knowledge from further destruction by the colonisers and their descendants.
Mayan blue is a fine example of how an indigenous pigment merges into a new culture as a colour and a symbol.
Among both the indigenous people and the Iberian rulers, blue represented the higher powers in the Upperworld and Underworld. For the Maya, the colour symbolised the indomitable powers of heaven, earth and water; it was the sacred colour for ritual sacrifice, including that of humans, especially from around 250 to 1520 CE. Spanish 16th-century chronicles describe how prisoners were smeared with blue paint before they were pulled backwards onto a sacrificial block, upon which their hearts were cut out while still alive or before they were thrown into the sacred well to drown. All to please and honour Chac (or Chaac), the god of rain, lightning and water. Protector of agriculture, the generator of this agricultural community.

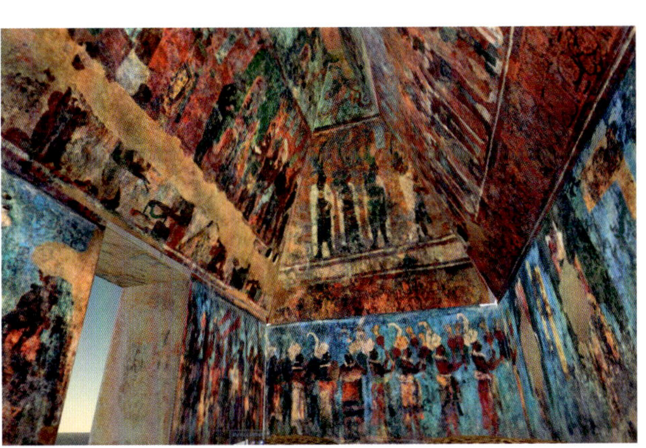

Wall paintings in the temple complexes at Bonampak, 580-800, Chiapas, Mexico

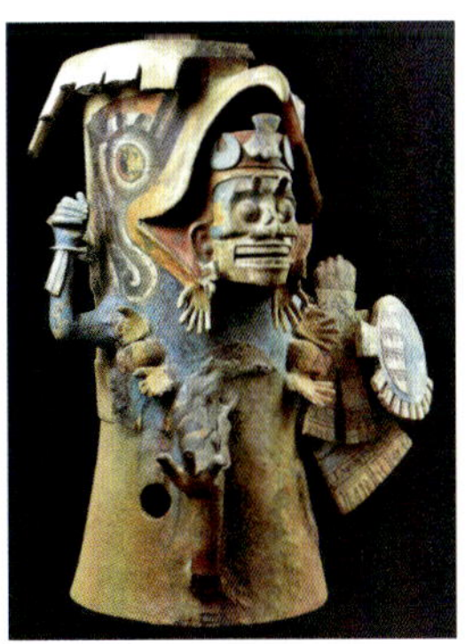

God of the Underworld, Mayan incense burner, 1428-1521, h. 99 cm, Museo Nacional de Antropología, Mexico City

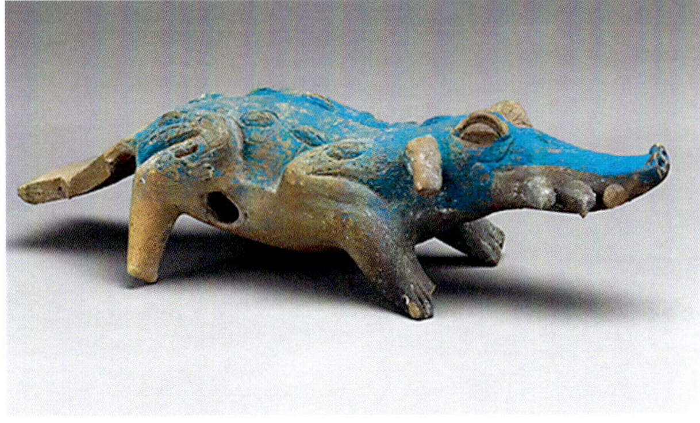

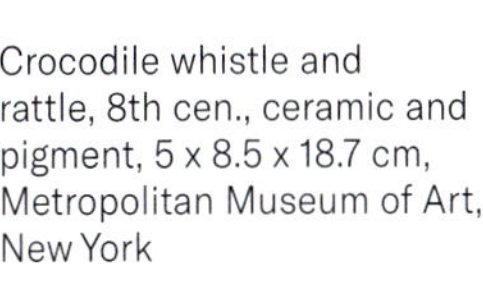

Crocodile whistle and rattle, 8th cen., ceramic and pigment, 5 x 8.5 x 18.7 cm, Metropolitan Museum of Art, New York

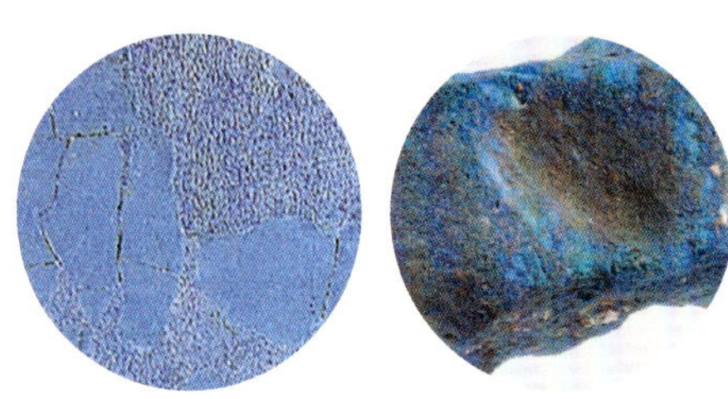

Egyptian Blue

The blue of the Ancient, for with the fall of the Roman Empire this beautiful blue disappeared from view. Unfathomable, as it is a versatile and stable pigment, which was only rivalled by the emergence of cerulean in the 19th century.

Egyptian blue is the calming, opaque blue seen in practically every museum that houses Egyptian, Cretan, Greek, Etruscan, Roman and Levantine antiquities, which is why its common name, Egyptian blue, is too limited.

Another name for the pigment is Pozzuoli blue, after the city where it was produced in Roman times. More recent names are Roman and Pompeian blue, referring to the colourful murals that surfaced during the rediscovery of ancient ruins in Italy. The pigment was most likely invented by chance, sometime around 3200 BC, during the production of glass or glazed ceramics. This blue is created by heating a mixture of calcium carbonate, copper oxide and potash. The common copper ore makes it a colour which is easy to manufacture almost anywhere. This too was a welcome replacement for the scarce and costly natural ultramarine.

Varying the proportions in the mixture, the temperature of the kiln and modifying the final product's grind size, produced a range of diverse colour nuances. A coarse grain has more tinting

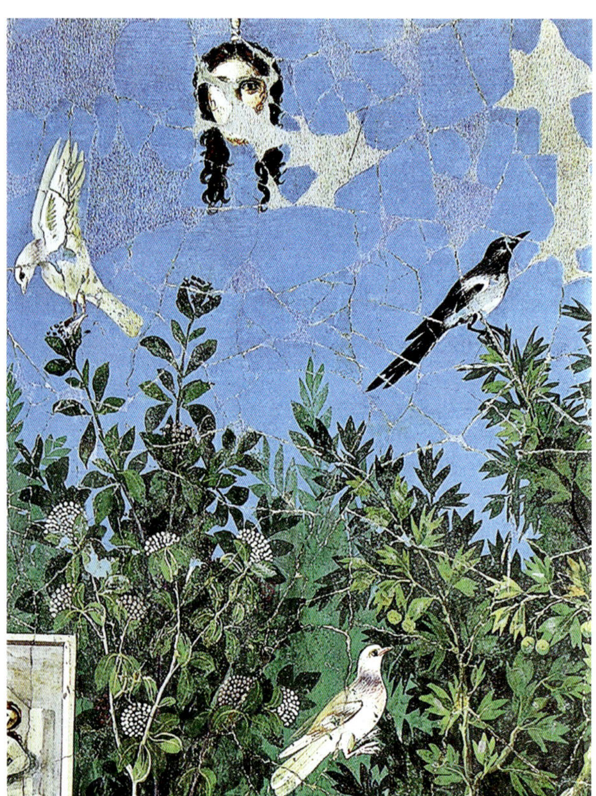

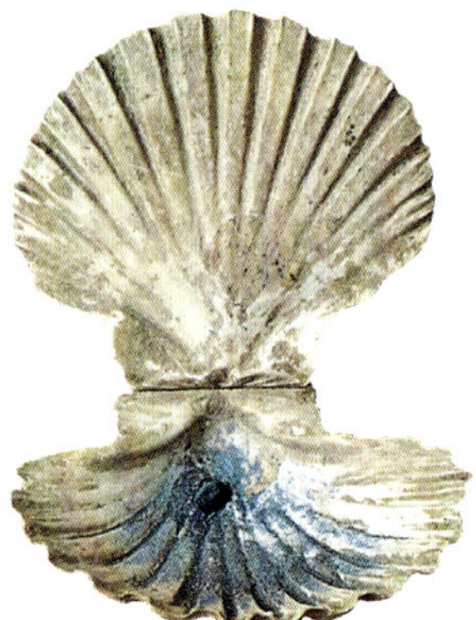

Garden with Birds, detail, c. 30 AD., fresco, House of the Golden Bracelet, Pompeyï

Shell with Egyptian blue, burial gift, Cyclades, c. 2500 BC

Egyptian blue scarab 600-570 BC, 1 x 0.7 cm

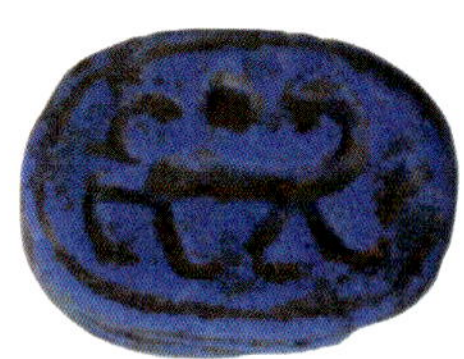

strength, while fine grinds have a much lighter and greyer appearance.
From Egypt and the Egyptian sphere of influence, the pigment and its recipes spread to Europe, Asia and numerous parts of Africa through the widespread trade networks. A route partly in reverse to the long road lapis lazuli travelled. As far as we know, its use reached Scandinavia in the north, and China in the east.
We know the latter thanks to research, which in 1982 revealed that the cerule-an-like blue employed in paintings from the Han period (206 BC-220 AD) is virtually identical to Egyptian blue.
To paint murals and decorate sculptures and terracotta, the dry pigment was mixed with lime or plaster. And for the murals, the wealthier the patron, the better the quality of pigment, and the higher the number of paint layers. This explains why preserved paintings from ancient Roman villas are still so legible, in contrast to paintings in tombs, on which less energy and material was spent.
Egyptian blue belongs to the stable colours and does not react to other pigments. Even after thousands of years of exposure to light, it will retain its tinting strength. Despite all this, it can appear dull and dark, as is the case of Nefertiti's once dazzling blue crown. This is due to grime that has adhered to the paint layer or penetrated the porous material below the painted surface.

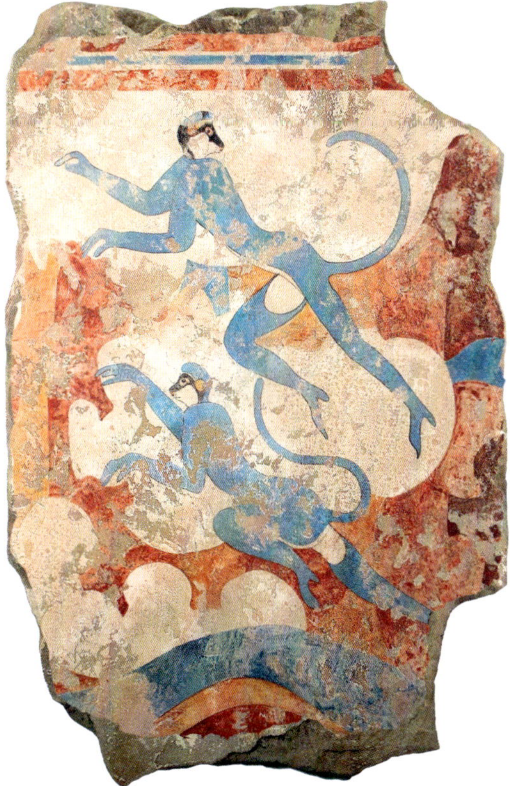

The Blue Monkeys, 2nd millennium BC, Minoan mural, Akrotiri

Nefertiti, buste c. 1700 BC, limestone and painted plaster, Neues Museum, Berlin

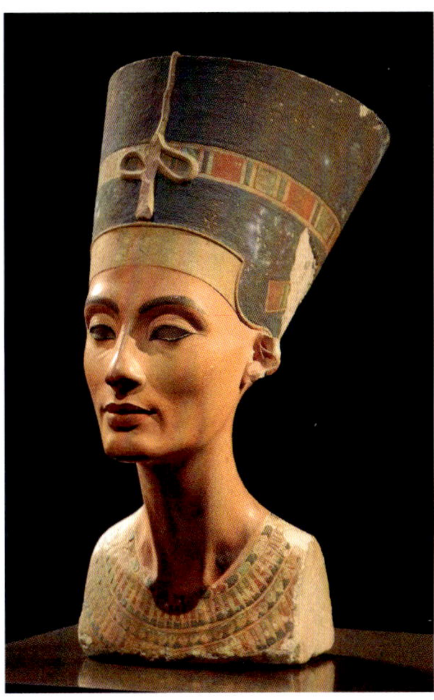

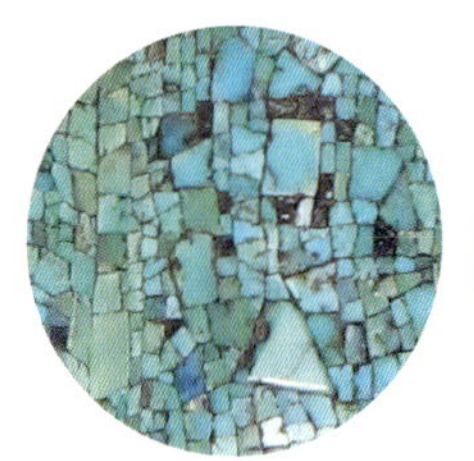

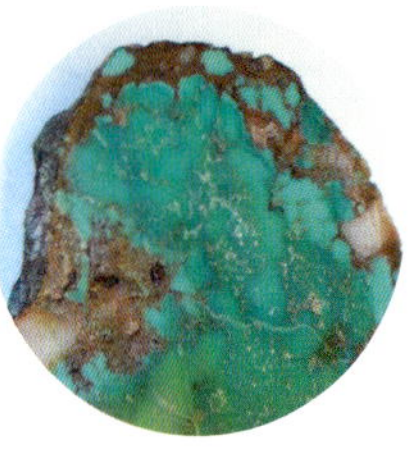

Turquoise

The word turquoise establishes the link with Turkey or Turkistan, the historical transit and deposit sites of the mineral.

The stone, the colour and the pigment, all carry the same name and refer to the popular semi-precious stone found in a range of green-blue or blue-green hues. Therefore, the colour cannot be categorised into a fixed colour group, which can be frustrating for the neurotic, Western, pigeonhole thinking.

Turquoise, like the related azurite and malachite, is a worldly colour. In many cultures representatives of intangible forces humans are destined to live with. In the West, turquoise is best known as the bright blue-green ornamental stone, employed in so many ways over the centuries that an entire book could effortlessly be devoted to it. Additionally, it is a colour of significance in its use as a glaze in ceramics. A much lesser-known fact is that turquoise was, and still is, employed in painting, especially outside Europe. Categorised as 'exotic', it is generally omitted in historical pigment overviews and is rarely illustrated in professional literature.
In Asia, in any case the Tibetans, and in the Americas, the Navajo, among others, used it on their palettes. As a result of ongoing research, other cultures will most likely be added to the list. Ancient

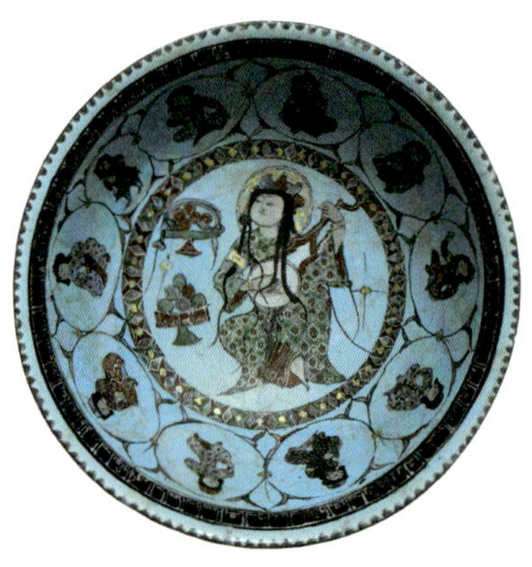

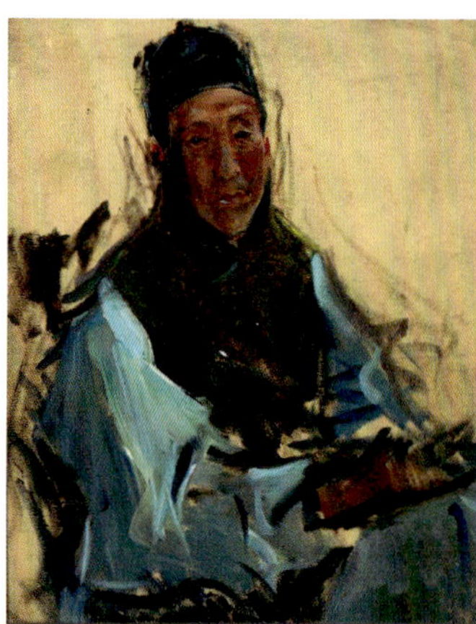

Turquoise Bowl with Lute Player, Iran, 12th-13th cen., earthenware, glazed and gilded, diam. 19.7 cm, Metropolitan Museum of Art, New York

Konrad Krzyżanowski, *Chinaman*, c. 1903, oil on canvas, 77 x 65 cm, National Museum, Warsaw

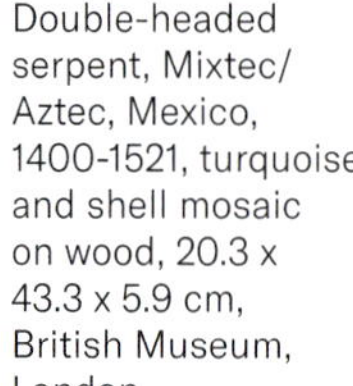

Double-headed serpent, Mixtec/Aztec, Mexico, 1400-1521, turquoise and shell mosaic on wood, 20.3 x 43.3 x 5.9 cm, British Museum, London

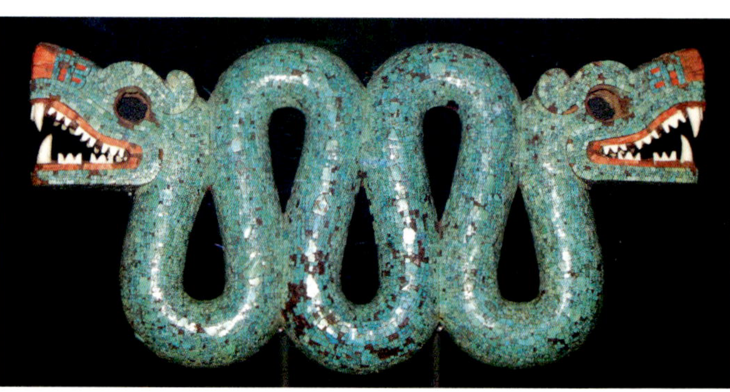

examples of turquoise mining and processing are in the Middle and Far East. As early as around 5000 BC, since the earliest Egyptian dynasties, Sinai, also known in Arabic as *Ard Al-Fayrouz* (the land of turquoise), has been the source of copper and copper-bearing minerals, including turquoise. It is a commonly employed stone in death masks, such as that of Tutankhamun, and in figurines, jewellery and furniture.

The Egyptian primordial goddess Hathor was nicknamed 'Mistress of Turquoise'. The goddess of life and fertility, depicted celestially as the earth-spanning cow, with the Milky Way spraying from her udder, and the blue-green turquoise as her symbolic colour.

In ancient Persia, the sacred colour stood for heaven on earth, representing victory and prosperity. Countless poets in Persian literature have sung about it, and since around 7000 BC, the stone has been an important funerary gift for anyone who could afford it. Today, turquoise can still be seen in abundance, in decorations and as a leading colour in mosques and palaces.

At first sight, the pigment resembles chrysocolla, a different blue from the rich copper family. The type of stone determines the colour and whether it can be used as a pigment. For the vast majority, this is not the case. Some varieties even become slimy mush after pulverisation. The turquoise pigment can still be purchased from specialist paint suppliers.

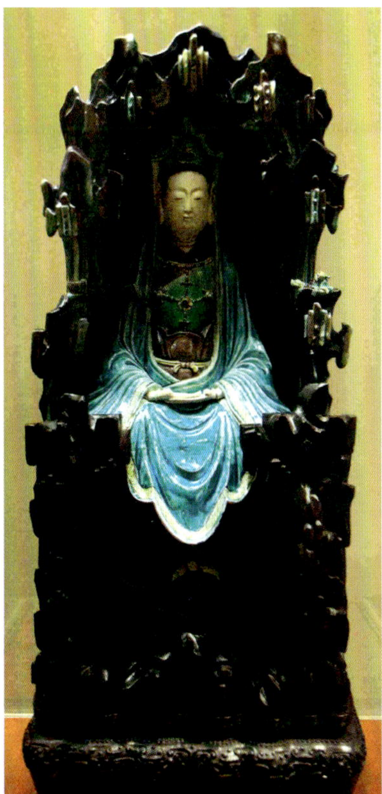

Guanyin, ceramics, Musée Guimet, Paris

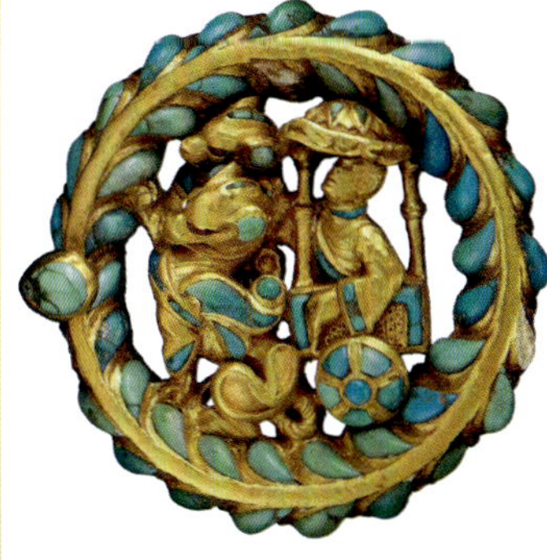

Boot buckle, Tillya-tepe, tomb IV, gold, turquoise, carnelian, diam. 5 cm, National Museum, Afghanistan

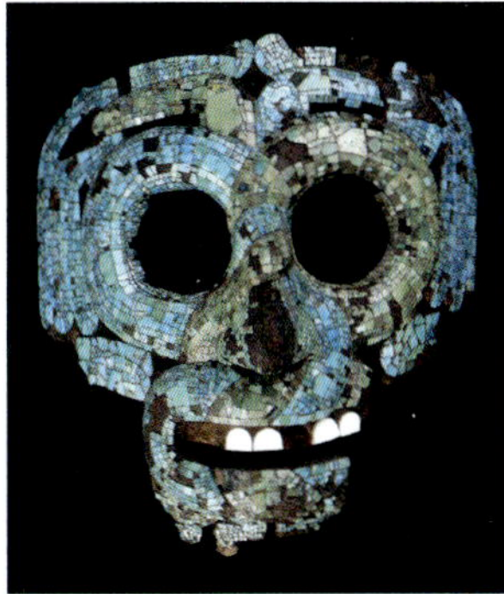

Serpent mask of Tlaloc, 15th-16th cen., shell mosaic and two-coloured turquoise on cedro wood with pine resin adhesive, Mixtec/Aztec, Mexico, 18 x 16.5 cm, British Museum, London

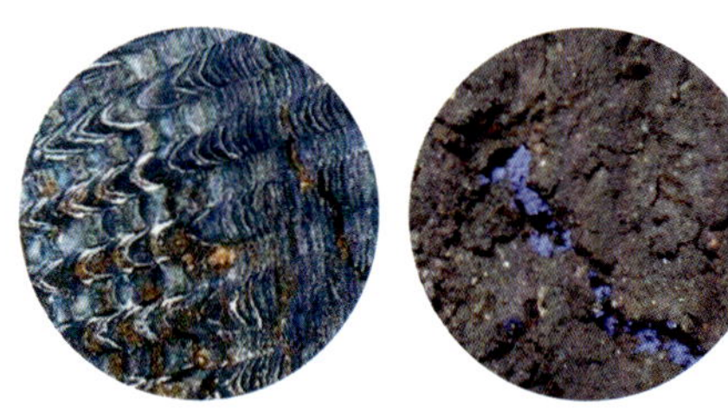

Vivianite

You won't see it. At least, not if it has been on a canvas for a while, as it will have lost its colour. That is why this blue literally disappeared from view and memory, until its rediscovery in the 19th century.

It is not a dazzling colour, more of a dull blue-grey, recognisable in old names such as blue ashes and blue ochre, two of the various aliases in circulation. The lack of brightness probably contributed to the inglorious end of this old pigment.

Vivianite is originally a soft, whitish-yellow phosphate substance that turns blue when in contact with oxygen, or into a glass-like blue crystal. It develops in oxygen-deficient marshes and pools wherein large quantities of nutrients, such as decayed bones and plant material, have accumulated. This can take on surprising forms, as was seen in Switzerland's Lake Brienz. There, a floating torso surfaced in 2010, enveloped in a white cocoon covered with a blue haze. Further investigation revealed that the corpse was at least three hundred years old. Due to the conditions of the site, the remains of a drowned man never decomposed but was converted into the so-called Adipocere (corpse fatty tissue). Small earthquakes in the area caused the torso to emerge after centuries, and after making contact with oxygen turned its surface into vivianite.

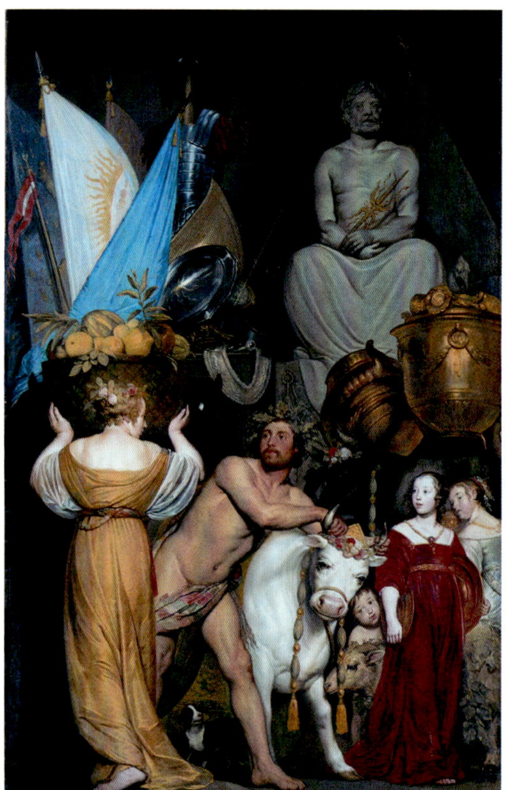

Pieter de Grebber, *Triumphal Procession with bull for offering*, detail, 1660, oil on canvas, 390 x 263 cm, Huis ten Bosch, The Hague

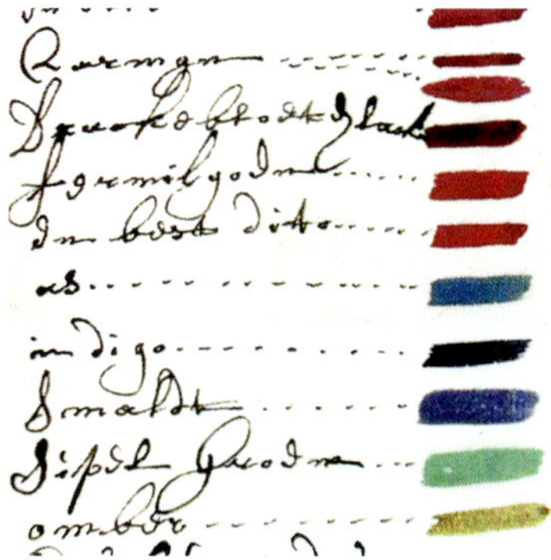

Simon Eikelenberg, colour table from *Aantekeningen over Schilderkunst*, 17th cen.; the blues are the threesome ash, indigo and smalt, of which the ash is probably vivianite.

Due to high phosphate use in modern, intensive agriculture, vivianite can increasingly be found in both forms in fields. Local blue ashes seemed a good alternative to solve the constant nuisances of the better historic blues – the natural ultramarine, azurite and smalt. Vivianite was cheap and, for inhabitants of wetlands, readily available.

It has been used for all forms of painting and paintings and is compatible with a plethora of binding mediums. It is described in old painting manuals as reasonably stable and, according to written sources, shows no specific flukes when combined with binders. But, regarding its long-term survival, people were obviously far too optimistic.

As far as we know, Roman artists worked with it, it is found on panels from the Middle Ages and was employed by painters such as Lucas Cranach the Elder, Albert Cuyp and Carel Fabritius. The latter two, living in the Rhine Delta, basically lived directly on top of the source: peat. In the 17th century, large areas of low moorland were excavated in Holland for the benefit of the expanding cities, uncovering blue ashes.

Vivianite can be recognised as a yellowed or browned colour, as can be seen in Fabritius' 1664 self-portrait. In the reconstruction I turned the sky into its original blue, allowing you to see what it looked like when the painter put down his brush.

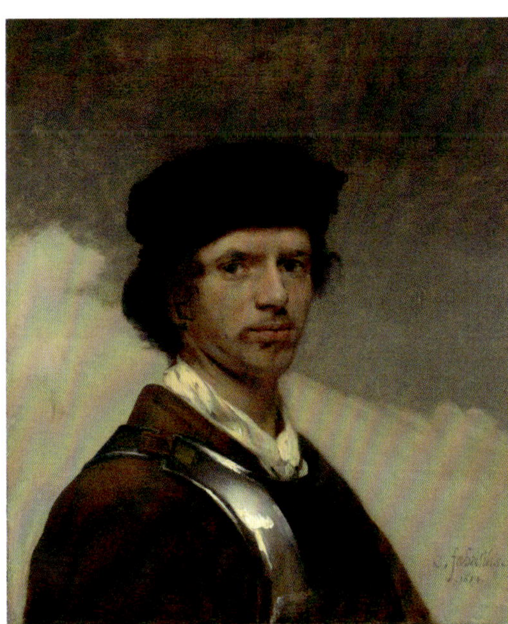

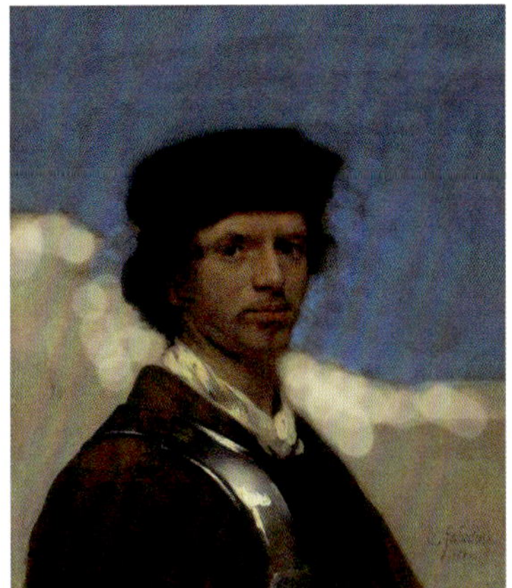

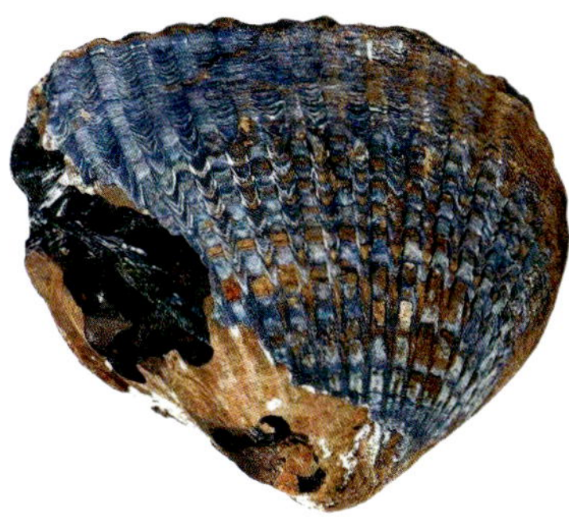

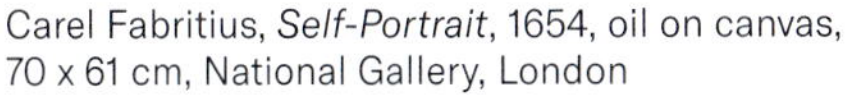

Carel Fabritius, *Self-Portrait*, 1654, oil on canvas, 70 x 61 cm, National Gallery, London

Reconstruction of the vivianite blue sky by the author

Vivianite forming on a shell

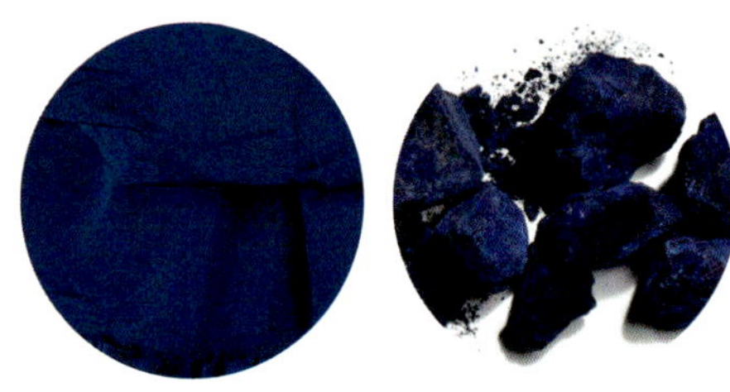

Prussian Blue

The revolution on the palette begins! Prussian blue is considered the first pigment of the modern era, appearing on the market in the very beginning of the 18th century.

Of all the blues, it probably has the most aliases. Aliases associated with the many slightly differing chemical compositions or referring to the places it was produced. One could fill a full sheet of paper with these names, which would even include 'ultramarine', 'indigo' and 'cobalt'.

The discovery of the pigment that became Prussian blue was once more a matter of pure coincidence. In his Berlin workshop, Johann Konrad Dippel produced the so-called Dippel's Oil, a kind of miracle oil made from boiled hooves, horns and hides, that would cure various ailments in humans and animals. The pigment maker Johann Diesbach, who worked at the Dippel company, was at one point preparing Florentine Lake based on cochineal (lice) when he discovered he had insufficient potash. He borrowed it from Dippel and, to his amazement, saw not red but a blue dye emerging. It was later discovered that the potash was contaminated with blood. Like an inkblot, the news and the pigment spread first across Europe and then the rest of the world. In 1709, the director of the Royal Academy in Berlin sent samples to various artists in Europe, and in 1714,

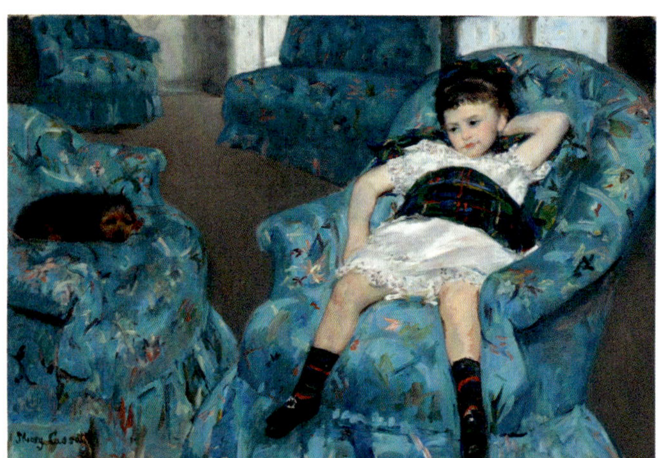

Mary Cassatt, *Little Girl in a Blue Armchair*, 1878, oil on canvas, 89.5 x 130 cm, National Gallery of Art, Washington D.C.

Utagawa Hiroshige, *Tobiuo and Ishimochi Fish*, from the series Uozukushi Tobiuo c. 1840, woodcut, 25.7 x 37.2 cm, Metropolitan Museum of Art, New York

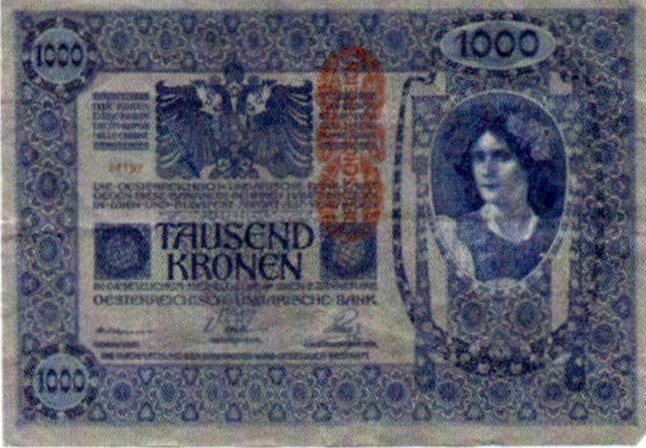

Banknote printed with Prussian blue, collection of the author

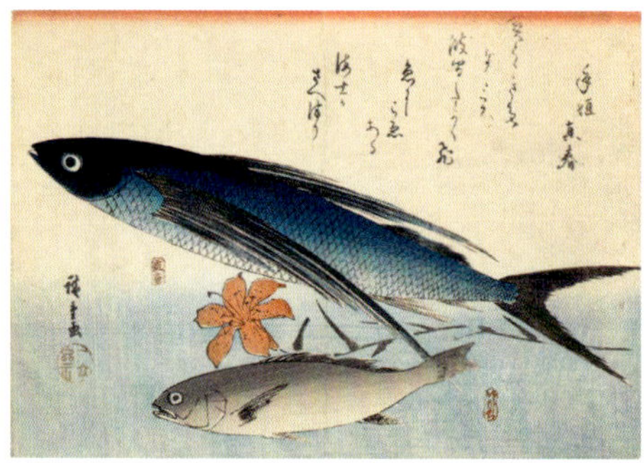

the manufacturer dispatched a small quantity of pigment to Paris. By 1716, it was already on sale in St Petersburg and Armenia, followed by the unstoppable march towards Asia, Africa and the Americas.
You can tell immediately whether a painting dates from before or after this crucial point in time: the inexpensive Prussian blue makes the palette considerably cooler in tone. Like indigo, it leans towards black in its pure form and needs an opaque spot colour to be perceived as blue, as can be seen in Cassatt's painting, with its excess of Prussian blue mixed with white. And not just as paint, as she displays the new colours that became possible in interiors and clothing thanks to Prussian blue.
The same applies to printing, graphics, ceramics and other related products. For a painter like Auguste Renoir, this cool blue was unacceptable, and never included it on his palette. This decision proved to be wise because you need to use it very carefully. Too often, one can see paintings in which the Prussian blue has absorbed the original colour scheme. The infamous bleeding, as can be seen in Picasso's blue period and Van Gogh's 'The Potato Eaters'. Bleeding means that sooner or later the Prussian blue will wriggle its way through the other colours. This is due to the very fine pigment particles spreading through and over the coarser pigment of, for example, ochre. Irreversible.

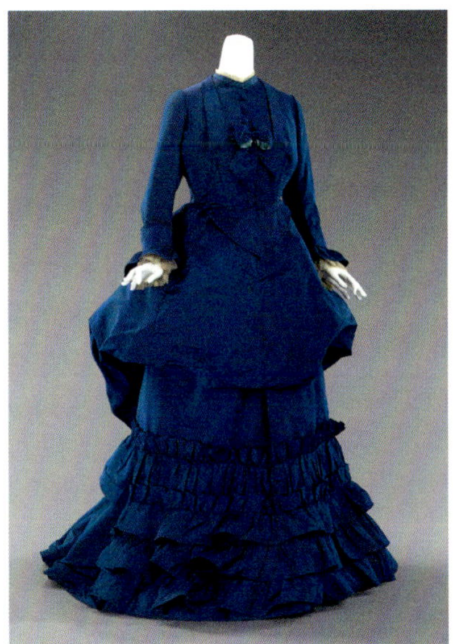

Evening gown, silk in Prussian blue, c. 1872, House of Worth, Metropolitan Museum of Art, New York

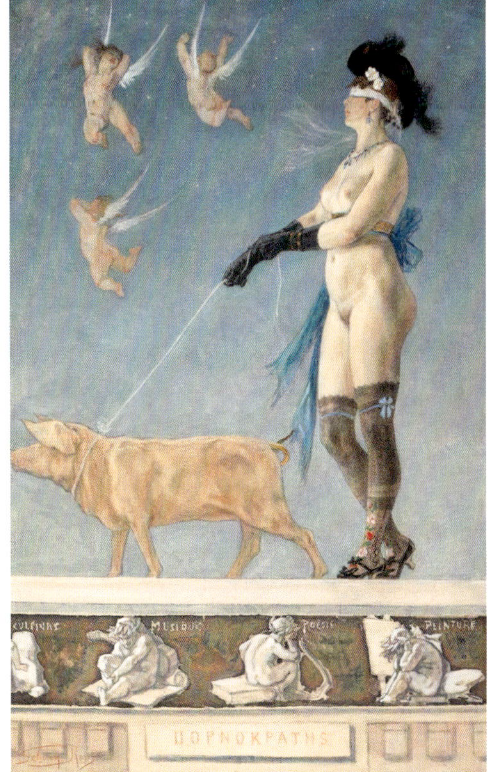

Félicien Rops, *Pornocrates*, 1878, watercolour and gouache, 75 x 48 cm, Musée Félicien Rops, Namur

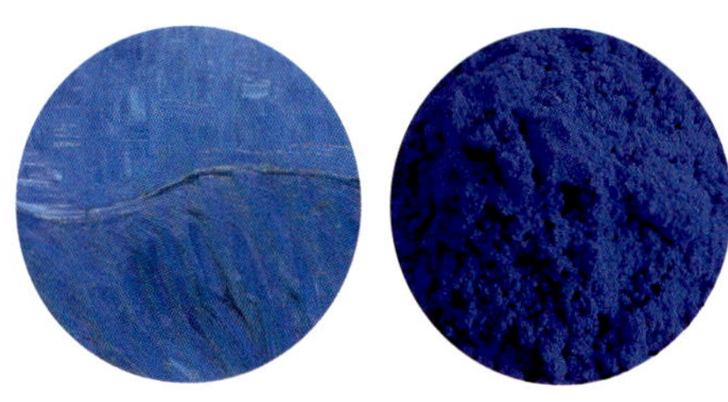

Cobalt Blue

'A divine colour,' Van Gogh called it. Despite its high price, Van Gogh was a fervent user of cobalt blue because it is more serene than ultramarine and far brighter than Prussian blue. It is ideal for a palette based on reds, yellows and blues and is perfect for mixing with other colours. It is indeed an exceptional blue – semi-transparent in its original version, neither too red nor too green.

Cobalt blue owes its existence to Napoleon's advancing troops looting foreign churches, monasteries and palaces. In the late 18th century, an enormous number of works of art were moved across Europe towards the French capital. The works that would become the foundation of the Louvre Museum.

In rudimentary and insufficient packaging, these works were transported via ships or via oxcarts and horse-drawn carriages over largely unpaved roads.

Not surprisingly, many artworks did not survive the journey unscathed. Because of the government's rush to exhibit as much loot as quickly as possible, a *Conservatoire du Musée des Arts* was set up under the direction of the artist Fragonard to repair the damage.

When repairing the blues, azurite or the natural ultramarine, lapis lazuli, the restorers faced the age-old problem of scarcity or even a complete lack of raw materials. Chemist Louis Jacques Thénard

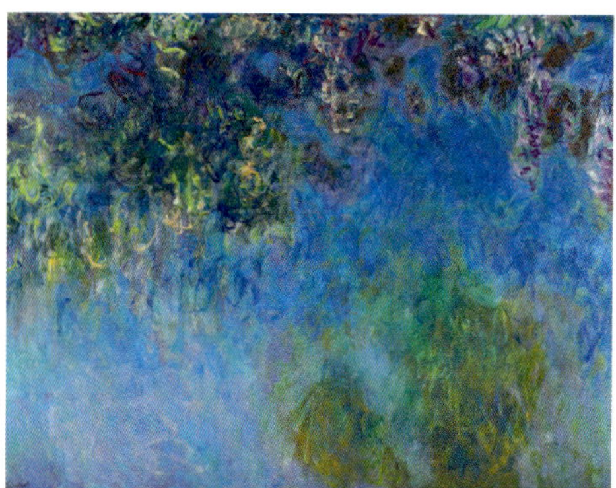

Claude Monet, *Wisteria*, 1917-1920, oil on canvas, 150.5 x 200.5 cm, Kunstmuseum, The Hague

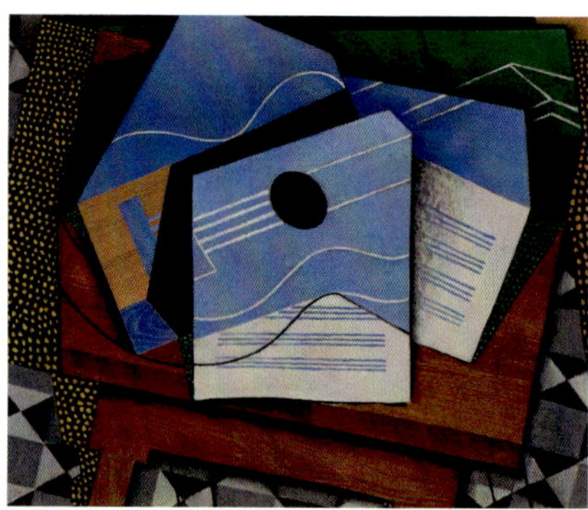

Juan Gris, *Guitar on a Table*, 1915, oil on canvas, 73 x 92 cm, Kröller-Müller Museum, Otterlo

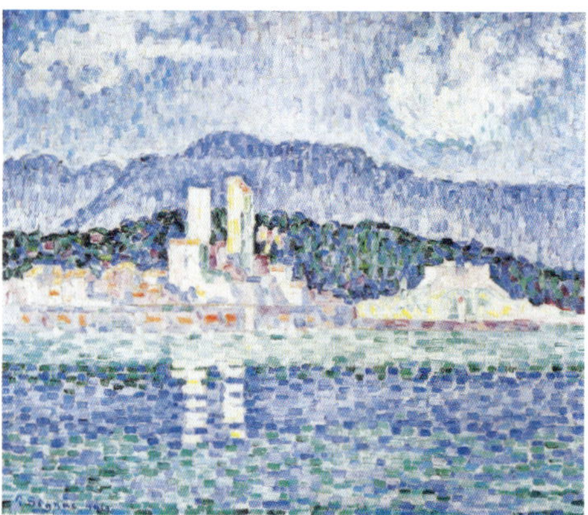

Paul Signac, *Antibes, thunderstorm*, 1919, oil on canvas, 46 x 55 cm, Albertina Museum, Vienna

was ordered to find a solution as quickly as possible. Looking for a possible answer, Thénard turned to the obvious basics: the blue of smalt based on cobalt ore. The source for the warm blues in both ceramics and glass. By making a chemically identical mixture and adding aluminium, Thénard created the long-sought alternative for natural ultramarine much faster than expected.
The production costs were higher than those of Prussian blue, but cobalt blue was still seventy times less expensive than natural ultramarine. Even today, there is no such thing as a cheap cobalt blue.
At last, painters could ignore the somewhat greenish azurite and the cool Prussian blue. As a result, the colour temperature in Western painting rose again. It facilitated the development of the Impressionist colour scheme, which became the basis for a different approach to the perception of colour – perfect for a new take on landscape painting.
Research into the various cobalt blues employed in Van Gogh's work revealed that only cobalt ore from Tunaberg in Sweden produces the much-coveted bright blue because it contains the least impurities. The quantity necessary for artists' paint is minimal. The vast majority disappears in industry, with the colossal grain silos in the United States as probably its most overwhelming example.

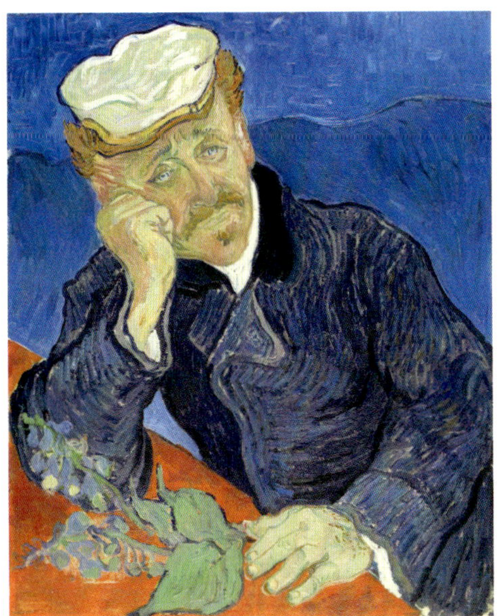

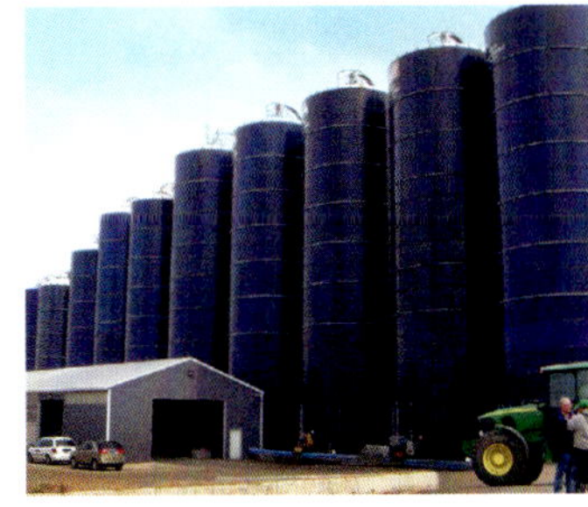

Enamelled cobalt blue Harvestore silos in the US

Vincent van Gogh, *Portrait of Dr. Gachet*, 1890, oil on canvas, 67 x 56 cm, Musée d'Orsay, Paris

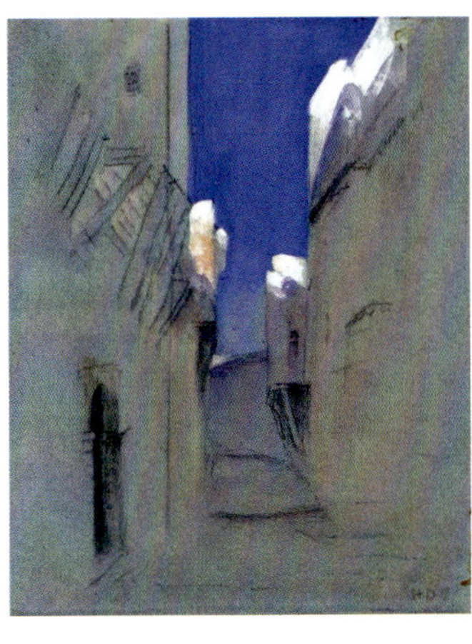

Hercules Brabazon, *Street scene in Egypt*, drawing with gouache, 28 x 22 cm, British Museum, London

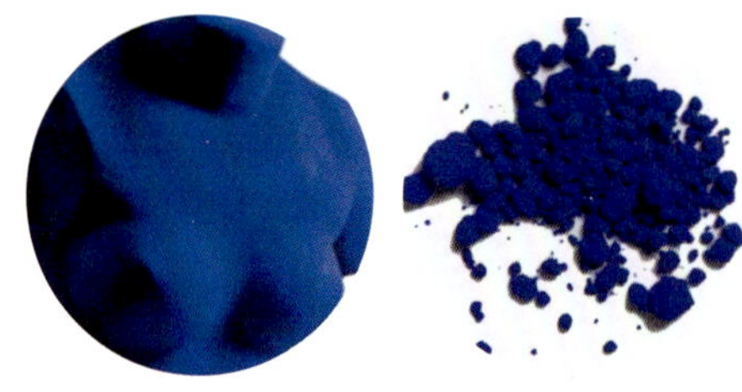

Ultramarine

A marriage is partly responsible for our current overabundance of ultramarine. In 1824, chemist Jean Baptiste Guimet wed Rosalie Bidauld, a painter and the daughter of an artist. Their alliance greatly influenced Guimet's view on pigments. He experienced first-hand how paint and colour determine the 'chemistry' on the palette and what causes restrictions. Including the everlasting lack of a warm blue.

Because of that shortage and the growing knowledge regarding the manufacturing of synthetic pigments, the *Société d'Encouragement pour l'Industrie Nationale de France* set up a targeted competition in 1824. The challenge was to develop a method that would allow large-scale production of synthetic ultramarine, with a retail price of no more than 300 francs per kilogram.

Guimet enters the contest. His experience as a pigment manufacturer, combined with his knowledge of chemistry and professional literature, proved to be a beneficial combination. By October 1826, he already produces the first samples of ultramarine. As there are no real competitors, he decides to refine the process further. Upon achieving the quality pigment he envisages, Guimet asked a few artists to test the paint. In July 1827, his ultramarine is on the palette of Ingres,

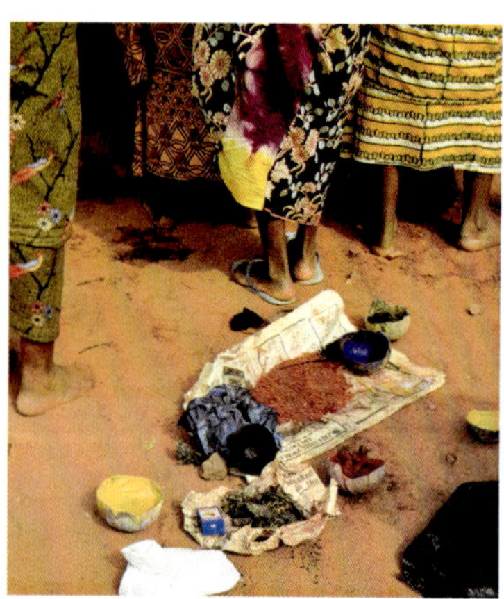

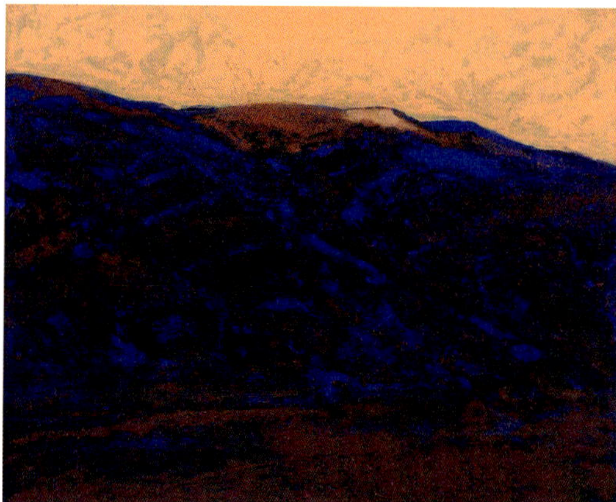

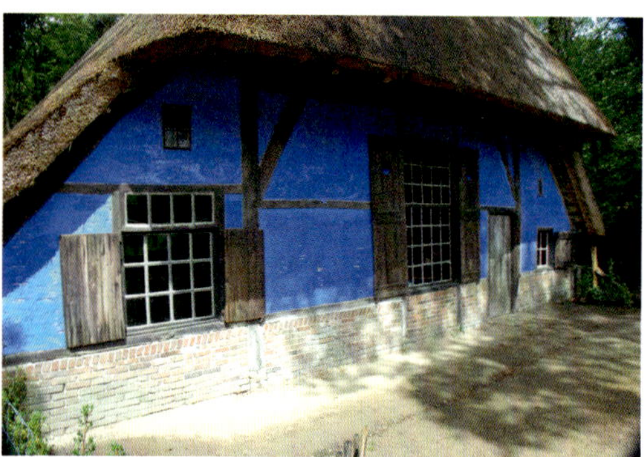

A group of Ibo women decorating the walls of a local temple, with, below, a packet of bluewash, Nri, Nigeria

monica rotgans, *Rising Light*, 2019, relief painting with ultramarine, hematite, ochre and acrylic paint on panel, 50 x 40 cm, artist's collection

Harreveld Farmhouse with blued walls, Nederlands Openluchtmuseum

among others, and in February 1828, Guimet reports to the institute with his ultramarine in hand.
After examination of the chemical components, production possibilities, and the opinions of the test painters, Guimet is awarded the prize.
A German chemist viciously disputes Guimet's victory, but his protests are to no avail and do not prevent the new ultramarine from being marketed as 'Ultramarine Guimet'.

Thus, thanks to the initiative of a competition, forty years on, the impressionists would be scolded as 'those blue painters', by a public accustomed to earth colours and yellowed varnish. They were shocked by what they considered the blinding quantities of ultramarine and cobalt.
Ultramarine manufacturing skyrocketed when it began to replace cobalt in the production of white paper. Sales rose further with the emergence of the professional laundry industry, in this case, services specialising in washing white goods. They employed the optical trick we can also use at home by adding Reckitt's blue or a related bluewash to white laundry.
The power of pure, high-quality ultramarine is astonishing. Yves Klein used it extensively, in combination with a special binding medium to preserve its intensity and brilliance. I achieved the same effect in my 'earth' panels. In *Rising Light*, I combined pure ultramarine pigment with natural haematite.
Ultramarine is the proof that blue is not synonymous with cool. An everlasting misunderstanding causing blue to be wrongly presented as a cool colour in colour theories.

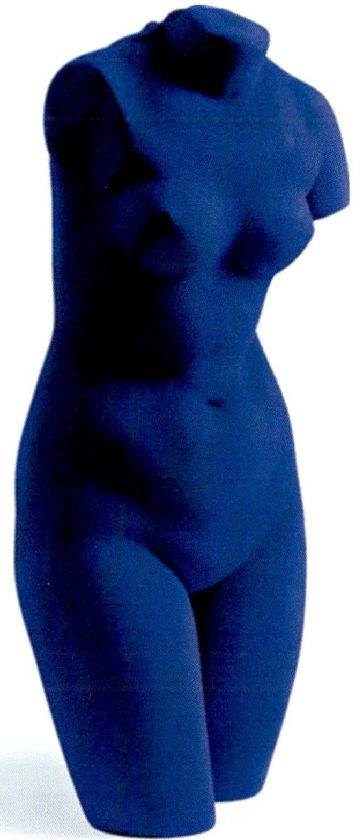

Yves Klein, *Venus Blue*, c. 1961, painted plaster, h. 67 cm, Metropolitan Museum of Art, New York

Sulka hemlaut mask, Bismarck Archipelago, h. 75 cm, Wereldmuseum, Rotterdam

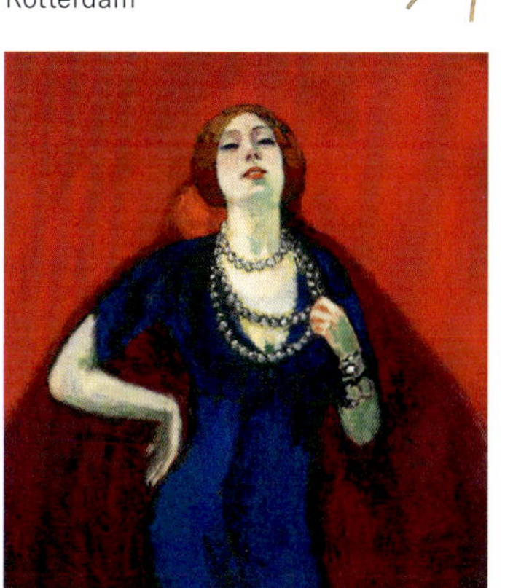

Kees van Dongen, *Portrait of Guus Preitinger*, 1910, oil on canvas, 146 x 114 cm, Van Gogh Museum, Amsterdam

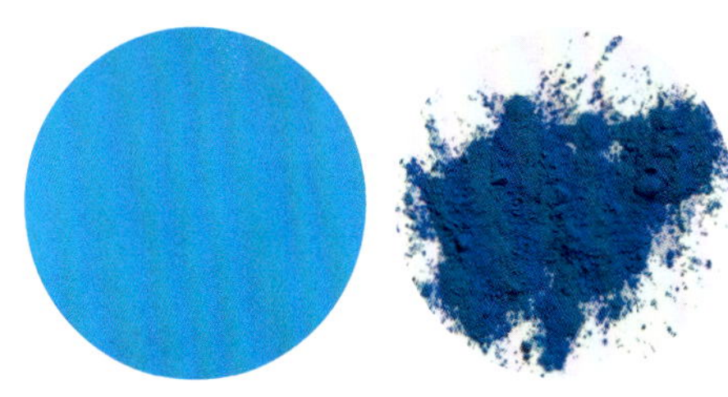

Manganese Blue

Ice blue. The coolest light blue the chemical industry can produce. It's better known as pool blue, that almost luminous blue that suggests paradise with tropical seas and palm trees. We know it thanks to Hollywood movies, basically the birthplace of the modern, luxury, private swimming pool. Tinting the cement for pools is one of the most popular uses of manganese blue in architecture, hence its moniker cement blue.

This will be a short chapter on the extremely short life of a colour unlike any other. In 1907, German chemist Bong developed the pigment basis, which was enhanced by IG Farben around 1935. After that, its production as an artist's paint took off. Lefranc introduced it in 1938 as a new pigment in its assortment under the name *bleu azural*, followed by the other paint manufacturers.

By 1970, production had already been phased out due to the high costs and environmental and health risks. Contact with the pigment via inhalation, the skin, or swallowing dried dust can have serious and negative effects on the nervous system. Manufacturers naturally searched for a less hazardous alternative. An imitation manganese was developed with the harmless, greenish phtalo as its base. Even though it comes close, it misses the intensity of the original pigment.

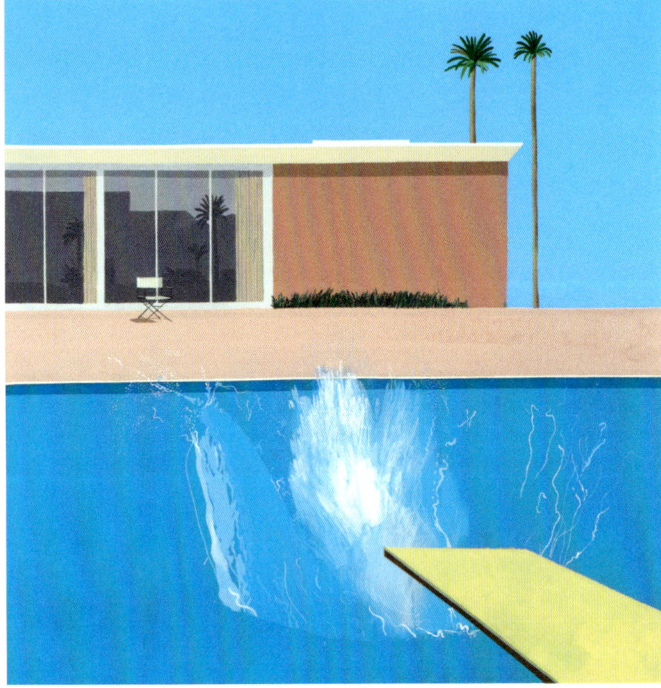

David Hockney, *A Bigger Splash*, 1967, acrylic paint on canvas, 242.5 x 243.9 cm, Tate Britain, London

Some paint manufacturers can still offer the original pigment from remaining stocks, under the motto "last chance!". As with cobalt blue, the price tells you whether you are dealing with the real thing: cheap original manganese blue pigment does not exist.

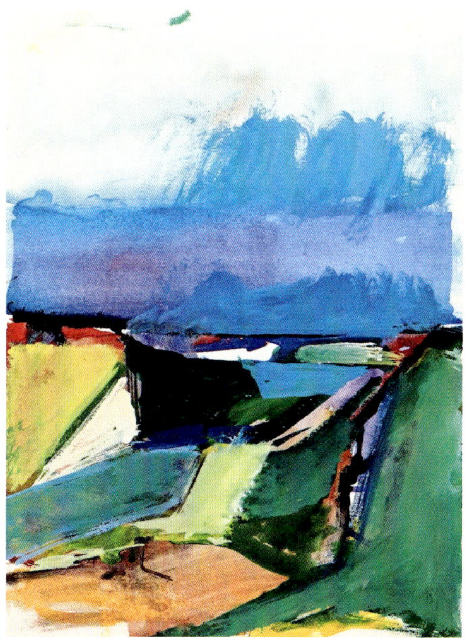

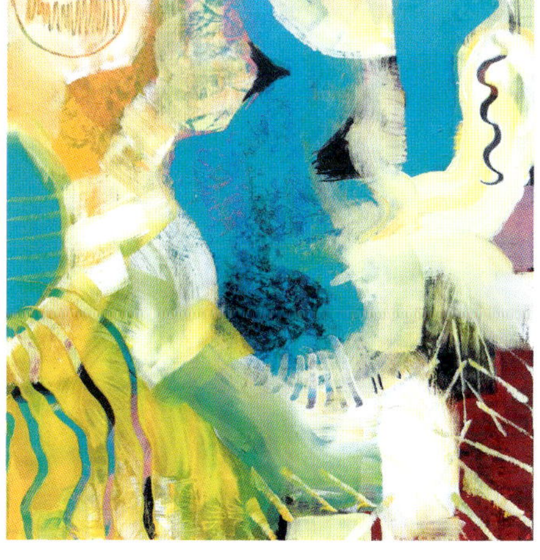

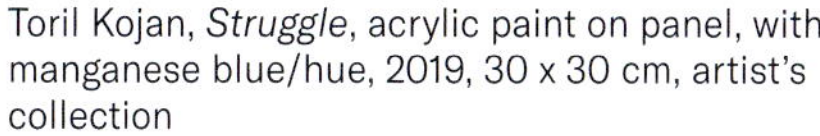

Toril Kojan, *Struggle*, acrylic paint on panel, with manganese blue/hue, 2019, 30 x 30 cm, artist's collection

Richard Diebenkorn, *Untitled*, from sketchbook #10, p. 13, gouache and watercolour on paper with artificial manganese blue, 2nd half 20th cen., Kantor Arts Center, Stanford

monica rotgans, *Breathless*, 2020, manganese pigment, natural ochres and acrylic paint on panel, 60 x 30 cm, artist's collection

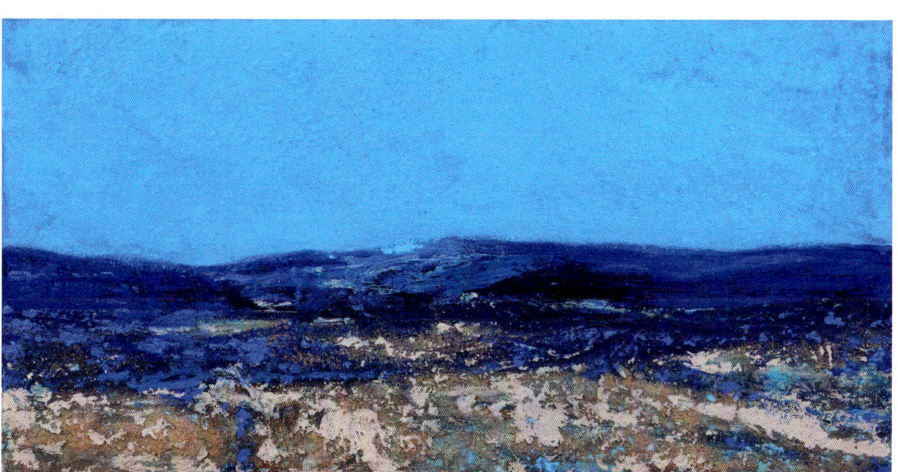

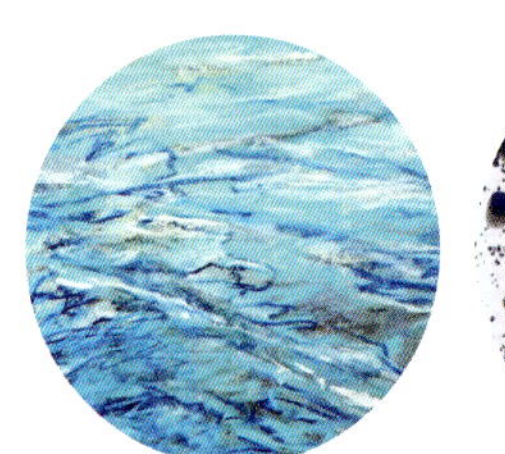

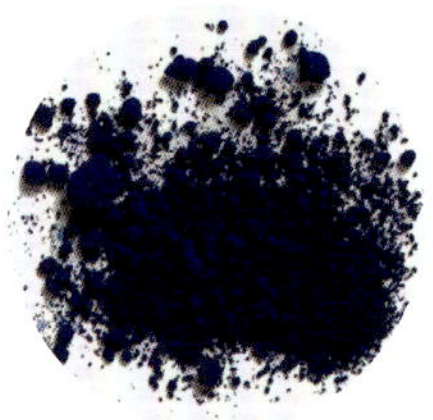

Phthalo Blue

Officially, phthalocyanine blue. A blue with countless aliases, including English and blood blue. The latter refers to the structure of the pigment, which resembles that of red blood cells. For anyone who paints, the term 'blood' is a stark reminder: beware of the infamous bleeding!

The pigment's colour and characteristics are very similar to Prussian blue. It is just as popular and just as risky.

Its popularity is mainly due to its captivating colour depth. Phtalo is very appealing to the eye. It is available in various hues, ranging from reddish to greenish, with seemingly unlimited possibilities.
To give an idea of the strength of that bleeding: if you paint a line on a wall with phthalo blue and apply a solid layer of cement over it, over time you will see that line emerge through the cement. The same happens with an underdrawing or underpainting executed with phthalo. When you put your brush down, the painting will look good. But soon, blue lines will begin to shine through, progressively becoming more obtrusive. And like Prussian blue, it tends to bleed into and darken the surrounding areas of colour. Again, it is a pigment discovered by accident. The name English blue refers to the site of this 1928 discovery at the

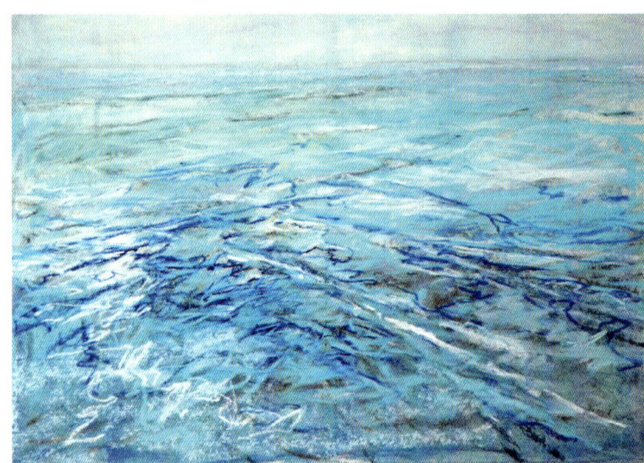

Lex Goes, *Kust (Shore)*, 2022, pastel, 35 x 49 cm, artist's collection

monica rotgans, *Deep Blue Surf*, 2010, oil on canvas, 140 x 60 cm, artist's collection

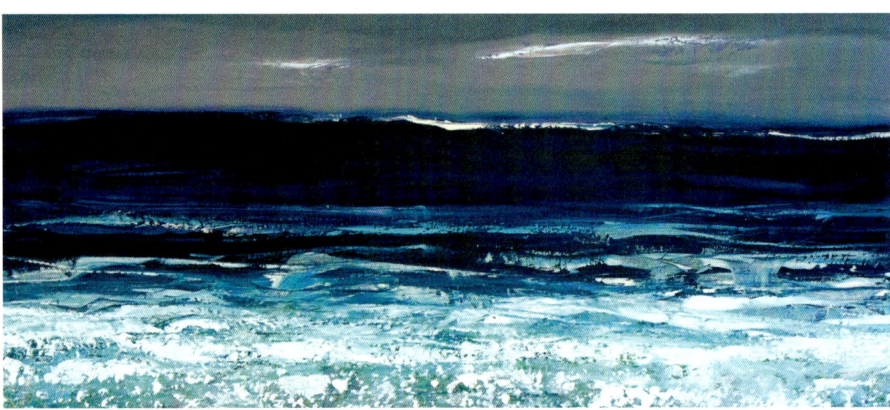

Scottish Dyes Ltd. in Grangemouth, England. During the production of white phthalimide, a bluish discolouration appeared in one of the kettles. It was revealed that a piece of enamel had broken off, which caused the raw material to turn blue through direct contact with the iron. It took another seven years before the commercial production of this new blue began. These days, phthalo blue has almost completely replaced the once-popular Prussian blue. In terms of convenience, Phthalo blue easily beats its three predecessors, cobalt blue, synthetic ultramarine and Prussian blue, due to its great resistance to acids and heat.

After World War II, phthalo blue became the leading pigment in art, house and school paints. Since the 1990s, the greenish variant has been used as a substitute for the toxic manganese blue. Phthalo blue is, therefore, abundantly present in post-1950 painting. If you pay attention, you can always see it around you in one form or another. Not only as a paint, but also in printer inks, textiles, car paints and plastics. It is the basis for imitation indigo and known as cyan in the graphic world.

Additionally, like many pigments, it is employed in the medical industry as a dye and as a medicine. Phthalocyanine is used as a photodynamic agent to combat tumours in cancer therapies.

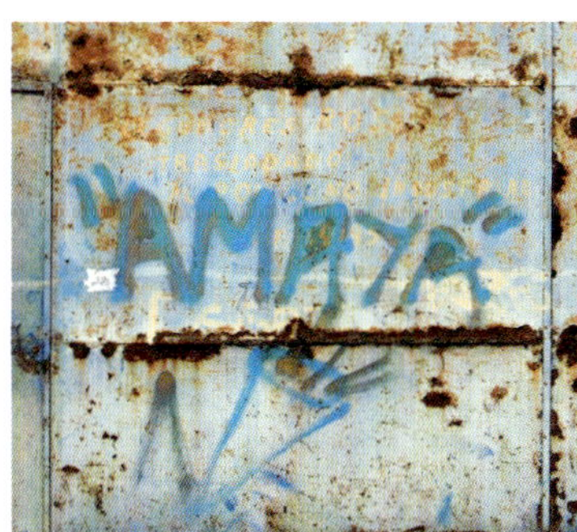

Graffiti, Crete

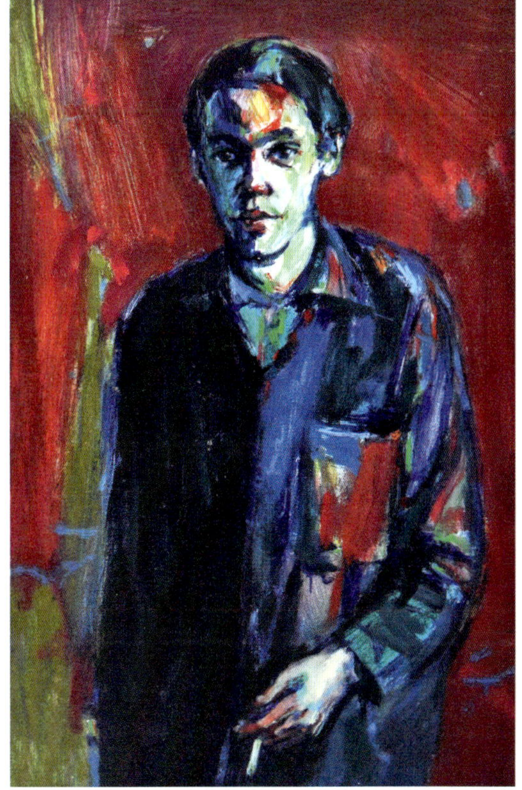

Norbert Olthuis, *Reinhardt Priesnit*, 1963, oil on canvas, 90 x 60 cm, private collection

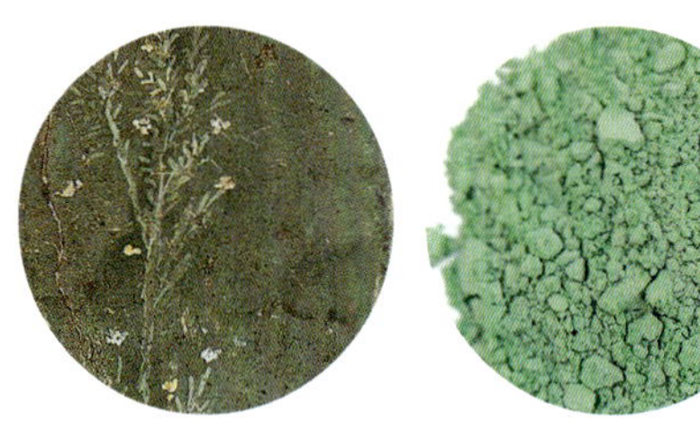

Green Earth

Green earth is the collective name for various minerals, of which celadonite and glauconite are the best known. There is no single green earth, its colour ranges from warm olive to a cool blue-green.

Green earth belongs to the ancient paints, but little is known about its use on the different continents. In India, the paintings in the Ajantâ caves are among the scarce examples found in non-Western painting. In Europe, Bohemian green from Germany and Veronese green are the best known. The latter was found near Lake Garda in Italy and marketed via Verona, hence the name.

It is a stable and almost indestructible pigment, making it easily recognisable in ancient murals even after hundreds of years. Through burning or heating, you can produce various soft browns.

Green earth has somehow become the ugly duckling among the greens: modest, transparent, and, best known as a tool to enhance other colours. It is a reliable and inexpensive alternative to the more bluish copper greens.

Once you know, you will recognise it in many old paintings. For example, green earth is evident in works by Vermeer, who employed it for the shadows in his figures and interiors.

Thus, he joins a long tradition that began, long before 1 AD. The same tradition from

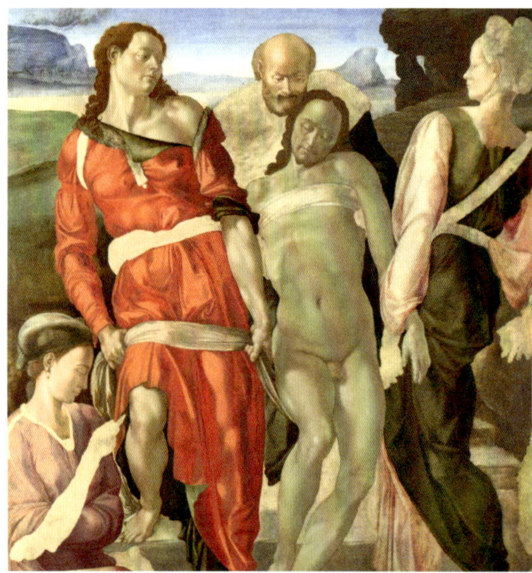

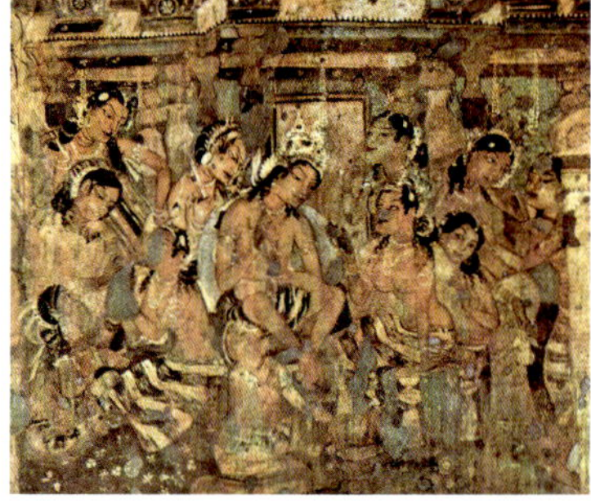

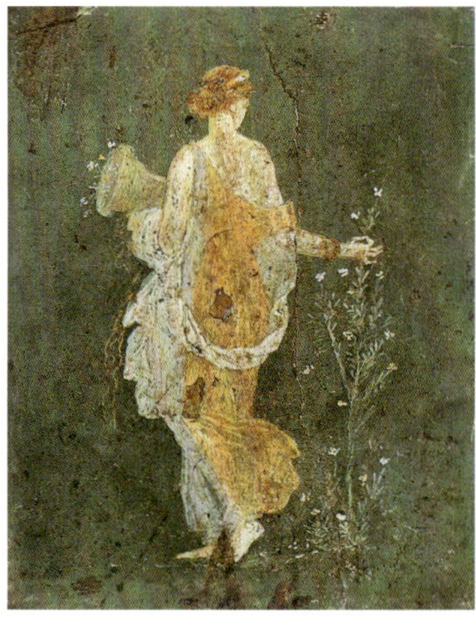

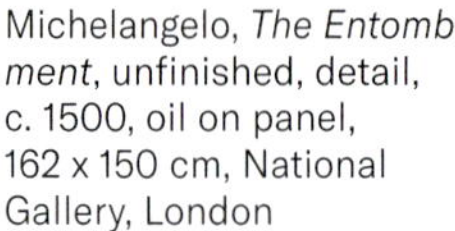

Michelangelo, *The Entombment*, unfinished, detail, c. 1500, oil on panel, 162 x 150 cm, National Gallery, London

Master of Mahâjanaka Jâtaka, wall painting, 7th cen., Ajanta caves, present-day Maharashtra, India

Primavera di Stabiae, 1st cen., 38 x 32 cm, fresco from Villa Arianna, Museo Archeologico Nazionale, Naples

which originated the icon painters, who used (and still use) the same system for their classical panels. Thanks to excavations, we know that muralists around the Mediterranean and in the Middle East likewise had green earth as a standard colour on their palettes. Little jars with celadonite and green serpentine have been found in Greek Delos and in the remains of a painter's workshop in Pompeii.

As in neighbouring Herculaneum, it hasa prominent place in the abundant wall decorations.

From the Roman palette, it entered, without interruption, the workshops of medieval painters. It became the effective underpainting and shade for the incarnate, the white and reddish skin colour. From this period, the term *verdaccio* originates, the name for a green underpainting.

The dead body features prominently in Christian art – just think of the many pictures of the crucifixion. This forced painters to depict the difference between dead and living skin convincingly. As Michelangelo shows, green earth is particularly suited for this.

The optical disappearance of the skin colour through aging and thinning, especially of the lead, is the cause for the sometimes almost uniformly green faces of Holy Virgins and saints. In these examples, the green earth changed from being an underpainting to the dominant colour.

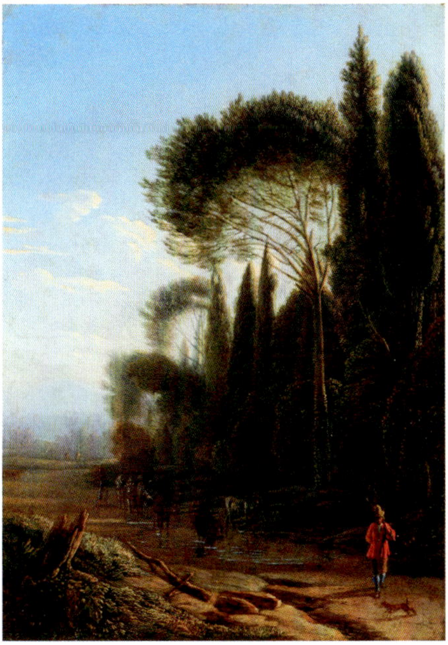

Jan Willemsz Lapp, *Italianate Landscape*, c. 1680, oil on copper, Mauritshuis, The Hague

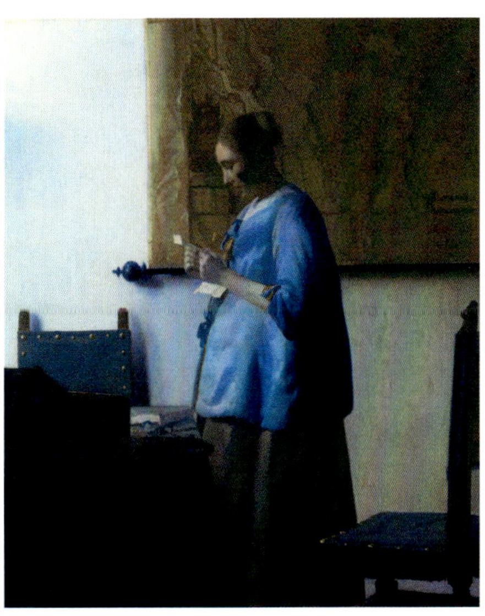

Johannes Vermeer, *Woman Reading a Letter*, c. 1663, oil on canvas, 46.5 x 39 cm Rijksmuseum, Amsterdam

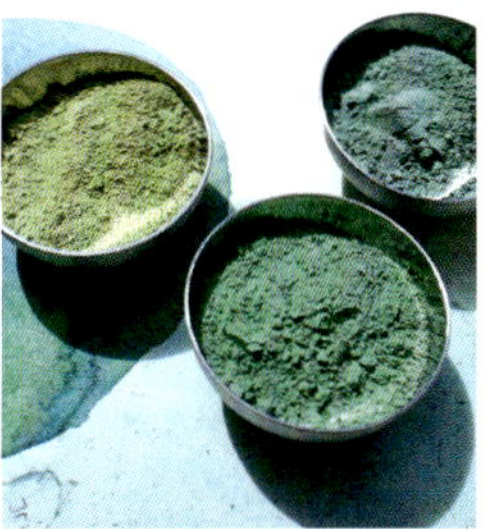

Warm Bohemian earth and cool Verona green and the colours that can be made with them

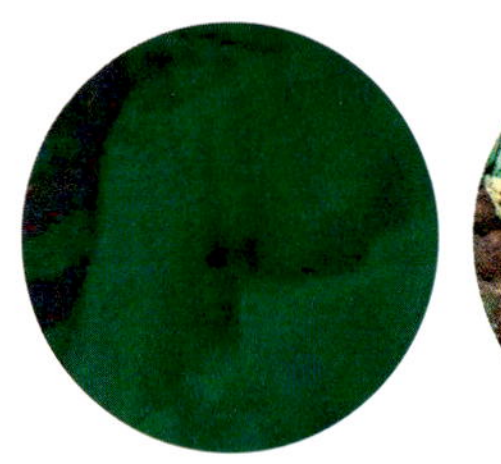

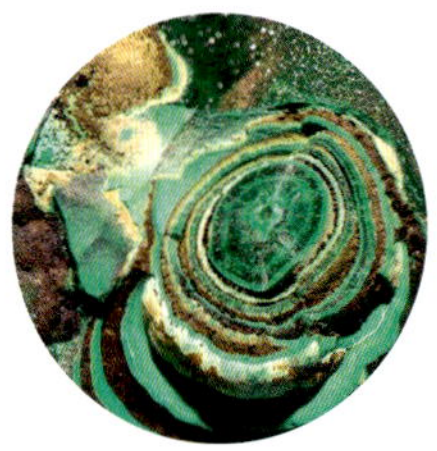

Malachite

The Venus or midwife's stone. As a stone and a colour, it was and still is the symbol of fertility and new life in several cultures.

Malachite and azurite, the other ancient copper pigment, are similar in chemical composition and are often found together. The name sounds classic but only became standard in the 17th century, slowly but surely replacing its many former aliases. Malachite is a semi-precious stone and has long been considered one of the precious pigments, for which a customer could be charged extra.

Like azurite, it is a global colour available on all continents. It can be found in most mountainous regions in Europe, with the Urals being the source of the famous Russian Romanov malachite. It is the raw material for the imposing and often metres-high decorations and adornments in the interiors of the Kremlin in Moscow and the Hermitage in St Petersburg. A colour of status. Today, the main deposits are in the so-called copper belt of Africa, the southern United States, Central America, Asia and Australia.

Large parts of the world are covered with green forests and fields, but as a pigment, green is a rarity. For thousands of years, malachite was the only source for a pure, deep green. That's why, in old paintings, it stands out immediately because its tinting strength is much stronger than

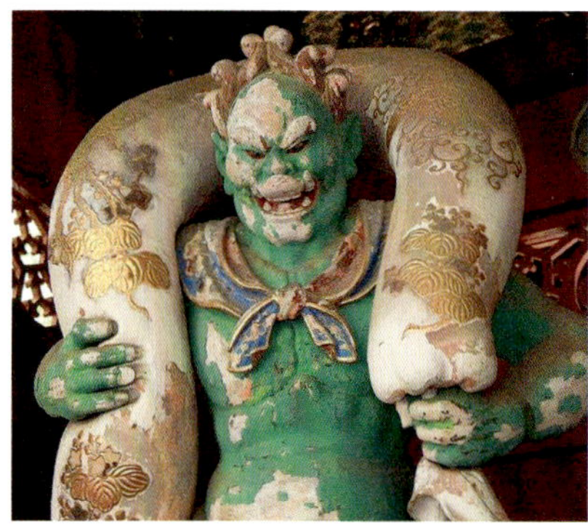

Statue of Fūjin, the god of the wind, Nikko, Japan

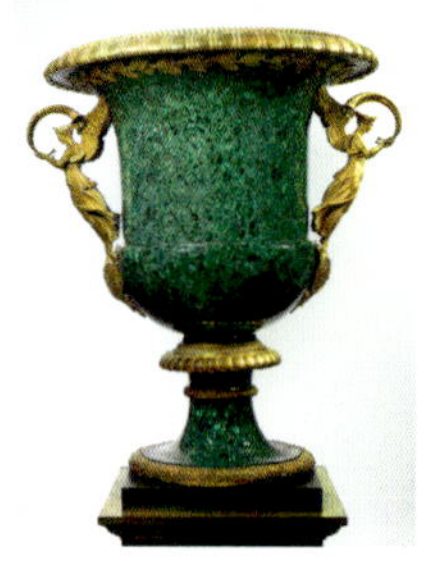

Monumental Vase, Italian/French, 19th cen., Russian malachite, gilt-bronze mounts, Metropolitan Museum of Art, New York

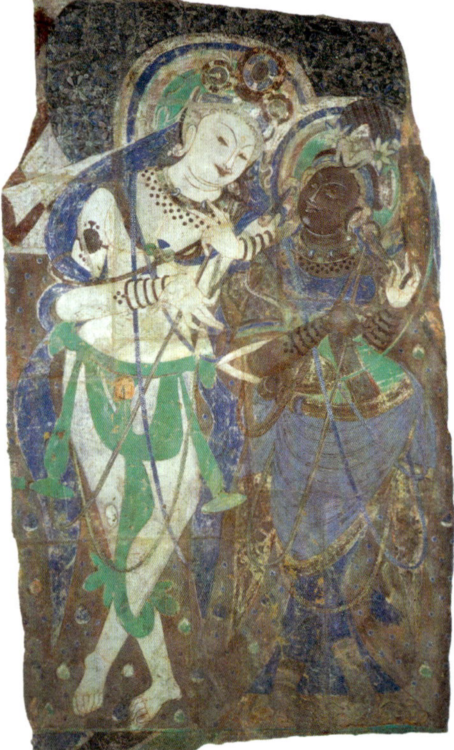

Cave painting, Kizil (China), 400-800 AD, malachite, azurite and lapis lazuli, Dahlem Museum, Berlin

that of the subtle green earths or the opaque Egyptian green.

The illustrations make it evident how old and widespread the use of malachite is. As paint, medicine and make-up, it has been combined with multitudes of binding mediums, including, egg white, gum, resin, oil and beeswax. To maintain its colour strength, a fine grind must be avoided, as the finer the grain, the less vibrant the colour. This graininess makes it easily recognisable in paintings. When blended with lime, it remains bright green in a fresco, but it darkens significantly if mixed with linseed oil and can even turn completely brown.

In pre-Columbian America, malachite was not only used as a pigment but also as a raw material for other decorative purposes such as (as a part of) sculptures and even inlays for teeth.

In Europe, it figures prominently in 15th and 16th-century painting. This might have something to do with the fact that the transparent malachite green works so well on a white ground, as is obvious in Bronzino's portrait. In contrast, on coloured grounds, which became more *en vogue* from the 16th century onwards, it loses clarity and power. Malachite briefly returned as a painting pigment in the 19th century. Renoir's flower still-life, painted on a bright white gesso ground, is a fine example.

Malachite is still used in Asia and is available at paint shops in the three basic hues and the different grain sizes.

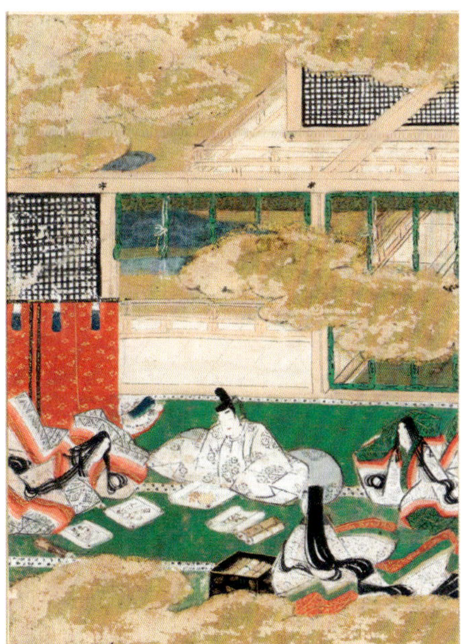

Tosa Mitsunobu, *The Picture Contest (Eawase)*, illustration to Chapter 17 of the Tale of Genji, c. 1510, 24.3 x 18.1 cm, ink on paper, Harvard Art Museums

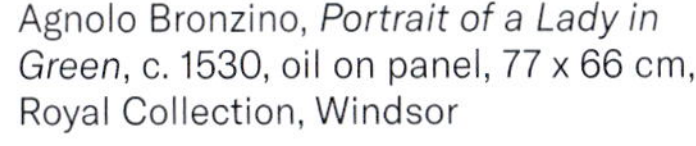

Agnolo Bronzino, *Portrait of a Lady in Green*, c. 1530, oil on panel, 77 x 66 cm, Royal Collection, Windsor

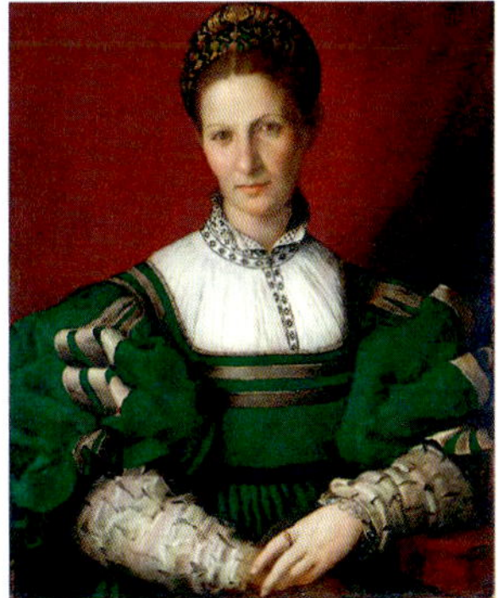

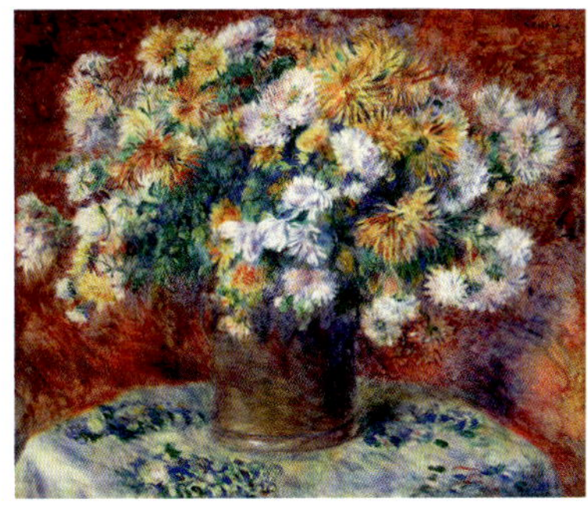

Pierre Auguste Renoir, *Chrysanthemums*, 1881-1882, oil on canvas, 55 x 66 cm, Art Institute of Chicago

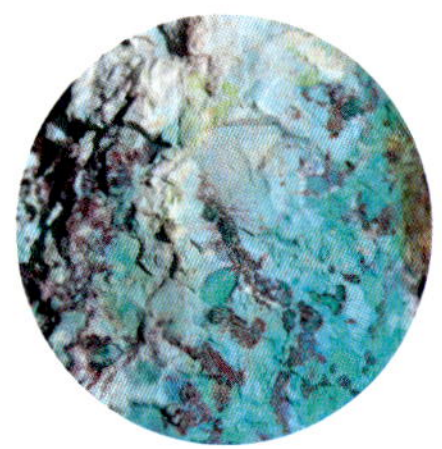

Verdigris

The other copper green, based on copper ore. An easy to make, cool, blue-green pigment. It belongs to the oldest, man-made, pigments. Because of its age and use almost everywhere, it has had a string of aliases, with the name verdigris 'only' in use for about six hundred years.

The term *Verd-de-gris* appeared in Europe in the 14th century and is a corruption of the Old French *vertegrez*, *vert-de-Grèce*, i.e. literally meaning green from Greece. Not the country as we know it today, but the region that was part of the former Eastern Roman or Byzantine Empire, with its capital Constantinople, where verdigris was a common paint and ink. Verdigris is an important medicine and pigment. Like anything made with copper, it kills bacteria and has been used since immemorial time for wood protection.

You cannot overlook it in museums that display art up to the 19th century. It is that strange cool blue-green or dark brown in landscapes and floral still-lifes. The basis for what once was a beautiful, true-to-nature warm green, of which little remains today. This is mainly due to how the painter composed the green. Two methods were employed to turn verdigris into a natural green: a yellow glaze or adding oil. For the glaze, a transparent, warm yellow was laid over the cool verdigris. The yellows used were rarely lightfast and

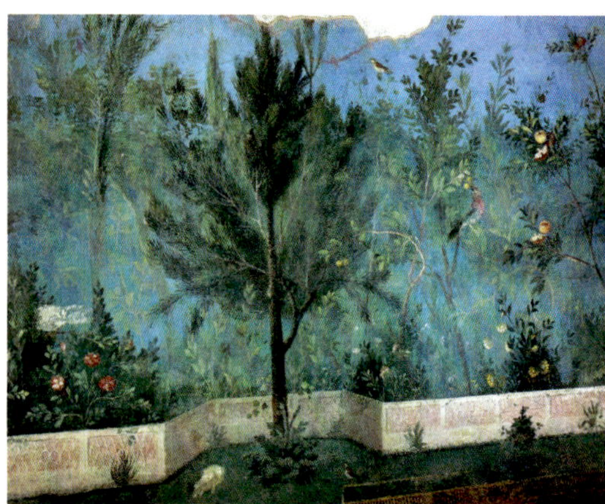

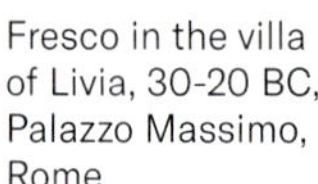

Fresco in the villa of Livia, 30-20 BC, Palazzo Massimo, Rome

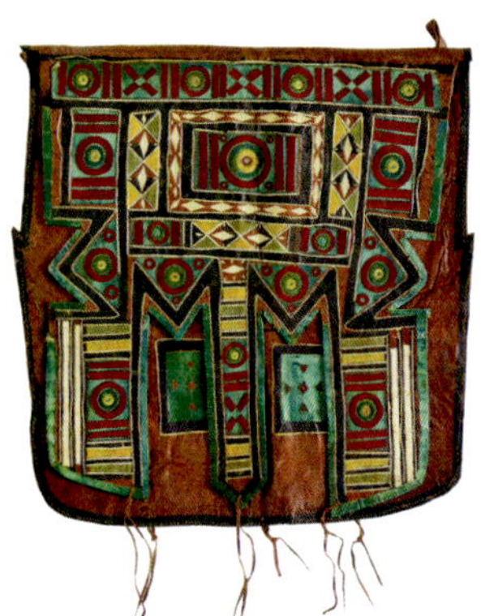

Eljebira saddlebag, Tuareg peoples, Agadez, Niger, early 20th cen., goatskin, silk, Verdigris and other pigments, 70 x 58 x 3 cm, Musée du Quai Branly, Paris

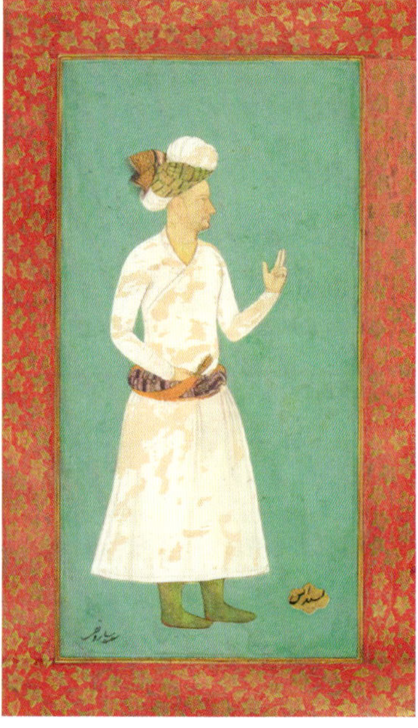

Bishandas, *Saru Taqi, a Safavid courtier*, c. 1618, watercolour, ink and gold on paper, 21.6 x 14.3 cm, Smithsonian's National Museum of Asian Art, Washington D.C.

vanished with time (see Stil de grain yellow). The other method is adding additional yellow linseed oil. This gives a magnificent, full effect when freshly applied, but is short-lived. Linseed oil turns brown as it dries, changing green into autumnal browns. With the apparent result that quite a few painters had a preference for depicting autumn scenes. As Leonardo da Vinci noted: 'the beauty of verdigris vanishes like snow in the sun if it is not varnished immediately.'
The work of Jan van Eyck and his colleagues proves that it can be done differently. Here, the warm greens were able to withstand the test of time because the verdigris, including the glaze, was isolated immediately upon application. Verdigris is easily made by oxidising copper plates for several months with an acid such as wine vinegar, urine or manure. The same green is then created that develops naturally through oxidation or acid rain on copper towers, roofs, bronze statues and, for example, at home, on brass candlesticks.
From the 17th century onwards, commercial production of verdigris increased considerably, and recipes for 'home-made' verdigris vanished from painting manuals and the artists' workshops. After the introduction of Prussian blue, the cheaper blending pigment for mixing greens in the 18th century, and the 'new' greens of the 19th century, verdigris fell into disuse in the visual arts.

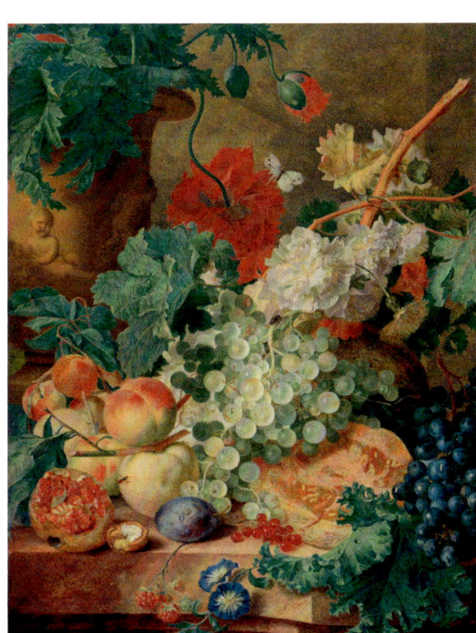

Jan van Huysum, *Still-Life with Flowers and Fruit*, c. 1721, oil on panel, 81 x 61 cm, Rijksmuseum, Amsterdam

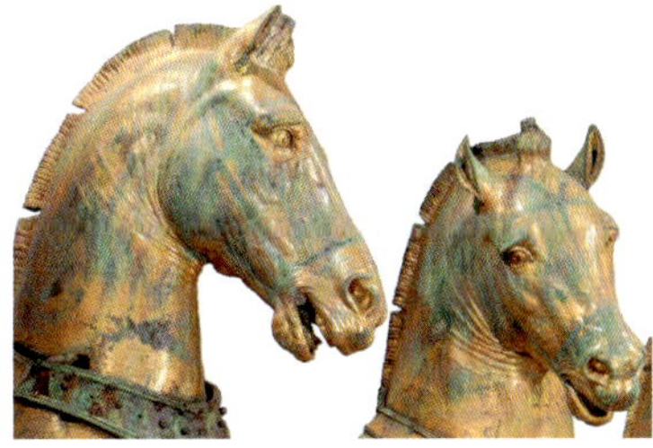

Horses of Basilica San Marco, gilt-bronze, h. c. 230 cm, Venice

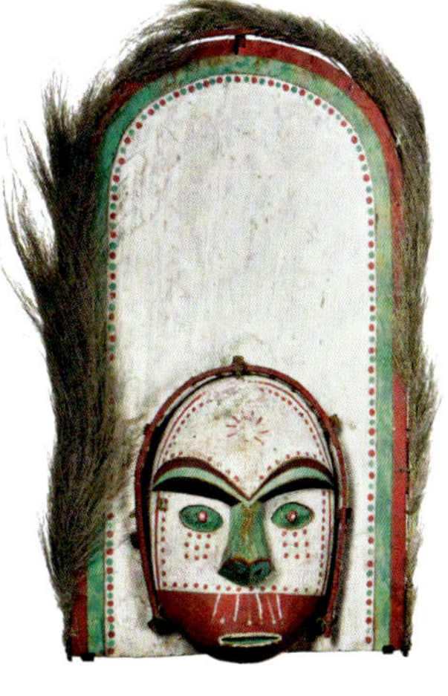

Alutiiq mask, Native American, Kodiak Island, Alaska, 19th cen., reindeer hide, wood and pigment, 44 x 25 x 10 cm, Musée du Quai Branly, Paris

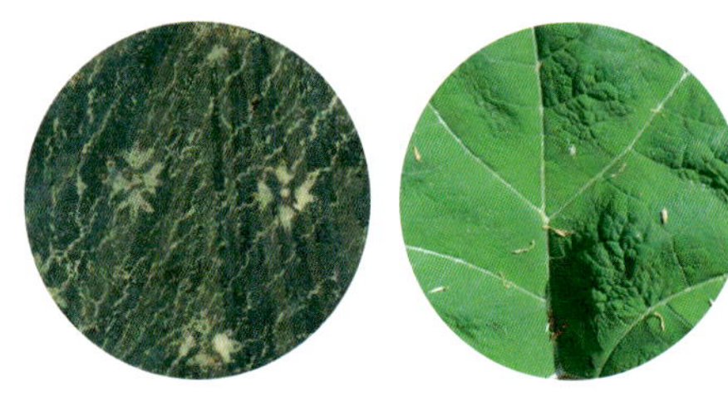

Plant Green & Sap Greens

Wild plants are the most common source of green paint. They can be found in most climate zones, where they can be harvested everywhere for free. Why would such abundant greenery not deliver a great paint? In this case, appearances can be deceiving.

However dazzling and brilliant fresh sap greens may seem on a white surface, they can quickly fade or become an undetermined colour once exposed to oxygen or moisture. This is neither effective nor desirable, especially when an exclusive and luxurious colour of status is required to convey how much wealth has been invested. This applies to both painters and textile dyers.

Still, sap greens are ranked among the traditional, historical dyes because, for a long time, the finer and more expensive green pigments were far from available to all. To make sap greens, people used what grew and flourished locally. This could vary from (unripe) berries, raw coffee beans and conifer needles, to herbs, vegetables (spinach, for example), reeds, flowers and leaves.

It was used to dye textiles but was also employed for painting and script by turning it into watercolour and ink.

The preparation was simple: the plants were dried, pulverised, sifted, and, if

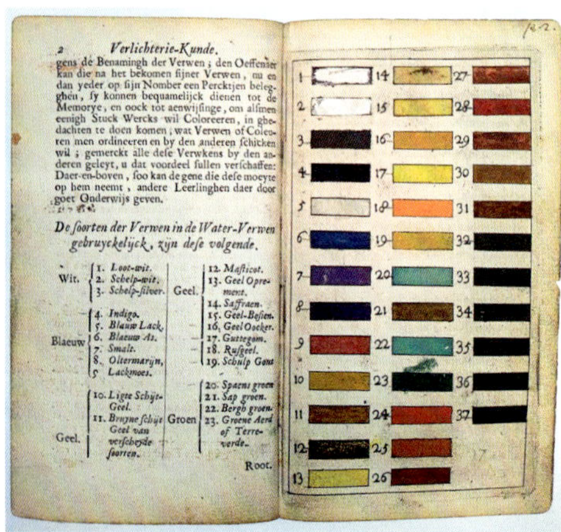

2 *Verlichterie-Kunde.*

gens de Benamingh der Verwen; den Oeffenaer kan die na het bekomen fijner Verwen, nu en dan yeder op sijn Nomber een Percktjen beleggheu, sy konnen bequamelijck dienen tot de Memorye, en oock tot aenwijsinge, om alsmen eenigh Stuck Wercks wil Coloreeren, in ghedachten te doen komen; wat Verwen of Coleuren men ordineeren en by den anderen schicken wil; gemerckt alle dese Verwkens by den anderen geleyt, u dat voordeel sullen verschaffen: Daer-en-boven, soo kan de gene die dese moeyte op hem neemt, andere Leerlinghen daer door goet Onderwijs geven.

De soorten der Verwen in de Water-Verwen gebruyckelijck, zijn dese volgende.

Wit. 1. *Loot-wit.* 2. *Schelp-wit.* 3. *Schelp-silver.*

Blaeuw. 4. *Indigo.* 5. *Blauw Lack.* 6. *Blaeuw As.* 7. *Smalt.* 8. *Oltermaryn.* 9. *Lackmoes.*

Geel. 10. *Ligte Schyt-Geel.* 11. *Bruyne schyt Geel van verscheyde soorten.*

Geel. 12. *Masticot.* 13. *Geel Operment.* 14. *Saffraen.* 15. *Geel-Besien.* 16. *Geel Oocker.* 17. *Guttegom.* 18. *Rusgeel.* 19. *Schulp Gout*

Groen. 20. *Spaens groen* 21. *Sap groen.* 22. *Bergh groen.* 23. *Groene Aerd of Terre-verde.*

Root.

Wilhelmus Goeree, *Verlichterie-kunde, of recht gebruyck der waterverwen*, no. 21 with a browned sap green, 1668

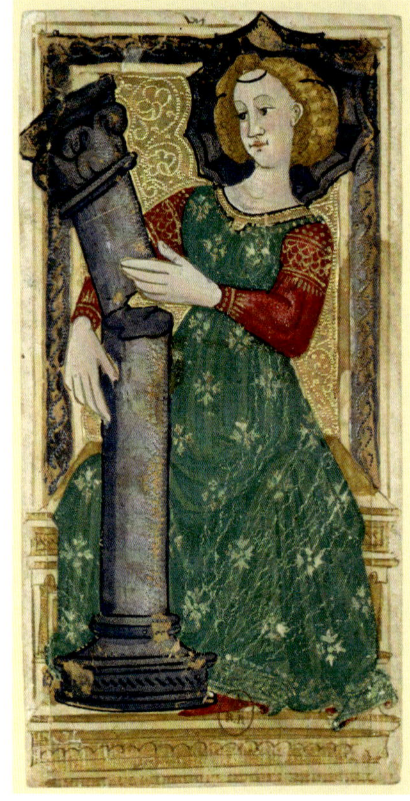

Strength, The 'Charles VI Tarot Cards', late 15th cen., egg tempera on paper, 18 x 9 cm, Bibliothèque Nationale de France, Paris

necessary, boiled with the addition of alum or some other mordant, after which they were ready for use. The ripe berry of buckthorn was, and still is, a favourite in Europe, along with the juice of aloe, lily, leek and various other native plants. It is usually a soft and transparent green, generally employed for darkening and increasing the intensity of greens, as rose madder was utilised for deepening vermilion or red earth. A discoloured sap green may be (partly) to blame in paintings with once vibrant but now browned flora. Sap green watercolour paints are still available for purchase, but it is essential to determine whether it is an organic plant green or a synthetic substitute. For some time, sap green was popular for the colouring of paper.
The growing interest in non-industrial dyes has led more people to look to nature and old pigment recipes to find the raw materials for their handmade paints. For example, the artist Helena Arendt is represented here with her nettle-painting, painted with nettle-green.
Plant green can also be used in an entirely different manner for a work of art. As a living, ever-evolving colour preserved in its original form in the depiction, shown here in Norbert Hinterberger's moss sgraffito piece and Anna Garforth's graffiti.

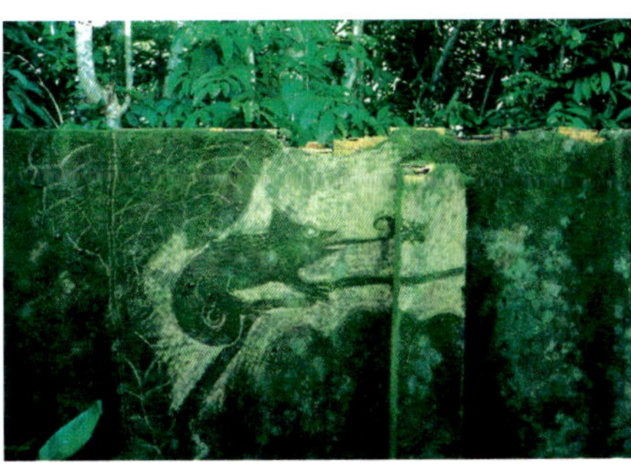

Norbert W. Hinterberger, moss-sgrafitto, Brazil

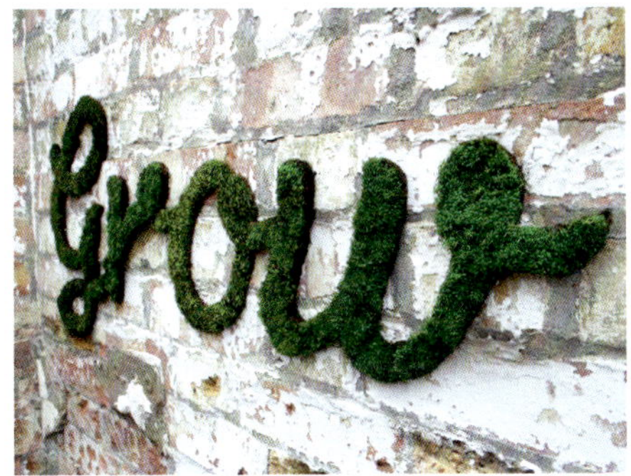

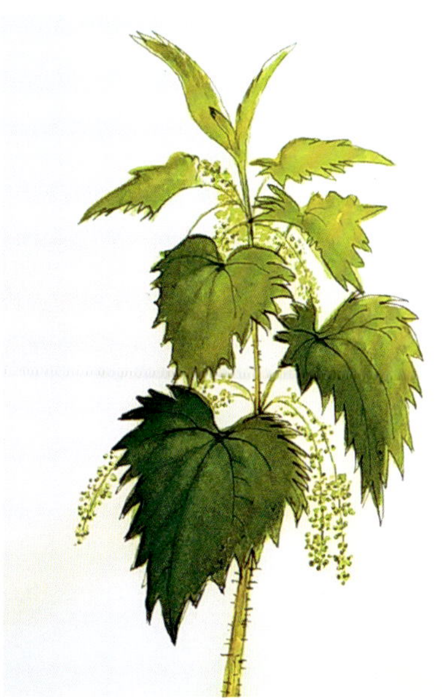

Helena Arendt, *Nettle*, drawing coloured with paint made from nettle

Anna Garforth, *Green graffiti*, moss graffiti, created with a spray based on moss; a mix of moss, beer and sugar that continues to grow after application.

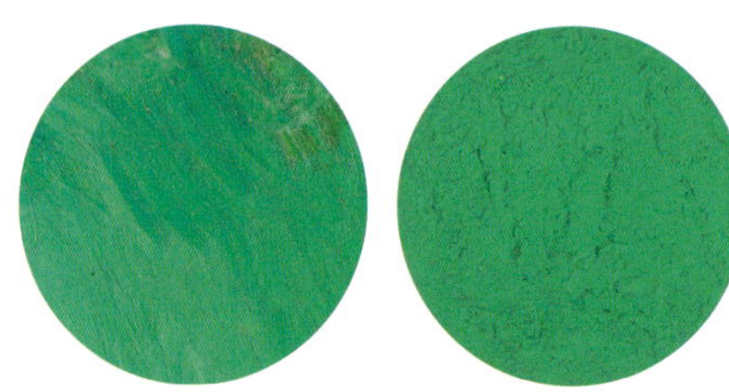

Scheele's Green & Schweinfurter Green

The true poisonous greens, with arsenic as their base. They are, therefore, related to the historical orpiment and realgar. Suitable for horror stories, as there are probably no other pigments that have claimed so many victims in such a short time.

Nevertheless, I can easily imagine an artist ignoring the risk due to the chronic and frustrating lack of bright greens. These are the first intense, opaque greens. Tints that are impossible to make by mixing the blue and yellow pigments available at the time. Scheele's green was developed in the 18th century by the Swede Carl Wilhelm Scheele. It was soon replaced by the better-quality Schweinfurter green, invented by Wilhelm Sattler of Schweinfurt, Germany. Sattler maintained a monopoly on his recipe until 1822, after which others succeeded in copying the procedure.

More and more small factories sprung up, and the colour spread like an inkblot, first across Europe and then to the other continents. Due to the many trade routes, the new, extremely popular emerald green came into the possession of anyone who worked with paints, inks and dyes via the

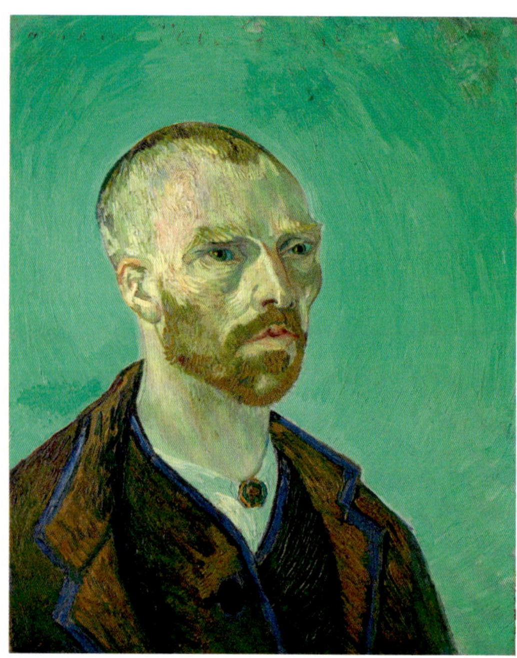

Vincent van Gogh, *Self-Portrait, dedicated to Gauguin*, 1888, oil on canvas, 60 x 49 cm, Fogg Art Museum, Cambridge

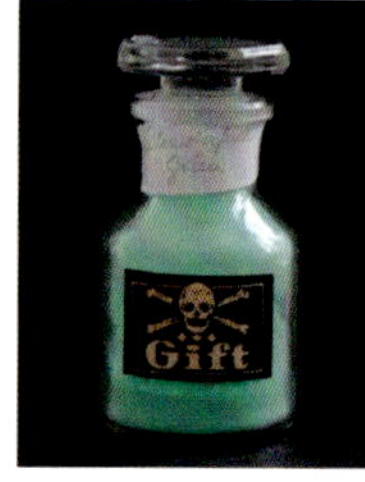

Bottle of Schweinfurter-green pigment

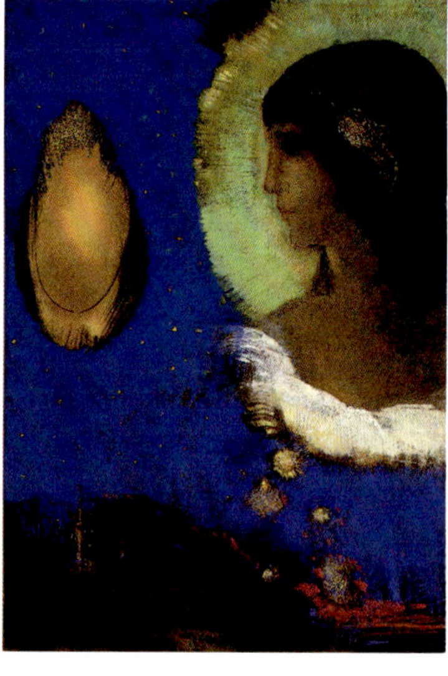

Odilon Redon, *Sita*, c. 1893, pastel over charcoal, 53.6 x 37.7 cm, Art Institute of Chicago

'colourmen' and pigment traders. This journey can be traced through works of art in the Americas, Africa, Oceania and Asia. Due to its high production, Schweinfurter green was not expensive. It was employed by most artists until the 19th century when it was taken out of production as pigment. Turner painted with it as early as around 1830, Constable followed a bit later. It can be found in Manet's *Déjeuner sur l'herbe*, in works by Arnold Böcklin and Vincent van Gogh, to name but a few of its many users. This pure green must have been quite a miracle for the Impressionists and their later colleagues, allowing much more direct and powerful work. Especially in the increasingly popular *en plein air* painting. Yet many, often ghastly, examples can be found showing the consequences of the indifference or ignorance with which the two pigments were handled. Causes of victims' suffering and death included green-dyed sweets, cakes and confectionery, green candles, as well as paper, carpets and rugs, wallpaper, and garments. Additionally, something as simple as a green price tag on a batch of plums at the greengrocer's could cause the poison to seep from the label into the moist fruits.

After its use as a pigment was banned, it was still available as a pesticide and poison control for both winged and wingless pests. It took some time before its effects on humans and the environment became apparent, and its production was completely prohibited.

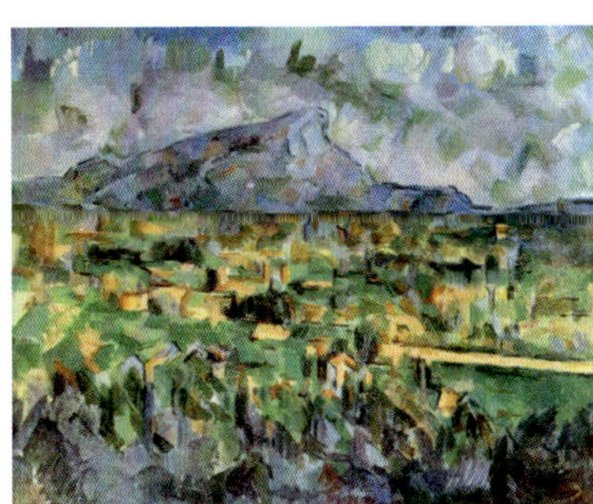

Paul Cézanne, *Mont Sainte-Victoire*, 1902-1904, oil on canvas, 73 x 91.9 cm, Philadelphia Museum of Art

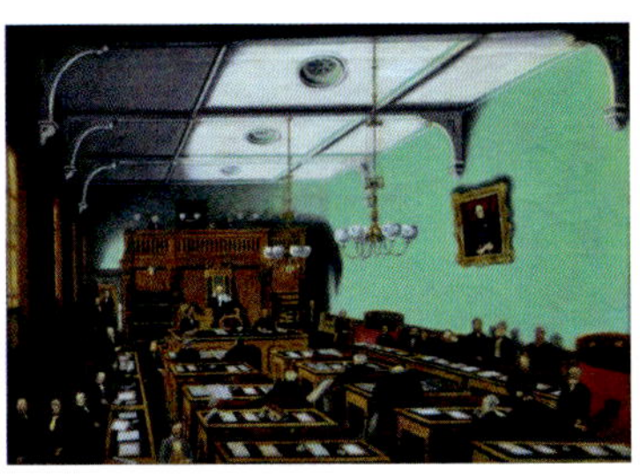

James Shaw, *South Australian Parliament; the House of Assembly*, c. 1867, oil on canvas, 64 x 93 cm, Art Gallery of SA, Adelaide

Gustav Klimt, *Portrait of Amalie Zuckerkandl*, 1917, oil on canvas, 128 x 128 cm, Galerie Belvedère, Vienna

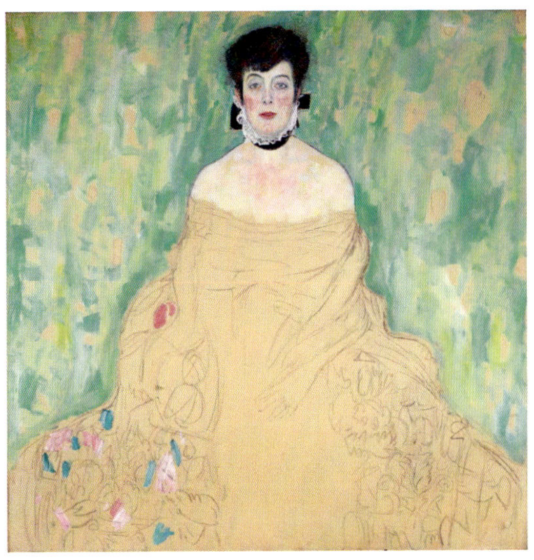

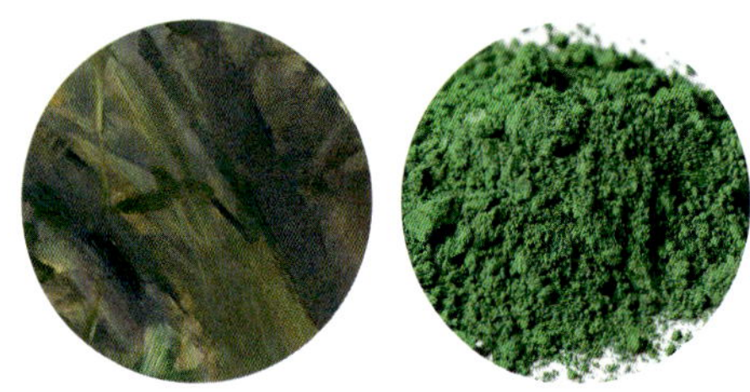

Chromium Oxide Green

Chromium oxide green is the denominator for several soft and opaque greens. All developed and brought on the market in the 19th century.

There are a few chemically slightly different versions, causing some to be more transparent and others the better known opaque dull green. To further complicate matters: what was (and sometimes still is) sold under the name chrome green can actually be a mixture of chrome yellow and Prussian or Phtalo blue. Because of the lead it contains, it is toxic.

Chromium oxide green finally meant a realistic plant green at artists' disposal, for the first time since the dawn of painting. And at the right time, as, in the 19th century, landscape art takes a leading role in painting.

Around 1830, in reaction to the dust-covered policies of the *Salon* and inspired by the work of William Turner and John Constable, a group of young French painters decided to devote themselves to depicting a more realistic landscape. They left their studios to paint outside, to study the interaction of light, sky, land and the people and animals. Quick sketches, which could further be worked out into larger studio canvases. This group became known as the School of Barbizon,

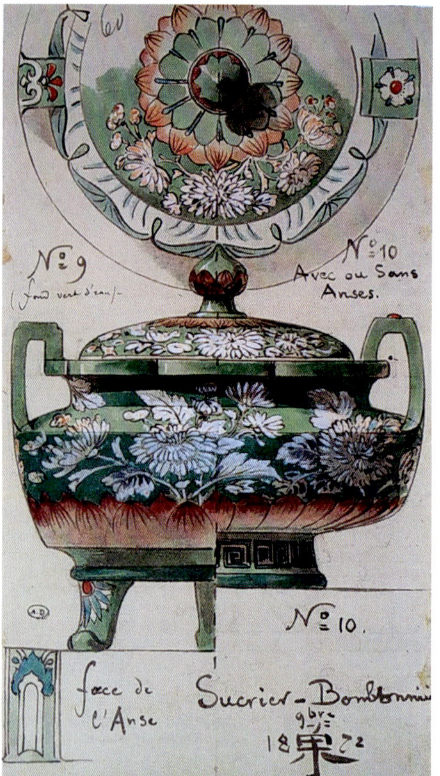

Émile Reiber, 'sucrier-bonbonnière', design for a sugar pot, 19th cen., charcoal, gouache, pen and brown ink on parchment, Musée des Arts Décoratifs, Paris

Enamel colander

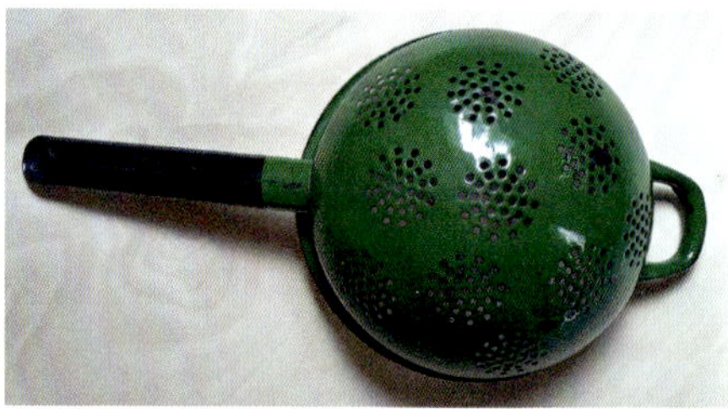

A.C.A. Rotgans, preliminary design for a decoration, 1900, watercolour on paper, collection of the author

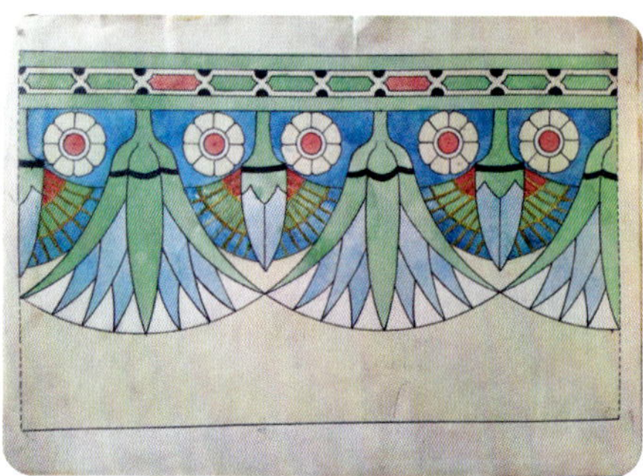

named after the village that became their artistic base.
In everything, they represented the very opposite of the austerely academic, romantic conceptions of art, in which historical pieces, with an often rigid and glorified depiction of patriotic and mythological subjects, were paramount. Artworks in which nature was at best a set piece. The Barbizon group inspired painters all over Europe, and later even in America, with as its Dutch offshoot the Hague School. They were the driving force behind the introduction of the landscape into Dutch academic training, from which landscape painters like Piet Mondrian and Leo Gestel emerged.
Chrome greens can still be seen around us. It has been used abundantly in public buildings, waiting rooms, hospitals, schools, institutes and prisons. One can wonder why. Because this dull green has a calming, almost sedating effect, which would help keep people tranquil in more or less involuntary group settings. The colour is also omnipresent in a wide range of industrial products; from trucks, trains and tractors to kitchen items such as colanders, buckets, cans and pans. And, of course, the predominant colour for most militaries.
Around the beginning of World War I, the British and French army began to replace their colourful, but much too conspicuous, traditional military uniform with muted ambient colours: *camouflage*. Today, camouflage is the military standard. It is difficult to imagine that not too long ago, soldiers were sent off to the battlefield in brightly coloured uniforms.

Berthe Morisot, *Young Girl in a Ball Gown*, 1879, oil on canvas, 71 x 54 cm, Musée d'Orsay, Paris

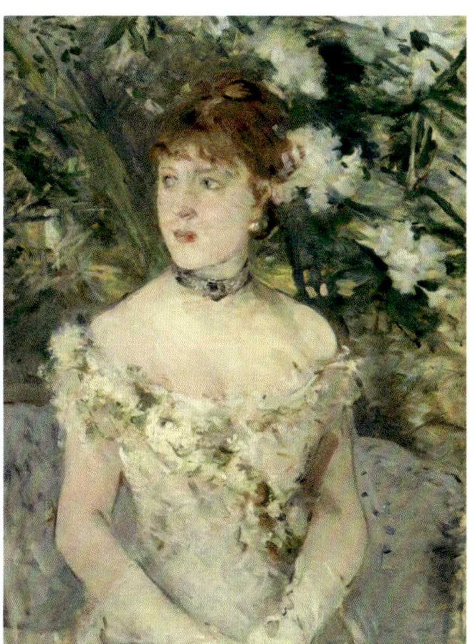

Camille Corot, *Pond in the Woods*, 1840-1875, oil on panel, 32 x 52 cm, Rijksmuseum

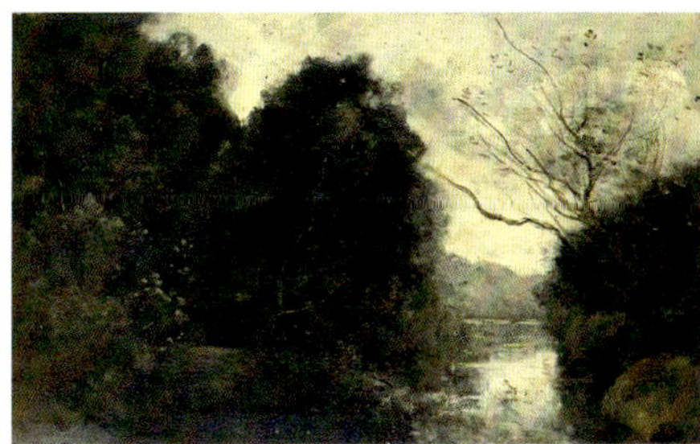

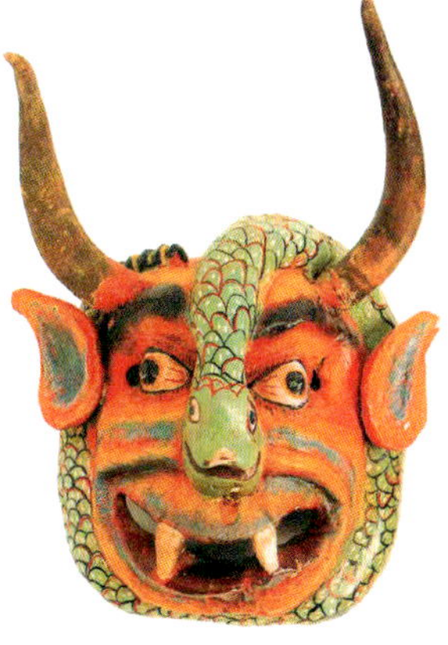

Mexican devil mask, c. 1950, painted wood with cow horns, Wereldmuseum Amsterdam

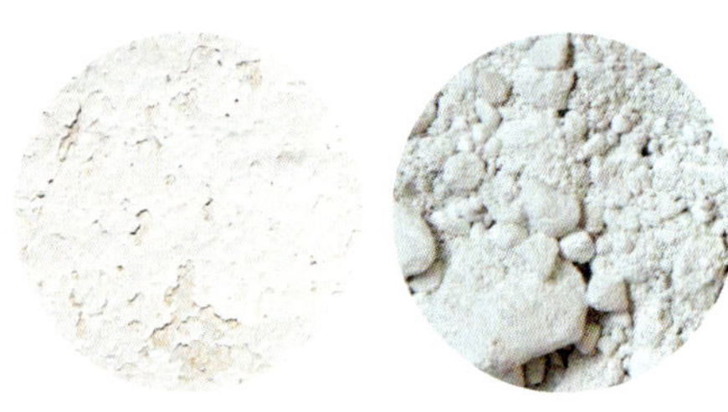

Chalk & Kaolin

Two ancient whites connecting pre-history with the present day. Existent on almost all continents, they were and still are used to decorate and protect the body and ritual objects, and to create images.
As colours, they represent the All and Nothing, the pure, immaculate, the good as well as evil spirits.
Death and mourning.

There are books full of theories discussing whether 'white' is an everything or a nothing.
Is it even a colour? As a pigment, the answer is a definite yes. White covers the whole range from cool to warm.
Chalk and kaolin are not interrelated. The former is a product of the sea, the latter from the land. Chalk consists of the microscopic plankton skeletons and shells of marine life, while kaolin is a clay produced by weathering of feldspar-bearing rock. Feldspar may seem complicated term, however, sixty per cent of the earth beneath our feet is feldspar.
The origin of the word chalk is unknown. The Latin term for it was *crēta*, meaning sieved earth. It probably refers to the ancient custom of purifying white wool (*cernere*) with sifted chalk powder. It became the name of the island with the coastline of chalk cliffs, Crete.

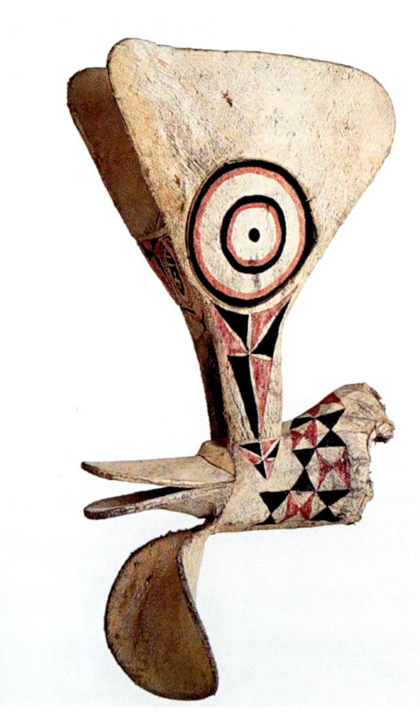

Uramot Baining people, Kavat Mask, bark cloth, natural pigments and rotan, h. 90 cm, Linden Museum, Stuttgart

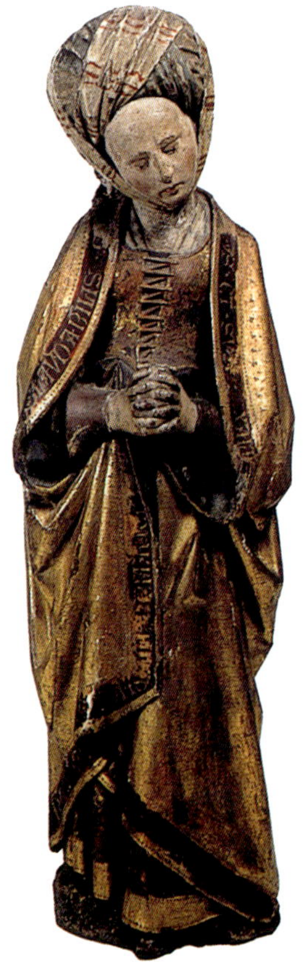

Mourning Woman, c. 1480, polychrome on gesso on wood

Chalk is the silent force in the world of painting. It was a crucial tool for anyone working with paint since the beginning of time. It is the basis of the original gesso ground, a mixture of chalk and an animal binder, occasionally with added lead white. A layer of gesso can transform the surface of coarse materials like stone and wood into a light and silky-smooth surface. In its top quality, it is as soft and white as the shell of a chicken's egg.
You can see it on sarcophagi, on icons, panels, frames and on countless painted wooden and stone sculptures on nearly all continents. It is an exceptionally beautiful and efficient ground and was adopted for painting on canvas with the advent of linen. Chalk is an excellent pigment for murals. Moreover, in water-soluble paints such as gouache, water colour and casein paint, it carries all colours except Prussian blue and the copper pigments. Soft pastels and ordinary drawing chalks, the word says it all, we owe to chalk.
The expression 'to chalk it up' refers to the old custom of keeping credit or score with chalk on a slate or a wooden board. It is useless when employed for linseed oil paint, as it adopts the colour of the oil and becomes a yellowish grey. With that distinctive colour (and scent) of putty, the universal sealant and filler.
For several years now, I have been using raw chalk as a pigment because of its magnificent and vivacious texture. It helped me discover in just how many shades and in how many places it can be found.
The list of official sites is long. In Europe, for example, the best quality 'paint chalk' comes from the chalk quarries of the French Champagne region and the German coasts. On Germany's Baltic Sea Island of Jasmund, about a million tonnes of chalk is mined each year.

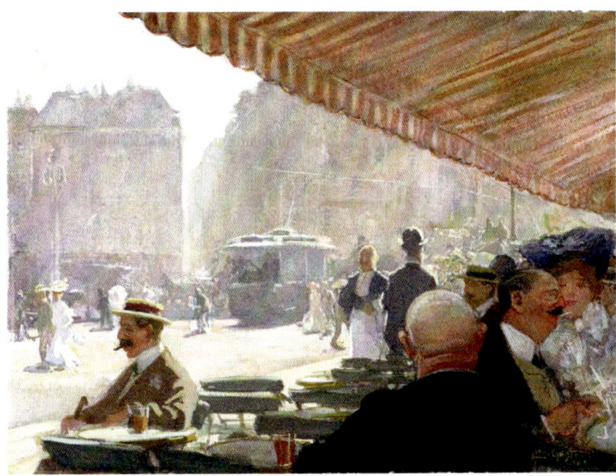

Leo Gestel, *Café Terrace at Rembrandtplein*, Amsterdam, 1906, pencil and water-colour, 24.1 x 33 cm, City Archives Amsterdam

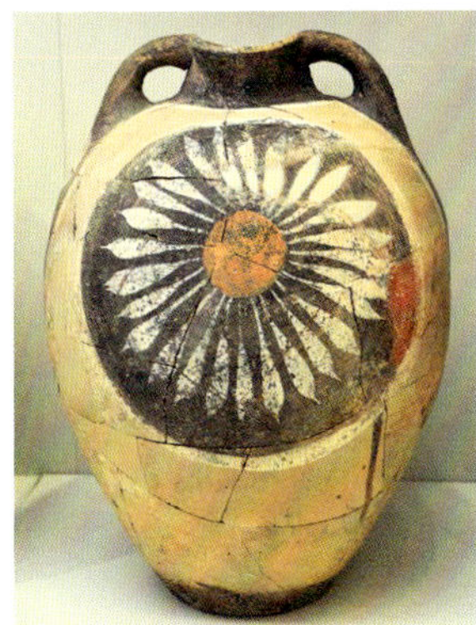

Amphora decorated with floral motif, 1800-1700 BC, Heraklion Archaeological Museum, Heraklion

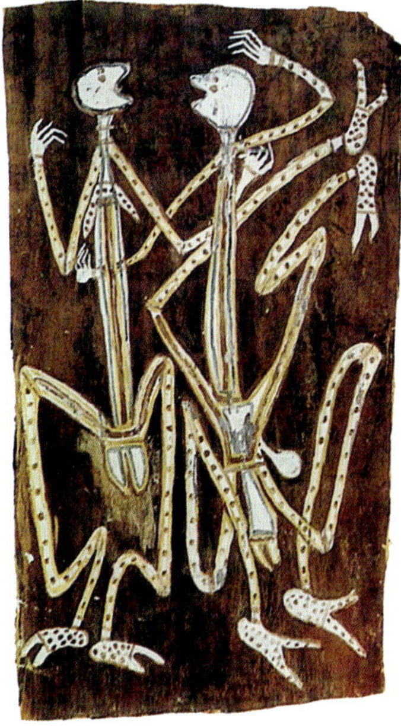

Bark painting, Arnhemland, Australia, Musée du Quai Branly

It is carved out in large blocks, which are left outside during winter to become pulverised. This grit is then rinsed several times with water, finally sorted by quality, and sold.
An extra-fine type of chalk, a plaster, is the so-called Champagne chalk from the Paris Basin. Unlike common chalk, this is formed from minuscule soft marine algae. It figures prominently in historical painting recipes because, due to a special processing, it does not clump and is therefore ideal for creating a smooth surface. Among other things, lime can include burnt chalk and is then called quicklime. Mixed with water, it is called slaked lime.
The well-known whitewash which, without proper adhesion, can turn back into chalk through contact with air and then gives off at the slightest touch.
To get a very fine grain, slaked lime was left in a barrel of water for at least two years.
Cennino Cennini advised the following procedure in the 15th century: '... put it into a little tub for the space of eight days, changing the water every day, and mixing the lime and water

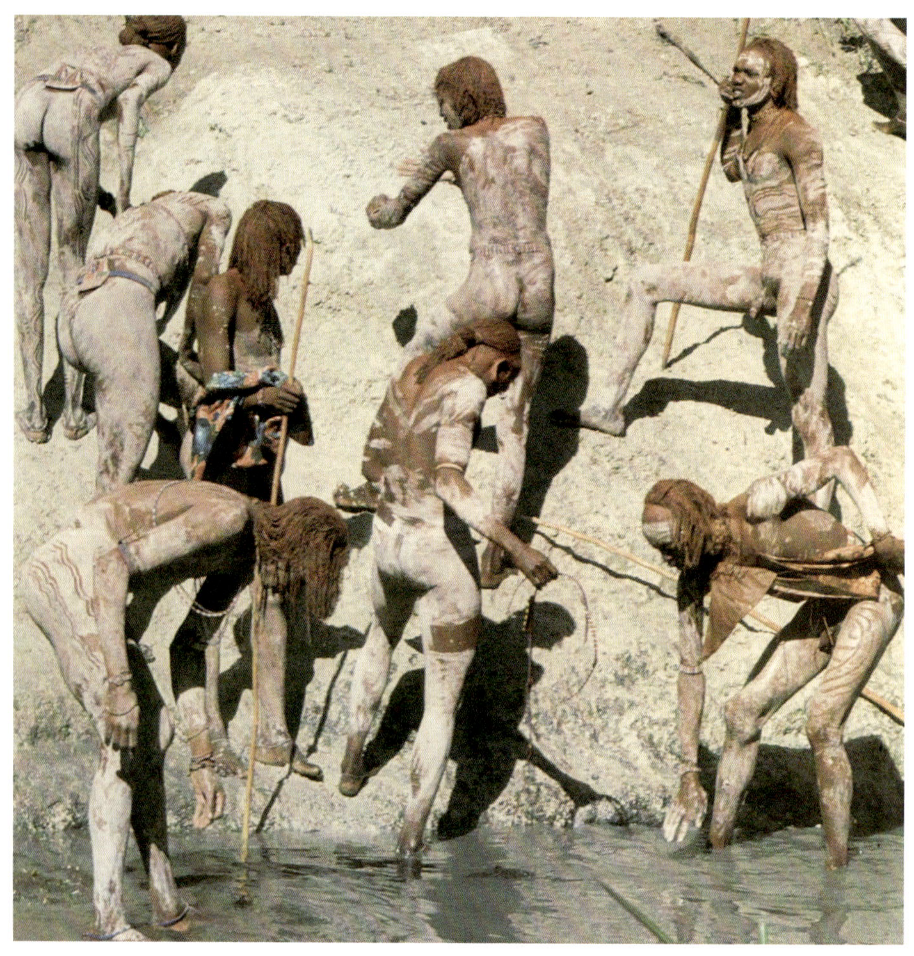

Masai warriors, Tanzania, body painting with kaolin

well together, in order that it may throw off all unctuous properties (grassezza). Then make it into small cakes, put them upon the roof of the house in the sun, and the older these cakes are, the whiter they become.' In fact, according to Cennini, it is of such a good quality that it is suitable to work with it directly on a wall, and '...without this colour you can do nothing... you cannot paint flesh, or make tints of the other colours which are necessary in painting on walls, namely, in fresco.'

Kaolin is a corruption of the Chinese word *kaou-ling*, meaning high mountain range. It is a white, fine and oily clay. Like chalk, it is found in water paints and putty and is similarly unsuitable as a pigment in oil paints. Along with many other pigments, it belongs to the group of ancient medicines, which is still used for treating haemorrhages and diarrhoea. Its moniker, porcelain earth, already reveals what it is renowned for: porcelain, the highest quality pottery.

These days, it is added to a range of products. It is indispensable for the paper industry to produce white paper and is employed as a filler for cardboard, it is found in car tyres, toothpaste, cosmetics such as powder, lipstick and skin masks, as additive E559 in foodstuffs and as a filler in paints. Kaolin is still commercially available as a modelling clay of superior quality.

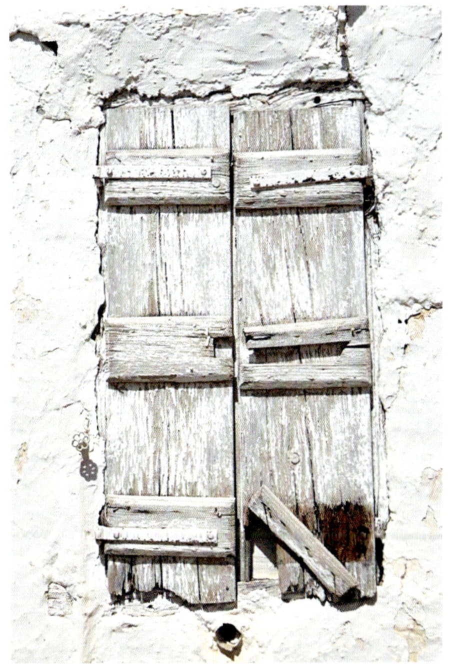

Whitewashed façade of a house, Crete

Wall painting in the tomb of Tutankhamun, c. 1323 BC, chalk, ochre, red and green earth, Egyptian blue and soot black on stone

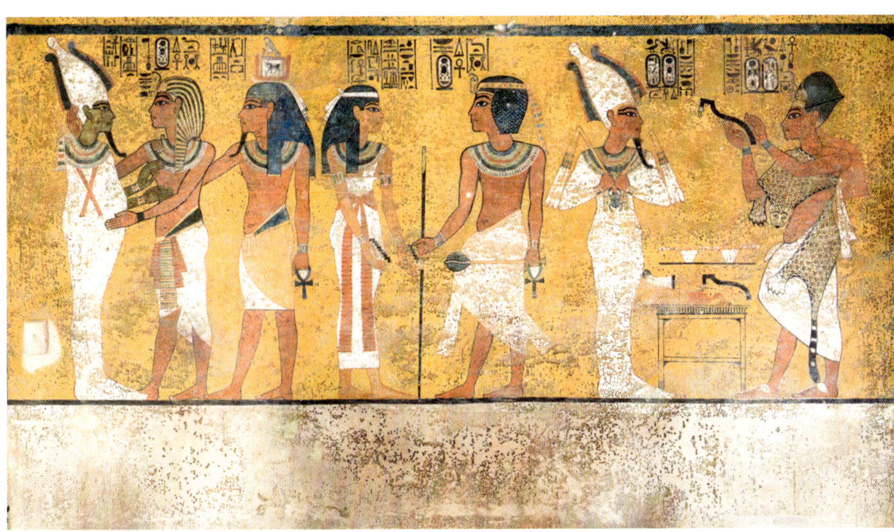

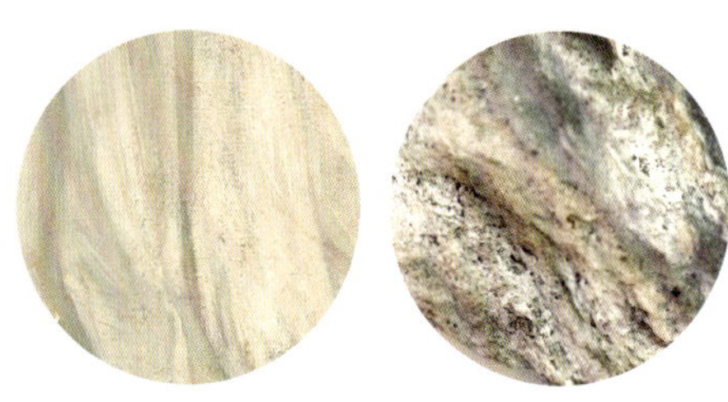

Lead White

A smooth and warm white. Until the 19th century, the only strong white on the palette, the image-setter in Western oil painting. The Spanish painter Sorolla, the master of light, is a brilliant example.

Its great disadvantage is its toxicity, like all lead-based pigments. The main reason why it was almost entirely replaced by the less toxic and stronger titanium white in the 20th century.

Lead white belongs to the group of historic synthetic pigments. It has been in use longer than the preserved recipes from both Greco-Roman times and 300 BC China. It is easy to make. Take a piece of lead and suspend it over a layer of vinegar or urine in a sealed jug. Over time the fumes will form a white crust: the pigment. Don't try it yourself because lead took many lives!

In 1970, the remains of the painter Giotto were discovered during excavations in Florence, which, upon analysis, were found to be full of toxins, including lead. Spanish artist Goya was another victim, as he habitually modelled paint with his fingers. Non-artists also died of lead white poisoning by using it as body paint or make-up. From early antiquity into the 19th century, the secular elite powdered their face with lead powder for 'chic' white skin. Which explains the large

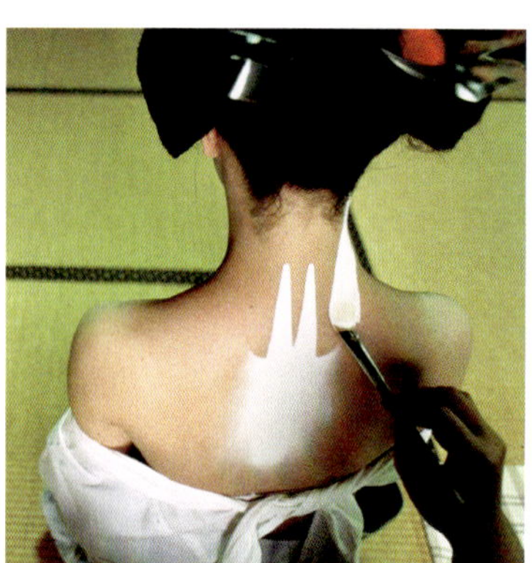

Neck adornment of a geisha, previously painted with lead white

Joaquín Sorolla Y Bastida, *Hooking the Boat, Valencia*, 1899, oil on canvas, 82 x 108 cm, Museo de Bellas Artes de Asturias, Asturias

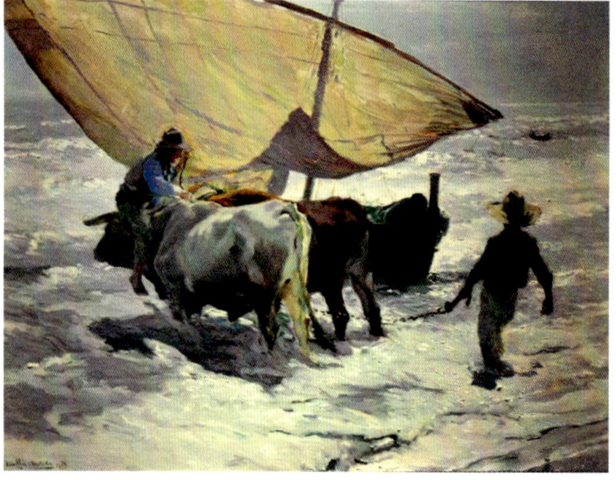

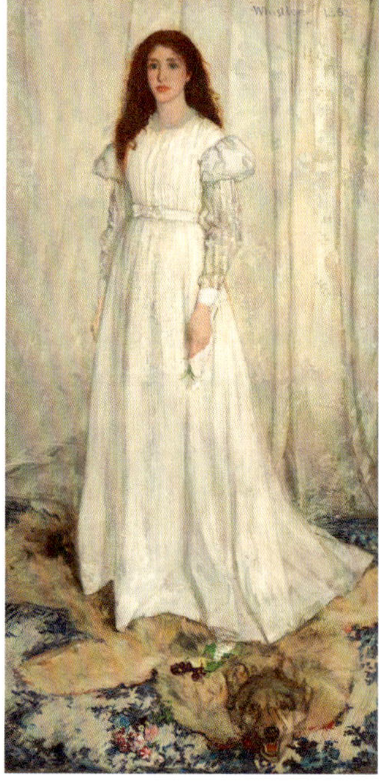

James McNeill Whistler, *Symphony in White no. 1: The White Girl*, 1862, oil on canvas, 213 x 107.9 cm, National Gallery of Art, Washington D.C.

number of pale women in society portraits.
The mining of the ore, as well as its production and processing, were equally risky. Fatalities were caused by inhaling lead dust and the inevitable direct skin contact.
Lead white has been on the market in various qualities, with the quality being determined by the percentage of admixed, and therefore cheap, fillers. Rubens and his pupil Van Dyck set high standards of purity. For them, this was the absolute requirement for achieving the maximum result. In addition to quality, particle size plays a role: fine particles have a different effect than coarse, allowing for special effects in painting.
Lead white is primary in recipes for skin tones, modelling figures, and skies. Applied thickly, it stays put, allowing extra relief to a form. This is well illustrated in Rembrandt's late self-portraits, which you can almost 'grab by the nose'.
Lead white can eventually disappear optically, partially or completely, when applied too thinly. This is a well-known occurrence in older painted art, as can be seen in the translucent ends of Coorte's asparagus. Lead-white is unusable in frescoes, as it changes back through a chemical reaction into its original colour, lead grey. It's flexibility and toughness made it a popular exterior paint.

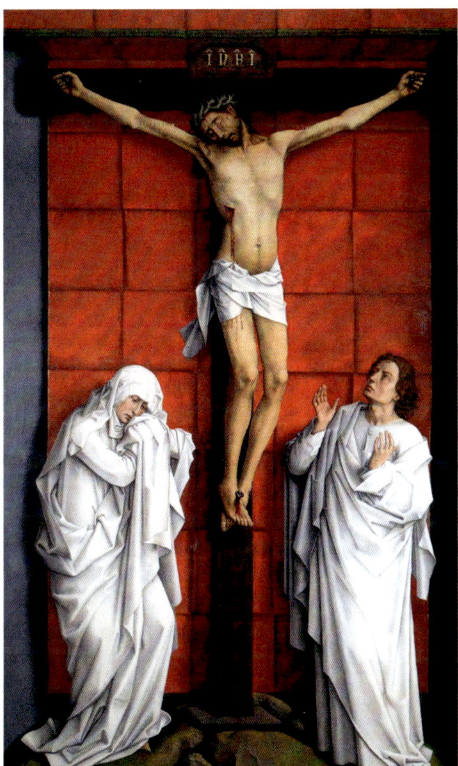

Rogier van der Weyden, *The Crucifixion*, c. 1457, oil on panel, 325 x 192 cm, Abby of Escorial, San Lorenzo de El Escorial

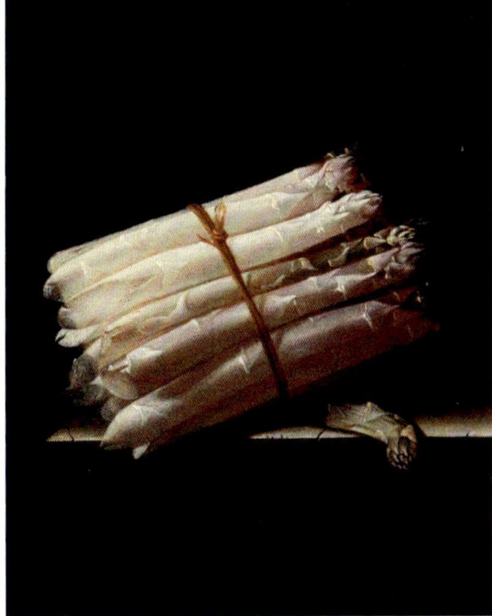

Adriaen Coorte, *Still-Life with Asparagus*, 1697, oil on paper on panel, 25 x 20.5 cm, Rijksmuseum, Amsterdam

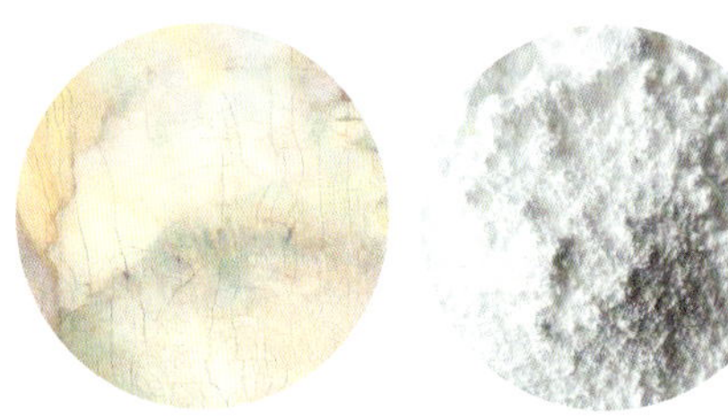

Zinc White

A safe and easy-going white. Due to its slight blue cast, it is visibly cooler than lead white. Zinc white is a slow dryer, which is why it is fittingly nicknamed *Drögnicht* in German.

A perfect pigment for the wet-on-wet painting of portraits, nudes and landscapes. A technique in which the painter applies various colours in one session to achieve the intended result. It is also ideal for painting outdoors.

The two whites were often simultaneously put on the palette: the opaque, fast-drying lead white, along with the more transparent, slow-drying zinc white. Its moderate covering power makes it one of the few whites that can be glazed. However, its tendency to become brittle and crack is a disadvantage.

There are two methods for the production of zinc whites: directly from the ore or indirectly using clean zinc. When and how the first zinc white was produced, is still uncertain. It was probably extracted from pure zinc ore in ancient Persia as early as the sixth century, after which it became known in India and China.

The rise of the various East Indian Companies and the expansion of trade between Europe and Asia enabled the German alchemist Andreas Libavius to obtain a zinc sample from China in 1595. However, it would take 100 years before

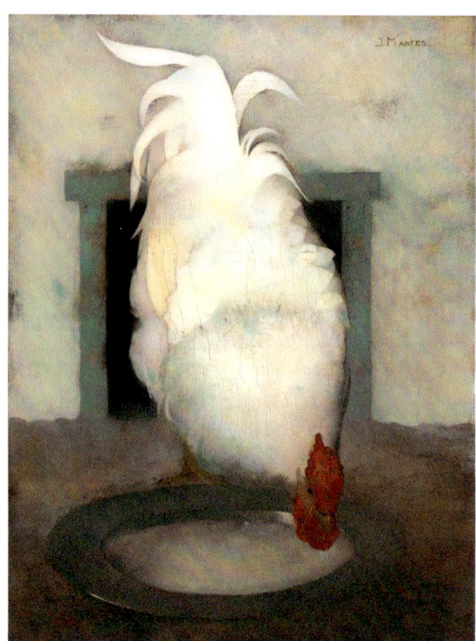

Jan Mankes, *Wyandotte Cockerel with Pewter Plate*, 1913, oil on canvas, 40.5 x 31 cm, Museum Belvédère, Heerenveen

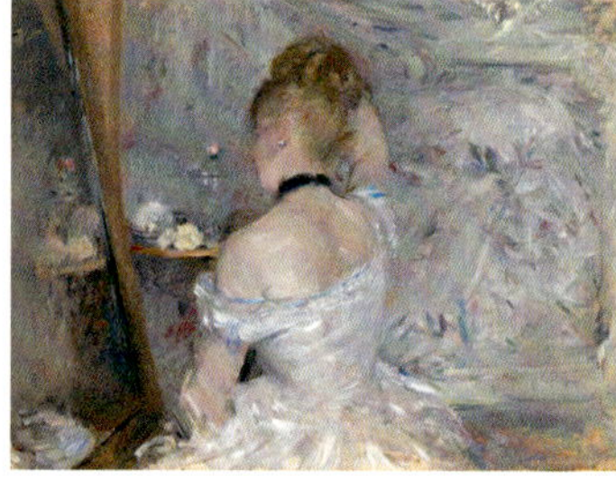

Berthe Morisot, *Woman at her toilet*, 1875-1880, oilpaint on canvas, 60.3 x 80.4 cm, Art Institute of Chicago

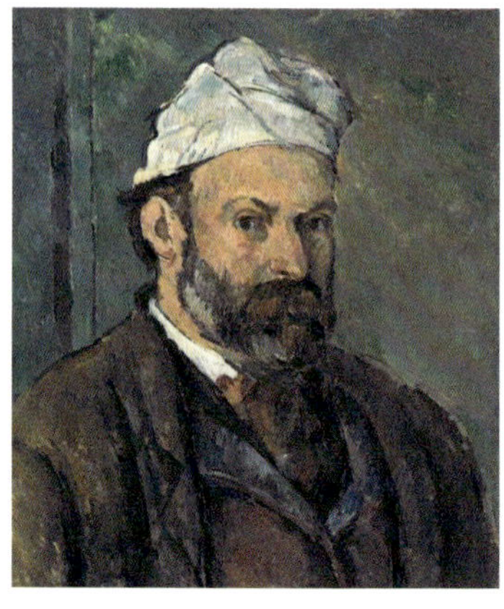

Paul Cézanne, *Self-Portrait with White Turban*, c. 1882, oil on canvas, 55.5 x 46 cm, Neue Pinakothek, Munich

the first, more or less viable, zinc production got underway in France.
In the 18th century, further attempts were made to produce zinc white on a larger scale in Germany and France, but both were unsuccessful due to high costs.
In 1834, Winsor & Newton marketed a so-called Chinese white based on zinc oxide. It was the first reliable white watercolour. Parisian painter Edme Jean Leclaire followed in 1844 by successfully opening a profitable factory, after years of experimentation, and zinc white became lead white's serious competitor. As with lead white, a system of quality labels was established for the market to indicate different gradations. The Schiedam zinc factory, for example, sold three grades categorised by label: a white seal for the highest, green for the secondary, and red for the lowest quality and, therefore, also the cheapest.
Zinc powder belongs to the group of traditional medicines and is used both internally and externally. One of its best-known uses is as a topical ointment, an effective remedy for infections and wounds. Comparable to chalk and kaolin, it is a multi-purpose whitening agent in multiple industries: it is used in paper, cosmetics, fillers, glazes, pharmaceuticals and for dental fillings.

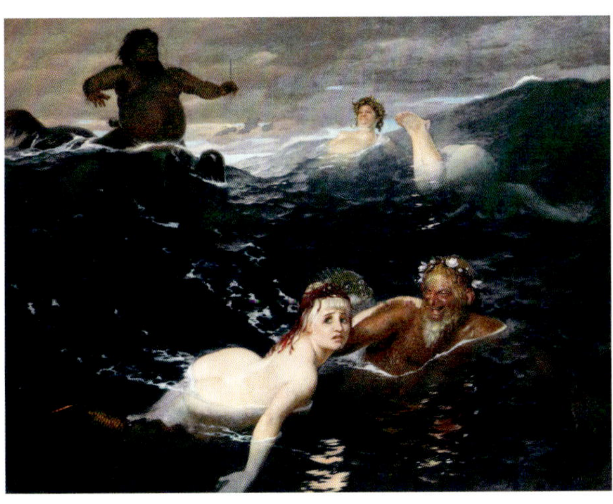

Arnold Böcklin, *In the Play of the Waves*, 1883, oil on canvas, 180 x 238 cm, Neue Pinakothek, Munich

Ferdinand Hodler, *The Life Weary / The Weary of Life / Tired of Life*, 1892, oil and tempera on canvas, 149.7 x 294 cm, Neue Pinakothek, Munich

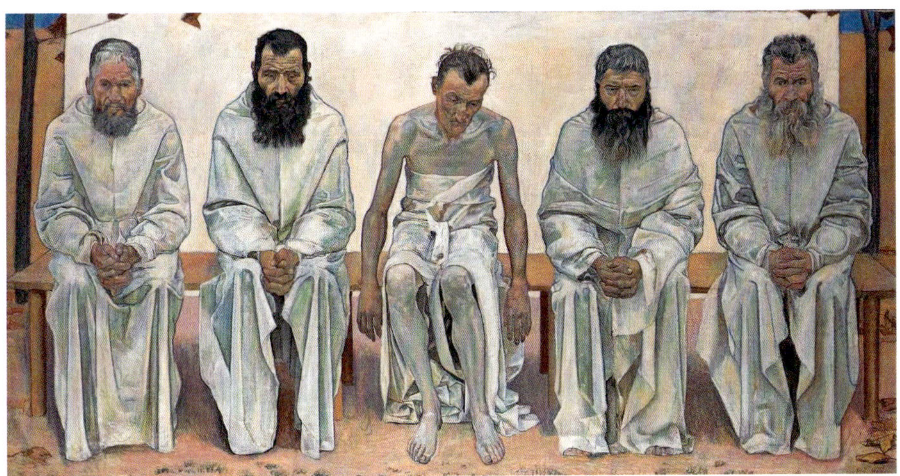

Titanium White

The new white, which today has surpassed its forerunners in nearly all areas of colour. More brilliant, lightfast, and without the hassles of the old whites. Its coating power is twice that of lead white. You can assume that the whites in works of art created after the 1980s are mainly titanium whites.

Its use in Japanese *urushi*, the art of lacquer, sparked a real revolution. For some 9,000 years, until World War II, the Japanese craftsmen had to manage with the extremely limited palette defined by the technology of the time. The introduction of titanium white as a carrier for the multicoloured new dyes, made the entire range of modern colours available. Resulting in a complete metamorphosis.
The element titanium is found in many places in one form or another, the best known of which are the minerals rutile and ilmenite. The Urals, Scandinavia, North America, Australia, India and Malaysia are home to many deposits. But titanium is also naturally present in us, in plants, in meteorites, the sun and the moon.
It unites an entire universe.
The clergyman and amateur chemist William Gregor discovered titanium by coincidence in 1791 during a stroll on the black beach of Cornwall. He realised that half of the magnetic sand under his feet consisted of a white metal. Four years later, German chemist Heinrich Klaproth

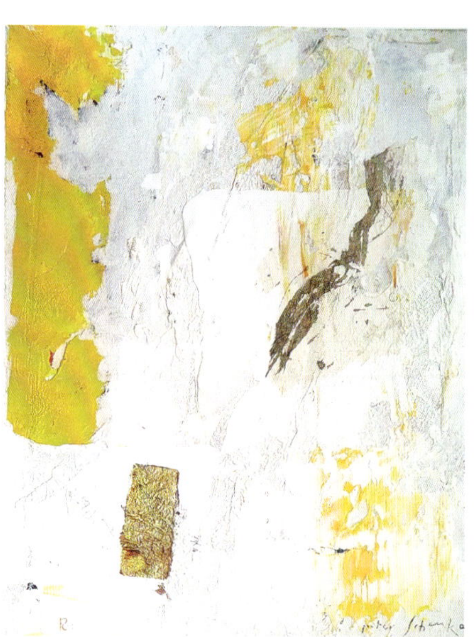

Peter Schenk, *Three Elements*, 2009, mixed media on canvas, 40 x 50 cm, private collection

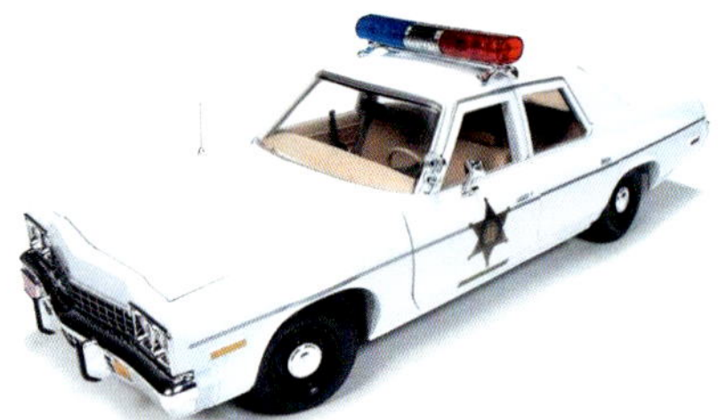

Toy car

Uesugi Gakusui, incense container, chōshitsu lacquerware, 42 x 7 cm, collection Ben Janssens

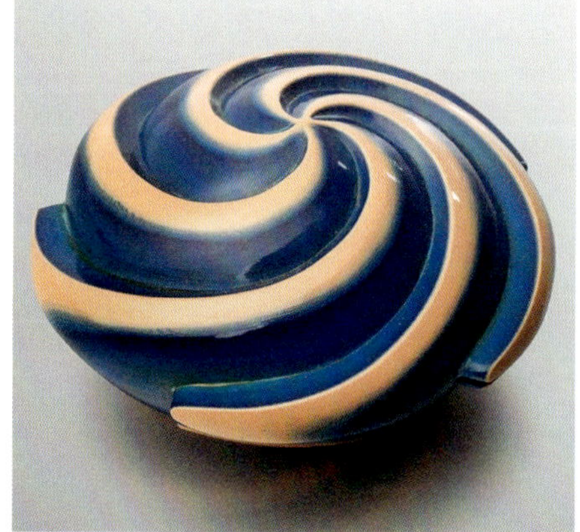

detected the same phenomenon in rutile and named the new substance after the Greek primordial gods, the Titans. Nevertheless, it would take until 1831 before the pigment was successfully isolated. In 1916, in Norway, at large deposits of ilmenite, the Titan Co. A/S was founded. The name says it all: the prelude to the global commercial production in the 20th century.
Titanium white eventually became the frontrunner of white pigments from World War II onwards and is why it can now be found in road and automotive paints, house paint, text correction fluid, cement, inks, glass, rubbers, cosmetics, sunscreen, medicine, paper, ceramics and as E171 in toothpaste and chewing gum. After research in 2019, France banned titanium white in foodstuffs. Either way, it is advisable to be careful when working with the dry pigment.

New generation pigments such as titanium white can be useful instruments in exposing counterfeit art. A good example is the case of Beltracchi. For years, this German painter and con artist sold artworks supposedly by great artists such as André Derain, Max Pechstein and Fernand Léger, including impeccably forged documents and photographs.
Thanks to technical investigations in 2010, the man was exposed. The pivotal evidence for his forgery was the discovery of titanium white in the paint, which could not possibly have been employed by these artists in their time.

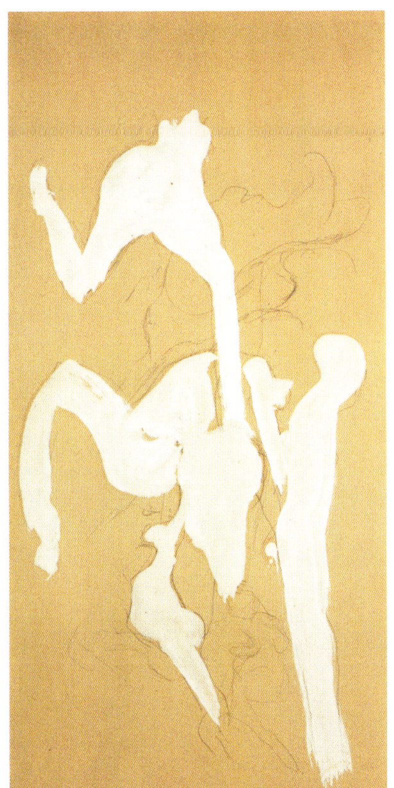

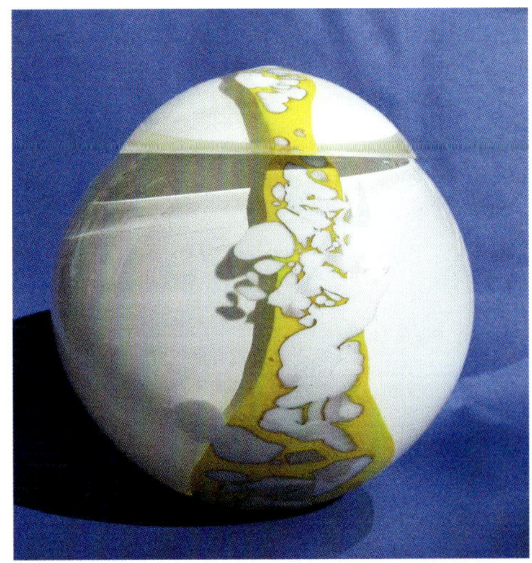

Joseph Beuys, *Untitled (Women)*, 1961, graphite / pencil and white gouache, 48 x 23 cm, private collection

monica rotgans, urn, layered glass, Onze Lieve Vrouwe Kapel / OLVG, Amsterdam

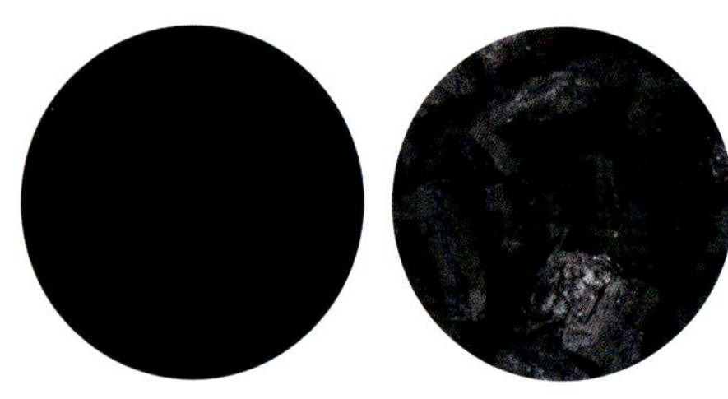

Charcoal & Soot Black

Made by fire, the primordial blacks. Representatives of a colour surrounded by positive and negative energies. In visual culture, the darkest contrast for the lightest light.

The Dutch word, *zwart*, stems from the Latin *sordeo*, meaning dirty and soiled, prompting associations with poverty and disease, such as the Black Death. Related terms are black market, blacklist, to blacken and black sheep. Black is the underworld without a glimmer of light, worse than the red, flaming Hell. In contrast, in ancient Egypt, black Osiris represented fertility, life, the colour of the annually submerged and fertile dark Nile banks. A similar interpretation is that of the Pygmies, for whom black represents the jungle's shadow. Once the core of the Pygmies' existence, depicted in paintings made with fruit-stone black. Additionally, black is linked with asceticism and seriousness, it is the colour of existentialism, as well as power. The latter association is conveyed through the exquisite black garments in portraits of the elite. Before the 19th century, a black dye that was strong enough to dye textiles a deep black in one take, did not exist, automatically making the colour a luxury product (see *Composite Blacks*).

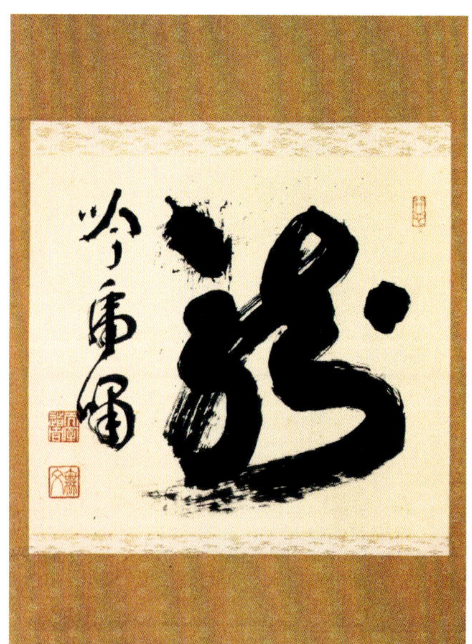

Anonymous, calligraphy, 19th cen., Japan

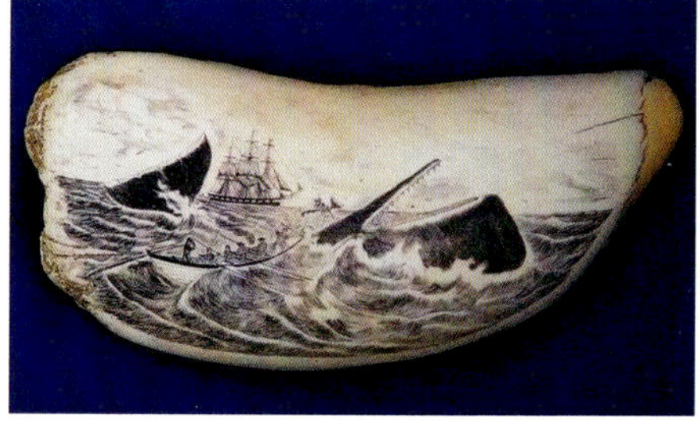

Scrimshaw of a whale's tooth, 19th cen., Azores

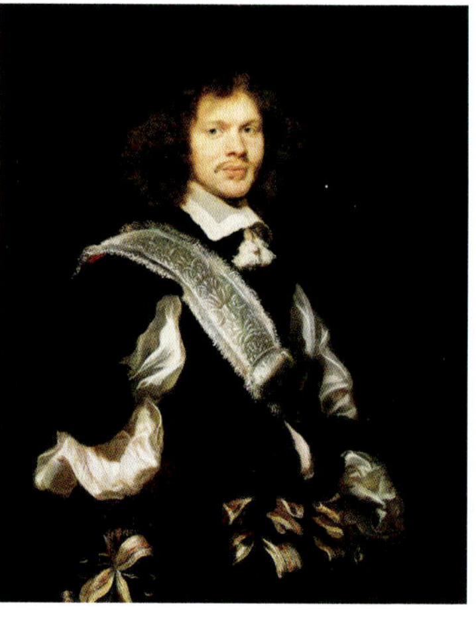

Frans Luijckx, *Portrait of a Young Man*, c. 1650, oil on canvas, 107 x 86.5 cm, Museum of Fine Arts, Budapest

Around 500,000 years ago, our early ancestors, predecessors of Homo sapiens, discovered how to manipulate fire, which marked the very beginning of the ever-growing environmental problems. It started simply, with fire as a source of light and heat. Our knowledge of those earliest activities is thanks to soot deposits and charred wood from fires found in caves where Neanderthals, and even earlier homonins, sheltered for shorter or longer periods. And where they used charred wood to draw on the walls. Charcoal is basically any piece of burnt wood suitable for drawing. Nowadays, we know it mainly in the form of rather fragile sticks. Soot and crushed charcoal turn into paint by mixing it with a binder. In its finest form, it is ink.

Charcoal is a very common material that has been produced and used for tens of thousands of years. Charcoal for drawing is the specially crafted variant for the artist. It is made of carefully charred twigs of wood types that differ per region: in Western Europe, mainly willow, lime, beech, cork oak and maple. It has recently come to light that the magnificent drawings in the *Grotte Chauvet* were made by Neanderthals around 30,000 years ago with pine charcoal.
Charcoal can be black, brown or greyish, and warm or cool in colour, depending on the wood. In principle, a wide range of blacks can be made by burning different types of wood.
The 14th-century Italian painter Cennino Cennini describes how charcoal was crafted in his time: 'Take some slips of willow, dry and smooth, and cut them into pieces as long as the palm of the hand… then divide them like matches, and fasten them together like a bundle

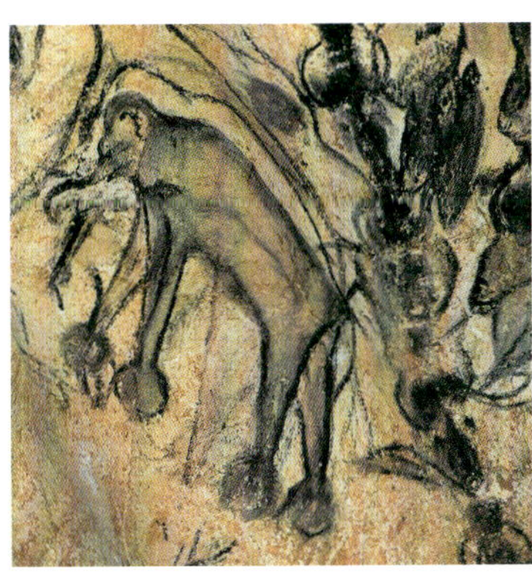

Grotte Chauvet, *Elephant*, detail of the cave wall with lions, charcoal, c. 30.000 BC

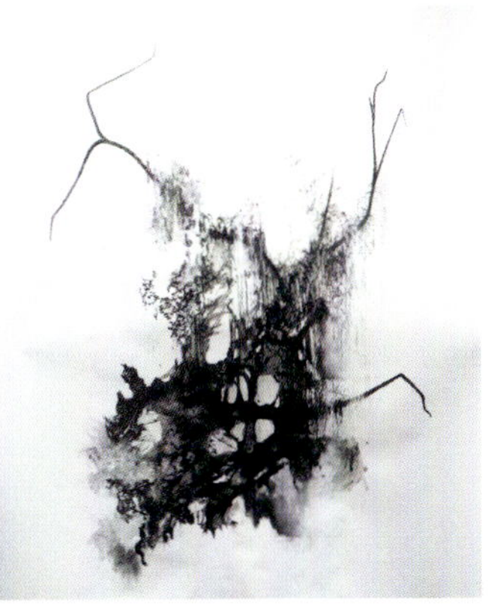

Lisanne Sloots, *Ecocide 2*, 2021, elm charcoal on museum board, 150 x 123 cm, artist's collection

Arthur Streeton, *Fatima Habiba*, 1897, oil on canvas on board, 29 x 27.4 cm, AGSA, Adelaide

of matches; but first polish and sharpen them... Thus, laying them in bundles, bind each bundle in three places, that is, by the middle and each end, with a fine copper or iron wire; then take a new pipkin, and fill the pipkin with them; put on an earthen cover, and lute it round with chalk or clay, so that no air can enter.
Then go to the baker in the evening... when he has finished baking the bread, and put this pipkin in the oven, and let it remain till morning; then look whether the crayons are well burnt and black...
If the crayon works freely on paper it will do; if it is too much baked it will not keep together in drawing but will split to pieces.'
It sounds simple, but you get a truly workable result through experience.
When used as an underdrawing in painting, it must be fixed to prevent contamination of the paint. When mixed with lead white and gesso, it is the historical mid-tone for oil paint ground.
Soot black is the blackest black. Chimney stones, torches, oil lamps, and anything in contact with smoke through combustion is a source. Scrape the inside of an older chimney and you will have the raw material for soot black. With Indian ink as one of the main products.
Ink is so common it is hardly noticed. Because of ink, we can communicate through written characters. Calligraphy and the letterpress were invented because of ink. The modern variant being the toner, printing ink, which enables us to read this text.
Ink was and still is made by mixing soot and sometimes additional other black pigments with hide glue, Gum Arabic or a modern binder. The best-known is probably Chinese ink, produced in solid blocks to be dissolved just before use.

Robert Motherwell, Elegy to the Spanish Republic, 1970

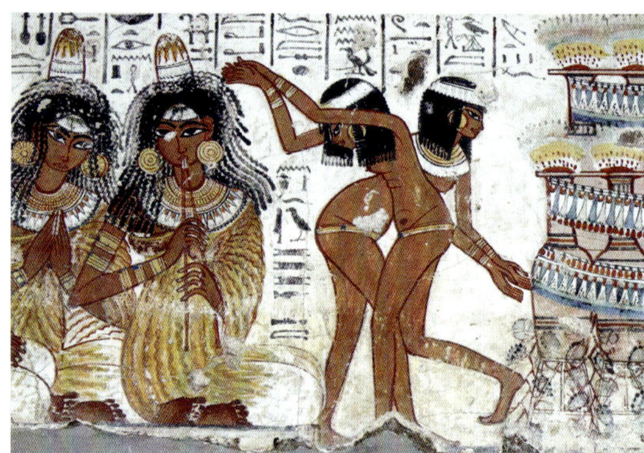

Detail of a wall painting in the tomb of Nebamun, Thebes, Egypt, 14th cen. BC, British Museum, London

For the (art) painter, soot black is listed as one of the dangerous pigments. Due to its fineness, it can instantly affect other colours, comparable to Prussian blue. Giorgio Vasari noted in the 16th century that Raphael's last canvas, *The Transfiguration of Christ*, was severely darkened by it: 'And if he had not on some whim or other used printer's black (which, as has often been pointed out, becomes gradually darker with time and damages the other colours with which it is mixed) this work would be as fresh as when it was first executed...'

Soot black is one of the great pollutants of modern times. It is everywhere, from wildfires to the emissions from chimneys and exhausts. It settles onto earth and in our bodies. It is found in all kinds of printed matter, pencils, cosmetics and medicines. About 90 per cent of the industrial production goes into the manufacture of car tyres (!).

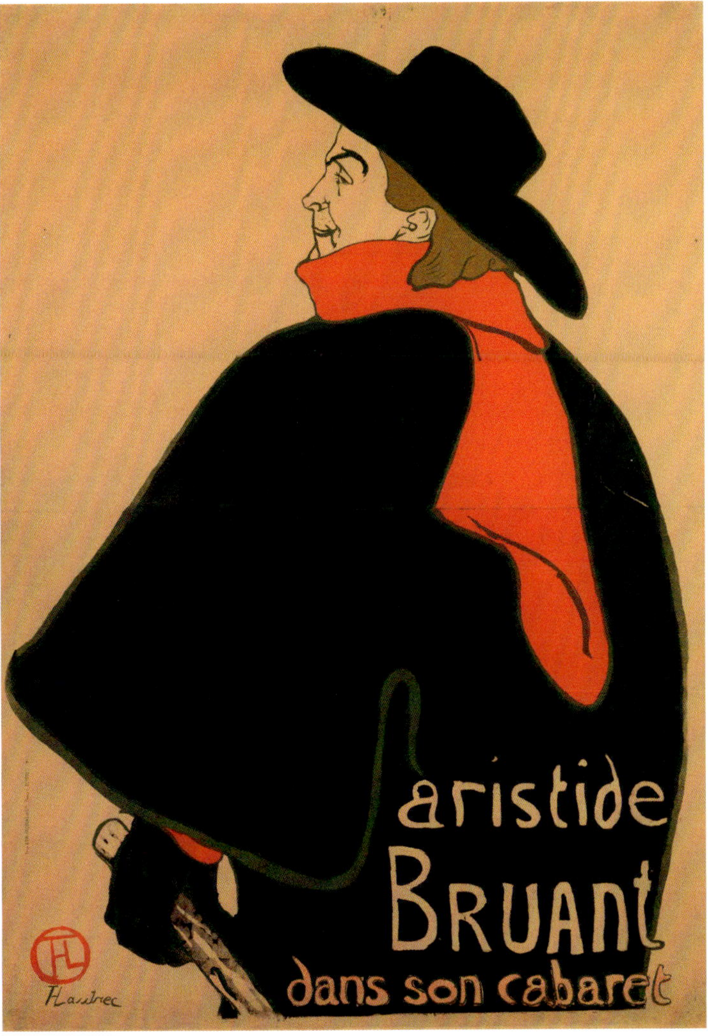

Henri de Toulouse-Lautrec, *Aristide Bruant in his Cabaret*, 1893, lithograph, 127 x 92.5 cm, Museum Boijmans Van Beuningen, Rotterdam

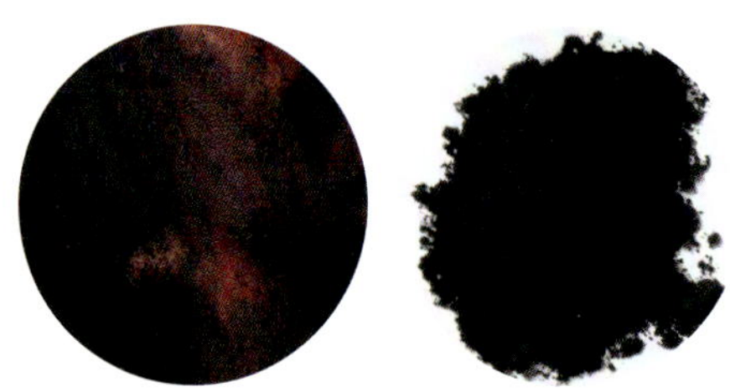

Stone Black & Black Oxide

The mineral, i.e. inorganic blacks, belong to the group of stone black and black oxide pigments. These are the red, yellow and brown earths blackened by firing and the modern-day synthetic varieties. Oxide refers to the oxygen (*oxygenium*) that is an essential partner in the process. Black slate is a natural stone black, available as pigment or processed into a drawing pen.

To begin with the latter, slate is that smooth, flat stone composed of thin sedimentary rock layers, commonly visible as a roofing material. It is, in fact, compressed fine-grained clay, hardened over millions of years and aptly coined in its old name, 'clay slate'.

Until the mid-20th century, slate was *the* writing board of choice. It was reusable and much cheaper than paper. One wrote on it with a lighter-coloured stone, chalk or a stylus, a pen usually made of a softer slate. When the slate was full, it was wiped clean, and one could continue 'with a clean slate'. Black slate has fallen out of use, but most Renaissance artists had it in their tool kit. It is the black of the so-called *technique à trois crayons*, whereby a red, white and black crayon was used to quickly and efficiently draw a sketch or design. It is still available in France under the name *pierre noir* (black stone).

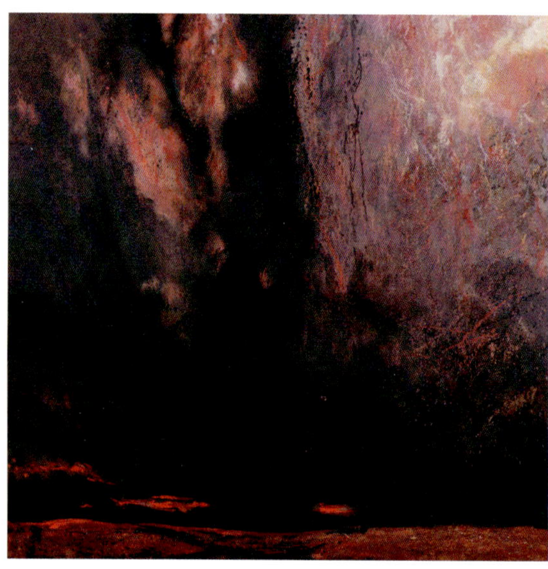

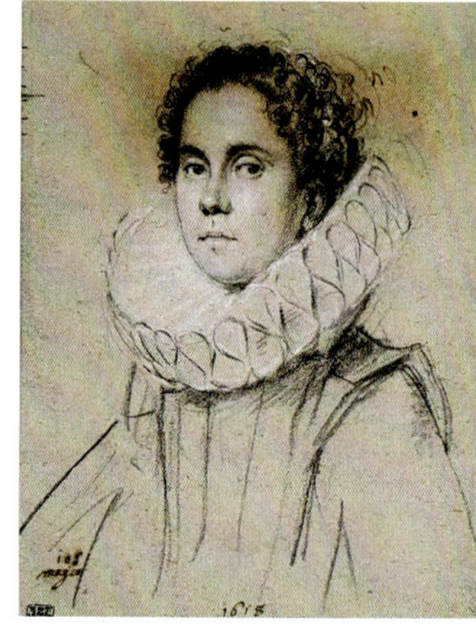

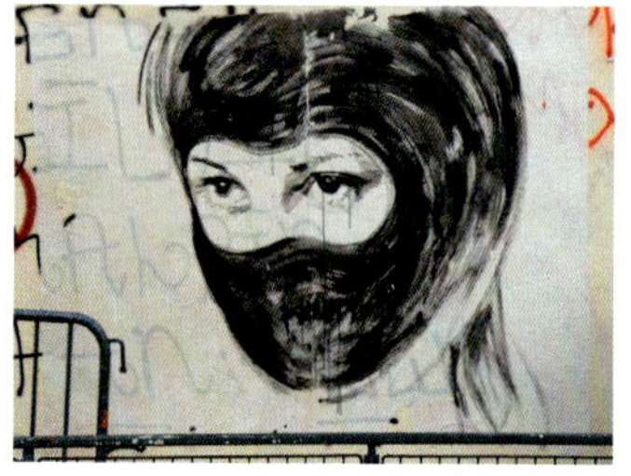

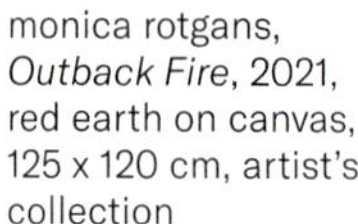

monica rotgans, *Outback Fire*, 2021, red earth on canvas, 125 x 120 cm, artist's collection

Ottavio Leoni, *Portrait of Olimpia Maidalchini Pamphili*, 1618, black and white chalk on originally blue paper, 23 x 16 cm, Musée des Arts Décoratifs, Paris

Graffiti, Paris

The pigment is made from crushed, ground and rinsed slate – or rather, it is returned to its original form: dry clay powder. A superb example of this is the pre-digital blackboard. Essentially, a large piece of slate made of wood coated with slate black. Slate is also a suitable ground to paint on directly with opaque paint.

Oxide black exists in a form known since antiquity and in a contemporary version. Originally, it was made by burning earth containing iron- and manganese oxide at temperatures between 800°C and 1100°C. The modern variants are the product of burning discarded metals. Ancient oxide black can be found in the deep black patterns and depictions on antique Mediterranean ceramics. The oldest pieces to date (from around 4000 BC) were discovered at Tell Halaf at the current border of Syria and Turkey.

The synthetic pigment has superseded historical black in Europe, mainly due to the growing scarcity of manganese-rich soil.
In parts of Africa, a form of oxide black is extracted from discarded lithium batteries. A modern but very unsafe raw material for traditional painting.
The so-called *Nero di Roma*, a brown-black soil found near Rome and Venice, is also sometimes called oxide black. However, when searching for it online, bone black pigments are for sale under the same name despite being entirely different. In short, in terms of names, the world of pigments is a labyrinth.

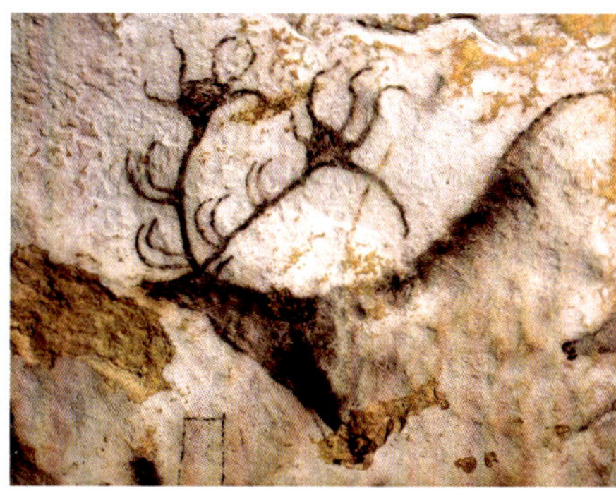

Cave of Lascaux, cave painting of a prehistoric deer, detail, c. 20.000 years old

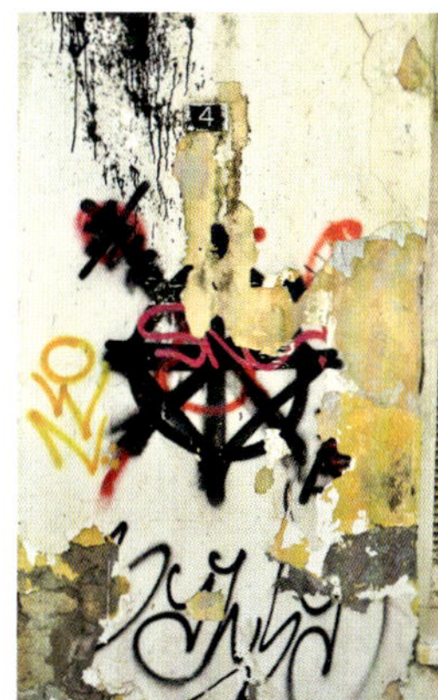

Graffiti, Crete

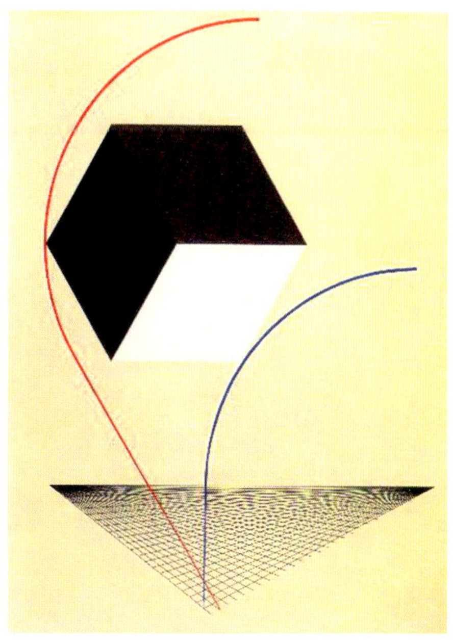

El Lissitzky, *Proun*, c. 1925, pen, ink and watercolour, 64.6 x 49.7 cm, Museum of Art, Rhode Island School of Design

Bone Black & Ivory Black

In any case, they are both of animal origin, regarding the names, it is a confusing mess. Verifying whether you are dealing with true ivory black or bone black, is extremely difficult. The latter is significantly cheaper than the former, but ivory black was and is also called bone black and vice versa.

The pigments and paints that pass for ivory black these days are usually bone black. You can easily make both using slaughterhouse waste such as bones and teeth. For water-based wall-painting neither bone nor ivory blacks were recommended because of the bleeding, inherent to fine-grained pigments. In the past, the pure and original bone black was recognisable by its typical brown hue. It was originally (and still is) made from charred animal bones. A variant would have been made by replacing the bones with the skeletal remains of fish. Believed to be the main ingredient of the historical Chinese ink.

Bone black has a deeper tone than soot black and can be found in abundance on the palettes of painters since the 16th century. Unlike bone black, high-quality ivory black has a blue tinge and is somewhat transparent. The Greek painter Apelles called it *elephantinum*, perhaps because it was made from elephant tusks,

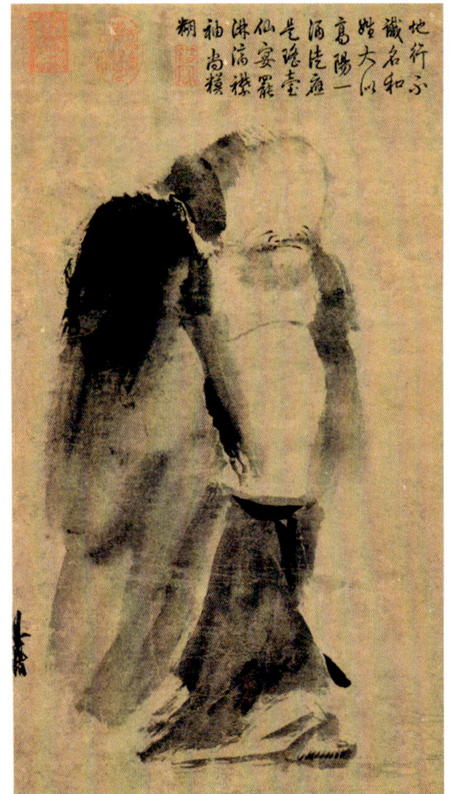

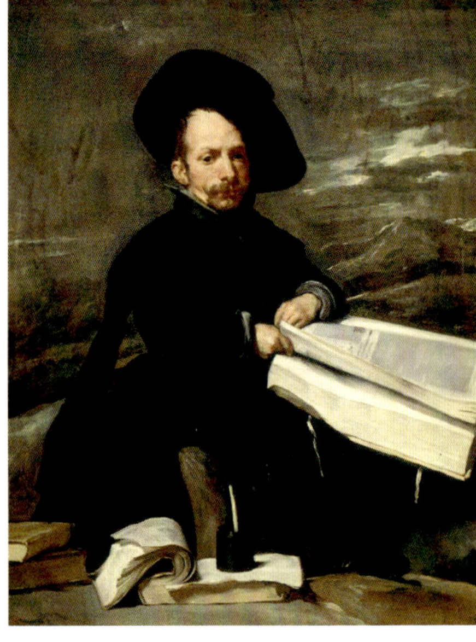

Liang Kai, *Immortal in Splashed Ink*, 13de cen., ink on paper, Nationaal Paleis Museum, Taipei

Diego Velázquez, *The Jester Don Diego de Acedo*, c. 1645, oil on canvas, 106 x 83 cm, Prado, Madrid

of the waste remaining after they were turned into ornamental objects. Like bone black, it has been found in prehistoric paintings. To make it yourself, you roast pieces of ivory in a pan. These can be all kinds of teeth, objects made from ivory, such as combs, and the waste of ivory carvers. Horns and antlers were occasionally used, despite them not being ivory. Kurt Wehlte provides a fine description of the firing of real ivory after visiting the factory in Schweinfurt, founded by Wilhelm Sattler in 1925. At the time, the factory was renowned worldwide for its excellent ivory black and Wehlte arrives to gather information for his standard work on artists' materials. He notes that the remains of ivory are heaped in iron pots as airtight as possible and then sealed with clay. Once the kiln has reached the right temperature, the pots are put in. He obviously wants to know at what temperature and how long the firing time needs to be and inquires with the old and experienced fire master.

In reply, the latter wordlessly places the back of his hand up against the kiln, at shoulder height: it is all about feeling, listening and experience. Four years later, the curtain falls on the factory, and the celebrated ivory black disappears from the palette.

(Circle of) Jan van Scorel, *Portrait of a Venetian man*, c. 1520, oil on panel, 45 x 33.5 cm, Niedersächsisches Landesmuseum, Oldenbrug

Floris Verster, *Dead Crow* 1907, oil on canvas, 55,5 x 37 cm, Dordrechts Museum

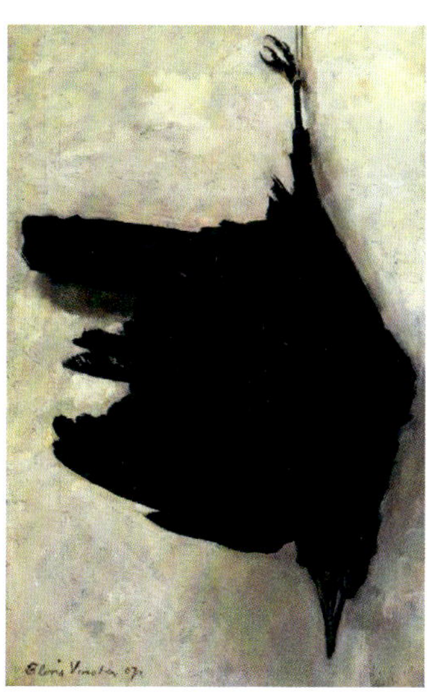

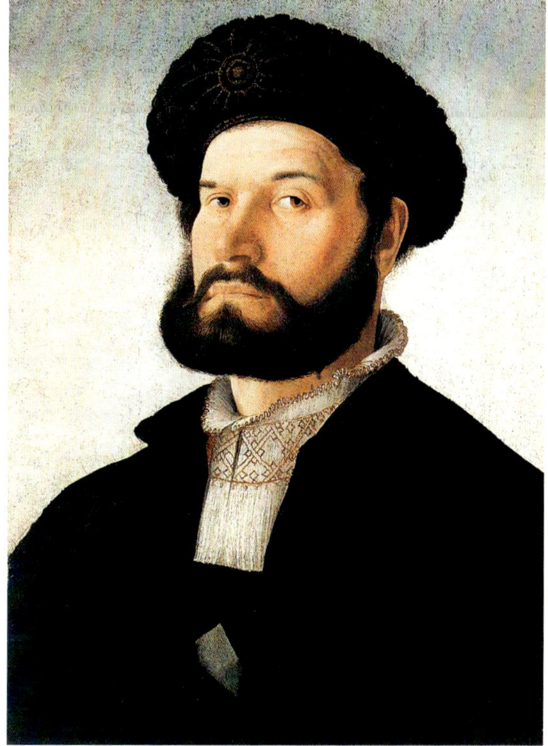

Graphite

A pencil is a mixture of fired graphite and clay in a wooden rod. Offered in twenty hardness from 9H to 9B, ranging from very hard to very soft. A few manufacturers offer twenty-four gradations.

There is a discussion regarding who exactly created this code in the 19th century. The letter H stands for *hard*, F for *firm* and B for *black*. Some say that H refers to Hardtmuth, B to Budweis, and F to Franz Hardtmuth. Names associated with one of the oldest pencil manufacturing families and factories, founded in 1790 in Vienna by Joseph Hardtmuth and established in 1816 in Budweis, today's České Budějovice in the Czech Republic. The above hardness grades apply specifically to the European market, as different codes are used in the United States, Russia, Japan and some other countries. The first graphite pens were the direct result of the 16th-century discovery of a large quantity of pure graphite deposits in Cumbria, northwest England. The first and only time such pure graphite would be found in Europe. The graphite was easy to cut into pieces and was therefore thought to be a type of lead. In 1778, the chemist Scheele (of the earlier mentioned Scheele's green) proved that this soft black-grey material was not lead but a form of carbon related to coal. It took another ten years before mineralogist

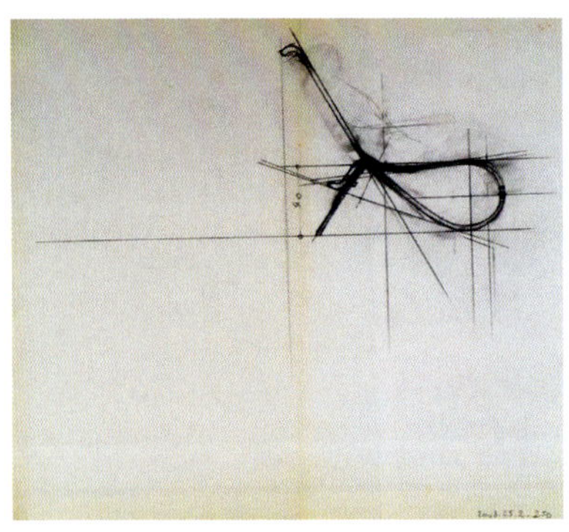

Jean Burkhalter, *Adjustable armchair* 1928, pencil on paper, 29 x 32 cm, Musée des Arts Décoratifs, Paris

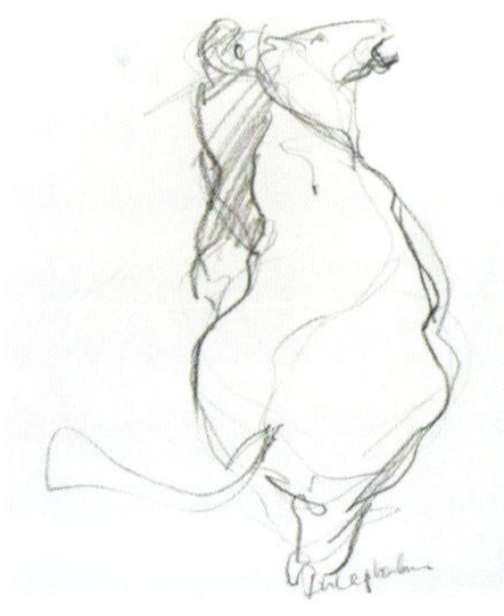

monica rotgans, *Bucephalus*, 1992, pencil on paper, 24 x 25 cm, artist's collection

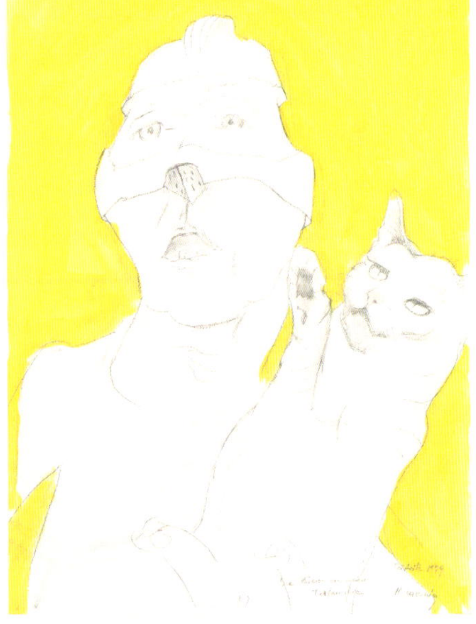

Maria Lassnig, *The Illusion of My Animal Family*, 1999, Albertina, Vienna

Abraham Gottlob Werner suggested the name graphite, derived from the Greek *graphein*, writing.
Because graphite is brittle and stains, these early pens were wrapped in string or sheepskin. Towards the end of the 16th century, the Italian couple Bernacotti devised the idea of encasing graphite in hollow cypress twigs. An idea that was quickly improved by placing the graphite rods between two hollowed-out planks and gluing them together.
The war between England and Napoleonic France ended graphite exports to Europe, and the search for alternatives began. Joseph Hardtmuth developed a process in which graphite dust was mixed with water and clay and fired in a kiln: the birth of the modern pencil.
Pure graphite is a material from which you can also carve a sculpture.

Lead, chalk, slate and coal have been used since early antiquity in one form or another as basic materials to express oneself in image and idea to communicate. The ancient Egyptians had already invented the concept of filling reed and papyrus cane with lead 5,000 years ago. The Dutch word *potlood*, stems from this older variant, the lead stylus, made with molten lead; the cheaper version of a silverpoint stylus. Neither one is as strong as graphite.
The English word pencil was derived from the 14th-century pence, which, in turn, stems from the Latin *penicillus*, brush.

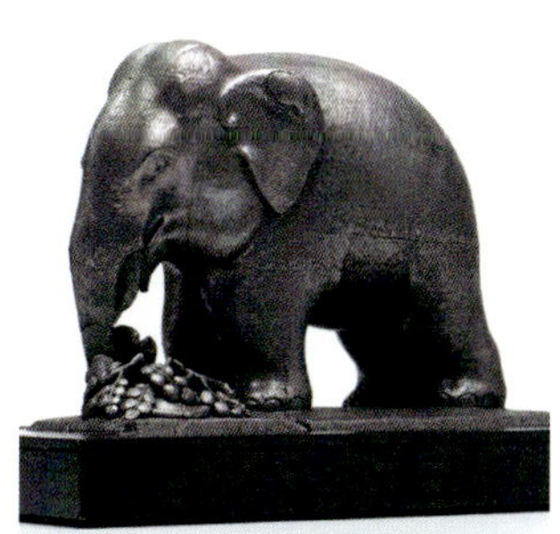

Anonymous, *Elephant*, c. 1875-1880, carved graphite, Ceylon, Powerhouse Museum, Sydney

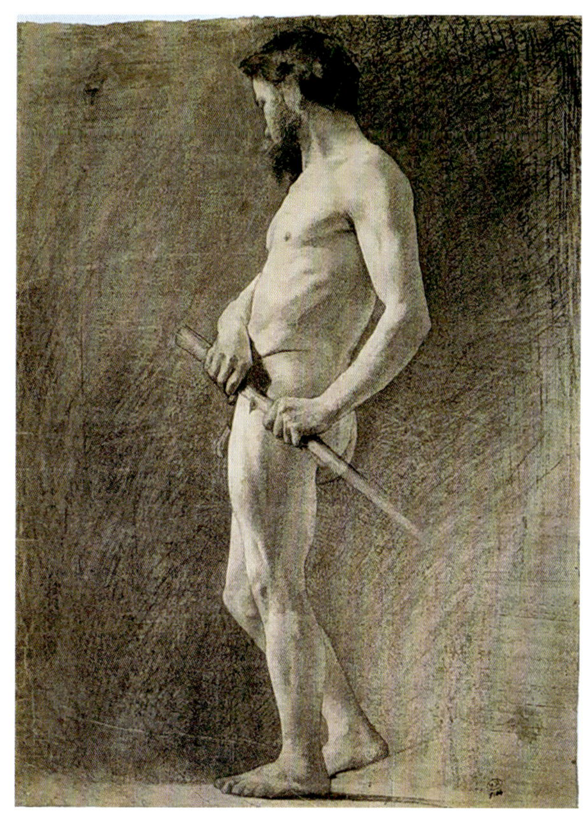

Auguste Rodin, *Study of a Man*, c. 1854-1857, pencil on paper, Musée Rodin, Paris

Composite Blacks

It seems a simple colour, black. The black pigments described earlier are fairly evident in terms of origin and character. But many more blacks were made than there is space here to discuss them.

In the 16th century, 27 different fruitstone blacks were known as pigment. These blacks were derived from charring the pits of stone fruits such as peach, plum and apricot, with each variety producing a slightly different tint.

An unfathomable abundance compared to today's limited range. One way of nearing that colour range is to compose blacks by mixing or overlaying colours. That way, you can create various red, green or blue and warm and cool blacks. The advantage is that it allows you to keep a nice consistency with a limited palette, because the colours are connected and not spoiled by an additional black paint.

A palette composed of, for example, madder, ultramarine, burnt sienna, and white ranges from cool (madder) to warm (ultramarine and sienna) and from light to dark. With the dark colours as potential mixing colours for blacks.

In Blechen's landscape, I believe the combination of burnt sienna and Prussian blue is to blame for the browns in the foreground. Prussian blue can lose its

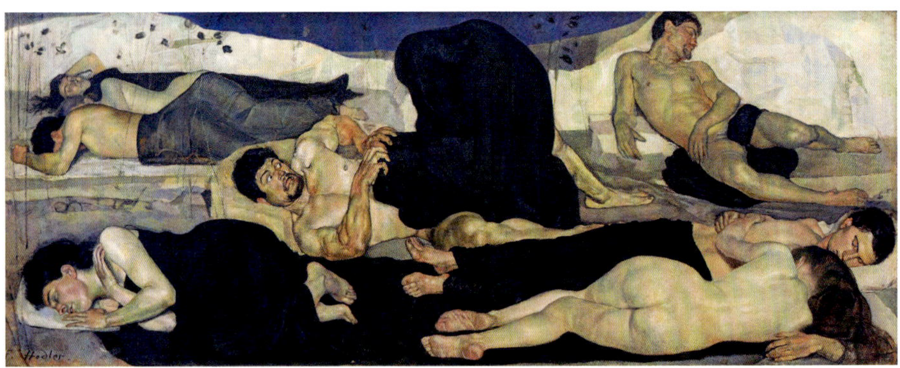

Ferdinand Hodler, *Night*, 1889, oil on canvas, 116,5 x 299 cm, Kunstmuseum, Bern

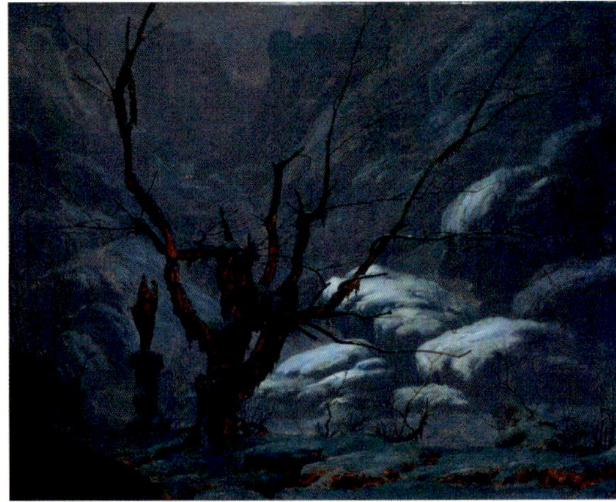

Carl Blechen, *Mountain Gorge in Winter*, 1825, oil on canvas, 98 x 127 cm, Alte Nationalgalerie, Berlin

colour, and here, it could be possible that the thin blue glacis over the burnt sienna has disappeared, so we no longer see the original black.
This combining of pigments can be compared to mixing blacks for the dyeing of fabrics. Black, deep black clothing symbolised status.
In contrast to how a deep blue can be made with indigo, no dye existed that produces a proper, black with depth. To achieve deep blacks, fabrics must alternately be dyed in, for example, a blue and a red dyebath. This is a labour-intensive and precise method, with only the most exquisite fabrics allowing the richest colour. It sounds quite simple, but, like all handicrafts, it takes time to achieve the desired result. The same applies to preserving the black in fabrics. Regardless of how fine or expensive a new garment is, black remains a sensitive colour and will rapidly fade with wear. Therefore, the portrait of Philip the Good left nothing to be doubted: here stands a mighty man.

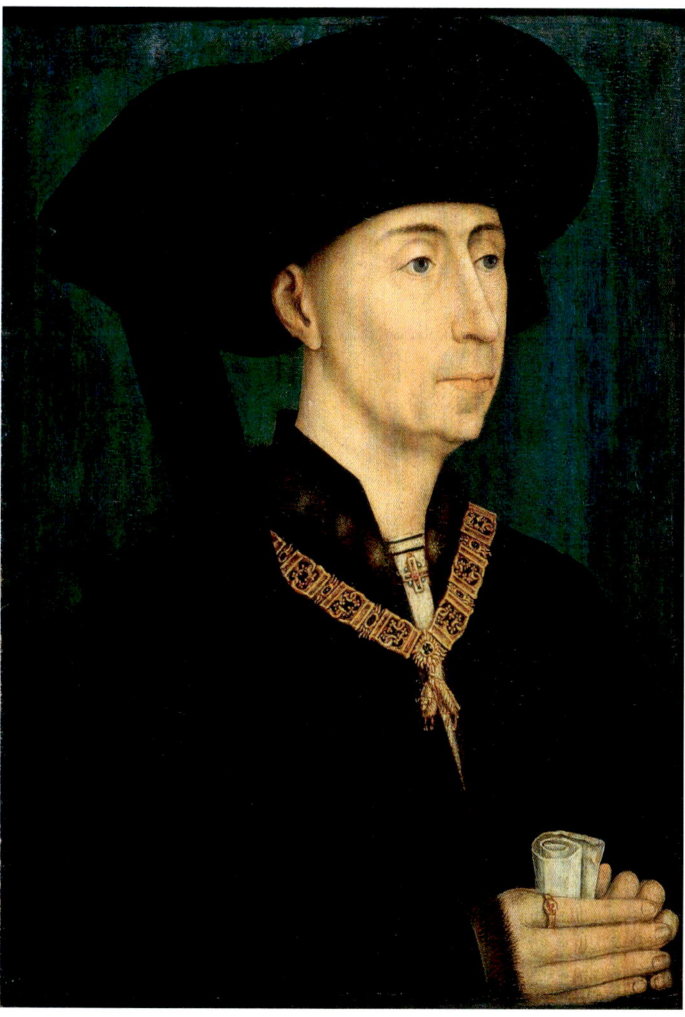

Rogier van der Weyden, *Portrait of Philip the Good*, c. 1450, oil on panel, 29.6 x 21.3 cm, Musée des Beaux-Arts de Dijon

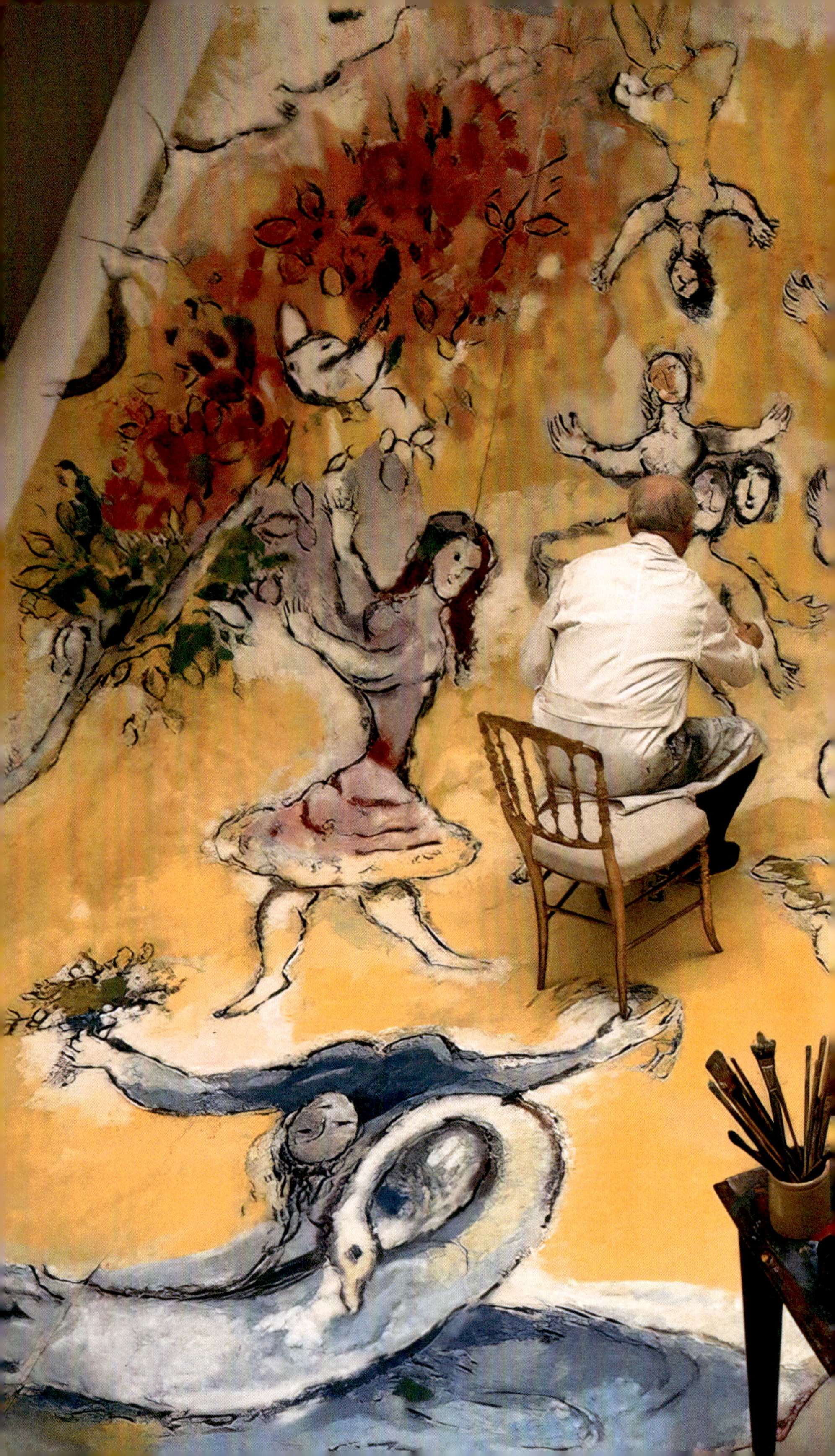

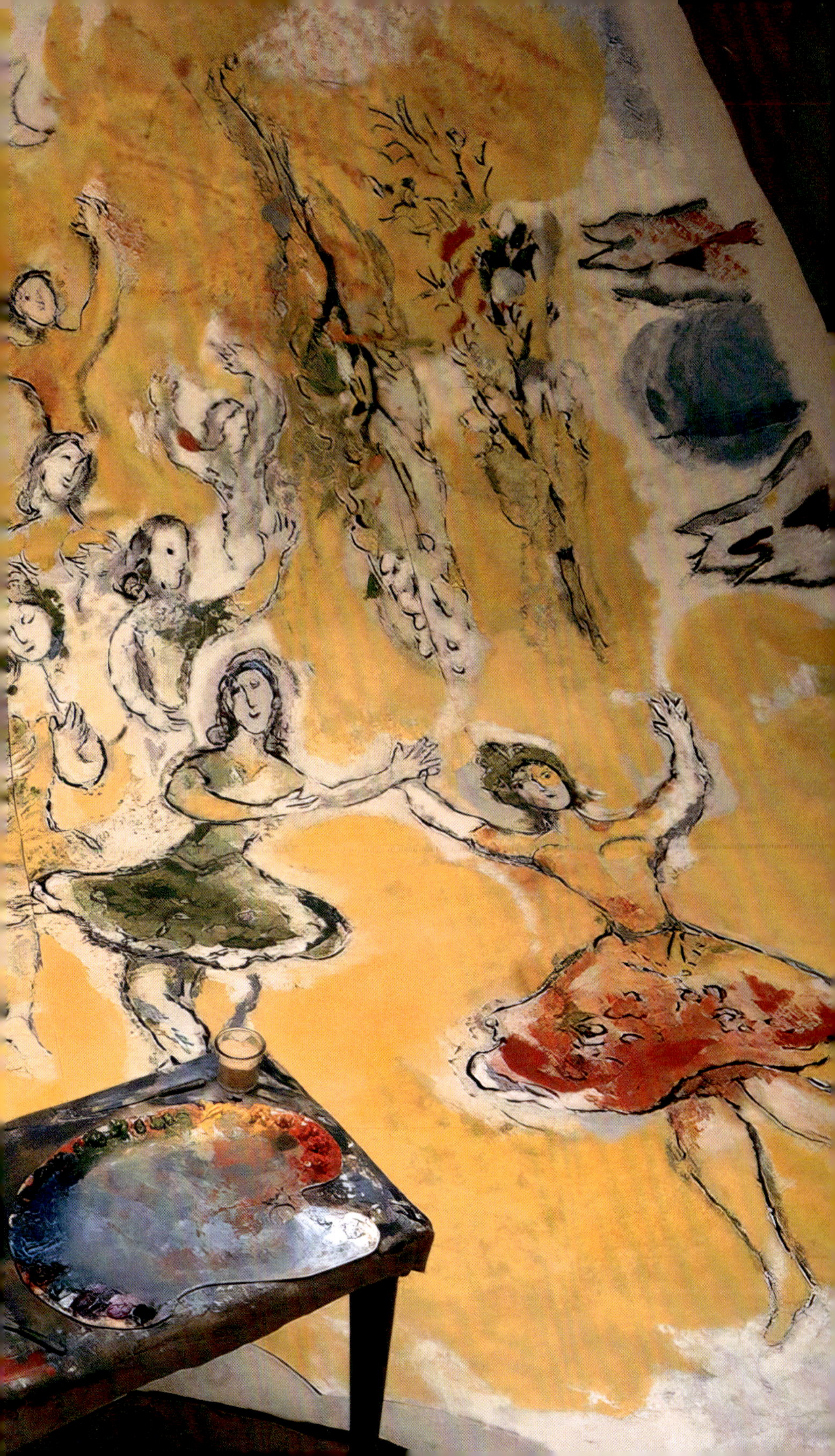

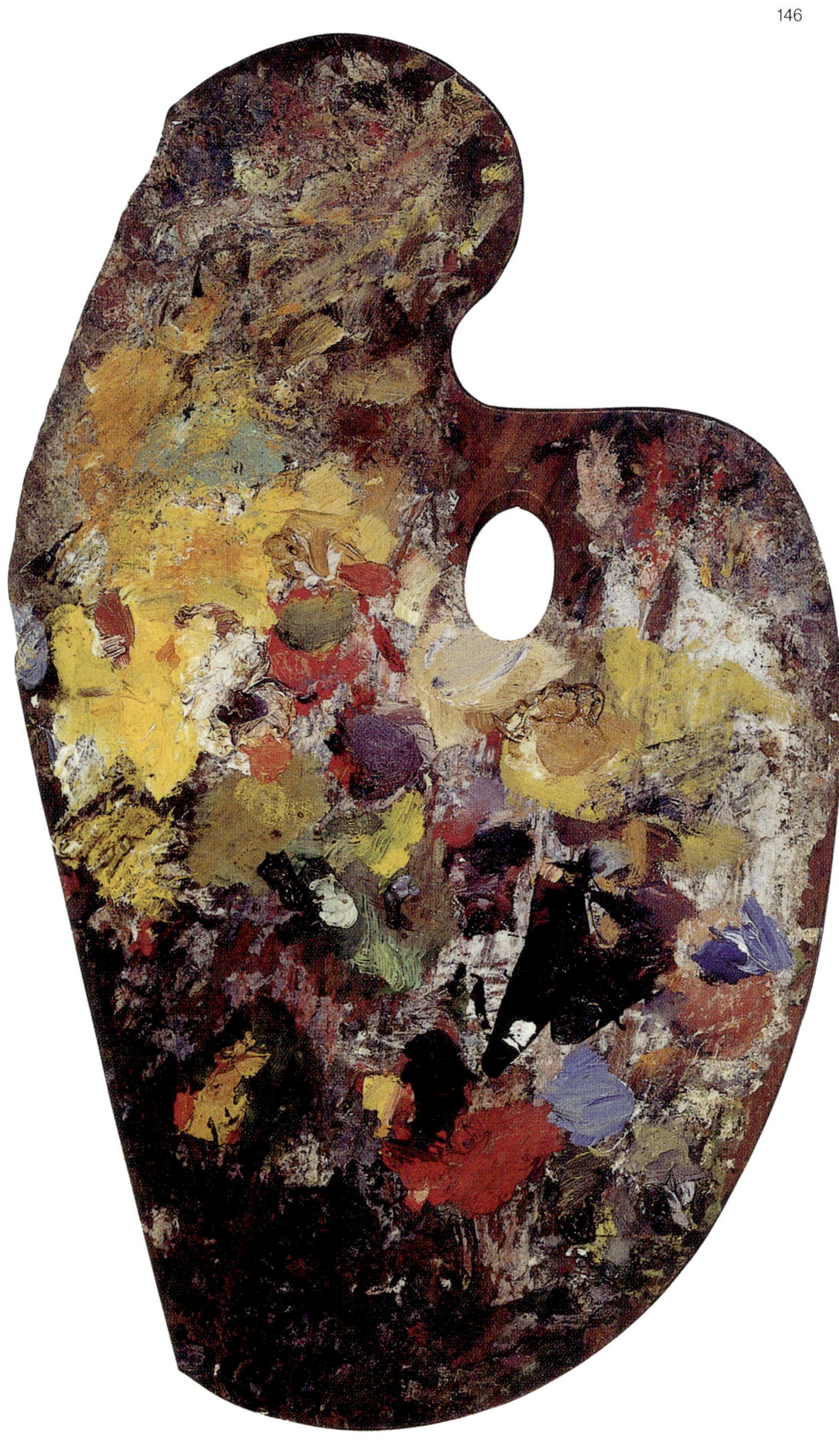

Conclusion

'The laws of colour are inexpressibly splendid precisely because they are NOT *coincidences.*'

Vincent van Gogh, 1884

The palette has a temperament of its own. Be it a board with paint or, figuratively, the sense effect of the colours. For everyone working with colour, in whatever way, the composition of the palette will determine the final result. Whether it is via pigments, pixels, or fibres.

The most important colours and raw materials in the existence of the human species have been illustrated in previous chapters. Some lasted for many millennia, others vanished after a short, occasionally brief, period of time.

Prior to approximately 150 years ago the basic palette consisted of a clearly defined number of colours. A core of earth pigments supplemented by a black and a white. Strong reds, blues, greens, and yellows, as required, could be added or blended. This system was in practical use all over the world. In our modern era it completely changed.

< Monet's palette

Diego Velázquez, *Self-Portrait*, detail of *Las Meninas*, 320.5 x 281.5 cm, oil on canvas, Prado, Madrid. In every way a small palette for a great work. Earth colours, vermilion, ivory or soot black and lead white.

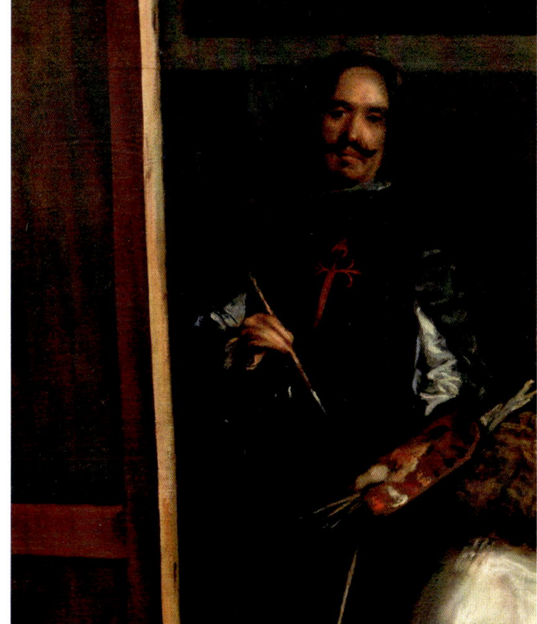

Previous pages: Marc Chagall's palette for the creation of the Mozart fragment of the ceiling painting in the Opéra Garnier in Paris, it incorporates the entire colour spectrum. From black, to cool and warm violets, ditto blues, greens, yellows and reds, with the whites separated to avoid contamination.

Traditionally, the palette is a product of the local environment. Palettes are shaped by time and place, by the paints the artist can afford, and by the mood and possible message to be conveyed through the work of art. Nowadays, we don't need to take these factors into our consideration. The availability of materials is unlimited, we have good alternatives for expensive pigments, and no longer must our art take a subservient role. Does this mean that with our limitless palette, we will achieve better results? Not necessarily, too many colours together can nullify each other. This is the reason for the innumerable recipes and methods for rendering skin, skies, landscapes, clothing, objects, and more. To give colour and form their most effective representation.

Colours come into their own right, as do people, when in harmony. Various colour theories have been developed during the past centuries to gain an oversight of this harmony. The French chemist Eugène Chevreul (1786-1889) had enormous influence with his theories on the art of painting. A great pioneer of the 'new palette' in the 19th century, Chevreul's 1839 published treatise, *De la Loi du Contraste Simultané des Couleurs*, laid the theoretical foundations for painters such as Delacroix, the impressionists, and the pointillists, establishing the fertile ground for the modern visual arts.
At age 17, Chevreul departs Angers for Paris to study chemistry. Some years later, he becomes assistant to Nicolas Vauquelin (1763-1829), the pharmacist and chemist who, at that time, has several newly invented pigments to his name. In 1813, Eugène Chevreul is appointed professor of chemistry at the Lycée Charlemagne. This appointment is followed by a directorship at the renowned *Ateliers Gobelins*. Here he also is responsible for the coloured yarn with which the frequently large tapestries (known as *gobelins*) are produced. Soon, he encounters the complaints made regarding the mediocre colouring of the tapestries. Apparently, it is not so much a chemical as an optical problem. A black that has been much criticised, itself a perfect

Chevreul's colour wheel. At the left with the original yarns that were dyed at the Gobelin factory and have now lost their original colour strength. Beside it the same wheel in watercolour on white paper.

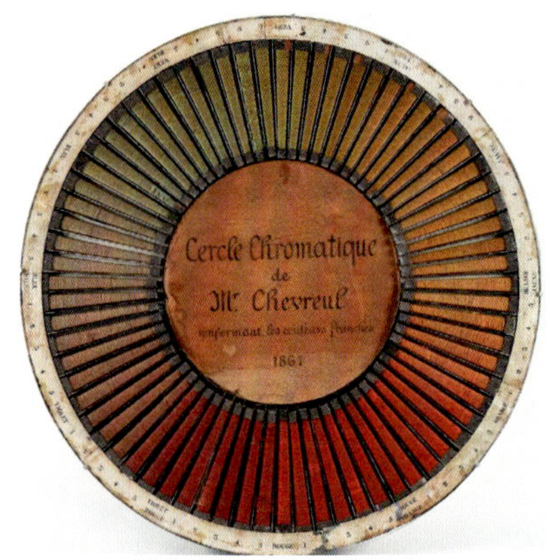

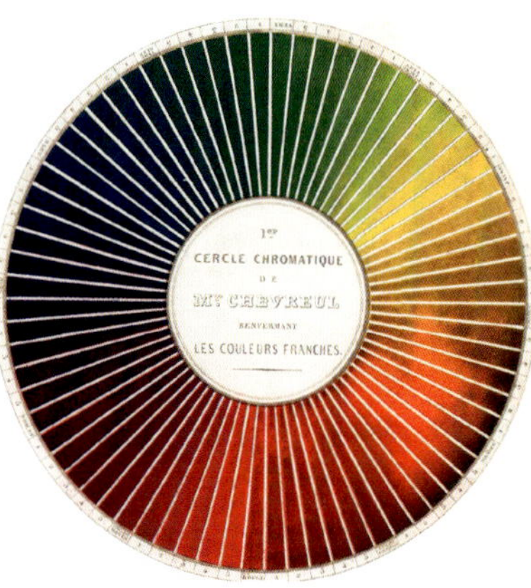

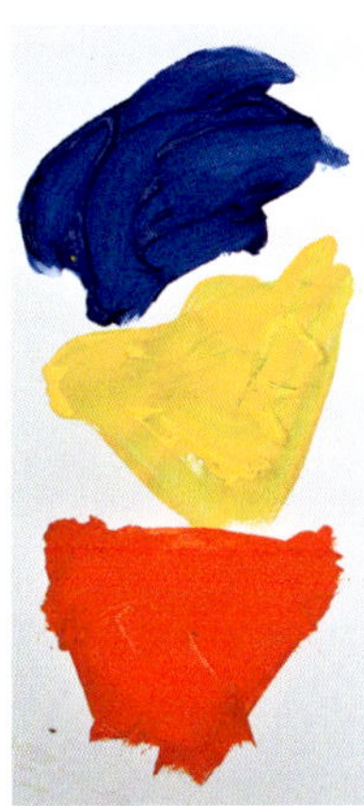

The primary colours blue, yellow and red

colour, when placed adjacent to a blue appears to change into a weak, reddish black. Chevreul's research into the interaction of colours results in the description of what he refers to as the simultaneous contrast of colours: a phenomenon occurring when we look at a certain colour, and our eye or brain wants automatically to add a complementary colour. You could evoke this, for example, by focusing your eyesight on a red shape and then onto a white wall where you may then see the same shape present as green. Chevreul's theory, and his colour wheel it brought forth, subsequently gave painters a holdfast, enabling them to work with the hitherto unusual colour combinations.

On the right-hand side illustrated circle diagram, colours appear to easily merge into each other. In painting, this is achieved only with the use of a warm and a cool variant for each 'primary' colour. To have colours successfully working together, this specific phenomenon, colour temperature, is of utmost importance.
In Chevreul's diagram, reds emerging from the warm blues and purples are cool. Closer to yellow, the reds turn warm orange. Near blue the yellow becomes cooler and greener, so-called lemon yellow. Each colour, in terms of temperature, covers the spectrum from warm to cool. Keeping this in mind provides a good basis for the setting up a palette. For example, when mixing colours with a limited palette. To obtain purples you will need a warm blue (ultramarine) and a cool red (madder). Vice versa, using a cool blue (phthalo blue) blended with a warm red (cadmium) will give you a brownish grey. It is preferable to use transparent colours; with opaque paint, the colours lose their brightness and strength. This principle clearly deviates from the contemporary approach based on three primary colours with a limited colour temperature: blue is cool, and red and yellow are warm. It is a useless classification for painting, which is still taught at (art)schools and academies. Paint manufacturers, grasping this opportunity, offer so-called basic sets with one blue, one yellow, one red, a white and black, adding a catch phrase like: 'all colours can be made with this set'. You might recognise this from primary school. Children were (are still) given paper and three bright dots of primary colours that gradually dull during painting, resulting in a sheet of paper covered with obscure browns to take home.

Self-portraits, including their palettes, may offer more insight to better understand what does work. They provide an idea of the colours used to create what you see. I have chosen two examples from approximately the same period: self-portraits by the Belgian Magritte and by the German Dix. In every respect, they are opposites. Magritte chose to use, for his painting *La Clairvoyance*, an earthy palette. A red, a yellow, and a brown earth, white and black: none of the so-called primary colours. It is literally and

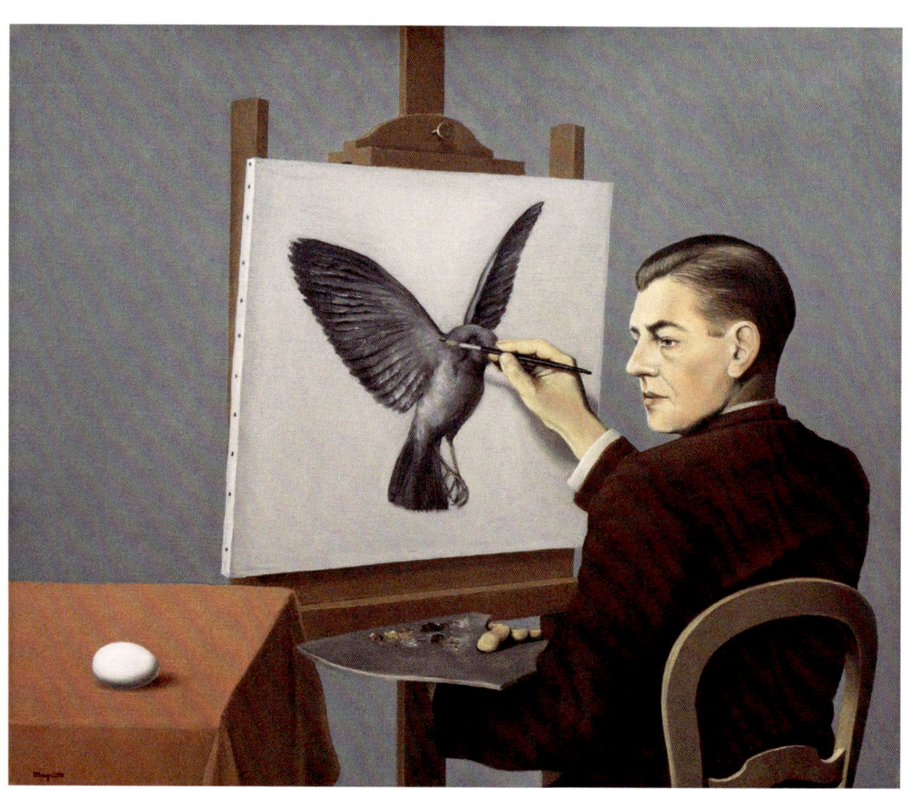

René Magritte,
La Clairvoyance,
1936, oil on canvas,
54 x 64.9 cm,
private collection

figuratively a small palette with a cool and distant atmosphere. Similarly, Otto Dix opted for a limited palette, though with a different temperament: intense and emotional. Warm cadmium red is the leading colour, supported by a cool rose madder, a warm burnt sienna, a cool Prussian blue and a white. The green landscape was painted at an earlier stage with an additional yellow. A grim self-portrait made when Dix was banned by the Nazi regime, his art labelled as *entartet* (degenerate art) with the world on fire: World War II. Both artists were professionals and masters in the use of their materials. Magritte's skills enabled him to make a living during that same period with forgeries of De Chiricos, Picassos, and Braques.

Working as an artist is a wonderful, at times difficult, and very old, profession. The more knowledge acquired, the more facets of the craft mastered, the more space made possible for the creative process. With the colours in this book, and through the materials and palettes of artists, I hope to have given you a whole new perspective on art.

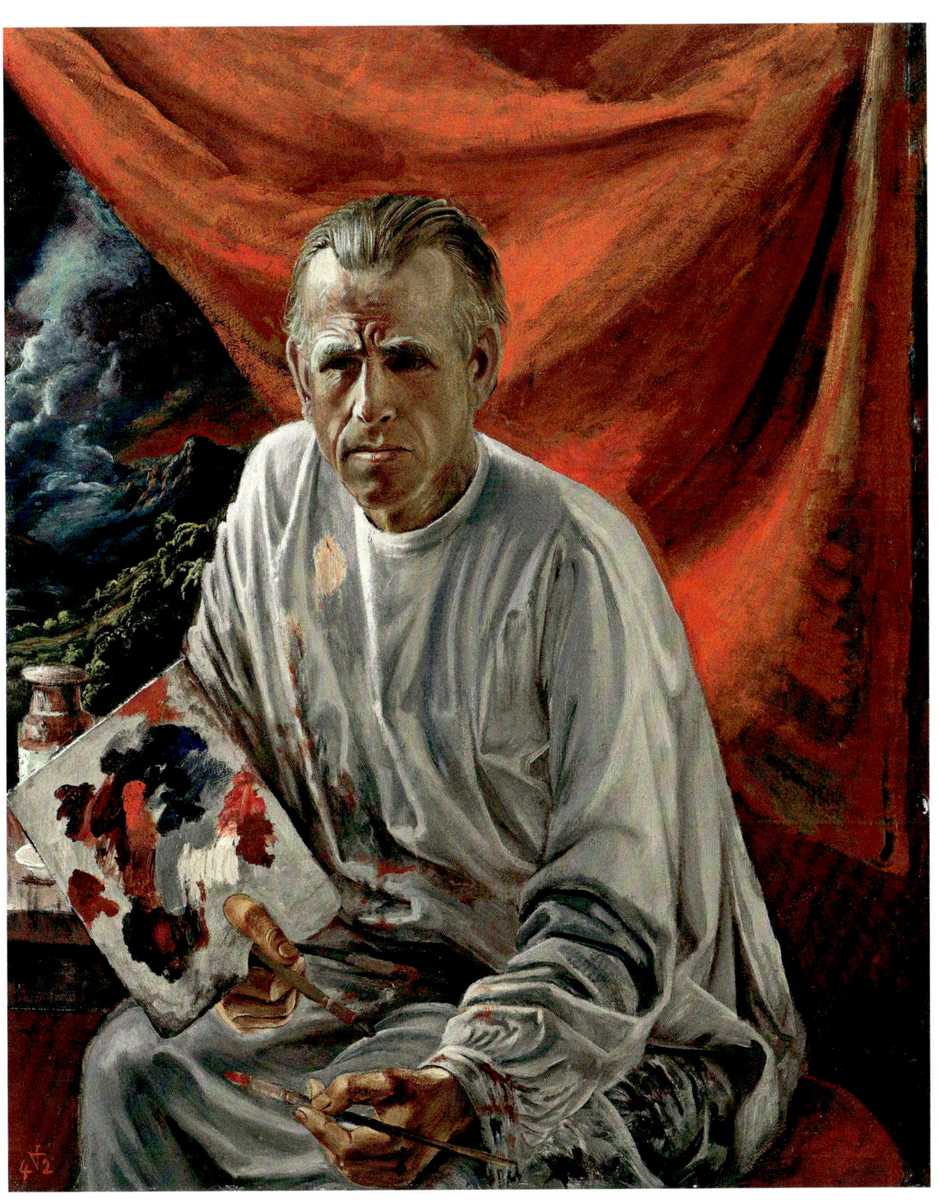

Otto Dix, *Self-Portrait with a Palette before a Red Curtain*, 1942, oil on panel, 100 x 80 cm, Kunstmuseum Stuttgart

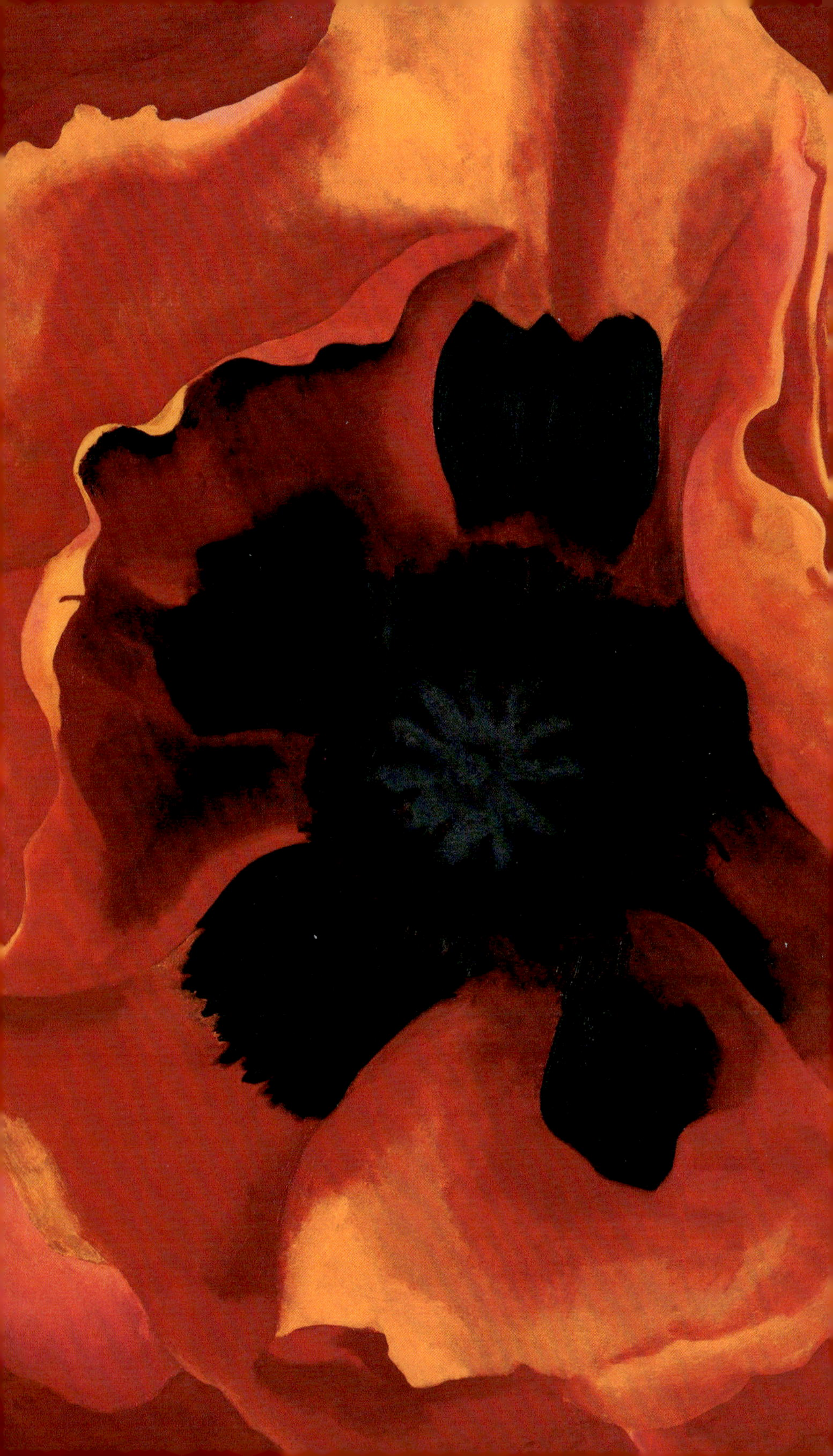

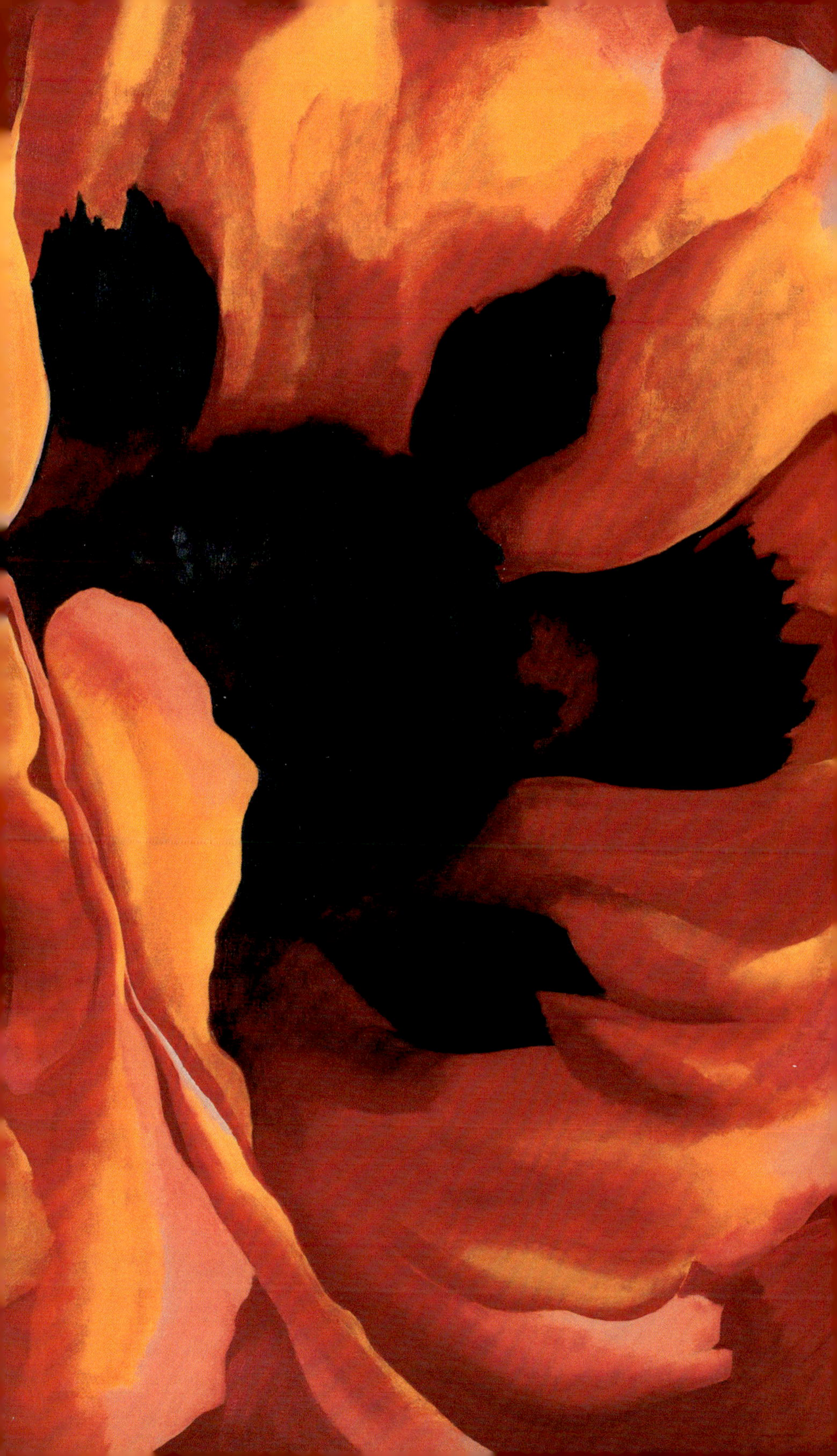

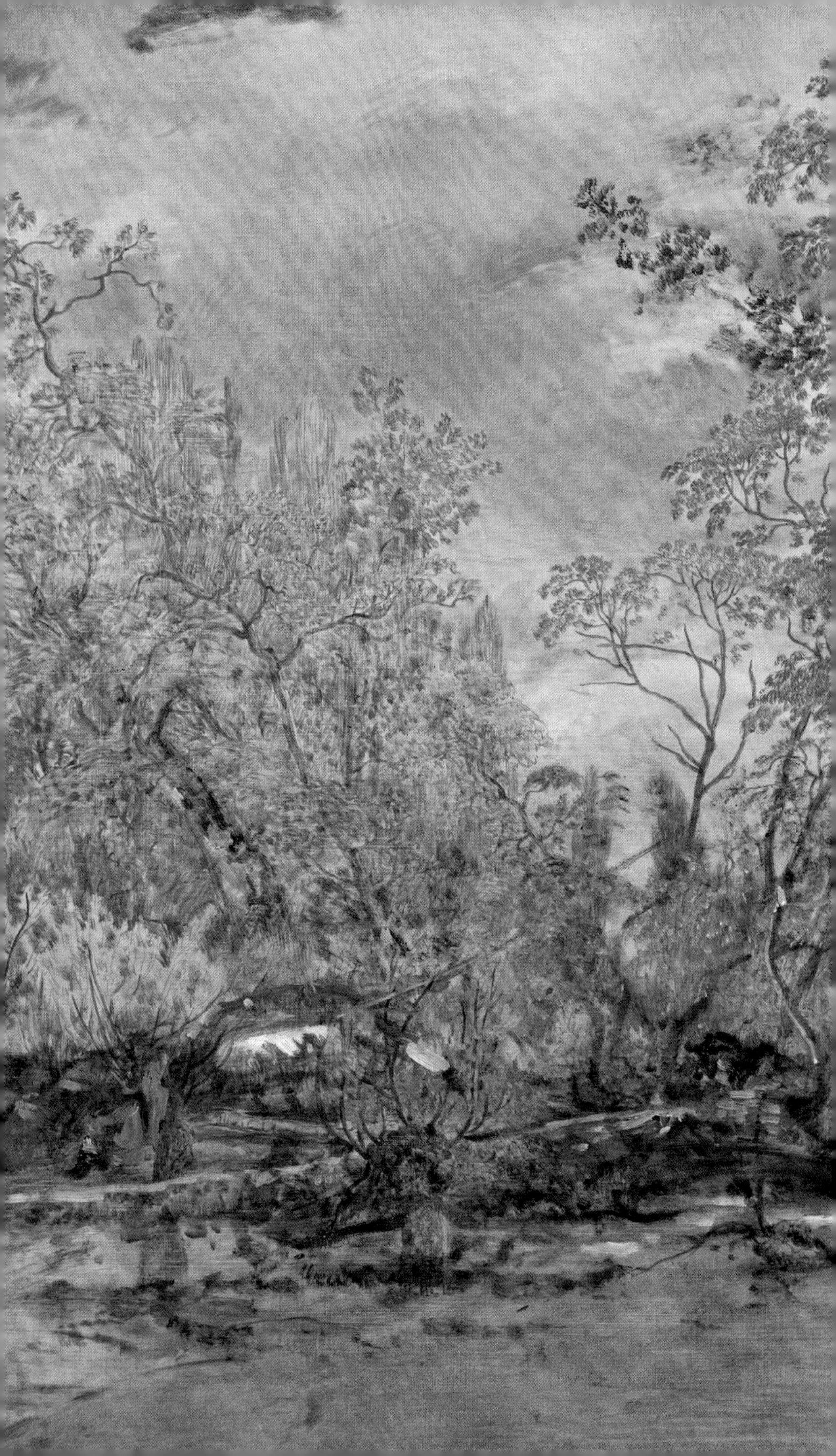

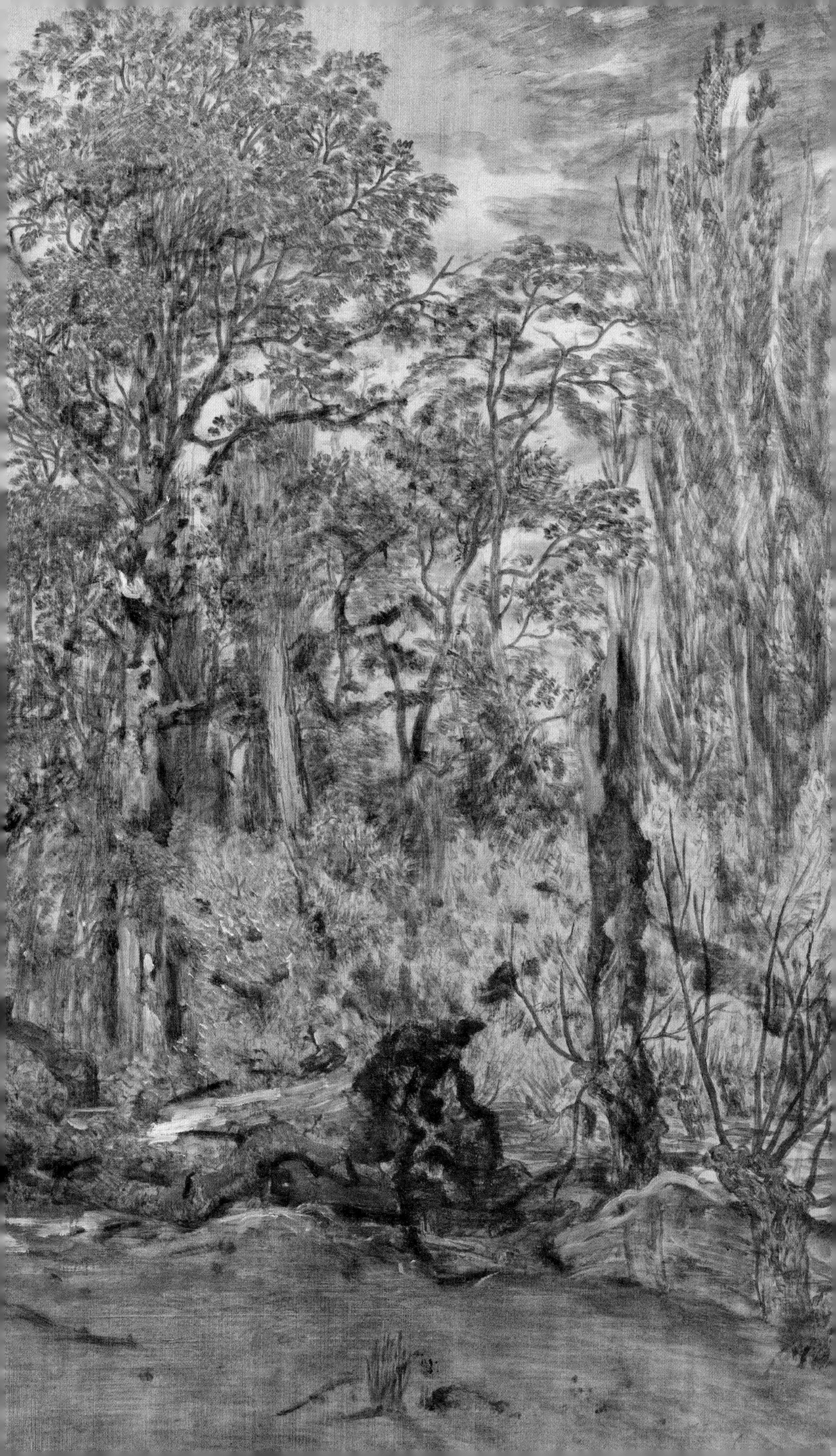

Glossary

Binder
A liquid used to 'bind' dry matter into a workable substance.

Bleeding
Suffusion of fine pigment particles into or through a paint layer, affecting the original colour.

Bolus ground
A painting ground containing reddish clay, called bole.

Colour temperature
Classifying colours from warm to cool. For painting, we distinguish between a warm and a cool variant for each primary colour.

Craquelure
The appearance of small and larger cracks in a paint layer.

Decorator
A painter specialised in the colouring of sculpture and ornamental architecture.

Dye
A substance used to colour textiles and objects. They can be used with a liquid solvent which adheres easily to a surface.

Dyer
A craftsman who dyes cloth and other materials.

Fresco
A type of mural painting executed upon fresh plaster. Water is used as the vehicle for the pigment to fuse with the plaster.

Glaze
A (semi-)transparent paint layer, generally applied to enhance an underlying colour. For example, red lake/madder over cinnabar.

Gouache
A fine, opaque water colour. Also, the name for the painting made with it.

Inorganic
Not consisting of live matter (i.e. neither animal nor vegetal).

Halftones
A tone whose grey value is between white and black. Can be made by mixing blues, browns and other dark colours with a white, or varying the thickness of a colour on a light background.

Hue
In colour theory 'tint'. For paint manufacturers a means to indicate a non-original pigment, resembling the original colour.

Illuminator
A limner, a painter of ornamental decorations in manuscripts and books.

Lake
As in lake pigments, for example madder. Mostly organic.

Mural
A painting on a wall with any kind of paint.

Opaque
Not transparent, lacking lustre. Pigments can be naturally opaque, such as yellow earth and chalk. Paints like gouache and poster paints are always opaque.

Organic
Derived from something living. From plants, animals and other living organisms.

Parchment
Prepared animal skin for writing and painting.

Pigment
A fine-grained, coloured, non-soluble, substance.

Pigment number
The so-called *Colour Index*, an international colour system, uses generic names for each pigment and a unique pigment serial number to clarify the pigment used in a product.

Potash
A mixture of salts, mainly potassium carbonate.

Painter
A person working with paint. Includes art painters, house painters and advertising painters.

Grinding
The rubbing and mixing, of dry pigment with oil or glue to make a paint, on a flat slab of stone or piece of glass.

Siccative
An agent to help paint dry faster.

Solvent
A substance that can break down a soluble material. For example white spirit, not to be confused with turpentine, a thinner.

Tempera
A distemper paint with a matte finish. The best-known form is based on egg yolk.

Gouache, Poster Paint
An opaque semi-permanent water colour. In the better form, gouache.

Thinner
A generally volatile liquid used to dilute paint or varnish, without influencing the original character.

Transparent
See-through, used in painting to refer to lake pigments.

Varnish
A transparent hard, protective coating applied over paint or other materials to seal and protect the surface against mildew, moisture or light. Also provides gloss and intensifies brilliance and depth of colours. It existed in numerous variations with natural ingredients. Modern, synthetic, varnishes are solvent based. A pigment can be added for extra effect.

Vellum
Fine parchment of the highest quality.

About the Author

monica rotgans is a visual artist, researcher and author and has been active in various disciplines for more than forty years. She has previously published *Blauw Groen* (Blue Green) and *Verf* (Paint), now a standard work.

Further Reading

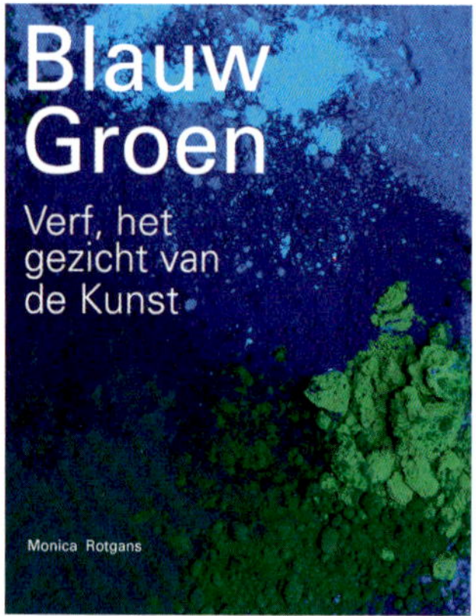

www.monicarotgans.nl
7colours.monicarotgans.nl
www.artiscreation.com
www.wildpigmentproject.org
www.webexhibits.org/pigments
www.kremer-pigmente.com
www.okhra.com
www.thisiscolossal.com/2018/01/werners-nomenclature-of-colours
https://paintingbynumbers.dxlab.sl.nsw.gov.au/
www.earlyfutures.com
www.seilnacht.com

Credits

Publishers
Waanders Publishers,
Zwolle

Author
monica rotgans

Translation
Claire van den Donk,
edited by Emily O'Shea
Eugene Jacques Petit
(Introduction and Conclusion)

Design
Studio Berry Slok,
Amsterdam

Lithography
Benno Slijkhuis,
Wilco Art Books, Amersfoort

Printing
Wilco Art Books,
Amersfoort

Photography
Maurcio Abreu: 132 r.a., Helena Arendt: 111 b., Izis-Manuel Bidermanas, Adagp, Paris: 144-145, Jodi Cobb: 126 l.a., M. Courtney-Clarke: 6, 26 l., 104 l.a., Lox Goes: 108, Van Gogh Museum (Vincent van Gogh Stichting): 35, 71, 105 Norbert Hinterberger: 117, Eugene Jacques: 50 b., Mathilde Karrèr (schilderijen monica rotgans): 10-11, 15, 49, 53, 74, 104, 107, 108, 136, 140, Toril Kojan: 107, Claus Meyer: 43 l., Nick Neddo: 82, Fabby Nielsen: 91 b., Philip Poupin: 84 b., Mirella Ricciardi: 124, monica rotgans: 13, 30 r.a., 31 l., 41 r., 42 r., 44 r., 49 l.b., 52, 67 l.a., 70 o. en l.b., 81 b., 83 b., 99 r.a., 100 l.b., 104 b., 199 l., 120 r.a. en r.b., 125 r.a., 126 b., 131 r., 133 r., 137 b., 149, Lisanne Sloots: 133

p. 1 Jan Sluijters, detail of *Portret van Greet van Cooten*, 1910, oil on canvas, 41 x 33 cm, Singer Laren, gift the Nardinc Collection
p. 2 Piet Mondriaan, *No. 2*, 1927, oil on canvas, 50.2 x 35.2 cm, private collection
p. 3 Anonymous, detail of *Wilg met mussen*, c. 1920, copper greens, mica, gold, ink and gofun on silk, 98 x 135 cm, coll. Kristan Hauge, Kyoto
p. 4-5 Jacobus van Looy, *De tuin*, 1893, oil on canvas, 93 x 137 cm, Teylers Museum, Haarlem
p. 6 The women of the Soninke paint exclusively with their hands and with pigments sourced around the Senegal River.
p. 8 Detail of p. 32
p. 10-11 monica rotgans, *Ochre Hills*, 2019, earths and chalk on panel, 51 x 40 cm, coll. artist
p. 24-25 See p. 61
p. 152-153 Georgia O'Keeffe, *Orientaalse klaprozen*, 1927, oil on canvas, 101.6 x 76 cm, Weisman Art Museum, Minneapolis
p. 154-155 Théodore Rousseau, *Moord op de onschuldigen*, 1847, oil on canvas, 95 x 146.5 cm, The Mesdag Collection, The Hague
p. 160 Detail of p. 70

ISBN 978 94 6262 601 0

This publication has also been published in a Dutch edition.
ISBN 978 94 6262 432 0

NUR 640

www.waanders.nl

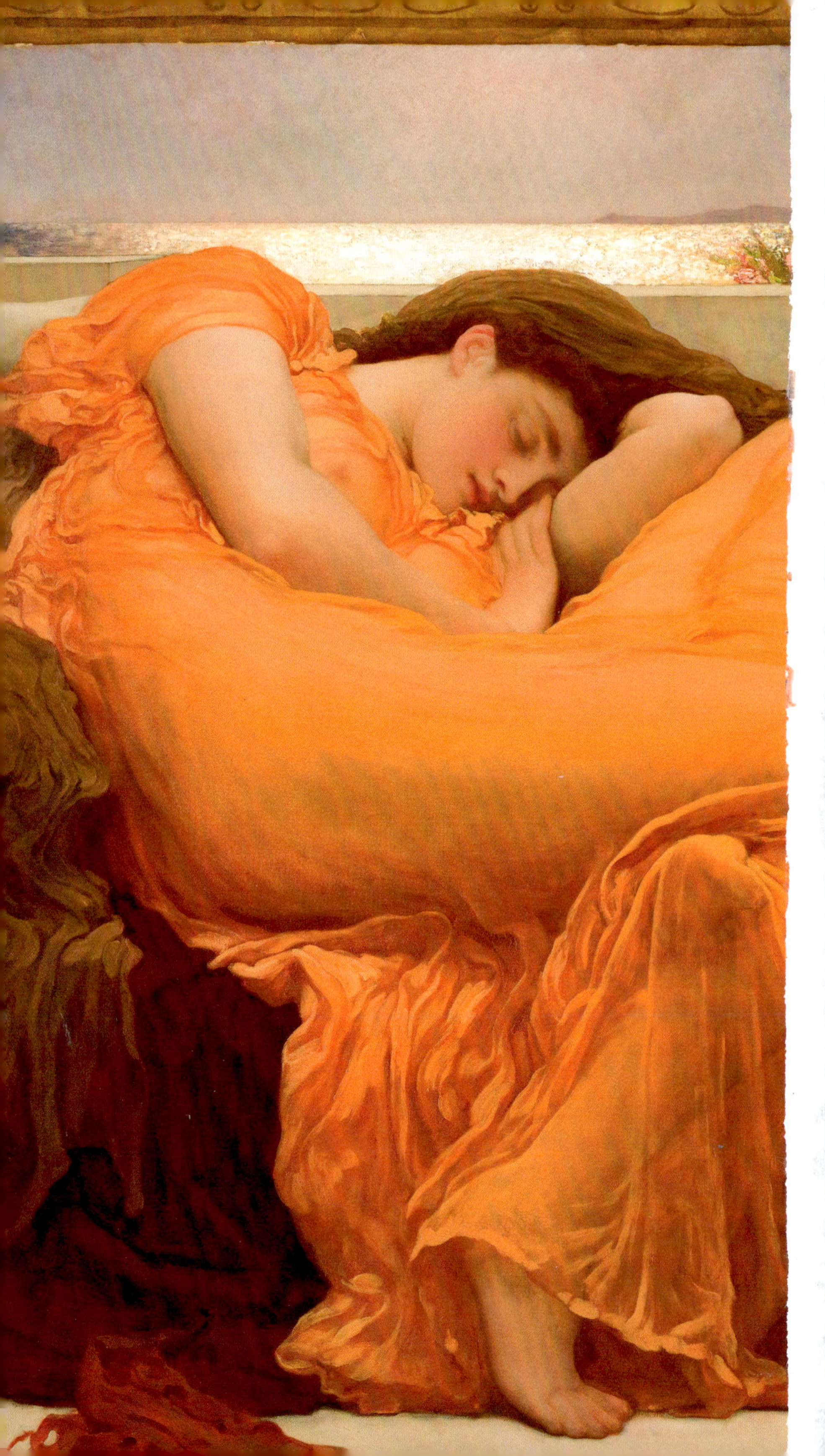